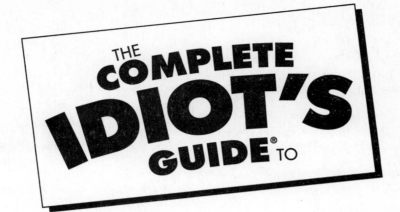

THE COMPLETE IDIOT'S GUIDE® TO

Exploring God

by Jeffrey B. Webb, Ph.D.

ALPHA

A member of Penguin Group (USA) Inc.

ALPHA BOOKS

Published by the Penguin Group

Penguin Group (USA) Inc., 375 Hudson Street, New York, New York 10014, U.S.A.

Penguin Group (Canada), 10 Alcorn Avenue, Toronto, Ontario, Canada M4V 3B2 (a division of Pearson Penguin Canada Inc.)

Penguin Books Ltd, 80 Strand, London WC2R 0RL, England

Penguin Ireland, 25 St Stephen's Green, Dublin 2, Ireland (a division of Penguin Books Ltd)

Penguin Group (Australia), 250 Camberwell Road, Camberwell, Victoria 3124, Australia (a division of Pearson Australia Group Pty Ltd)

Penguin Books India Pvt Ltd, 11 Community Centre, Panchsheel Park, New Delhi—110 017, India

Penguin Group (NZ), cnr Airborne and Rosedale Roads, Albany, Auckland 1310, New Zealand (a division of Pearson New Zealand Ltd)

Penguin Books (South Africa) (Pty) Ltd, 24 Sturdee Avenue, Rosebank, Johannesburg 2196, South Africa

Penguin Books Ltd, Registered Offices: 80 Strand, London WC2R 0RL, England

International Standard Book Number: 1-59257-429-7
Library of Congress Catalog Card Number: 2005929452

07   06   05   8   7   6   5   4   3   2   1

Interpretation of the printing code: The rightmost number of the first series of numbers is the year of the book's printing; the rightmost number of the second series of numbers is the number of the book's printing. For example, a printing code of 05-1 shows that the first printing occurred in 2005.

Printed in the United States of America

Note: This publication contains the opinions and ideas of its author. It is intended to provide helpful and informative material on the subject matter covered. It is sold with the understanding that the author and publisher are not engaged in rendering professional services in the book. If the reader requires personal assistance or advice, a competent professional should be consulted.

The author and publisher specifically disclaim any responsibility for any liability, loss, or risk, personal or otherwise, which is incurred as a consequence, directly or indirectly, of the use and application of any of the contents of this book.

Most Alpha books are available at special quantity discounts for bulk purchases for sales promotions, premiums, fund-raising, or educational use. Special books, or book excerpts, can also be created to fit specific needs.

For details, write: Special Markets, Alpha Books, 375 Hudson Street, New York, NY 10014.

Publisher: *Marie Butler-Knight*
Editorial Director: *Mike Sanders*
Senior Managing Editor: *Jennifer Bowles*
Senior Acquisitions Editor: *Randy Ladenheim-Gil*
Development Editor: *Lynn Northrup*
Senior Production Editor: *Billy Fields*

Copy Editor: *Susan Aufheimer*
Cartoonist: *Shannon Wheeler*
Cover/Book Designer: *Trina Wurst*
Indexer: *Heather McNeil*
Layout: *Ayanna Lacey*
Proofreading: *John Etchison*

Contents at a Glance

Contents

Foreword

The search for greater understanding into the nature and meaning of God is perhaps one of the most universal and perennial pursuits of humankind. Whether one looks at the world historically, culturally, or geographically, one finds that people and societies everywhere have held to a notion of God or gods with reverent fascination and awe. Such notions of God bind the individual not only to community and culture, but also to the world of Nature and the cosmos. Belief in and understanding of God is often that central idea wherein the answer to the meaning of life and one's place in this universe is grounded. Individuals and societies alike define themselves in reference to their understanding of God. Thus, readers of this book are embarking upon a truly noble and meaningful human enterprise.

Students and adults alike come to this topic not as blank slates devoid of any idea of God but as individuals having their own histories, cultures, and backgrounds. Whether through family or clergy, most of us have at some point been "taught" about who and what God is. But few of us go on to discuss what this might mean to us personally and intellectually. Few of us learn, for example, alternative views of God or the reasons other people hold such different ideas. We may not even have learned the rationale for what we ourselves were taught, leaving us in the rather difficult position of thinking everything we learned requires purely a leap of faith. Thus, when we later return to the topic of God, whether due to academic or personal reasons, we inevitably bring with us a number of unresolved questions gathered in the interim—questions arising from our inability to easily fit together what we have been taught with the complexities of everyday life.

For this very reason you have done well in selecting *The Complete Idiot's Guide to Exploring God*. Through an honest and objective presentation of a remarkable breadth of cultural and historical content, author Jeffrey Webb's text provides an excellent overview of the topic. The emphasis here is upon a thorough presentation of the history, rationale, and implications of each of the world's diverse ideas of God—a discussion that encompasses not only living religions of the world but also those that, although long dead, influenced those that survived.

As such, this book will serve well as a personal guide into the complexity and richness of the world's thriving discussions of God. It will undoubtedly leave the reader with a greater understanding of his or her own beliefs and ideas regarding God, as well as, importantly, those of others. This book will also prove very useful to teachers of comparative religion in search of a highly readable and comprehensive textbook for their students to learn and gain from.

Scott David Foutz (MDiv, STM, ABD) teaches courses in Comparative Religions, Religious Studies, and Technology at North Park University of Chicago, Illinois. He serves as principal editor of *Quodlibet Online Journal of Christian Theology and Philosophy* and is the founder of *TheologyWebsite*.

Introduction

Let me make an admission right up front: More than anyone else, I realize it takes a certain mix of recklessness and gall to write a book called *The Complete Idiot's Guide to Exploring God*. Probably a dash of irreverence as well. There's no subject more complicated, more impenetrable, and more mystifying than the subject of God. And there's no subject that generates more contention and controversy. But that's easy enough to explain.

There's no other subject that people care more about.

God provides comfort, meaning, and purpose to billions of people around the world, and of course God has been the focus of the longest-running conversation in the history of mankind. If you could keep track, you'd likely find that God has been written about more than any other subject. Certainly it would take more than a few lifetimes to read the God-related books that have been preserved down to the present day, in their many different languages, from their many cultures; not to mention the many lifetimes you'd need to read all the books that haven't survived the ages.

With this endless sea of books, and with the dangers lurking in wait for the writer, why do we need another book about God? If you're like me, you would certainly benefit from an easy-to-read introduction to an important, if not the most important, topic in the contemporary world (and perhaps in any other time). Getting started on the subject of God is like taking a proverbial drink from the fire hose. The glut of books you come across bowl you over, leaving you wondering where to begin.

Another problem lies in the passion with which believers approach the subject. Of course their passions are perfectly appropriate and even praiseworthy. But the literatures of different religious traditions sometimes campaign vigorously for their conceptions of God. This partisanship begs the question, Who can you trust to tell you about such an important subject? And if you start over here, will it color your view of what you discover when you move over there?

I must offer several disclosures in this connection: I am a believer in God—a Christian, actually—and I belong to a community of other believers. As such, I am under no illusion that I can turn off my faith like a switch and write in a completely disconnected and disembodied way. As a check, I have continually asked myself, would a Buddhist describe Buddhism like this, or would a Native American describe her faith like that? Though imperfect, my approach helped me to be sensitive to other faiths as lived by their adherents. My desire to be objective also led me to leave out highly uncharitable depictions of rival faiths that you often encounter within the different traditions. In the end, I trust you will find my efforts evenhanded and fair.

Taken as a whole, this book offers a starting point for investigating the various concepts of God in world religions and in different theological and philosophical traditions. The emphasis in that sentence is *starting point*. Think of this book as a trail map. It shows you where you can find the different trailheads leading into the forest, and it shows you where the signposts are located so you can orient yourself along the way. And like any good trail map, it highlights points of interest that are worth the extra time and attention.

A few words about what you *won't* find here: This book isn't an answer to the riddle of heaven. Throughout you will find discussions of spirituality in various religious traditions, but not practical suggestions for finding the path to enlightenment. It is not a comprehensive treatise on the nature of divinity, either, though you will find out why, and to what effect, various thinkers have written extensive treatises on divinity. Finally, it is not an argument for continued belief in God. There are lots of persuasive books that explain why faith in God is reasonable and justified in the modern world. This isn't one of them.

Rather, this book provides an introduction to the different ways God (or the Absolute) has been described and experienced in different times and places. You'll discover the faith of ancient Greeks, Hasidic Jews, and Zen Buddhists. You'll compare the vision of Christianity with the vision of Islam. You'll start to appreciate the richness of the Hindu tradition in all its beauty, mystery, and complexity. Throughout the book, you'll learn how various rituals and observances came into being across the religious landscape as seekers struggled in their progression toward the divine. Much is covered here, but given the nature of the subject, I hope you'll understand that much will end up being left unsaid as well.

Here's What You'll Find Inside

This book is divided into six parts:

Part 1, "Concepts of God," provides some insight into how experts interpret the phenomenon of belief in God, along with an introduction to the problem of using words and concepts to depict an unfathomable God. It also introduces you to conventional categories that scholars use to help understand religious belief and behavior.

Part 2, "The Concept of God in Judaism," tells the story of how ancient Hebrews fashioned the Jewish faith through belief in Yahweh. It tracks the concept of God as it emerges in the Hebrew scriptures, develops in the work of Talmudic scholars, and arrives in the hands of modern, and strikingly diverse, Jewish communities throughout the world.

Part 3, "The Concept of God in Christianity," highlights the Jewish background of the Christian faith and introduces you to Jesus of Nazareth, the figure at the center of Christianity. You'll also take a tour through the history of Christian thought, ending with an account of recent efforts to extend the conversation about God within the Christian tradition.

Part 4, "The Concept of God in Islam," offers an introduction to the world of Muhammad ibn Abdallah and to the Qur'an, the sacred text of the Muslim people. This part offers a beginning point for an excursion through the Islamic tradition, taking note of the major division between Shi'ites and Sunnis, and renewal movements intended to invigorate the faith, such as Kalam, Sufism, and Wahhabism.

Part 5, "The Concept of God in Eastern Religions," surveys the vast landscape of Asian religion and philosophy, starting with the common roots of Hinduism and Buddhism in the ancient Vedic religion. You'll begin to understand the meaning of concepts such as Brahman, atman, karma, dharma, Nirvana, and Zen. And that's just the beginning, because we'll also explore the concept of the Absolute in other Chinese, Japanese, and Southeast Asian religions.

Part 6, "Keeping the Faith," explains how the modern case against God took shape in the last few centuries, and how believers chose to respond. You'll also discover why belief in God thrives in the contemporary world, and how God provides help in time of need. But you'll also come to grips with some of the problems that arise when believers equate their imperfect visions of God with the actual Supreme Being or Absolute of the universe.

Extras

Because this book deals with the vast subject of God, there's always more to say than can be said in a limited space. So I've packed a wee bit more information into sidebars throughout the book. These self-contained boxes include definitions, tips, quotes about God, and other miscellaneous tidbits of information.

Word to the Wise
Here you'll find quick and handy definitions for the most puzzling terms you'll encounter in conversations about the divine.

Pearls of Wisdom
These boxes introduce you to the language of believers as they reach for words and phrases to capture their sense of the divine.

Divinations

These boxes offer tips and take you further into discussions of people, places, and things to add shading and color to our depictions of religious groups.

Take Heed!

Check these boxes for cautions against common misconceptions, and suggestions for handling difficult, confusing, and sometimes misleading information.

Acknowledgments

I would like to acknowledge a debt of gratitude to Jessica Faust of BookEnds, LLC; to Randy Ladenheim-Gil and Billy Fields of Alpha Books; and to Lynn Northrup and Susan Aufheimer, for their considerable professionalism and dedication, without which this book could not have been written.

While researching and writing this book, I received cheerful encouragement, and at a number of crucial points expert advice, from my gifted colleagues at Huntington University. It is impossible for me to recount the ways they helped to improve the quality of this book, though I alone bear responsibility for any and all of its shortcomings. They are, in no particular order: John Sanders, Del Doughty, Todd Martin, Jack Heller, Paul Michelson, Dwight Brautigam, Chaney Bergdall, Mark Fairchild, Beth Felker Jones, Tom Bergler, Kevin Miller, Norris Friesen, and Dwight Simon. I would also like to thank Rev. Robert Leach, Rev. Nathan Ahimbisibwe, the members of First Presbyterian Church of Bluffton, First Presbyterian Church of Huntington, and the Huguenot Society of Indiana for helping me address various issues relative to the subject at hand. Special thanks to my sons Christian and Aaron for sustaining me through the writing process; and to my wife Jill, who shows me every day what it means to be a true partner and friend.

Special Thanks to the Technical Reviewer

The Complete Idiot's Guide to Exploring God was reviewed by an expert who double-checked the accuracy of what you'll learn here, to help ensure that this book gives you everything you need to know about the subject of God. Special thanks are extended to David M. Woodruff, Ph.D.

Trademarks

All terms mentioned in this book that are known to be or are suspected of being trademarks or service marks have been appropriately capitalized. Alpha Books and Penguin Group (USA) Inc. cannot attest to the accuracy of this information. Use of a term in this book should not be regarded as affecting the validity of any trademark or service mark.

Part 1

Concepts of God

Among the more arresting book titles to appear in the last few years is this one: *God Is Not: Religious, Nice, One of Us, an American, a Capitalist* (Brazos Press, 2004). The authors of this collection provide a useful caution against the human tendency to describe God in ways that look an awful lot like ourselves, and to claim God's allegiance to our different human undertakings. But it's a whole lot easier to say what God is "not" than to say what God "is." If God is the most important entity in the universe, God is also the most difficult to describe. Is God a single thing, a multiple thing, everything, or not a "thing" at all? Is God part of us, inside us, surrounding us, or somewhere in the distant cosmos? Is God changeless and eternal, or is God subject to change like everything else in the universe? These are tough questions, and here you'll discover how people in different cultures and historical periods have struggled with them and a host of other questions that arise in conversations about God.

Search for the Divine

In This Chapter

- Why billions of people believe in the existence of God
- The basic questions of human existence that fuel the search for God
- How God has been described and experienced through history
- The difficulties many people encounter in describing God

There's nothing harder to put into words than a description of God. Even though God, or what some describe as the transcendent being or ultimate reality of the universe, enables billions of seekers to find meaning and purpose in life, we find it nearly impossible to adequately describe what God is like and how God relates to people. This problem has vexed priests and poets, conjurers and spiritualists, theologians and philosophers, and countless other people throughout the ages.

And yet this doesn't stop people from searching for the divine. And it doesn't shake their belief that if God can't be fully understood, then at least glimpses of God's nature can be seen in the universe, in human affairs, in sacred texts, and in many other ways. Finally, it doesn't stop people from pursuing an intimate encounter with the ultimate reality through meditation, prayer, ritual observances, incantations, hymn-singing, dancing, and a bevy of other spiritual practices. Finding language to describe God is next to impossible, and yet that is precisely where we're headed.

Theism and Its Critics

Most people believe in the existence of God, or in some transcendent reality beyond the world of our senses. Of course, within this vein of thought you can find lots of variation. Some think of God as a distant, impersonal force that initiated the laws of physics governing the universe. Others see God as a very active, personal being who is intimately involved in human affairs. Still others say that God isn't God as such, but a kind of eternal principle that gives structure and meaning to existence.

> **Word to the Wise**
>
> **Theism** refers to a system of belief in which God is depicted as the sole creator and sustainer of the universe, unified in form and perfect in nature. It also conceives of God as spiritual in essence, separate and distinct from the material world.

Probably the idea of God that pops into the heads of most people living in the West is what experts call *theism*. Although meanings of the term vary, theism is the combined work of Jews, Christians, and Muslims through the ages, and refers to a conception of God as a perfect, all-powerful and all-knowing being, possessed of a changeless and eternal nature and existing outside the confines of the material world. This God is the creator of the universe, but also the sustainer and governor of creation. This God hears prayers, grants blessings, punishes evildoers, and otherwise acts in ways that are not altogether unlike human action.

Traditional theism presumes a lot. It presumes that we can know and understand—if imperfectly—the nature of God. It presumes that God is a being who has particular kinds of attributes. It presumes that God, in a rather humanlike way, has wants and desires, and takes pleasure in the companionship of people. Scholars have concluded in light of these tendencies that theists have veered toward anthropomorphism, which means assigning to God human traits like compassion, jealousy, determination, and even angst.

It's hard to resist the extreme conclusion that some could reach from this line of thinking: that because people describe God in rather human-sounding ways, they have merely invented a being who doesn't actually exist. Karl Marx thought this way, and so did Friedrich Nietzsche and Sigmund Freud, among others. Ancient and medieval theists responded to skeptics with rational proofs of God's existence; today theists are as likely to say that asking for proof is to play according to the rules of rationalism and scientific thought, when in fact the God they worship exists above and beyond these rules. Keep in mind that the main objective of this book is not to respond to God's critics with a case for continued belief. At many different points the people of God have been compelled to explain why they believe what they believe, and these instances are given lavish attention here. To cite one example, you'll find St. Thomas Aquinas's arguments for God's existence in Chapter 14. These accounts are not the main subject of this book, but rather serve its larger purposes, which are to illustrate the manner by which God came to be understood by different believers in different places around the world.

Michelangelo pictured God in man's own image.

Take Heed!

People often ascribe to God rather humanlike attributes. Be careful not to conclude from this fact that God is a figment of someone's imagination. The impossibility of describing the indescribable quite naturally results in the use of expressions that are familiar to human experience. How could it be otherwise? You'll discover alternatives to anthropomorphic depictions of the divine in the major Eastern religions, the subject of Part 5 of this book.

Questions and Answers

So what brings a person to believe in God? Contemporary scholars of religion tend to consider belief in God as a natural human response to the glaring uncertainties of life. These scholars could have a point. Human beings are certainly unique for having the power to marvel at their own existence, question their own suffering, and ponder their future destiny.

I happen to like a passage in *Oration on the Dignity of Man*, written by Renaissance thinker Giovanni Pico della Mirandola. God, "the supreme Architect," had fashioned the world with all its creatures, but then "kept wishing that there was someone to ponder the plan of so great a work, to love its beauty, and to wonder at its vastness." The result, according to Mirandola, was that God created people with their special capacity to contemplate the mysteries of existence.

Mirandola's *Oration* poetically illustrates our fundamental desire to know the meaning of life. This desire is universal, extending backward in time and across all regions and cultures. As the writer of the ancient Hindu text *Svetasvatara Upanishad* asks, "what is the source of this universe," and "by what power do we live?" These questions are as fresh today as they were 2,500 years ago when the writer penned them in ancient Sanskrit. We'll discover more about the Hindus and the Upanishads in Chapter 21.

But answers to the questions that we most want answered continue to elude us. In a useful book titled *The Universe Next Door* (see Appendix A), written by James W. Sire, we are introduced to seven basic questions that help us compare major worldviews in different cultures. These questions are pretty much a digest of the existential questions that fuel belief in God. Sire's questions are these:

- What is prime reality—the really real?

- What is the nature of external reality, that is, the world around us?

- What is a human being?

- What happens to a person at death?

- Why is it possible to know anything at all?

- How do we know what is right and wrong?

- What is the meaning of human history?

Responses to these questions have taken a variety of forms ranging from cave paintings to complex philosophical ruminations. There's more on that in upcoming chapters. For now, Sire's questions teach us that human beings are meaning makers. We ascribe blessings and curses to forces that lie outside our perception and control. We place our lives in broader contexts of cosmic struggle and spiritual progression.

Whether by divine intention or biological accident, we seek to understand our position in relation to the larger universe that surrounds us.

So whether you believe in God or not, you probably recognize that the vast majority of people who are alive today, and who have ever lived, have decided that God offers a way to address fundamental questions that we have always wanted answered.

The Spiritual Impulse

People who believe in God have no trouble explaining why they believe. They'll tell you they believe because God can be proven through logic or history. Or maybe they'll say they believe because they feel God's presence in their lives. Whatever the case, the experts have a more difficult time explaining why people believe in God.

Scholars tend to observe believers from a distance, and then say this belief comes from a natural process of socialization as children are raised to adulthood. They might also attribute belief to group solidarity, as in the case of Albanian Muslims who cling—as the theory goes—to belief in Allah in order to avoid being absorbed into the Croatian, Serbian, or Greek cultures that surround them in the Balkan region.

Or perhaps body chemistry explains belief. I recently came across a story about a molecular geneticist by the name of Dean Hamer who believes he might have discovered a "God gene." The theory goes like this: A particular gene, identified as VMAT2, regulates the flow of certain chemicals to the brain. These chemicals—monoamines—alter your consciousness and make it possible for you to have—or seem to have—spiritual experiences. Dr. Hamer discovered an association between VMAT2 and test subjects who say they are more likely "to see everything in the world as part of one great totality." (For more, see *The God Gene: How Faith Is Hardwired into Our Genes*, Anchor, 2004.)

It probably ought to be mentioned that Hamer's evidence doesn't impress his scientific critics, and religious leaders complain that belief can't be reduced to biological factors. This story shows that the scientific mind wants and demands empirical evidence for claims made about belief in God, while most believers place the Absolute outside and beyond empirical boundaries.

Within these boundaries, we might ask whether there's a spiritual impulse latent within each person. One of the more astute observers of religion, William James, said yes. In his book *The Variety of Religious Experience* (see Appendix A), he found that somewhere in the human consciousness you can find "a sense of reality, a feeling of objective presence, a perception of what we may call 'something there'" that is more deep and general than the senses we use to perceive the material world around us.

Pearls of Wisdom

In one of William James's illustrations, a 43-year-old man explained his belief like this: "God is more real to me than any thought or thing or person .... I talk to him as to a companion in prayer and praise, and our communion is delightful. He answers me again and again, often in words so clearly spoken that it seems my outer ear must have carried the tone, but generally in strong mental impressions .... That he is mine and I am his never leaves me, it is an abiding joy. Without it life would be a blank, a desert, a shoreless, trackless waste."

James's ambitious exploration of the spiritual impulse is a good starting point for outsiders who are interested in the psychological dimensions of religion and spirituality. However, keep in mind that believers don't need to be told that their belief is rational or explainable in empirical terms. They will simply go on believing in God, the Absolute, the eternal principle, or the many other expressions of the ultimate reality.

God and Religion

Early scholars of religion had a theory that belief in God comes from the need to prevent society from lapsing into chaos. Religion, they said, provides this controlling element. Judaism, Christianity, Islam, Hinduism, and other religions supply humankind with moral codes, and with terrifying deities that are disappointed and angry when humans fail to observe those codes. Living in fear of divine wrath, people follow these rules and thereby produce an orderly, cohesive, and stable society.

It is true that most, if not all, belief systems link a deep sense of the Absolute with a plan for right living. That's because believers consider their ideas about God to be only one part of a holistic approach to life. Ancient Israelites were expected to honor Yahweh by observing the *mitzvot* (commandments), just as Muslims follow the true path by performing *sunnah*, or practices modeled by the prophet Muhammad. In fact, the Arabic word *islam* in the Qur'an actually means complete submission to the will of Allah in both thought and deed.

So belief systems combine belief and behavior into an integrated whole, producing religion. You can see this in Buddhist teaching, for example, in the Eightfold Path that leads to nirvana (the eternal state of nonbeing), which encourages the seeker to acquire right views of the Noble Truths, then right thought, right speech, right action, right livelihood, right effort, right mindfulness, and right concentration. Buddhists ascend toward nirvana through meditation on eternal truths, but also through avoidance of hatred, cruelty, killing, gossip, lying, theft, and other behaviors that tear at the fabric of human relations.

Buddhists share this holistic approach to life with other major world religions. Authentic belief entails commitment to core truths, but also sacred observances and moral duties that align the believer with the will of God, or in the case of Buddhists, enable the seeker to attain the eternal state free of suffering, ignorance, and death. Modern scholars understand that believers do not promote morality and ritual—and hence religion—for their own sakes, but for reasons related to believers' understanding of ultimate reality.

Is God a Thing?

The major world religions hold some things in common. They teach ultimate truths, promote moral behavior, encourage sacred observances designed to enhance the spiritual experiences of believers, and so forth. But there are some fundamental differences in how they perceive the nature of ultimate reality. Perhaps no division is more pronounced than the division between religions that depict God as a divine being, and religions that reject the idea that God is a "something" that can be described like any other object.

Historically, the three major monotheistic religions of Judaism, Christianity, and Islam conceived of God as a divine being. Their sacred texts depict God as an active agent in the universe, creating, sustaining, controlling, intervening, and so on. Listen carefully to St. Augustine, an important Christian theologian, who wrote in *The City of God*, "Of all visible things, the world is the greatest; of all invisible, the greatest is God." In this simple statement Augustine reveals much. Reality is divided into two realms, one visible (material) and one invisible (spiritual). This is called *dualism*. Then, Augustine sets God in the invisible realm and depicts God as a thing. God takes a particular form that can be described in particular ways.

Word to the Wise

In relation to belief in God, **dualism** most often refers to the division of reality into two realms: matter and spirit.

But adherents of some forms of Buddhism and certain strands of Hinduism protest that God is not something separate from the world. In fact, they believe that God is not a being as such, but rather, the source of all being, or Being itself. Early Hindus, for example, came up with the concept of Brahman to account for the fundamental reality of the universe. It lacks a will, a plan, a personality, or any other attribute that would make it seem humanlike. Those who believe in Brahman say it cannot be described in normal language, since it transcends human reason.

The result is pretty clear. Those who perceive God as a being encounter a bevy of paradoxes that are not easily explained away. How can God transcend reality, but also permeate all of existence? How can God be perfect and unchanging, but nevertheless respond to human concerns and actions? Perhaps most centrally, how can an incomprehensible and infinite God nevertheless allow itself to be confined within the boundaries of human thought?

Early Jewish and Christian thinkers responded to these paradoxes by making an important distinction between God's essence on one hand, and God's abilities or powers on the other. God's very nature is unfathomable, they claimed, while God nevertheless allowed himself to be perceived in *theophanies*, or in the design of nature, or through outright interventions in human affairs (such as the parting of the Red Sea in Exodus). This distinction didn't erase the paradoxes completely. What it did was allow conversation about God to proceed, and to provide believers with an object of awe and reverence worthy of worship.

> **Word to the Wise**
>
> A **theophany** is a special appearance of God in the presence of a human being, such as God's visitation with Moses on Mt. Sinai, or Ezekiel's vision of a burning metallic figure.

If those who believe God is a divine being have their difficulties, then so do those who believe God is a nonbeing. Theirs is the problem of finding appropriate language to express their understanding of the ultimate reality. This produces descriptions of the Absolute that most people living in the West would describe as vague and evasive. Of course, adherents of these traditions respond by pointing out that imprecise language is necessary in order to avoid reducing the Absolute to human measures.

Naming the Ultimate Reality

In the briefest excursion into the world's religions, you discover at once the difficulty that God's people experience in naming and describing the ultimate reality. Part of the problem is the nature of language itself. Words are merely symbols that represent something else, such as the word "table" used in reference to a material object with a flat surface and legs, useful for holding things like plates, glasses, and eating utensils. Words will always imperfectly capture the essence of the objects they intend to represent.

A second-century Christian, Justin Martyr, spoke for most of the people of God throughout the world and through all time when he wrote, "God cannot be called by any proper name, for names are given to mark out and distinguish their subject matters, because these are many and diverse; but neither did any one exist before God who could give him a name, nor did he Himself think it right to name Himself, seeing that he is one and unique." Words are used to differentiate and distinguish; God, however, is infinite, ultimate, and Absolute. The ancient Hindu text *Kena Upanishad* agrees, noting enigmatically that Brahman is "what cannot be spoken with words, but that whereby words are spoken."

> **Pearls of Wisdom**
>
> Lao Tzu, thought to be the founder of Taoism, wrote:
>
> The way that can be spoken of
> Is not the constant way;
> The name that can be named
> Is not the constant name.
>
> —Tao Te Ching, 1.1.1

Sometimes believers resort to describing God as ineffable, which means incapable of being expressed in words. When Moses asked God to provide a name for himself that Moses could use with the Israelites, God replied, "I am who I am," which in Hebrew language formed the acronym YHWH. Vowels were added by translators, and YHWH became Yahweh. In addition to not allowing himself to be named, Yahweh also refused to allow images. No name, no statuettes or idols. This is why ancient Hebrews and most believers today think of God, or the ultimate reality, as ineffable.

Even so, people have given God a thousand names. Ancient Hebrews referred to Yahweh as Elohim and Adonai, among a variety of other names (see Chapter 6); Muslims famously identified 99 beautiful names for Allah (see Chapter 16). When you add this to the countless other names that the ultimate reality has been given, you get a sense that God is ineffable, to be sure, but people have nevertheless chosen to name the unnamable and describe the indescribable.

Islam, Judaism, Christianity, Hinduism, and other religions give God names that reflect the attributes they consider God to possess, or the nature of the relationship they have to God. In Hebrew scriptures, Yahweh is sometimes identified as El Shaddai, which means mighty God, revealing the Hebrew sense of God's power and strength. There's a similar move in the Qur'an; the Arabic word Al-'Azeez, one of the 99, means the mighty one. The multiple names offer believers a way to express and appreciate God's qualities, while nevertheless holding to a belief in God's incomprehensibility.

What should we make of representations of God in words and images? They are representations of God as processed by the minds of human beings, rather than exact replicas of the divine in its essence. When Morgan Freeman walks across the water alongside Jim Carrey in the film *Bruce Almighty*, we are given a way to imagine an experience of God that is, to all intents and purposes, impossible to express in language or pictures. We can immediately object to statues, paintings, symbols, word pictures, concepts, and so forth that purport to represent God—all are inadequate vehicles for presenting the true infinite and Absolute. But we must concede that if God is to be comprehended and experienced at all, God must take a form that human beings can understand and value. In the words of Montesquieu, "If triangles had a God, he would have three sides."

The Least You Need to Know

- ◆ Belief in God is fueled by existential questions about the origins of the universe and the meaning of life.

- ◆ Believers tend to distinguish between God's essence, which is unknowable, and God's attributes, which can be discerned, admired, and adored.

- ◆ Many believers give God names and attributes that seem rather humanlike, which scholars call anthropomorphism.

- ◆ Many believers shy away from naming and picturing God because they believe words and symbols would do injustice to the infinite and absolute character of God.

God Is Everything: Pantheism

In This Chapter

- ◆ All creation as a unity
- ◆ Nature and the environment in pantheist religious practice
- ◆ The importance of sacred places
- ◆ Differences between pantheism and animism

A good place to begin working on the key concepts in the study of God is pantheism. Pantheists believe that everything that exists is a unified whole, and this unified whole is God itself. This is a very old idea, but it has many modern adherents. Pantheists claim kinship with a disparate group of thinkers that includes Lao Tzu (considered the founder of Taoism), Roman emperor Marcus Aurelius, seventeenth-century Dutch philosopher Baruch Spinoza, and contemporary physicist and author Stephen Hawking. And pantheists are well represented among modern poets, novelists, and film stars.

The reason pantheism is a good place to begin is because pantheists tend to disregard the complicated metaphysical ruminations that accompany belief in divine beings, as in the case of polytheism and monotheism (which I'll discuss in Chapters 3 and 4, respectively). Believers who follow the pantheist route often simplify things considerably. Once you understand their perspective on God, you'll be ready to bring the complications of other faiths into the mix.

What Is Pantheism?

Pantheism came into use to describe believers who conceive of all reality as a unity, then identify this unity as God or divine. The word pantheism combines the Greek terms for "all" (*pan*) and "god" (*theos*), though it seems to have been used in only the last few centuries. Philosophers and theologians wanted a handy way of linking certain religious and philosophical traditions that stress the oneness of reality, and so they came up with pantheism.

The word *pantheist* seems to have been first used in 1705 by John Toland, an Irish freethinker, to describe the work of Baruch Spinoza. Why did philosophers invent the term? And would people who philosophers identify as pantheists think of themselves as pantheists? Good questions. Hundreds of thousands of people actually use the term to describe themselves, but not every person who scholars would classify as a pantheist recognizes or accepts the label. It is essentially a concept that helps observers to organize disparate believers into a group to help us understand the nature of their vision.

Word to the Wise

Pantheism refers to the belief that all reality is one, and this one is God.

That's right: Believers ranging from Zen Buddhists and adherents of Advaita Vedanta (a tradition within Hinduism) to New Age seekers and naturalistic pantheists have something in common that makes them different from believers in other traditions, which is a belief that God does not exist apart from our earthly reality. They disagree with Jewish, Christian, and Islamic adherents who see God and human beings as distinct and separate entities; in pantheist traditions, human beings are *manifestations* of the divine unity.

Some accuse pantheists of atheism, since they are said to have equated God with the universe, making God irrelevant. But believers in this tradition have not merely created another name for the universe by invoking the word God. On the contrary, God is that which gives reality its fundamental unity in many pantheistic schemes. That is not the same as saying that God does not exist.

One Realm or Two?

At the back of most every conception of God (and therefore most every religion) is a particular understanding of the structure of reality. It is conventional in the study of religion to see believers as conceiving of reality in one of two ways: dualism and monism. Dualism, as you learned in Chapter 1, divides all reality into two realms or principles, as with the division between matter and spirit. In this connection, dualism creates a strict separation between God and the physical world.

As you can probably guess, believers of various stripes throughout history have objected to this division. They see all of reality as a seamless whole, interconnected and interdependent. The technical word for this view is *monism*. Some of the earliest recorded expressions of belief in God were monistic in their vision, and the *Upanishads* again supply a good illustration:

> Far spreading before and behind and right and left, and above and below, is Brahman, the Spirit eternal. In truth Brahman is all. (*Mundaka Upanishad* 2.2.11)

> All this universe is in truth Brahman. He is the beginning and end and life of all. As such in silence, give unto him adoration. (*Chandogya Upanishad* 3.14)

The *Upanishads* imagined a universe in which behind all reality is Brahman, the source of being, with each person connected to Brahman through Atman, the fundamental nature of each individual person. This concept lies at the center of most strands of Hinduism, especially Advaita Vedanta, a tradition started in the eighth century C.E. *Advaita* means "not two," in reference to the unity of Brahman and Atman, which is as clear a rejection of dualistic notions of reality as you can get.

Advaita Vedanta and its spiritual cousins also taught the idea of God's immanence, a general concept that envisions the divine as present within every living thing, including the human mind or soul, or perhaps present in the world. Immanence is usually contrasted with the idea of transcendence, a concept in which God is seen as distinct and separate from creation. Some element of immanence exists in almost all religions. To give just one of many examples, Quakers in the Christian tradition are fond of saying "there is that of God in everyone" connecting each person to every other person. They refer to this as the Inner Light.

God and Nature

The principle of unity in pantheism appears to have great consequences for how we think about the natural world. Former Soviet Premier Mikhail Gorbachev might be said to be speaking in a pantheist way when he offered this confession: "All of us are linked to the cosmos. So nature is my god. To me, nature is sacred. Trees are my temples and forests are my cathedrals." From Gorbachev's words it might be easy to conclude that pantheists are nature worshippers.

Divinations

The Greek god Pan (the flute-playing man-goat) was associated with the forest and flocks of sheep. This connection between "all" and nature offers some insight into the primitive beginnings of pantheistic belief.

This could be true for a small number of believers within the pantheist tradition, such as Thoreau, Whitman, and other writers in the transcendentalist community of the nineteenth century, and for followers of ecognosis, gaiasophy, and naturalistic pantheism today. But the larger share of pantheists don't worship nature; rather, they venerate the entity of which we are all a part, which is at the same time wholly present in our innermost being.

So how did all the rocks, trees, birds, and people get here? Buddhists believe this question is unanswerable, and the Buddha himself famously refused to give an answer when asked whether the universe had a beginning or whether it was limitless in space. Others, for example Taoists, see the universe as a product of emanation, the belief that the natural world flowed out from a divine source. The Taoist scheme goes like this: "The way [Tao] begets one; one begets two; two begets three; three begets the myriad creatures." (*Tao Te Ching*, II.42.93) In this concept, reality emanates in stages from the Absolute.

The Importance of Place

The tendency among believers in God to designate certain places as sacred is nearly universal across religions. You might remember the passage in Exodus 3:5, when Moses encountered God in the burning bush and God asked him to take off his shoes because the ground upon which he stood was holy. The same sense of sacred places is at work when Muslims pray in the direction of Mecca, Hindus journey to Benares to bathe in the Ganges, and Jewish pilgrims stick written petitions into Jerusalem's Western Wall.

"Go back to the darkest roots of civilization and you will find them knotted round some sacred stone or encircling some sacred well," wrote G. K. Chesterton in his book *Orthodoxy*, published in 1908. And why? Pantheists believe they have an answer—because all of us are connected to everything in nature, and everything together—you, me, the tree over there—is a manifestation of the unifying principle or power.

Pantheists don't necessarily see spirits in the landscape or on the faces of woodland creatures. Pantheists aren't any more inclined than other believers to think of forest paths or mountain shrines as the best means to enter into communion with the divine. In fact, many pantheist traditions, especially the Buddhist forms, are just as likely to teach yoga and meditation as effective ways to escape pain and ignorance and enter the eternal state.

But pantheists remind us at every turn of the importance of sacred space in the minds of the people of God. The Taos Pueblo of New Mexico aren't pantheists, but they demonstrate the importance of place in their belief that the Blue Lake possesses sacred power. They gather annually at the water's edge to initiate new members into the kiva, which expresses the dual importance of community and place to the Taos people. The Taos believe the Sacred Mystery permeates all of creation, making the geological features of the landscape literally alive. The Taos see the natural world as numinous, or filled with a supernatural presence. And just as the Black Hills of South Dakota are sacred to the Lakota of North America, Mt. Fuji is considered sacred by followers of Shinto and Buddhism.

> ### Pearls of Wisdom
>
> Huixang of Langu, a Buddhist monk, felt the sacred power of the Wutai Shan mountains in Shanxi Province, China. In 677 C.E., he wrote the mountains were occupied by many beings who chose to preserve the dharma of the ancient buddhas, and so "Manjusri has manifested his traces, reached out to people's spiritual capacities, and come to attend to the needs of us sentient beings."

Diversity of Opinion

There's a certain frustration awaiting those who want to apply the concept of pantheism to the many religions of the world. Few traditions could be identified as a pure type. And pantheism, as applied by various experts, can be a rather large tent, sheltering a diverse range of belief systems and religions. The term is useful mainly as a way of showing how believers across cultures and through time have come to see the oneness of all reality, and the divine nature of that unity. This gain in understanding, though, comes with the risk of overlooking the quite substantial differences among these traditions.

A good example is Hinduism and Buddhism. Both can be included in discussions of pantheism, and yet they harbor significant disagreements about some important issues. For example, Siddhartha Gautama, or Buddha, disagreed with the Hindu idea that each person leads a series of lives with a continuous, transmigrating soul that ultimately can be freed from the cycle of rebirth and reach a state of harmony with the Absolute. Today, most Buddhists share a belief in reincarnation with most Hindus, but do not think of human souls as permanent, continuous, and transmigrating. You'll learn more about the complicated Buddhist understanding of reincarnation in Chapter 23.

There are other substantial points at issue in the Eastern religions, such as whether one can return from the eternal realm, or whether it does any good to worship deities. And any basic course in either Hinduism or Buddhism will tell you right from the outset that neither one is a pure type; elements of pantheism, panentheism, polytheism, henotheism, and monotheism are evident in the Hindu tradition, and Buddhism simply defies categorization. Both Hindu and Buddhist visions help us see something fundamental about the religious impulses of pantheism, but their visions are nonetheless distinct.

Related Concepts

Some of the confusion associated with the term pantheism can be minimized by introducing a few closely related terms.

Panentheism

Some scholars believe that religions frequently put in the pantheist category are really panentheist—the belief that everything in the universe is part of God, but that God is more than the universe. The word derives from a combination of Greek words for "all," "in," and "god," and seems to have come into use during the nineteenth century by scholars who were busy sorting religions into categories to understand their common features.

Perhaps as good a statement of panentheism as any comes from Black Elk (1863–1950), a spiritual leader of the Oglala Sioux in North America. In *The Sacred Pipe* (University of Oklahoma Press, 1989), Black Elk expresses the Sioux conception of God this way: "We should understand that all things are the work of the Great Spirit. We should know that he is within all things; the trees, the grasses, the rivers, the mountains, all the four-legged animals and the winged peoples; and even more important we should understand that he is also above all these things and peoples."

In panentheism, believers find a way to emphasize the union of God and creation. They see the material world and the divine as mutually supportive and interdependent. But they also find a way to affirm the supremacy of God over the natural world.

> **Take Heed!**
>
> The concept of pantheism came about in large part as a response to the work of Dutch-Jewish philosopher Baruch Spinoza (1632–1677). Spinoza pushed the idea of unity to its limits, arguing that God is the infinite, self-existing, and unique substance of the universe, and "Whatever is, is in God, and nothing can be or be conceived without God."

Animism

From time to time, you might come across a religion or set of beliefs described as a form of animism, a word that comes from the Latin word *anima*, meaning "breath of life," or "soul." In common use, animism refers to religions that perceive everything in existence to contain spirits, including living things such as humans, animals, and plants, and also rocks, water, sky, and even meteorological phenomena such as lightning or thunder.

Today, scholars are less likely than they were a century ago to see native religions in Africa, Polynesia, the Americas, Australia, and elsewhere as examples of animism, because now scholars prefer to talk about traditional religions in noncategorical ways. Much more is known about the central role of religion in the lives of traditional peoples, and with this increased knowledge comes increased difficulty in making generalizations.

We get a glimpse of this complexity in traditional Yoruba (Nigeria) belief. Yorba believe in a chief god, Olorun (or Olodumare), who conferred upon humans their fates. Men can negotiate with Olorun through Esu, a sort of messenger god. But Yoruba also see reality as infused with *ase*, or divine energy, and believe that within each person is an *orisha*, or spirit, who acts as guardian and mentor. Since Yoruba believers perceive the divine as a supreme being, a hierarchy of gods, and a unified reality infused with ase, they resist classification. And certainly it would be a mistake to call the Yoruba animist.

Neo-Paganism

In recent decades, readers in the West have grown accustomed to reading news coverage of neo-pagan groups, particularly druids and Wiccans. But technically, any group that wishes to revive the ancient religious traditions of pre-Christian Europe would be identified as neo-pagan. This includes groups seeking to rediscover ancient Norse religion, the Greek pantheon, and Egyptian deities.

Neo-pagans show up in lists of pantheists because they tend to speak of an intimate connection with nature and the natural rhythms of the earth. Druids, for example, stage celebrations at the changing of the seasons, and of course at the solstices and equinoxes. Wiccans observe the seasons and cycles, too, and add special initiation ceremonies and herbal medicines to their practice.

But more fundamentally, neo-pagans see an elemental power uniting all of reality, with every living thing as a manifestation of that power. This power is seen most vividly in natural phenomena and in the cycle of life, death, and rebirth; hence the neo-pagan tendency to follow closely the phases of the moon, the rotation of the sun, and shifting constellations of the night sky.

The Least You Need to Know

- The concept of pantheism came into use to help observers see certain common features in many religions.

- Pantheism is commonly understood to mean belief in the unity of all reality and the equating of this reality to God.

- To most pantheists, human beings are not distinct and separate from the divine, but are manifestations of God.

- The concept of pantheism can help us clarify certain ideas within the various religious traditions, but it can obscure some important elements of these traditions as well.

God Is Many: Polytheism

In This Chapter

- ◆ The mythology behind the belief in multiple gods
- ◆ The famous Greek pantheon
- ◆ Blurring the lines between gods and mortals
- ◆ The involvement of the gods in human affairs
- ◆ How believers of polytheism choose a god to worship
- ◆ Why Hindus worship Brahma, Shiva, Vishnu, and the lesser deities of the Hindu tradition

Another strange word you often hear in conversations about God is polytheism, a word that describes belief in multiple gods. According to polytheists, there isn't a single being called God, and God isn't the sum total of everything. Instead, polytheists perceive a set of divine beings, typically thought to wield different powers or possess different attributes. In some cases a high god rules over these divinities; in other cases all gods are equal in status.

This chapter covers some important terrain on the subject of divinity. A little exposure to the polytheistic traditions reveals just how complicated some perceptions of the divine can get. It also gives us a stronger sense of the common threads that run through various religious traditions, ranging from parallel accounts of creation to the nature of human interaction with the Absolute.

The Mythic Vision

A common starting point for discussions of *polytheism* is ancient mythology. In the ancient world, myths developed as a way to celebrate great heroes of the past, but also as a way to talk about natural phenomena that otherwise defied explanation. Long before advanced tools of measurement and handy theories of electricity,

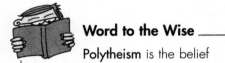

Word to the Wise

Polytheism is the belief in multiple gods.

Norsemen saw lightning and heard the tribal *skald*, or storyteller, spin tales of Thor and his thunderbolts. Greeks saw lightning too, and conversed with one another about the anger of Zeus. Farther east, Polynesians felt the earth shake and explained that Ruau-Moko, the unborn child of the earth goddess Papa, had stirred inside the womb.

Myths gave people a way to talk about lightning, earthquakes, changing seasons, and even the color of flowers. More fundamentally, they addressed the enormous existential questions of life and death. Ancients asked how the stars, the sun, the moon, and the earth came into being. They also wondered why human beings appeared to be so different from other animals. Quite naturally, people reflected on the future, and what happens to a person at death.

In the absence of scientific explanations, the poets and storytellers engaged these questions, finding in their stories a way to exercise the imagination and give expression to human creativity. Science is ill-equipped to address many of these questions, such as how something came out of nothing, or how life entered lifeless matter, so many scientists leave the answers to the poets, philosophers, and theologians.

Explaining the Beginning

Mythological explanations for nature and religious belief in the divine occupy adjacent territory; in fact, their borders overlap. A look at some ancient mythological schemes can help us understand a little better how polytheistic belief took shape in earlier periods of human history.

Sumerians' Myths of Creation

The earliest human cultures, such as the river societies of the Tigris-Euphrates, Nile, and Indus, illustrate the overlap between myth-making and polytheistic belief. In the stretch of land between Basra and Baghdad in present-day Iraq, ancient Sumerians and Babylonians experienced the violent forces of nature and the fragility of human life, and came to see them as part of a larger cosmic drama. The story, as told in the epic poem *Enuma Elish*, starts with the emergence of three gods—Tiamat, Apsu, and Mummu—from primordial chaos. This triad then produced a series of gods, in couplets actually, through a process you learned about in Chapter 2, emanation.

At some point, Anu and Ea arrived on the scene, and that's when the trouble began. Ea uncovered a plan by Tiamat to kill all her divine offspring. Ea rebelled, and in the process killed Tiamat's consort, Apsu. Enraged at Ea's insurrection, Tiamat bred an army of monsters to confront him, setting the stage for a dramatic climax. This came after a general meeting of the gods ordered Ea's son, Marduk, to battle against Tiamat's monster army, to be rewarded with Marduk's appointment to the headship of the pantheon. Marduk won, and thereby became the chief deity.

Marduk's victory and ascension also offered an explanation for the origins of the human race. In victory, Marduk split Tiamat's dead body into two halves, one half becoming the sky and the other half becoming the earth. Tiamat's water formed the clouds and the source of the Tigris-Euphrates. Another of Tiamat's consorts, Kingu, died in battle, and Marduk mixed Kingu's blood together with some dust to create human beings. By the way, Norse mythology tells a similar story of the earth and sky being formed from the body and head of a slain giant, Ymir.

Divinations

In polytheism, gods tend to be identified with certain elements or forces of nature. Many cultures perceive the moon, the sun, and the stars as gods. The sun god is known by the following names: Ra (Egyptian), Huitzilopochtli (Aztec), Apollo (Greek), Amaterasu (Shinto), Shamash (Mesopotamian), Surya (Hindu), Belenos (Celtic), Maelare (Polynesian), and Wi (Lakota Sioux).

But telling the Mesopotamian creation story this way flattens out much of its richness and meaning. It's important to know that Mesopotamians linked the gods to various aspects of nature. When you realize that Apsu was associated with fresh water, Tiamat with salt water, and Mummu with the womb, you get a better feel for how Mesopotamians perceived the interplay of natural forces and elements. Marduk, by the way, is associated with the sun. So it goes for a wide variety of ancient mythologies that came to associate a particular feature of the natural world with a particular god, or a specific human trait with a particular deity.

The Greek Variation

The Greeks had their own version of the creation of the universe and the beginnings of humankind, though experts have had to piece together the Greek story from a number of texts, including Homer's *Iliad* and *Odyssey* and Hesiod's *Theogony* and *Works and Days.* Greek plays, such as those of Aeschylus, Sophocles, and Euripides, help to round out the picture.

The general outlines of the Greek myth of creation include a primitive Chaos, with five elements emerging out of it. One of these elements, Gaia (Mother Earth) bore a son named Uranus (the sky). Together they gave birth to the Titans (incest was not a taboo in Greek mythology), the Cyclopes (one-eyed monsters), the Hecatonchires (beasts with a hundred hands and fifty heads), and the Furies (gods of punishment and revenge).

Divinations

The Judeo-Christian account of creation depicts a void, or nothingness, that existed before the material elements of the universe. Creating something out of nothing is known as creation *ex nihilo.* The notion of ex nihilo differs from the Mesopotamian and Greek accounts, which depict a kind of primordial goo, or slop, that gains definition and complexity through the creation process.

Displeased with the Cyclopes and Hecatonchires, Uranus banished them to the bowels of Gaia, who resented this treatment of her children. She asked Cronus, youngest of her male children among the Titans, to castrate Uranus, which he accomplished with a very large sickle. Blood from Uranus's wounds dropped into the sea, creating a foam out of which came Aphrodite, goddess of love. Cronus and his wife (and sister) Rhea took over control of the gods and began producing children themselves.

Cronus discovered that he was fated to be killed by one of his own progeny, so he began to swallow them at birth. Rhea saved the sixth child by switching him with a stone. This son, Zeus, returned from hiding and poisoned his father, which induced him to vomit up the children he had eaten. War ensued, and with Zeus's victory the Titans were banished to the lower world. Zeus and his regurgitated siblings Hera (also his wife), Hestia, Demeter, Poseidon, and Hades, removed to Mt. Olympus and established dominion over the universe. While living on Olympus, Zeus continued to populate the Greek pantheon with his issue, some born to Hera and others born to various consorts. You might be interested to know that Athene, goddess of war, sprang from Zeus's head, which is a rather unusual emanation.

And what about humanity? Several Greek myths speak to the origins of the human race. One myth involves Prometheus, a Titan who actually fought alongside Zeus. Prometheus was directed by Zeus to form a man from soil and water. Prometheus grew so fond of his creation that he wanted to give him special status among the animals, so he gave him fire stolen from Zeus's thunderbolt. When Zeus discovered Prometheus's treachery, Zeus created the first woman, Pandora, and sent her to live with man. Along with her came a box that she was not to open, but being curious, she opened it anyway. Out of it came all the troubles of humanity, such as plagues, famines, diseases, crimes, and so on. So the story of Prometheus accounts for the human race, but also the beginnings of evil as well.

The Idea of a Pantheon

Myths offered ancient Greeks a way to converse about thorny, existential questions, and their mythological figures bore associations with features of the natural world, mysterious forces of nature, and even uncontrollable human desires and passions. Given the multiplicity of the elements and forces of nature, it follows that the heavens would be populated with a multiplicity of gods.

This is how we get the notion of a pantheon, a term that combines the Greek words for "all" and "gods." In the Greek system, the emanation of the gods from primitive Chaos through Gaia, the Titans, and finally the Olympians resulted in a differentiation of function. The traditional 13 Olympian gods acquired these attributes:

- Zeus, god of the sky and earth
- Hera, wife of Zeus and mother of gods
- Hestia, goddess of home and family
- Demeter, goddess of agriculture and fertility
- Poseidon, god of the sea
- Hades, god of the underworld
- Aphrodite, goddess of love and beauty
- Athena, goddess of wisdom
- Apollo, god of light, music, poetry
- Hephaestus, god of fire

- Ares, god of war

- Artemis, goddess of hunting and the moon

- Hermes, god of trade and messenger of the gods

But there are many, many more gods in the Greek pantheon than simply the Olympians. There were Muses, daughters of Zeus and Mnemosyne (goddess of memory) who provided inspiration to poets, musicians, and philosophers; Charities, daughters of Zeus and Eurynome (a sea nymph) who graced lucky mortals with charisma and beauty; and the Horae, daughters of Zeus and Themis (goddess of order) who regulated the seasons and the cycle of plant life. The gods themselves feared the Moirae, or Fates, who were thought to determine the destiny of every individual.

Divinations

Ancient Greeks and Romans credited many different gods with the birth and continuation of the universe, and in fact feared angering any number of possible gods by not identifying them in the pantheon. At times the Greeks and Romans paid homage to an "unknown god" as the force behind unexplainable occurrences, lest "it be a god or goddess" who caused the events.

The Greek pantheon was cluttered with scores of deities for every occasion. Other pantheons could be equally profuse; Egyptian divinity numbered its gods at more than 2,000. An ancient writer in the last days of Rome put the number of gods in the Roman pantheon at 30,000! Experts believe the large number was the result of imperial policy, whereby Rome sought to maintain control by absorbing the gods of other cultures, rather than imposing its pantheon upon subjugated territories.

Gods and Mortals

It's safe to say that the ancient mythic imagination blurred the line between the physical and spiritual worlds. Greek mythology again offers the most striking examples, such as when Zeus impregnated a mortal, Semele, to create Dionysus (god of wine and fertility), one of the chief deities of ancient Greece and Rome. Achilles, the Greek hero in Homer's *Iliad*, was the son of Peleus, a mortal, and Thetis, one of the sea nymphs who along with Poseidon ruled over the waters. In the Greek mythological world, the gods existed in a scale that operated within the compass of human measurement. African, Indian, Asian, and Middle Eastern history provide numerous illustrations of human beings turning into gods, or at least being worshipped as divine.

Greek sculpture helped to blur the lines between mortals and immortals, since the gods were represented in human form.

(Courtesy of the Hellenic Ministry of Culture)

Though blurred, the lines between gods and mortals in mythology are nonetheless evident. Achilles himself might have become immortal were it not for his mother's mistake in holding his heel while dipping him in the river Styx to make him invincible. This undipped spot took an arrow from Paris before the walls of Troy, and so Achilles followed other mortals into death. One popular method of interpreting mythology and polytheism is to consider the gods of the pantheon as exemplary heroes—but still actual people—who became the subject of tales that became more fantastic in the retelling, with feats growing ever more supernatural as the figures receded deeper into historical memory.

If you recall from Chapter 2, pantheism depicts all of reality as a unity, and then identifies that unity as God. Polytheism, on the other hand, perceives the divine in plural terms, usually as beings separate from humanity. This is the case even if certain polytheistic schemes permit frequent interaction between the gods and mortals. Furthermore, polytheistic traditions perceive the gods as having some point of beginning—a birthday. This distinguishes them from the monotheistic traditions, such as the Hebrew, Christian, and Islamic faiths, which depict God as timeless and eternal, with no beginning and no end.

Division of Labor

Inside many of the polytheistic systems you'll discover a basic division of labor. One god might govern the waters while another supervises the growing cycle. A third might sway the fortunes of armies in battle. Various beings safeguard the rivers and forests, or direct the prevailing winds.

What you get when you range across these literatures is a number of commonalities that aren't that easy to dismiss. The study of these commonalities preoccupies experts in the fields of comparative mythology and religion, and one of the pioneers in this area is James Frazer. Frazer discovered thematic similarities among ancient and pre-modern mythological schemes in his book *The Golden Bough* (originally published in two volumes in 1890).

In one particular case, Frazer and others discovered that it's hard to find a polytheistic religion that doesn't assign to a particular deity the responsibility of fertility. It doesn't matter whether the god is named Diana (Roman), Artemis (Greek), Cybele (Phrygian), Freyr (Norse), Osiris (Egyptian), Deng (Dinka), Ala (Ibo), Nawang Wulan (Javan), or a dozen other names. Fertility is a central feature of human existence, because without the fertility of the soil, humanity would suffer, and without the fertility of the womb, humanity would disappear. The mythological vision thus included deities for fertility.

Of course, different cultures have widely differing perceptions of what the fertility gods, or any of the other gods, actually do. This brings us to a very important question: Do the actions of the gods actually affect people? Or another way of putting it, what is the gods' role in shaping human destiny? Did an ancient Egyptian think his crops were ruined or his wife's womb was barren because of the displeasure of Osiris?

The Olympian gods offer a good beginning on the subject of who plays what role in the drama of life. It is commonly thought that the Greeks actually believed in the existence of their gods—their gods were not merely imaginative fictions designed to entertain the crowd at feasts, for example—and Greeks revered them in a manner appropriate to their divine status. But the way that Greeks perceived the involvement of gods in human affairs was, well, complicated.

To be sure, the gods were thought to act only within the confines of their job description. Nobody would have attributed lovesickness to Poseidon, because that was clearly Aphrodite's territory (although an earnest suitor might have given the goddess of desire some help by supplying the object of his affection with an aphrodisiac). In another instance, when Hector and his armies were winning the Trojan War, the Greeks understood that their enemy had won the favor of Ares, god of war.

The gods provided solace, companionship, and sometimes even material help. But they didn't control human affairs. Greek polytheists didn't consider themselves to be robots acting out a divine script. A bereaved Athenian might bemoan the Fates who brought sorrow into her life, but to suggest that ancient Greeks believed events to be foreordained is to overstate the case. No doubt there was a division of labor among the gods, and between gods and mankind. Responsibility for human choices lay in the hands of people themselves.

> **Pearls of Wisdom**
>
> Euripides (480 or 485–406 B.C.E.) wrote, "Try thyself first, and after call in God. For to the worker God himself lends aid." (*Hippolytus, Frag., 435*) Apparently in the mind of this Greek playwright, God helps those who help themselves.

Henotheism: Many Gods, One in Charge

Frazer's work inspired scholars to seek out other commonalities, and they discovered that most polytheistic visions of the divine actually perceive the existence of a supreme being, with secondary divinities existing in a subordinate position. Technically, the term we use to describe the form of polytheism in which many gods are thought to exist, with one having exalted status, is *henotheism*.

This is clear in the Greek and Roman pantheons, where Zeus and Jupiter reign, respectively. It might also be applied to Norse and Egyptian religions, and to Rig-Veda (early Hindu) divinity as well. Some observers see the imprint of henotheism in many indigenous religions of Africa and the Americas. Henotheism is captured in the idea of a Great Spirit over and above the other spirits of the heavens and earth. In his book *Everlasting Man* (Ignatius Press, 1993), G. K. Chesterton recounts a story in which a European missionary came upon a group of aborigines, and after some discussion about this god and that god, the missionary started in on his sermon about a supreme being who judges the entire world. This apparently caused a buzz, and after the aborigines conferred among themselves, they cried "Atahocan! He is speaking of Atahocan!"

Another henotheistic motif is the concept of a creator god giving life to other spirit beings and to the natural world. This comes up in Egyptian polytheism in the figure of Ptah, who was said to have made everything, including the gods. Aztecs believed that Ometecuhtli and his wife Omecihuatl created the other gods, perhaps the source of the Aztec view of the duality of existence. Chinese mythology includes the tale of P'an Ku, a creator who emerged from a primordial egg and began the work of separating and differentiating, like male and female, light and dark, and soil and water. From this comes the Chinese principle of yin and yang.

An interesting twist on henotheism is a concept known as *monolotry*. This is a type of religion in which many gods are perceived, along with a supreme being, but only one is worshipped (usually the supreme one). This might explain the nature of ancient Hebrew religion. The earliest Hebrews perceived the divine in plural terms, but Yahweh commanded them to worship him alone, a commandment the Hebrews largely obeyed. From time to time, however, they slipped back into Baal worship, and so God chastised them for their unfaithfulness with military defeats, natural disasters, and captivity.

The Practice of Polytheism

Perhaps now we're ready to tackle some bigger questions, such as what turns myth into religion. To ask the question more narrowly, how did simple fables about the movements of nature translate into articles of religious belief?

The key difference between mythology and religion is the presence of devotion and piety in the latter, along with the material culture, sacred sites, and religious rituals that accompany devotion and piety. Mythology crosses the border between literature and religion when it goes beyond storytelling, and makes its gods the focus of sacrificing, praying, worshipping, and spiritual pilgrimage. In ancient Greece, temples were created to honor Zeus, Poseidon, Apollo, and Dionysus among many others. But a wide array of Greek gods still remained in the territory of myth. Of course in Greek religion, the Olympian gods were more likely to be objects of worship than earlier generations of gods (such as Gaia, Uranus, or the Titans).

So how did believers under polytheism pick a god to worship? Generally, ancients discerned an awesome power in nature, manifested in the four winds, the changing seasons, budding trees, and flooding rivers. The ancients personified these demonstrations of nature's power in the form of highly anthropomorphic gods. And these gods were thought to exercise a degree of control within their sphere. If drought induced a famine one year, you wouldn't be surprised if the residents of Achaia petitioned Demeter, goddess of fertility, for assistance the next. Prayers and ceremonies were efforts to form alliances with various deities, who might then come to the aid of their petitioners.

Generally, believers wouldn't risk angering the gods by worshipping one to the exclusion of the others. And yet the Greeks produced religious cults with secret initiation rites to honor certain gods such as Apollo and Dionysus. The cult of Dionysus, for example, staged festivals and feasts with participants dressed in laurels and robes, dancing to the music of flutes and cymbals. One particular rite apparently ended with the frenzied attack on a sacrificial bull. Participants, known as Bacchae because of Euripides' play by the same title, were sometimes depicted in literature and visual arts as drinking the blood and eating the raw flesh of the slain animal. The Greek and Roman cults of Dionysus and Bacchus were notorious for their orgiastic rituals involving drunkenness and revelry. Experts believe these cults were exceptions to the more common pattern of orderly worship at local temples.

> **CAUTION**
>
> **Take Heed!** _____
>
> Although today we think of such practices as barbaric, sacrificing animals or even people to the gods was considered necessary by ancient peoples to keep the gods alive or to revive them when their powers weakened. Contrary to common belief, the Aztecs practiced human sacrifice to sustain the rhythms of nature, not to appease angry divinities or take vengeance on particular people.

The choice of which god to worship was often made easy because of tradition and place. If you were born in Ephesus (in present-day Turkey), for example, you were probably taught a pantheon of gods, but you might worship only Artemis, known in Ephesus as a fertility goddess, because she was special to the residents of the city. In fact, the Temple of Artemis was one of the Seven Wonders of the Ancient World. In the case of Roman polytheism, an ancient writer, Varro, talked about "select gods" in the Roman pantheon who elicited universal reverence. And yet Romans worshipped thousands of different tribal gods and the gods of their particular villages and regions. This illustrates the central role that family and lineage played in shaping Roman values.

Eastern Perspectives

It's easy to make the association between these ancient polytheisms in Mesopotamia, Egypt, Greece, Rome, and elsewhere, and the religions of South and East Asia that speak of the divine in plural terms. In Hinduism, especially, you'll hear about Brahma, Shiva, Vishnu, Kali, Ganesh, Parvathi, and assorted names for the avatars of Vishnu. The ancient Hindu sage Yajnavalkya answered the question of how many gods with a range of numbers from 3 to 3,300. One source of Hindu divinity, the *purâna* texts, puts the number at over 330 million. So should we include Hinduism in the category of polytheism?

Tricky question. We'll explore the nature of Hindu divinity in Chapters 21 and 22, but for now, keep in mind a few important points that make Hinduism difficult to categorize neatly. First, Hinduism is not a religion but a family of interrelated religious traditions. You'll find lots of variation within this family. Second, Hindus resist the Western impulse to systematize and codify religion, so there's no "authoritative" expression of Hindu doctrine to refer to here. Third, Hinduism accepts the growth and development of its traditions.

Given these points, you'd have to be very specific in time and place when making a reference to Hindu "polytheism." It might be more applicable in the earliest stages of development, when Hinduism wasn't really Hinduism yet, but something called Vedic religion, expressed in sacred texts called the *Rig-Veda*. *Rig-Veda* perceived a trinity of Brahma, the creator god, Vishnu, the sustainer, and Shiva, the destroyer. But this polytheistic vision grew weaker as Vedic religion moved through time, and came to be expressed in the *Upanishads* and the *Bhagavad-Gita*. In these later texts, the divine is perceived in more pantheistic terms, as Brahman, the unified Absolute. With the advent of this tradition, other gods came to be understood as manifestations of the ultimate reality. This understanding is captured in a quote attributed to Mohandas K. Gandhi: "I consider myself a Hindu, Christian, Moslem, Jew, Buddhist, and Confucian."

> **Pearls of Wisdom**
>
> With respect to the origins of the universe, the *Rig-Veda* sounded an agnostic tone:
>
> > He, the first origin of this creation, whether he formed it all or did not form it,
> >
> > Whose eye controls this world in highest heaven, he verily knows it, or perhaps he knows not. (*Rig-Veda* 10.129.6–7)

The Least You Need to Know

◆ Polytheism refers to the belief in a plural divinity, usually expressed as numerous gods.

◆ Polytheism gained greater definition through the mythologies of the ancient Near East and Greco-Roman civilization.

◆ One variation of polytheism is henotheism, or the belief in many gods, with one designated as supreme.

◆ Ancient mythologies developed into religions when the gods became the objects of worship and devotion.

◆ The concept of polytheism is not alien to the religious visions of the East, but most Hindus and Buddhists do not accept the label.

Chapter 4

God Is One: Monotheism

In This Chapter

- ◆ The roots of belief in one God in the religions of the ancient Near East
- ◆ Greek philosophers weigh in
- ◆ The power of one God
- ◆ Basic similarities among the major monotheistic faiths: Judaism, Christianity, and Islam
- ◆ Core disagreements among the monotheistic traditions that survive to the present day

Among the more consequential developments in the ancient world was the emergence of the monotheistic traditions of Judaism, Christianity, and Islam. They gave religion in the Mediterranean world a new birth. Greek and Roman religion had grown stale amid the rise of skepticism and rationalism, and seekers came under the spell of mystery cults imported from Persia, Egypt, and other points east. With the advent of a new vision of the divine, of a single, supreme being governing the universe, came an entirely new outlook on the natural world, the problems of humanity, and the whole question of the destiny of humankind.

Monotheists perceived the divine as a perfect, all-powerful, all-knowing, self-existing being. They understood God to be separate from the material world, though fully capable of intervening in that world. Although good, the unitary God of the early monotheists was jealous. God was prepared to chastise believers or deny them blessings should they turn toward other gods. But with great commitment and sacrifice came great rewards; monotheists developed a fresh vision of a final victory of good over evil and an afterlife of eternal bliss.

Early Arrivals

There's no question that a shift in perceptions of the divine toward *monotheism* resulted in a revolution in worldview. But this shift was anything but sudden.

On the contrary, monotheism was a long time coming. In many accounts it existed alongside prehistoric polytheisms throughout the world, though playing second fiddle during the height of Mesopotamian, Persian, Egyptian, and Greco-Roman civilizations.

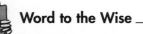

Word to the Wise

Monotheism refers to belief in one Supreme Being.

Egyptian Monotheism

A famous instance of primal monotheism occurred during the time of Pharaoh Amenhotep IV (1353–1336 B.C.E.). Amenhotep and his wife Nefertiti sought to completely transform Egyptian religious life, ending the tradition of polytheistic worship of Re, Osiris, Set, and a bevy of other gods in favor of worship of a single God, Aton. Aton referred to the sun disc, exemplifying its importance in ancient Near Eastern religion. Amenhotep changed his name to Akhenaton, meaning "one who is useful to Aton," and built a giant temple to Aton at Karnak.

Pearls of Wisdom

Akhenaton's "Hymn to Aton" evokes monotheism:

How manifold are thy works!
They are hidden from man's
  sight.
O sole god, like whom there
  is no other!
Thou didst create the world
  according to thy desire.

In the end, Akhenaton failed to make his reforms stick, and when King Tutankhamen followed him in office, he erased Aton worship and restored polytheism. Later, the temple at Karnak was destroyed. Even so, certain principles of divinity in Egyptian religion were later merged with the monotheistic conception of God in the Christian tradition. This would include Akhenaton's single-minded devotion to Aton, but also some of the attributes associated with Osiris, such as Osiris's death and resurrection and his role in meting out the final judgment of humanity.

Zoroastrianism

Further east, during a somewhat later period, a religious figure known as Zarathustra or Zoroaster (b. c. 570 B.C.E.) also perceived God as one. He sought to reform the polytheism of the Iranians, which bore similarities to the neighboring religion of the *Rig-Veda* with its numerous gods. Zoroaster came to understand the divine as Ahura Mazda, creator of all things and originator of Arta, the principle of good order.

Zoroaster and his heirs left behind a very complicated set of writings that further developed his concept of a single God. The basic problem Zoroastrian theologians had to tackle was the problem of good and evil, which vexed thinkers in other monotheistic traditions, too. If there's only one creator God, then the creator must have created evil as well. Zoroaster talked about two spirits, Spenista Mainyu and Angra Mainyu (bounteous and destructive, respectively) representing the opposing principles of the universe; later thinkers described the opposing principles as infinite time and time of long dominion (time of the sort that led to decay and death). These ideas roughly accounted for good and evil, even if it left Zoroastrianism rather untidy from a philosophical point of view.

Some Greek Philosophers

The appearance of formal monotheism in Near Eastern religions paralleled the advent of new thinking about the divine in Hellenic culture. In Chapter 3, I discussed the relationship between Greek mythology and religion. As this relationship evolved, a third strand of thought became entwined with developing perceptions of the divine, namely concepts coming out of Greek schools of philosophy.

Plato

Socrates and Plato were among the earliest to systematically investigate the area of thought known as *metaphysics*. Plato, as you learned in Chapter 2, believed in fixed, universal entities called forms, which exist independently of the material world. Human beings encounter these forms before the forms actually become human, as souls in the world of forms. When human souls become incarnate at birth, they bring mental imprints of the forms with them into their earthly lives. Plato's thinking later contributed to the development of monotheistic belief by philosophizing about two realms—the material world and the world of the forms—and locating the divine element in the latter world. This sort of dualism reinforced and catalyzed Jewish, Christian, and Islamic thinking about God.

Aristotle

Plato's most well-known student, Aristotle (382–344 B.C.E.), wrote extensively on the subject of metaphysics. In fact, one of his own students assembled a collection of writings that actually coined the term "metaphysics," around 350 B.C.E. In that collection, Aristotle said "all men suppose what is called wisdom to deal with the first causes and the principles of things." (*Metaphysics* 1.1) He then went on in the text to speculate about what things are and how they came to be, postulating the existence of a first cause, or unmoved mover behind the operations of the natural world. (*Metaphysics* 4.8) Again, monotheists had no trouble equating Aristotle's unmoved mover with the God of creation.

Word to the Wise

Metaphysics refers to the philosophical study of the ultimate nature of reality or being. It addresses questions such as what actually exists, and what are the fundamental principles of reality (for example, time and space).

The Stoics

Plato's Academy drew a number of talented thinkers to its halls, among them Aristotle, and it inspired others to follow its model of rational speculation. Zeno (335–263 B.C.E.) built a school and produced a distinctive body of teachings called Stoicism. The Stoics, including such luminaries as Roman emperor Marcus Aurelius of *Gladiator* fame, came to see an underlying principle in the universe, the principle of Divine Reason (logos). This principle was also planted within each person's soul. Happiness, according to Stoic teachers, lay in conforming one's will to the principle of Divine Reason. Clearly Stoicism might be more accurately described as pantheistic, but it did bequeath to monotheism the idea of a universal dominion and a universal truth underlying this dominion. More important, Stoicism contained the idea of a transcendent universal logos, coupled with an immanent, localized logos within each individual. You'll see this again in later Christian thought.

Plotinus

The formal connection between Greek philosophy and monotheism lies in the figure of Plotinus (204–270 C.E.), who worked out a complicated system of thought that bore a striking resemblance to the emerging Trinitarian conception of the divine within Christianity. Plotinus followed the tradition of Plato and the Stoics and perceived the One at the center of reality.

He believed it was folly to describe it, or even name it, and so he declined to do so. But the One can be perceived, Plotinus taught, so the One must have permitted emanations by which people can discern and appreciate the divine. He counted two distinct emanations: from the One came Mind (nous), and from Mind came Soul (psyche). These emanations provided the first principles and cognitive powers necessary for individuals to encounter God and to become reunited with the One.

> **Divinations**
>
> The work of the Stoics and Neo-Platonists such as Plotinus informed the thinking of later Christian monotheists, particularly the Trinitarians who helped to fashion the central tenets of the Roman Catholic Church and Eastern Orthodoxy. But their work nevertheless has a decidedly pantheist ring to it.

The Power of One

Trends in Greek philosophy appear to map neatly onto developments within a small tribe of Semitic nomads who came out of Mesopotamian, sojourned in Egypt and the Sinai, then settled in Canaan between the Jordan River and the Mediterranean coast. Over time, the Hebrews abjured the worship of Mesopotamian, Egyptian, and Canaanite deities and followed Yahweh, the divine being revealed to Abraham, Jacob, and Moses, and described in the growing body of Hebrew literature. The Hebrews perceived Yahweh in strongly anthropomorphic terms, even identifying times and places where Yahweh talked directly to human beings, or exhibited humanlike qualities of delight, regret, and jealousy. And however else Yahweh could be described, Yahweh was singular in nature and separated from the material world.

Unlike Greek and Egyptian polytheists, the Hebrews came to understand God as the driving force of history. Other religions spoke of the will of the gods, but not as an all-encompassing determinant of the trajectory of creation and eventual human destiny. Yahwehists conceived of human choice as a decision between following the will of Yahweh, or rebelling against this will and risking the consequences. And where the other local polytheists saw an array of fickle, mutable gods, Yahwehists talked about a *covenant* between themselves and God, which bound both parties to a contractual agreement offering an ordered and knowable future. As a result, they approached Yahweh with submissiveness and humility, but also retained confidence in God's jealous partisanship on their behalf in the struggle against neighboring powers such as Assyria and Babylon—but only so long as Yahwehists upheld the covenant.

You can see the ways in which Hebrew monotheism radically redefined the relation between the human and the divine in the ancient Near East. But there was much more to come. The followers of Jesus of Nazareth further developed monotheistic concepts within the Hebrew community and carried monotheism to Gentile populations throughout the Roman Empire. Christians came to believe that Jesus of Nazareth was the Messiah prophesied in Isaiah and other Hebrew texts, an *incarnation* of Yahweh and only begotten Son of God. Jesus himself referred to God as his "Father." Jesus' miraculous birth, supernatural miracles, and bodily resurrection after death attested to his claims to be the Son of God. Jesus' disciples carried his teachings and the message of his birth, death, and resurrection throughout Palestine, Asia Minor, and Greece, finally reaching the imperial center at Rome. These developments will be covered in Chapters 11 and 12.

> **Word to the Wise**
>
> A **covenant** is an agreement between two parties, usually involving certain expectations of responsibilities and privileges. An **incarnation** refers to the divine taking on a human form, which is derived the Latin word *carn*, meaning "flesh."

Of course, the Christian version of monotheism required a little more elaboration, and this is where Greek philosophy came in handy. Plato's dualism and Plotinus's concepts of oneness came to the assistance of early church leaders—sometimes called the Early Church Fathers—as they struggled to express the relationship between the Father, the Son, and the Holy Spirit, and to explain the relation between the human and the divine in the person of Jesus Christ. Through a series of councils, church leaders framed the basic concepts of Trinitarianism. This body of thought enabled Christians to perceive God in a variety of seemingly paradoxical, and perhaps even mutually exclusive, ways: as transcendent and immanent, infinite and finite, unitary and plural, and coexisting and emanating. (Not all followers of Christ considered themselves Trinitarians. In the third century C.E., a group called Monarchians were accused of anti-Trinitarianism, and more recently, Unitarians and Jesus-Only Pentecostals deny the triune Godhead, though for very different reasons.)

To the south, Muhammad ibn Abdullah of Mecca (c. 570–632 C.E.) began to receive new revelations about the divine in 610 C.E., which came to be called Allâh (English translation doesn't cut it, but the best it can do is "the God"). For 10 years Muhammad received further revelations that when gathered together formed the Qur'an (or Koran). The Qur'an, spoken to Muhammad in the language of Arabic, was the final revelation to humanity, and offered a vision of a perfect, eternal, all-powerful and all-knowing God who demands submission and obedience. Muslims who followed the Qur'anic teachings rejected Christian Trinitarianism as a violation of the principle of God's oneness, and they regarded claims of God's incarnation and resurrection in the person of Jesus as impious blasphemy, even as they affirmed Jesus' status as an important prophet.

Islam, the religion of the followers of Muhammad, contributed to the conversation about God within monotheism in several important ways. Islam reminded the community of the faithful of the inexpressible nature of the divine, cautioning against the dangerous anthropomorphic tendencies of Judaism and Christianity. According to Muslims, their close cousins tended to weaken the divine by limiting and dividing its power. To the Muslim mind, Allâh is wholly other, unblemished by any association with the material world and sinful human flesh. Muslims believe these principles are a necessary component of belief in the all-encompassing power of a unified God.

This sixth-century B.C.E. relief depicts Zoroaster's monotheistic God, Ahura Mazda, as a bird with a human head leading the Persian army into battle.

(Courtesy of Ugo Bardi)

Transcendence vs. Immanence

Judaism, Christianity, and Islam offer the clearest examples of the continuation of ancient monotheistic belief into the present day. Within each of the traditions, however, there's been a good deal of conversation on the subject of God's relationship to the world. Is God far removed, off in an inaccessible realm and uninvolved with humanity? Or is God very near, participating in creation, giving to and getting from those who call upon the divine? I'll be discussing all three perspectives in much greater detail in the rest of this book, but for now here's an overview.

Hebrew Perspectives

The ancient texts of Judaism indicate that the issue isn't an either/or proposition; God is both transcendent and immanent. At certain times in their history, Hebrew writers perceived God in strikingly transcendent terms, as when God told Amos in Amos 7:8 that a plumb line of separation divided them because of Israel's iniquity. At other times God was described as quite immanent, as in the episode in Genesis 32:24 where God grappled with Jacob and sprained Jacob's leg in order to escape. "The Lord, the Most High, is terrible, a great king over all the earth," the Psalmist wrote. (Psalm 47:2) But a few verses earlier, the Psalmist said with no apparent concern for contradiction, "God is our refuge and strength, a very present help in time of trouble." (Psalm 46:1) The Hebrew concept of God permitted this elasticity, which is one of the subjects we'll learn more about in Chapter 6.

> ### Pearls of Wisdom
>
> St. Augustine perceived God as immanent in his famous autobiography:
>
> I have learnt to love you late! You were within me, and I was in the world outside myself. I searched for you outside myself .... You were with me, but I was not with you. (*Confessions* 10.27)

Christian Perspectives

So what about Christianity? Christian monotheism must be viewed in light of the concept of the Trinity of Father, Son, and Holy Spirit. The Church Fathers endeavored to maintain the oneness of God by describing the divine as one essence in three persons, or personalities. As Father, God exhibits transcendence, while as Spirit, God exhibits immanence. As Son, God exhibits both at once, since Jesus Christ was perceived as fully divine and fully human. Later mystics such as St. Teresa of Avila and Meister Eckhart would describe intimate encounters with the divine, whereas deists such as John Toland and Thomas Jefferson closed off the possibility of God's continued supernatural involvement with nature and human affairs.

Islamic Perspectives

Islamic philosophers and theologians tended to remain faithful to the original Qur'anic vision of a transcendent divine being. Remember, this was one of the key points of departure in the revelation Muhammad received in the seventh century C.E. The Qur'an says: "Allâh is that Supreme Being Who is the Independent and Besought of all and Unique in all his attributes. He begets none and is begotten by no one. And there is none his equal." (Surah 112.2–4) Later thinkers attempted to capture a sense of Allâh's presence; Abu Bakr al-Baqillani (d. 1013 C.E.) theorized that material beings were composed of atoms that in turn were sustained by Allâh. Nevertheless, Islamic divinity continued to stress the absolute otherness of Allâh and the necessity of complete submission of humankind to his will.

Patterns of Belief

Despite differences of opinion on God's orientation toward the material world, you'll find some striking similarities among the major monotheistic religions. These similarities set monotheism apart from the ancient polytheistic schemes and from the Eastern religions as well.

Jews, Christians, and Muslims depart pretty significantly from other philosophical and religious traditions on the subject of time and history. Where Eastern religions stress themes of recurrence and cycles, the ancient monotheisms stress the linear nature of history. They perceive an omnipotent God who called the universe into being, then placed creation on a trajectory toward the final judgment, which will bring an end to historical time and the onset of eternity. This understanding of time relates to another core idea shared by monotheists, which is the historical revelation of God to humanity by means of a fixed, authoritative, and sacred canon of religious texts.

The Hebrew scriptures, called the Tanak, are unique because of their strongly historical content. The Tanak contains the sacred history of the Israelites, a narrative that offered confirmation of Yahweh's promises to Abraham, Moses, and others in the earliest epochs of human history. Ancient Hebrews came to understand the Tanak (what Christians call the Old Testament) as a holy text, containing an account of the sacred history of Israel's covenant relationship with Yahweh. Christians eventually defined their scriptures—the Hebrew Tanak together with the canonical books of the New Testament—as the very Word of God; biblical writers were inspired by the Holy Spirit to record divine truth. And Muslims affirm the idea of divine revelation and take it one step further, claiming that the very language of the Qur'an itself—Arabic—is Allâh's eternal thought and word. And not only are the concepts and ideas holy, but the vocabulary, syntax, and grammar are holy, too. Jews and Christians make no such claim for Hebrew or Greek (though Hindus do for Sanskrit).

And then there's the idea of spiritual disciplines. Ancient Hebrews spoke of the *mitzvoth* (commandments) and *halakhah* (law) required under the covenant, while Muslims practiced the duties outlined in the Five Pillars of the faith. Jesus told the disciples to practice the sacraments of baptism and the Eucharist (also known as communion). While not unique to monotheism, these disciplines offered confirmation of the special status of their practitioners, which sets monotheists apart from adherents of other religions. Each of these faiths perceives their believers to have a special, exclusive relationship to the divine.

Consequences of Monotheism

Experts have credited Judaism, Christianity, and Islam with many of the core values of Western civilization. They claim that the ethical standards of the West were codified by these ancient monotheisms, and the idea of a special relationship to God with duties and obligations gave their lofty ideals greater urgency. And these duties implied moral accountability and personal choice. This association encourages scholars to trace the Western ethic of self-determination back to the way human relationships with the divine were framed in monotheistic belief.

Besides individualism, monotheism is credited with the idea of progress because of its linear view of history. This idea of an ultimate purpose to history with an ultimate end has a technical name: *teleology*. Teleological perspectives on time and eternity are thought to have brought hope and optimism to these cultures, clearing the way for the Western idea of progress. To be sure, these monotheisms contain recipes for a just society and heavenly mandates to follow these recipes in reforming contemporary politics, society, and culture. Simply put, monotheism has been credited with the idea that humans should try to make the world a better place, and rightly so.

Word to the Wise

Teleology refers to the investigation of final, or ultimate, causes. In religious thought, it involves discussion of the origins of the universe, the destiny of humankind, and the resolution of the war between good and evil.

Still, tensions persist within these communities of belief. Monotheism gave rise to persistent philosophical difficulties such as the problem of evil and the relationship between divine control and human action. In both instances, monotheistic insistence on a perfect, all-powerful, all-knowing, self-existing being leads to the question of where evil entered into the system. Lots of attempts have been made to explain the source of evil, which will come up in subsequent chapters. A more esoteric debate involves the degree to which human beings have the capacity to freely choose and act, given an all-powerful and all-knowing God. Each religion has had its warring camps on the free will and determinism issue.

If monotheists have had their philosophical and theological difficulties, then so have the pantheists and polytheists. But the difficulties are certainly not enough to dissuade hundreds of millions of adherents from monotheistic belief, including the person who owns the car I spied in a pharmacy parking lot recently with the license plate that reads, "1 God."

The Least You Need to Know

♦ Monotheism is commonly associated with Judaism, Christianity, and Islam.

♦ The idea of a single God is very old, probably as old as the dawn of civilization.

♦ Monotheism blends divine transcendence and immanence together in creative ways, including the Christian doctrine of the Trinity.

♦ Monotheist religions believe their adherents have an exclusive relationship with God, which culminates at the end of a linear progression of history.

Chapter 5

God Is None: Atheism

In This Chapter

- Early skeptics and doubters from the Classical Era through the Enlightenment
- The onset of disbelief amid the disenchantment of the West
- Russell's arguments against the existence of a Christian God
- The difference between atheism and agnosticism
- Buddhism as a kind of atheism

Many, if not most, believers have at one time or another doubted the existence of God. Just as the famous doubting Thomas did in the Gospel of John, they question the reports of others who claim to have seen God, but they find enough faith to believe when they've experienced the divine firsthand. Yet these occasional doubts do not make them atheists. Atheists are not merely doubters; they are disbelievers.

Atheists affirm certain principles regarding the existence (or in this case, nonexistence) of the divine, ruling out the possibility that God is real. However, very few people who doubt the existence of God are technically atheists. Most are agnostics, because they are unwilling to completely rule out the possibility of God.

Idle Speculation?

You might be surprised to learn that *atheists* are very recent participants in the conversation about God that's been going on for several millennia. But atheists build on a long tradition of skepticism about the gods reaching back to at least classical Greece and beyond. In this era, as with every other since, thinkers rejected conventional wisdom about ultimate reality and advanced innovative concepts that endeavor to explain the mysteries of existence. Their voices are heard behind the bolder claims of modern atheists that God cannot possibly exist.

> **Word to the Wise**
>
> **Atheism** is the belief that gods or spiritual beings do not exist.

Xenophanes

In the beginning of the atheist tradition, skepticism was not atheism as such. The work of Greek philosopher Xenophanes (c. 560–c. 478 B.C.E.) is a great starting point for understanding what these early skeptics were up to. He resented Homer's treatment of the gods in the *Iliad* and *Odyssey*, and Hesiod's depiction in *Theogony*. He wrote: "Homer and Hesiod have attributed to the gods all sorts of things that are matters of reproach and censure among men: theft, adultery, and mutual deception." So the popular conventions in Greek divinity didn't sit very well with him.

If Xenophanes didn't like the impious treatment of the gods in popular literature, he also seemed displeased with the prevailing anthropomorphic tendency to assign the gods human attributes. In several surviving documents he took note of this phenomenon:

> But mortals suppose that gods are born,
> wear their own clothes and have a voice and body.
>
> Ethiopians say that their gods are snub-nosed and black;
> Thracians that theirs are blue-eyed and red-haired.

Instead, Xenophanes advocated a more impersonal, essentially pantheist conception of God. A later Greek, Theophrastes, described Xenophanes' position like this: "the all is one and the one is God." Xenophanes' work took its place among the work of Thales, Anaximander, and Anaximenes, who involved themselves with efforts to re-think the ultimate basis of reality, each identifying a different substance at the core of all material phenomena. Thales, for example, made the important distinction between reality as it is, and reality as we perceive it to be, and speculated that water is the unifying element of all reality. These Ionian Greeks, together with Xenophanes, left a legacy of speculation that challenged the accepted view of the divine in Hellenic culture.

Carneades

By the time of Carneades (213–129 B.C.E.), a formal school of thought had emerged in ancient Greece called Skepticism. Carneades, the most well-known Skeptic, directed his doubts not toward the divine as such, but toward the larger question of whether it was possible to know anything for certain. He believed it was impossible to conclude that mathematical principles are constant and absolute. And he held that the seeming order of the natural world provided no evidence for a supreme architect in the heavens. In effect, he doubted *both* reason and faith as a means to arrive at truth.

Saving Belief Through Syncretism

Clearly, in the three centuries before the appearance of Jesus of Nazareth the struggle for the soul of the ancient Mediterranean world reached fever pitch. Mythological, philosophical, and religious visions contended for the allegiance of seekers desperate for insight into the mysteries of existence. It was a pivotal time in the history of conversations about God.

In this period, several key figures attempted to blend together religious and philosophical visions. When thinkers try to pull disparate strands of thought together in this way, we call it *syncretism*. You can see this in the "Hymn to Zeus" by Cleanthes (c. 331–c. 231 B.C.E.), who tried to harmonize Greek mythology and Stoic philosophy. The Zeus of mythology shows up in the hymn when Cleanthes sees Zeus "shrouded in dark clouds and holding the vivid lightning." Zeus appears in the hymn as creator and sustainer of the universe. But Zeus manifests in very impersonal ways, too, as the "first cause of nature" and the force that guides "the universal Word of Reason which moves through all creation."

Word to the Wise

Syncretism is the practice of fusing different religious or philosophical concepts into one integrated system.

Cleanthes' hymn bears an unmistakable Stoic imprint, because it perceives the divine in universalistic ways (Zeus as a god "with many names") and identifies the divine with universal law or reason. And while the hymn offers praise and worship to this universal principle, the intent is to call hearers to greater virtue, to live in conformity with "God's universal Law." The effect is to empty Greek thought of magic and mystery, and to direct religious feeling away from the supernatural and toward the natural. When God is equated with reason, there's no real need to call God "God" anymore.

Reason and Revelation

The ancients, from Zeno and Cleanthes to Xenophanes and Carneades, left a legacy of rational speculation and religious syncretism to the Jewish and Christian philosophers of late antiquity and the Middle Ages. Within the Jewish tradition, Philo of Alexandria (c. 15–45 C.E.) worked to integrate Greek philosophical concepts into his reading of ancient Hebrew texts, while Christian theologians throughout Palestine, North Africa, and Asia Minor discovered Neo-Platonism very helpful in hammering out Trinitarian ideas regarding the substance and essence of the divine.

The essential problem for these metaphysicians and others to follow was what to do with our traditional concepts of God, which require belief in supernatural phenomena, when the insights we gain from our senses and from the workings of our minds appear to contradict those concepts, or fall short in explaining them to our satisfaction? During the Middle Ages, three philosophers, Maimonides, ibn Rushd, and Thomas Aquinas, brilliantly deployed logic and reason in their discussions of the divine, each within their own traditions (Jewish, Islamic, and Christian, respectively). Significantly, all three men worked from the ideas of Aristotle in their effort to establish the truths of their traditions upon a rational basis. You'll discover more about their work in later chapters.

In the work of Aquinas, though, you begin to see some of the pressures that will eventually come to menace the community of the faithful. Aquinas believed that people can know truth, but sometimes we know it in ways that are not easily explained. There is only one truth, and part of it is easily proved through logic and reason. But another part derives from divine revelation and must be taken on faith, although reason can help us to understand its meaning. For example, God's existence can be proven through reason, following Aristotle's proof of an unmoved mover. But the idea of the Trinity cannot, which doesn't make it less true for being beyond the capacity of humankind to either prove or disprove. Where human logic and divine revelation conflicted, Aquinas argued, it was a result of the misapplication of reason, or a misinterpretation of divine revelation.

Aquinas's approach was enormously successful, and largely shaped the way Christians went about justifying continued belief in God. And yet Aquinas unleashed forces that quickly became difficult to contain. In the thirteenth century, teachers at the University of Paris acted on Aquinas's prompts and looked deeper into Aristotle's work. They discovered some incompatibilities that seemed to defy harmonization, such as Aristotle's claim of an eternal material realm versus the Christian claim of creation *ex nihilo*. The Bishop of Paris condemned 219 propositions offered up by these teachers, including some propositions associated with Aquinas himself. It was only the beginning of a torrent of debate about faith and reason that grew through the Middle Ages and reached its height in the period known as the Enlightenment.

Divinations

In 2001, surveys revealed that some 900,000 people in the United States identify themselves as atheists. That's about 0.4 percent of the population. Some 990,000 claimed to be agnostics, which was up from 118,600 in 1990, a sevenfold increase in one decade. (American Religious Identification Survey, CUNY)

The Disenchantment of the West

History teaches us that the relationship between faith in God and the scientific exploration of nature hasn't been a very amicable one, at least since the time of Aquinas. But the modern suspicion of faith is a multifaceted and often contradictory impulse.

Anticlericalism

Much of the animus toward religion, in fact, is not actually the result of critical reevaluation of religious claims about the ultimate reality. Critics zero in on the hypocrisy of believers, political ambitions of church leaders, persecution of heretics, and various abuses of religious—and specifically clerical, authority. Because of its high profile, the Roman Catholic Church became an easy target of these critics in medieval and Renaissance Europe. Early critics were at least sympathetic to the church; new religious organizations such as the Franciscans and Brothers of the Common Life sprang up promoting reform to improve the practice of Christianity.

The Protestant reformers must be included here, too, though their reforms eventually produced schism in the church. Over time, critics became less sympathetic, unleashing savage attacks clearly not intended to make the church better.

Humanism

Through the Middle Ages and Renaissance, so-called Humanist writers began an effort to broaden and extend Aquinas's discovery of the ancient writings of Greece and Rome. Humanists such as Francesco Petrarcha (1304–1374) and Desiderius Erasmus (1469–1536) devoured Greco-Roman philosophy, history, drama, poetry, political commentary, and so on, discovering pre-Christian alternatives to Roman Catholic metaphysical and moral teachings. By the time of Michel de Montaigne (1533–1592), the mood in Western Europe had indeed changed. Montaigne wasn't a savage critic of the church so much as a thoughtful skeptic who doubted pretty much everything—Catholic dogma, Protestant reforms, even the reawakened rational outlook. He cautioned against both positive and negative attributions to God in the *Essays:* "To make judgments about great and high things, a soul of the same stature is needed; otherwise we ascribe to them that vice which is our own."

Science

Montaigne's pessimism was born of endless theological wrangling between Catholics and Protestants and of course the near-constant warfare over religious and territorial issues in the sixteenth century. And whatever intellectual and cultural unity remained in Europe was shattered in the wake of the revolution of ideas inspired by Johannes Kepler (1571–1630), Galileo Galilei (1564–1642), and a few years later, Isaac Newton (1642–1727). These men sought—and found—naturalistic ways to describe the invisible forces that sustained the workings of nature; even the powers that moved the planets and stars across the night sky had mechanical explanations. There was no longer a need to imagine an Atlas or even a Yahweh holding the Earth in his hands. But more was to come, because the ground had been laid for others to come along and further diminish God's role in the universe.

Freethinkers and Deists

People seeking to further diminish God's role in the universe arrived in the form of Freethinkers and *Deists* in the eighteenth century. John Toland, Voltaire, Rousseau, Thomas Jefferson, and many others led the way in casting doubt upon traditional explanations for the creation of the universe, the origin of sin, the meaning of Jesus' appearance on Earth, and the future destiny of humanity. Thomas Paine's *Age of Reason* (1794) is the most provocative expression of Deism. After affirming belief in one God (hence no Trinity), he said "I do not believe in the creed professed by the Jewish church, by the Roman church, by the Greek church, by the Turkish church, by the Protestant church, nor by any church that I know of. My own mind is my own church."

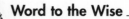

Word to the Wise

Deism, from the Latin *deus,* for "God," is the belief that God is revealed through reason and scientific inquiry, rather than supernatural or scriptural revelation.

The only insight into the divine that Paine would accept was the "progressive knowledge that man would gain, by the aid of science, of the power and wisdom of God, manifested in the structure of the universe and in all the works of Creation." To the Deists, God was uninvolved in the universe. God was rather like a clock maker who wound up the universe and then let it run of its own accord. What was true for the universe was true for human affairs as well. Enlightenment thinkers held that people were not inherently sinful, but were blank slates—*tabula rasa* in John Locke's famous phrase—and turned bad because of oppressive social and political institutions and lack of proper education. If people were to be made good, it would be accomplished by the work of people themselves, or not at all.

Reasons for Disbelief

The eighteenth century posed challenges for those who still believed that God created the universe and remained actively involved in the material world throughout history. Just as Christianity made it harder for people in the ancient Mediterranean world to look at a forest and imagine it filled with nymphs and satyrs, the Scientific Revolution and Enlightenment made it harder for modern Europeans to look at the countryside and imagine it filled with angels and demons. Simply put, the world had become disenchanted.

Not all doubting leads to disbelieving, but events of the last several hundred years might encourage many to make this assumption. The culmination of these developments in the intellectual world of Western Europe was the atheism of Karl Marx, Friedrich Nietzsche, and Sigmund Freud in the nineteenth century. We'll learn more about them in Chapter 26. Each had very curious ideas about the nature of religion, but none expressed the reasons for their disbelief as clearly as the atheist Bertrand Russell, whom we'll meet next.

The Problem of Causes

Bertrand Russell (1872–1970), a British mathematician and philosopher, believed that the argument from first causes, based on Aristotle's concept of unmoved mover, was not necessarily "proof" of God's existence. In a famous speech delivered in 1927 titled "Why I Am Not a Christian," Russell said, "if everything must have a cause, then God must have a cause." To him, the world might just as well have come into existence by itself, or not have had a beginning at all. The argument from causes, to Russell, doesn't hold water because it's only a failure of imagination on our part to insist that the world must have had a beginning.

The Problem of Natural Law

Going further in his speech, Russell attacked the inference that since universal laws govern the universe, there must be a lawgiver. He believed this was the by-product of a false association between the "laws" of physics and the laws of legislatures. In the latter case, parliaments make laws, which citizens decide either to follow or disregard. This isn't the same as natural law. In natural law, the principles of physics are descriptions of how nature is *thought* to behave, not how it *ought* to behave. The principles are conventions that human beings have derived in order to express what they perceive in nature. And when the principles are subject to real scrutiny, they don't reveal design so much as the "statistical averages of just the sort that would emerge from chance."

The Problem of Design

Christians had grown accustomed to arguing that nature offers proof of divine planning because it is so perfectly fitted together. In his speech, Russell had no patience for this argument, citing the parody of this belief in Rousseau's quip about the nose being perfectly designed for the holding of glasses. And drawing from Darwin, Russell argued that it's easier to believe people became suited to their environment through a process of adaptation, than to believe that the environment was designed to be suitable to people.

The Problem of Good and Evil

Universal morality provided no cover for theists either, according to Russell. In his speech, Russell rejected the claim that the concept of good and bad originated from God; if God is good, then "good" as a concept must be separate from and perhaps even superior to God. Furthermore, he rejected the idea that moral imbalances of the material world will be righted in the hereafter, because there's no reason to believe that moral imbalances do not exist in the hereafter as well. It would be more logical to assume that the other world is more or less like this world with all its sin, oppression, and injustice.

The Problem of Religion

Russell ended his speech with a number of comments about the teachings of Christ and the hypocrisy of Christians. He thought Jesus to be a poor teacher because one or two of his teachings were wrong—Jesus didn't return in the lifetimes of the disciples as he predicted, for example. He also thought Jesus wicked because he spoke of eternal damnation, and to Russell's thinking a perfectly good God could not be author of such cruelty. But Russell saved his most venomous condemnation for Christians. He believed that "the more intense has been the religion of any period and the more profound has been the dogmatic belief, the greater has been the cruelty and the worse has been the state of affairs," meaning inquisitions and witch burnings. And nobody seems to be turning the other cheek or selling their goods to give to the poor as Jesus had taught.

Divinations

Perhaps the most well-known promoter of atheism is Madalyn Murray O'Hair (1923–1995), founder of American Atheists and plaintiff in the famous 1963 Supreme Court case *Murray v. Curlett* that declared mandatory prayer in U.S. public schools to be unconstitutional.

It was "ignorant men" who devised the concept of God in order to terrify others into submission, at least according to Russell. He offers this prescription for the ills of society: "Science can teach us … no longer to look around for imaginary supports, no longer to invent allies in the sky, but rather to look to our own efforts here below to make this world a better place to live in, instead of the sort of place that the churches in all these centuries have made it."

Who Killed (What) God?

Russell's speech failed to impress the philosophers, but gained a wide and devoted following. This is because it neatly expressed the modern case against God, at least God as described by theists such as the Christians. It turns out that atheism really is the end product of a long-running but nevertheless very modern argument. This is

Divinations

In 1998, *Nature* published a survey that revealed that some 52.7 percent of the scientists in the National Academy of Sciences expressed "personal disbelief" in God in 1914, which rose to 72.2 percent in 1998. Those expressing "personal belief" declined from 27.7 percent to 7.0 percent in the same time period.

the argument between Western European and British clergy and theologians who hold to a classical theistic conception of the divine, and the free-thinkers, deists, and materialist philosophers who have had difficulty accepting certain propositions associated with that conception.

Traditional monotheism places God in a transcendent position with certain attributes such as perfect, eternal, unchanging, all-powerful, all-knowing, self-existent, and the like. These attributes naturally emerged from accounts of the Supreme Being Christians claimed to be worshipping since the time of Christ. It is not surprising that these attributes have created opportunities for creative minds to go to work, finding the apparent contradictions and inconsistencies that lie behind any finite account of an infinite entity.

When philosopher Friedrich Nietzsche (1844–1900) famously proclaimed, "God is dead," he didn't mean that what was once living—the creator and sustainer of the universe—is now dead (*The Gay Science*, 1882). What he meant was that there was no longer a need to retain the traditional, Western understanding of the divine in the face of the scientific mood of the modern age. It meant that the challenges to metaphysics were so significant that the West had begun to turn away and busy itself with material preoccupations. What died was not the Supreme Being itself, but the confidence that theistic belief in God is justified with rational "proofs" of God's existence, and that faith in God must serve as the grounds of human action.

Atheism and Agnosticism

What had happened, of course, was that many critical minds had turned away from confident belief to a sort of perpetual state of withholding assent. They didn't embrace disbelief, but instead hovered between two certainties—that God does exist and that God doesn't exist. The technical word for the belief that the evidence supports neither claim is *agnosticism*.

Significantly, this term was coined in the modern era during the debates inspired by the emerging materialist views of scientists and philosophers. In 1869, T. H. Huxley, biologist, educator, and defender of Darwin's theory of evolution, created the word *agnostic* and applied it to himself during a debate over Darwinism in London's Metaphysical Club. What he meant was that certain things are just not knowable; we cannot establish the truth or falsity of many things through processes of empirical investigation. Suffice to say that agnosticism, properly understood, does not preclude the existence of God.

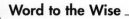

Word to the Wise

Agnosticism is a position that holds that one cannot know conclusively whether or not God exists.

This is where atheists and agnostics part company. Agnosticism is a position of neutrality in the face of imperfect knowledge. Atheism, on the other hand, is a position that affirms a proposition: God does not exist. Atheists then must take the same road as the Islamic, Jewish, or Christian theists and offer well-grounded reasoning in support of their proposition. Agnostics would probably say that they are equally disadvantaged for having framed an unanswerable question. Atheists and agnostics differ because an agnostic would ask an atheist, "What's your proof that God *doesn't* exist?"

Huxley might have coined the word, but if you've read this far in the book you will already have noticed that the roots of agnosticism run back to the prehistoric era. Every culture has produced its voices calling for humility in conversations about the divine. Perhaps it's sufficient to let the chief of all agnostics, Protagoras (c. 485– c. 410 B.C.E.), have the last word: "Concerning the gods, I have no means of knowing whether they exist or not or of what sort they may be. Many things prevent knowledge including the obscurity of the subject and the brevity of human life." This attitude, you should know, got him exiled from Athens and all of his books burned.

Eastern Perspectives

Perhaps you have come across the claim that Buddhists are atheists. The Buddhist concepts of God are very complicated and require extended reflection, which is the subject of Chapter 23. For our purposes here, it bears mentioning that Buddhists do not share the same perception of the divine that we associate with conventional Western theism in the Jewish, Christian, and Islamic traditions.

The Buddha sought release from suffering by overcoming desire and attachments and by seeking enlightenment. Buddha offered a diagnosis and a cure: misery and suffering on one hand, and knowledge on the other. He taught that those who successfully detached themselves from desire and attained enlightenment (via the Eightfold Path) could reach nirvana, the eternal state of nonbeing. Those who failed during this lifetime were doomed to continue the cycle of rebirth.

As you can see, gods never entered into Buddha's program. He thought all the talk about gods was rather a distraction from the true path of enlightenment. He chose to remain silent when asked various metaphysical questions about time and eternity and the nature of the human soul. In fact, Buddha believed that the worship of gods was just another attachment that must be overcome in order to reach nirvana. So you can say that Buddha was sort of agnostic on the question of God.

And yet Buddhists, as opposed to the Buddha, may have had other opinions. The Mahayana tradition within Buddhism began to teach that Buddha is divine, and that others who obtained nirvana and chose to remain behind to help others (bodhisattvas) are divine beings as well. Needless to say, that places the Mahayana strand outside the category of atheism.

The Least You Need to Know

- Ancient skeptics offered alternative conceptions of the divine, but didn't preclude the existence of God.

- Atheism is an outgrowth of religious and philosophical trends of the last two centuries.

- Many intellectuals in the last few centuries explained the origins and operations of nature without reference to divine activity.

- Noted atheist Bertrand Russell summed up the modern cast against the Christian concept of God in his speech "Why I Am Not a Christian."

- If the Buddha was agnostic on many questions related to God, his followers produced more definitive statements about the divine through the centuries.

Part 2

The Concept of God in Judaism

Israel means "wrestler with God," and this definition provides a clue to the Jewish concept of the divine. These chapters detail the remarkable history of the Hebrew people and their evolving relationship with Yahweh, starting with Abraham's conversation with God and ending with debates over the place of God in modern Israeli politics. The Jewish God is the God of history, working through historical events to reward or chastise those who perceive themselves as his chosen people. But Jewish voices throughout history have spoken of this covenant relationship in subtly different ways, giving rise to diverse literary traditions within Judaism. In these chapters you'll hear rabbis speak of God through the Talmud, Jewish mystics describe the ultimate reality in the Kabbalah, and scholars probe the connections between faith and reason in a philosophical movement known as falsafah. All these thinkers helped sustain an ongoing dialogue within the Jewish community, and between Jews and non-Jews, about the nature of the divine and how God might be experienced in light of changing times and circumstances.

Chapter 6

God in the Hebrew Scriptures

In This Chapter

- ◆ Learning about the saga of the ancient Hebrew people
- ◆ The meaning behind various names for the Hebrew God, such as El Shaddai and Yahweh
- ◆ The importance of the covenant idea to Jewish concepts of God
- ◆ Understanding the complex nature of Hebrew scripture
- ◆ How the ancient Hebrew religion turned into Judaism

Perhaps you've heard of the Tanak, or what many people outside Judaism know as the Old Testament. These texts record the thoughts and actions of the ancient Hebrews in Palestine. Inside, you get a very distinctive concept of God, one that gave rise to many of the core principles of theism, and particularly monotheism.

Throughout the Tanak, God is perceived as a creator God who brought the universe into being. But God is certainly not distant since he speaks directly to various people and even wrestles with Jacob in a famous episode in the Book of Genesis. God also acts in a highly partisan way, helping the Hebrews defeat their enemies and captors. But God also demands perfect loyalty and submission, with very real threats of divine retribution for offenders. In this chapter, you'll discover a picture of God in the Tanak as an absolute, sovereign, intimately involved, and perfectly just deity who maintains a special relationship with his chosen people.

Father Abraham

The Hebrew scripture contains the remarkable history of Hebrew people, beginning with the account of the universe's origins, then getting quickly to the story in Genesis of a Chaldean man named Abram who lived sometime before 2000 B.C.E.

A Surprise Visitor

One day Abram received a call from El Shaddai (in English, "God, the One of the Mountains," or "Almighty God"), instructing him to leave his hometown of Ur in the Tigris-Euphrates region and settle in Canaan, between the Jordan River and the Mediterranean Sea. The reason? God said "I will make of you a great nation, and I will bless you, and make your name great." Abram discovered he was to be part of God's larger plan to exalt the *entire* human race: "By you all the families of the earth shall bless themselves." (Genesis 12:2–3) Some scholars believe the El in the story of Abram is the same "El" worshipped by the ancient residents of Canaan. In Canaanite religion, El (High God) presided over a council of divinities that included Baal, Asherah, and others. (We'll explore these connections and scholars' disagreements over them a little later.)

Promises, Promises

We find out rather quickly in the Tanak that this is only the first of many promises God made to Abram and the rest of the Hebrew people. When Abram crossed into Canaan at Shecham, near the modern West Bank city of Nablus, God made a second promise: "To your descendents I will give this land." (Genesis 12:7)

These promises formed a covenant between Abram and God. In exchange for land and children, God demanded that Abram "walk before me, and be blameless." This covenant relationship was marked by the change of Abram's name to Abraham ("the father of many nations") and the requirement of male circumcision for Abraham and all of his tribesmen and descendents.

One of the more startling promises in Genesis included a promise to Abraham to provide a male heir through his wife Sarah, which brought Abraham to the point of laughter, given their ages (he 99, she 91). Interestingly, Sarah had earlier contrived to produce an heir through her maidservant Hagar, and Ishmael, the child Hagar bore to Abraham, was sent into the southern wilderness where he became the patriarch of the Arab people. At least this is what the Tanak teaches.

Promises Kept

Despite Abraham and Sarah's incredulity, God was true to his word. Soon Sarah conceived and gave birth to Isaac. The covenant was put to a test when God asked Abraham to offer up his miracle baby and sole heir as a human sacrifice. Abraham went through with preparations but when the time came for him to put Isaac to the knife, an angel of the Lord stayed his hand. God rewarded Abraham with further promises of land and children. From Isaac came Jacob (soon to be renamed Israel), and from Jacob came the twelve patriarchs who would establish the twelve tribes of Israel. God's promises were indeed fulfilled.

> **Divinations**
>
> There are numerous Mesopotamian records that provide evidence of a wandering group of Semitic nomads, called "Hapiru" in Sumerian cuneiform. Scholars believe this is where the word Hebrew comes from.

God of History

Abraham's story begins one of the most arresting sagas in human history. It leaves you on the edge of your seat, with cloak-and-dagger intrigue, mighty armies and epic battles, long chases and narrow escapes, and of course plenty of romance. But the story has a purpose, summed up in Deuteronomy 26:5–10. The writer tells the Hebrews to remember where they came from, and wrote up a sort of creed that begins:

> A wandering Aramean [Abram] was my father; and he went down into Egypt and sojourned there, few in number; and there became a nation, great, mighty, and populous. (Deuteronomy 26:5)

This passage in Deuteronomy stitches together Abraham's story with the story of another noteworthy Hebrew, Moses, who lived at a much later date. The account in Deuteronomy 26 continues:

> And the Egyptians treated us harshly, and afflicted us, and laid upon us hard bondage. Then we cried to the Lord the God of our Fathers, and the Lord heard our voice, and saw our affliction, our toil, and our oppression; and the Lord brought us out of Egypt with a mighty hand and an outstretched arm, with great terror, with signs and wonders. (Deuteronomy 26:6–8)

Word to the Wise

The **Torah** refers to the texts traditionally attributed to Moses, which comprise the first five books of the Tanak: Genesis, Exodus, Leviticus, Numbers, and Deuteronomy.

There's an important message here. Hebrews perceived the divine as a God of history, driving the forces of change toward some distant consummation at the end of time. The German scholars of the Tanak developed a concept for this mode of expression in the *Torah: Heilsgeschichte*, or salvation history of the Jewish people. Each major event in the Hebrew past was significant for what it revealed about the purposes of God, and each subsequent event was interpreted in light of this unfolding history.

There's More to the Story: Moses

The Hebrews established a connection between their history as a people and their growing commitment to the God of Abraham. This gets us to the story of Moses. The story includes Moses' vision of Yahweh in the burning bush, the miraculous delivery from the hands of Pharaoh, the revelation of the law (including the Ten Commandments) on Mt. Sinai, and the ultimate return to the Promised Land in Canaan. Clearly, it is no coincidence that Moses is a pivotal figure in the history of the Hebrew people *and* a pivotal figure in the emerging Hebrew concept of God.

Way Down in Egypt Land

The Hebrews went to Egypt during the time of Joseph, Abraham's great-grandson, who served as viceroy to the Pharaoh. The Hebrews lived in peace, but then Ramses II (1290–1224 B.C.E.) came to power and consigned them to slavery. The Book of Exodus records that Pharaoh feared Hebrew slaves would overcome the

Egyptians through natural increase, and so he ordered every Hebrew male infant to be killed. Moses, it seems, was spared when his parents hid him in the reeds along the Nile, only to be discovered by Pharaoh's daughter.

Moses grew up in Pharaoh's court, but when Moses killed an Egyptian for beating a Hebrew slave, he was forced into hiding again, this time among the Midianites. Then a remarkable thing happened—another divine visitation.

God Gets a Name

Hebrew scripture records that "the people of Israel groaned under their bondage …. And God heard their groaning, and God remembered his covenant with Abraham, with Isaac, and with Jacob." (Exodus 2:23–24) So God appeared to Moses in Midian, in a flame of fire out of a bush that seemed not to be consumed. The exchange that followed was extraordinary. The divine identified itself as "the God of your father, the God of Abraham, the God of Isaac, and the God of Jacob," and pledged to use Moses to lead the people of Israel from bondage.

But Moses wasn't so sure he was ready for leadership. When Moses asked what he should tell the people when they asked the name of the god that sent him, God identified himself as Ehyeh-Asher-Ehyeh, which has been translated variously into English as "I Am That I Am," "I Am Who I Am," and "I Will Be What I Will Be." This provided the basis for the Israelite name for God, YHWH, commonly pronounced Yahweh. Here Yahweh refuses to be identified with meteorological phenomena, celestial bodies, the cycles of nature, or features of the landscape. He will be what he will be, and that's the end of it.

Take Heed!

Among the more distinctive practices in Judaism is the restraint on naming or picturing the divine. If you see God written as G-d, it is not because Jews are commanded not to take God's name in vain, but out of concern that someone might come along and deface the word once it's written.

Are there two gods in the Torah, El Shaddai and Yahweh? This is a complicated question, but it touches on the strong historical consciousness of the Hebrews. Scholars explain the multiple names through critical examination of the manuscripts that we still have from the ancient period. Their theory is that the Torah was actually written by four writers in four different periods spanning an entire millennium. The first draft expressed the name of God as El Shaddai, but then a later redaction (critical revision) changed portions of the original and added new material, such as Yahweh's explanation that he was the God of Abraham, Isaac, and Jacob. The theory says that later writers knew God as Yahweh, and revised the earlier drafts to correspond with their perspective. This layering of revision upon revision introduced progressively "newer" elements into the tradition of Abraham and his progeny, elements that reflect the thinking of the Hebrews in later periods.

Believers don't think they need the scholarly explanation to make sense of the text—they simply believe that God has a number of different names that highlight various qualities or attributes, and particular passages of the Tanak should be read as parts of a larger, unified whole.

Yahweh the Deliverer

Yahweh's conversation with Moses in Exodus creates a rather odd picture—a God who refuses to be pinned down to a name or an image nevertheless conversing with a human being through a flame in a bush. We are introduced to an utter incomprehensibility—YHWH—but also a deity possessed of humanlike attributes.

And yet there was plenty more direct, divine action to follow. Yahweh punished Pharaoh for not heeding his instructions to free the Hebrews, eventually sending a plague to kill all the firstborn of the Egyptians. So Pharaoh relented, though he changed his mind once the Hebrews set out for Canaan. Of course Yahweh delivered once again, permitting the Hebrews to cross over into Sinai on dry land, then swallowing up Pharaoh's pursuing army in a watery grave.

Flagging Commitments

Both Hebrews and Egyptians experienced the awful power of Yahweh firsthand. In a song written after the narrow escape from Egypt, Moses described the deity in absolute terms, which should be read in the context of rival polytheisms in Egypt, Greece, and the Near East:

> Who is like thee, O Lord, among the gods?
> Who is like thee, majestic in holiness,
> terrible in glorious deeds, doing wonders?

But this didn't prevent the Hebrew people from complaining about their new situation in the Arabian wilderness, where they could find no food, water, or shelter. Having lived among the Egyptians and their gods for so long, some even said it would have been better to remain slaves in Egypt than die in the wilderness. The time had arrived for a renewal of the covenant.

The Covenant Idea

Hebrew carping and bickering in the wilderness served as a backdrop to Moses' famous encounter with God on Mt. Sinai. The Torah passages that record the Mt. Sinai encounter provide us with the clearest expression of the Hebrew concept of God, coupled with the fullest account of the special relationship between Yahweh and the Hebrew people.

A Terrifying Presence

In preparation for the event, Yahweh told Moses to consecrate his people, and warned him not to let anyone approach the mountain where he would appear. Death would come to those who crossed the border to Mt. Sinai. Then with thunder, lightning, and dark clouds shrouding the peak, Yahweh descended to the top of the mountain and called Moses into his presence. Yahweh reminded him of his work in delivering the Hebrews from bondage, and issued the Ten Commandments, along with a list of rules governing the religious, economic, and social life of the Hebrew people.

Here, Yahweh comes across as the Supreme Being of the universe, so absolute in holiness and power that those who merely cast a gaze upon him meet with instant death (Exodus 19:21). Yahweh demanded ritual purification prior to the encounter, signifying that the divine and the human must be thought of as fundamentally different things, with a wide ontological gulf separating them.

This idea of radical separation is the focal point of Isaiah's vision of the divine much later in the Tanak. Isaiah hears seraphim proclaiming "Holy, Holy, Holy is the Lord of hosts; the whole earth is full of his glory." (Isaiah 6:5) The Hebrew word for holy, *kaddosh*, can also be translated as "other." The Lord's otherness and holiness brings Isaiah to fear for his life: "Woe is me! For I am lost; for I am a man of unclean lips … for my eyes have seen the King, the Lord of Hosts."

Pearls of Wisdom

God has a number of names in the Hebrew scripture because the actual essence of the divine can never be named, only described in certain imperfect ways. Here are some of them:

- El (Strong One)
- Adon/Adonai (Lord)
- El Shaddai (Almighty God)
- Adonay Tzivaot (Lord of Hosts)
- El Olam (Everlasting God)
- Abir (The Strong)
- El Chai (Living God)
- Elohim (God)
- El Elyon (Most High God)
- Melech (The Ruler)

Terms of the Covenant

Although Yahweh is perceived as wholly other, he also sought to fashion a predictable, orderly, and in fact binding relationship with his people. The terms of the covenant are clear: Obey the law and receive divine favor. Yahweh's passionate desire for their loyalty and obedience comes through in this portion of the text: "I the Lord your God am a jealous God, visiting the iniquity of the fathers upon the children to the third and the fourth generation of those who hate me, but showing steadfast love to thousands of those who love me and keep my commandments." (Exodus 20:5–6)

Yahweh held forth with further promises of a "land flowing with milk and honey," but included warnings not to permit any of the previous occupants to remain. It seems Yahweh recognized the appeal of Near Eastern polytheisms and sought to remove the temptation of Canaanite, Hivite, Hittite, and Jebusite divinities once and for all. Yahweh instructed that once the people had been blotted out, "you shall not bow down to their gods, nor serve them, nor do according to their works, but you shall utterly overthrow them and break their pillars in pieces." (Exodus 23:24)

But take a look at the blessings that awaited the Hebrews should they prove faithful! Yahweh promised to bless their bread and water, to heal their sicknesses, and even to remove female infertility. And Yahweh promised to destroy all of the people who stood ready to prevent the Hebrews from realizing their destiny as a nation.

God Gets a House

In response, the people said, "All the words which the Lord has spoken we will do," which Moses recorded in the so-called "book of the covenant," later described as stone tablets handed down by Yahweh. Yahweh and his people sealed the agreement at an altar, complete with the bloody sacrifices common among Near Eastern religions that were thought necessary to bring humankind into communion with God. The Lord then asked Moses to build an ark, or chest, to contain the "testimony" of the covenant, and to build a tabernacle, "that I might dwell in their midst." (Exodus 25:8) Of course, those who built and maintained the tabernacle were directed to undergo the requisite purification rites. The ark and the tabernacle, along with the consecration of a priestly class and the performance of religious rituals, provided a venue for Yahweh to "dwell among the people of Israel." (Exodus 29:45)

Recent commentary on these passages sets the intimate scaling of the Tabernacle and the Ark of the Covenant alongside the story's spectacular personification of the divine, who engages in give-and-take with Moses, issues various instructions and commands, and agrees to dwell alongside the Hebrews. These intimate and personal aspects of the divine, scholars argue, provided a counterpoint to the frightening immensity and radical otherness of Yahweh.

God of the Heroes and Kings

The covenant had been established, but by no means was the story of the Hebrews complete. The rest of Exodus, Leviticus, and Numbers explain the development of Hebrew law and custom, and how the people struggled to maintain the covenant in the wilderness. Despairing of ever seeing the Promised Land, they resorted to worshipping Baal, the Canaanite god of storm and fertility. In Numbers 25:3, we read that "Israel yoked himself to Baal of Peor. And the anger of the Lord was kindled against Israel."

God ordered Moses to kill the tribal chiefs and all the Baal worshippers, though he relented when the priests made a proper atonement. Eventually Yahweh delivered great (though bloody) victories for Joshua over its current occupants; this is commemorated in the creed of Deuteronomy 26 as well:

> … and he brought us into this place and gave us this land, a land flowing with milk and honey. And behold, now I bring the first fruit of the ground, which thou, O Lord, hast given me. (Deuteronomy 26:9–10)

Other great heroes followed Joshua. David (d. c. 961 B.C.E.) and Solomon (d. c. 922 B.C.E.) together established Jerusalem as the political and religious center of the Israelite domain. Solomon's temple replaced the portable tabernacle, giving the Hebrews a monument to Yahweh to rival the other architectural wonders of the ancient world. And the writings attributed to David and Solomon signified a maturation of ancient Hebrew literature, particularly David's Psalms and Solomon's Ecclesiastes.

> **Take Heed!**
>
> Apparently the name Jehovah is a mistake. It's based on a poor transliteration of YHWH, the Hebrew derivative of Ehyeh-Asher-Ehyeh ("I Am Who I Am"). Though Jews do not pronounce YHWH (preferring to use Adonai, or Lord), scholars believe a better transliteration of YHWH would be Yahweh.

But try as they might, the Hebrews simply couldn't restrain themselves from worshipping local deities, despite Yahweh's many warnings and chastisements. Through the books of history—Joshua, Judges, Ruth, I and II Kings, I and II Samuel, I and II Chronicles, Ezra, Nehemiah, and Esther—we discover repeated instances of Hebrew faithlessness, none more notorious than the case of Ahab, one of the rulers of the northern kingdom of Israel 100 years or so after Solomon.

According to Hebrew tradition, Ahab built an altar to Baal and honored the Canaanite fertility goddess Asherah. Worse, he permitted his wife Jezebel to spread Baal worship among the northern tribes of Israel. In her wickedness Jezebel managed to have many of the prophets of Yahweh murdered. The Tanak records, "Ahab did more to provoke the Lord, the God of Israel, to anger than all the kings of Israel who were before him." (I Kings 16:33) As a consequence, Yahweh lifted his hand of blessing and permitted a severe drought to engulf Canaan. God had begun to deal with the Hebrew people in a collective fashion; that's the way the covenant worked.

God of the Prophets and Priests

It's difficult to know what the Hebrews found so appealing about the Canaanite gods. Maybe it was a vague memory of a tradition that existed prior to Moses' encounter with Yahweh on Mt. Sinai. Or maybe their idols seemed closer and more accessible than the ineffable Yahweh. Perhaps they just wanted to hedge their bets and pray to every available deity in order to ensure a successful growing season. The reasons for the lapse were of little importance, because the Hebrews ultimately broke their promise under the covenant and therefore deserved the calamities that befell them. That's a harsh message, though justice was served.

The job of delivering this message to the Hebrew people was taken up by a group of men called prophets. Among the first, Elijah, made it his business to instruct Israel that the reasons for the drought and famine lay in Ahab and Jezebel's apostasy. Elijah then staged a dramatic showdown between himself and 900 prophets of Baal and Asherah at an altar on Mt. Carmel. When Baal's prophets asked their god to come down and consume the sacrifice with fire, nothing happened. When Elijah called, Yahweh responded. This brought Israel back to faith in Yahweh, and the drought was lifted.

The prophets Elijah, Isaiah, Jeremiah, and Amos took on the job of refocusing the Hebrews' attention on the God of the Patriarchs. Isaiah, Amos, and Hosea even outdid Elijah by expanding their field of vision to include a variety of other grievances that the divine harbored toward Israel. Isaiah complained that the temple rituals were hollow and ineffective because the people who performed them didn't strive for moral perfection in their personal lives. Amos proclaimed a case against Israel for permitting social injustices among the people to spread unchecked. Hosea spoke of Yahweh's displeasure at the lack of feeling in Israelite devotion: "For I desire steadfast love and not sacrifice, the knowledge of God, rather than burnt offerings." (Hosea 6:6)

The prophetic voice offered a running commentary on the reasons for Israel's distress. Isaiah and Hosea associated the conquest of Canaan by the Assyrians in 722 B.C.E. with the immorality and dry ritualism of the age. The rise of Babylon and its conquest of Jerusalem in 587 triggered a spate of calls for repentance by a new generation of prophets such as Ezekiel and Jeremiah. But during the ensuing exile in Babylon, with the temple in ruins and the Promised Land in foreign hands, the prophets struck a note of hope. Because the Israelite God is a God of history, events can turn in their favor once again. Provided, that is, they demonstrate faithfulness to Yahweh. The parts of the Book of Isaiah written after the exile and the Book of Jeremiah point toward a future delivery of Israel from the hands of its enemies.

Scholars believe that the Babylonian exile and return to Canaan in 538 B.C.E. produced a noticeable shift in Hebrew perceptions of God. They detect in these last revisions of the Torah and in the new texts of the post-exile period a vision of Yahweh as creator and sustainer of the universe. Here, Yahweh also recedes from humanity a little, since the newer writings highlight the majesty of the divine, and move away from personal encounters like Jacob's wrestling match. Scholars think these redactions of the Hebrew scripture reflect the concerns of the priests who restored the temple and called the Hebrew remnant back to faith in Yahweh.

The priestly authors were more inclined to stress the cosmological supremacy of Yahweh over the old deities of Babylon and Canaan—hence the theory that the creation stories in Genesis were developed in this period. And they were more inclined to stress the *mitzvoth*, or extensive regulations for everyday life, which scholars believe were developed by post-exilic priests and written into revisions of the Torah. And the revisions include new passages that elevate the Sabbath to a position of first importance in Hebrew religion. If you were paying attention, you'd see why scholars believe that once the Israelites returned from exile, restored the temple, and revised and supplemented the Tanak, they actually worked the ancient Hebrew religion into the form we know as Judaism.

The Least You Need to Know

◆ In Hebrew scripture, God is master of history, working through historical events and processes.

◆ Ancient Hebrews perceived God as radically separated from humanity.

◆ Yahweh means I Am Who I Am, which suggests that the Hebrew God was not to be identified with sky, sun, moon, water, or any other cosmic, meteorological, or natural feature.

◆ Developments in the post-exilic period, like the emphasis on the mitzvoth, shaped the ancient Hebrew religion into a form more recognizable to modern observers as Judaism.

God in the Rabbinic Tradition

In This Chapter

- Pharisees and other sects of ancient Judaism
- Creation of the Hebrew canon of scripture
- The meaning of the Talmud
- How rabbis speak about God

The story of the ancient Hebrews is populated with character types such as patriarchs, prophets, and priests. As the story continues, we encounter the rabbis, who took over spiritual leadership of the Hebrews throughout the Middle East and the Mediterranean world. Rabbi means simply "my teacher" in Hebrew; those who held this title wore a lot of hats, from instructing the young to supervising religious observances to resolving conflicts among fellow Jews.

Rabbis didn't reinvent the Yahweh of the ancient Hebrews. Rather, they adapted the old divinity to the new realities of the Jewish Diaspora. The Diaspora refers to the worldwide scattering of the Hebrew people, starting with the Assyrian conquest of northern Israel in 722, proceeding through the Babylonian exile in 586 B.C.E. and accelerating after the destruction of the rebuilt Temple (or Second Temple) in Jerusalem in 70 C.E. In the dispersion, rabbis taught that God extends a healing hand in the face of suffering and despair, and lovingly embraces His wayward children when they choose to repent. Read on and you'll learn more about how rabbis perceived God, revealed mainly through a unique body of rabbinical teachings called the Talmud.

Leaving the Promised Land

The Hebrews were a history-minded people. They learned an important lesson from their own past—that Yahweh loved them and set them apart for a special purpose. When things went bad, such as their enslavement in Egypt or captivity in Babylon, the Hebrew people reasoned that it was because of their own failure to fulfill their covenant obligations. But when they repented and made the Lord their God, their sufferings ended and their blessings were returned.

This is how the Hebrews interpreted the Babylonian Captivity and the subsequent, seemingly miraculous, Persian conquest of Babylon in 538 B.C.E., which resulted in a new policy permitting the Hebrews to return to Palestine. Upon the Hebrew people's return, the priests insisted on strict adherence to the commandments, complete separation from non-Hebrews, and of course an end to any dabbling in Canaanite polytheism. The newly rebuilt Temple beckoned the scattered population of Hebrews back to Palestine; some heeded the call, others didn't.

Many Hebrews in exile maintained their national identity by living among other Hebrews and following the mitzvoth at a local *synagogue*. The word synagogue comes from the Greek word for "bring together," meaning place of assembly. So why did a Greek word come to be used as the name for Hebrew houses of worship? That was the work of Alexander the Great, who conquered Palestine in 332 B.C.E. and left behind rulers who used Greek language and practiced Greek folkways. Synagogues popped up wherever large enough concentrations of Hebrews could be found to support them in Palestine, Asia Minor, North Africa, and even in southern Europe.

Word to the Wise

A **synagogue** is where a congregation of Jewish people gather to worship God, usually under the leadership of a rabbi, a teacher who has studied the Torah.

The Greek rulers of Palestine, called Seleucids, tried to force the local Hebrews to convert to Greek polytheism, delivering severe penalties to those who refused. Antiochus IV Epiphanes further scandalized the Hebrews by ordering sacrifices to Zeus in the Temple. Some of the loyal Yahwehists took to the hills under the leadership of the priest Mattathias, whose three sons Judas, Jonathan, and Simon Maccabeus waged a guerilla war against the Seleucid armies, starting in 167 B.C.E. By the way, early in the war Judas reclaimed Jerusalem's Temple Mount and rededicated the Temple, an event that is commemorated today in the Hanukkah celebration.

Here's another instance in which the Hebrew people were persecuted and ultimately delivered, and as you can imagine the priests lost no time in connecting these recent events with the longer Hebrew history of captivity, exile, and deliverance. The pattern continued when Rome took control of Palestine in 63 B.C.E., instituting policies of religious tolerance for the Jews throughout the Empire, only to turn around and order the Temple destroyed and Jerusalem abandoned in the face of persistent attacks by Jewish rebels. Once the Temple was destroyed in 70 C.E., the rabbis carried the onus of explaining the meaning of these events to the Jewish Diaspora, and instilling hope of a brighter future for God's chosen people.

Occupied Palestine

The Jewish response to Greek and Roman control fixed the character of Judaism for the next eighteen centuries. A number of different groups emerged within the Hebrew community, each advocating a different response to the challenges at hand.

Zealots

Clearly, many Hebrews didn't accept Roman occupation, and so they followed the rebellious path of Judas, Jonathan, and Simon Maccabeus. The Zealots, a fanatical sect of Judaism, seemed to have organized themselves in the first century B.C.E., and readied themselves for open warfare on the Roman garrisons stationed throughout Palestine. They even attacked fellow Jews who collaborated with the Roman occupiers, and harassed those who seemed to get too comfortable with Roman folkways and policies.

The Zealots were militantly single-minded in their objective to rid the Promised Land of the Romans, picking up where earlier Hebrew kings and generals had left off. They maintained a low-grade guerilla war for much of the period, waiting for the right moment to strike. That moment came in the massive Zealot uprising of 66 C.E., which led to the Roman destruction of the Second Temple and the ethnic cleansing of Jerusalem. The uprising ended with the siege of the Zealot stronghold of Masada. When they could hold on no longer, 960 Zealots committed mass suicide rather than surrender to Rome.

Sadducees

The Zealots hated Jews who collaborated with Rome, and the Sadducees topped their list. The Sadducees took a different approach to the problem by assuming that the survival of Judaism depended on making peace with the Roman Empire. They were typically priests and wealthy landowners who had the most to lose in an all-out war with Rome. They accepted Roman occupation and adopted many Greek and Roman folkways in order to convince Rome of their peaceableness. In exchange for their acquiescence, Rome permitted them to continue Temple observances and favored them with certain political privileges. The Sadducees took a very strict view concerning God; the only scripture they accepted was the Torah (the first five books of the Bible), and they interpreted it in its most literal sense, as a record of Yahweh's direct intervention in natural and human history. Of course, their position of influence was weakened when the Romans destroyed the Temple, because this was their base of power and source of authority within the Hebrew community.

Pharisees

Both Zealots and Sadducees were wrestling with the same basic question: How should God's chosen people continue to practice their covenant obligations in the face of such trying circumstances, especially given the scattering of the people throughout the Empire? In answer to this question, the Pharisees took an entirely different approach. They spent their lives deep in the study of the Torah and the other ancient writings of Hebrew prophets, priests, and kings, making themselves into local authorities on the Hebrew faith in the synagogues throughout the region.

Divinations

The Pharisees, Essenes, and Nazarenes believed the coming of a Messiah would end the Hebrews' troubles. But the Pharisees disagreed with the Nazarenes that Jesus of Nazareth was the one. Interestingly, the Pharisees shared with the Nazarenes a belief in resurrection from the dead, which is something the Sadducees rejected.

The Pharisees were teachers. In their study and teaching, they propagated the idea that the Torah should be read in light of the viewpoints of other gifted interpreters in the Hebrew past. This meant that the written Torah was to be set alongside an "oral Torah," or body of instruction regarding the Torah handed down through the centuries. So their understanding of Yahweh was not locked down, as it was for the Sadducees, who held to a literal view of the events recorded in the Torah. They invigorated conversation about the covenant, and enjoined the people to observe the law in every aspect of life to win God's favor. The Pharisees weathered the tumult of the first century better than the Zealots or Sadducees; they influenced the inclusion of non-Torah texts in the Hebrew canon of scripture, and the further development of the oral Torah through the Talmud. More on that later in this chapter.

Essenes

The Pharisees engaged in intensive study of the writings of their Hebrew forebears, and taught a doctrine of conformity to mitzvoth that stood in stark contrast to the compromising ethos of the Sadducees. But if you want a real contrast, take a look at the Essenes. This group purified themselves through baptismal rites (literally immersing themselves in water) and separated themselves from their neighbors, whom they believed had become tainted by Greek and Roman culture. The Essenes resented the Sadducees' political compromises and their control of the Temple. The Essenes began to speak of a Temple of the Spirit that didn't require a physical dwelling. And they took seriously the prophetic passages of the Hebrew scripture foretelling the end of times, when a Messiah would appear to defeat God's enemies, establish true justice, and reward the faithful. The Essenes believed the end of the world was very, very near.

Other Groups

The Zealots, Sadducces, Pharisees, and Essenes disagreed on how to continue practicing the Hebrew religion in the face of captivity and exile. Plenty of other voices were heard, too, coming from maybe 20 to 40 distinct groups. For example, Samaritans, the multi-ethnic residents of the northern territories of Palestine, accepted the Torah but few other elements of post-exhilic Judaism, which seems to have accorded with the views of the Nazarenes. The Nazarenes came to believe that the priests and teachers of the post-exhilic period were wrong to concentrate on the mitzvoth, or outward religious observances. They called for an inner purity of the heart and total commitment to God. The Nazarenes were peculiar for holding the view that the much-anticipated Messiah was none other than Jesus of Nazareth. We'll come across them again in Chapter 11. As you can see, Hebrew people in the first century C.E.

could choose from quite a range of opinions regarding the nature of their faith and the proper way to practice it.

Rabbinical Schools

The period between the Maccabean Revolt in 167 B.C.E. and the destruction of the Second Temple in 70 C.E. was a chaotic time for the Hebrew people. Many died in suicidal attacks on the Roman Legion; others trailed off into movements such as The Way, which morphed into Christianity when it began to attract Gentile converts. Given these circumstances, it's a wonder the Hebrew faith survived at all. But then the Hebrews had a remarkable history of suffering, oppression, apostasy, and miraculous restoration.

With the Zealots and Essenes exterminated by Roman armies, and the Sadducees weakened with the destruction of the Second Temple, Hebrew leadership passed to the Pharisees. Since at least the Maccabean Period, Pharisees had studied and taught in the synagogues. Given that many were far removed from Jerusalem, they developed a view that devotion to Yahweh could be maintained outside the Temple. They personalized the mitzvoth and spoke of every family table as an altar of God. Devotion could manifest itself in purity of social interaction, diet, dress, and other matters of everyday existence. They taught the Hebrews to see God everywhere, and to think of Yahweh as approachable without priestly mediation or bloody animal sacrifices.

> **Pearls of Wisdom**
>
> In the Talmud you can find plenty of thoughtful sayings, like this passage that echoes the Golden Rule: "Anyone who judges others favorably will be judged favorably in Heaven." (Talmud, Sabbath 127)

The Pharisees who survived the chaos of the first century C.E. looked back to the work of two exceptional teachers from the time before the destruction of the Temple, Hillel the Elder and Shammai the Elder. Not much is known about either man, but they exerted enormous influence over the shape of Judaism because of the schools they left behind. Hillel is famous for his quip to a seeker who asked him to recite the Torah: "What is hateful to you, do not unto your neighbor; this is the entire Torah, all the rest is commentary." In light of this, he added, "Go and study."

Hillel and Shammai began a conversation about God that hardened into rival "schools" of interpretation. Shammai, it seems, applied principles of the Torah and rabbinical interpretation rather strictly to everyday issues and problems. Apparently Hillel was a little more broad-minded and liberal in his decisions. Later scholars identified some 300 areas of disagreement between these two figures. They produced divergent streams of thought about the Torah that eventually became known as the house of Hillel (*Bet Hillel*) and the house of Shammai (*Bet Shammai*). What's important here is that later rabbis perceived the give and take between the schools to be productive, not unsettling, because it oriented the Hebrew community toward the larger goal of sustaining a vital relationship with Yahweh.

The Hebrew Canon

One of Hillel's students, Rabbi Johanan ben Zakkai (dates unknown, but active in 70 C.E.), started a school at Yavneh (also known as Jamnia, in the present town of Jaffa near Tel Aviv), which persisted after the destruction of the Temple and the deportation of the Hebrew population of Jerusalem. His wisdom was sought on all sorts of questions such as why did God choose Babylon for the Hebrews' exile, or why are certain numbering schemes in the Torah contradictory? But he was most well known for founding the school at Yavneh, which was one of the most important centers of learning for the Hebrew people. It was this school that determined the extent of the Hebrew *canon* of scriptures sometime around 100 C.E.

> **Word to the Wise**
>
> **Canon,** a Greek word meaning measuring stick, refers to writings that are accepted as authoritative, mainly because they meet some standard of holiness or divine inspiration. This word is used mainly in connection with Hebrew and Christian scripture.

The Hebrew canon reflects the influence of the Pharisees over the selection of sacred texts: the Torah was included, but also the writings of prophets and historians (called Neviim), and the wisdom literature of Proverbs, Ecclesiastes, and Job (called Ketuvim). The origin of the word Tanak derives from a compilation of the first letters of Torah, Neviim, and Ketuvim.

The Talmud

When Rabbi Zakkai's students set the number of sacred books at 39, they didn't mean for the conversation about God to stop. On the contrary, they wished it to continue. To foster further dialog, they took the extraordinary step of putting into writing the oral Torah handed down for centuries from priest to priest and teacher to teacher, making it accessible to successive generations of Jewish readers. That step was the beginning of the Talmud.

The Oral Torah

The oral Torah is the tradition of commentary on the works of Moses (or written Torah), developed by the rabbis in light of the changing circumstances of the Hebrew people. The rabbis' collected opinions provided a steady hand amid the jarring dislocations of captivity, foreign occupation, and dispersion. The oral Torah taught that it was possible to live out the covenant with Yahweh despite repeated disruptions in Temple activities, or even in the absence of the Temple itself.

> **Divinations**
>
> The life of Rabbi Johanan ben Zakkai provides one of the more colorful episodes in rabbinical history. He fled Jerusalem in 70 C.E., narrowly escaping the clutches of Roman troops and Jewish rebels by hiding in a coffin carried by two of his students, Eliezer ben Hyrcanus and Joshua ben Hananiah.

One of the greatest of the early rabbis, Rabbi Akiba ben Joseph (c. 15–135 C.E.), realized that these teachings should be preserved for use among Jewish refugees throughout the Mediterranean world. When he looked closely, he discovered that these opinions could be gathered under six heads: agricultural laws, regulations concerning festivals, marriage and family laws, business and financial laws, Temple observances, and laws that cover issues of purity and impurity. Akiba's impulse to organize and commit to writing the oral Torah of the rabbis resulted in the Mishnah.

Mishnah

This set of writings preserves the rabbinical opinions of the first generations of rabbis, such as Hillel and Shammai, and was in use by the second century C.E. It is the centerpiece of the Talmud, which is a very large book that also contains the written opinions of later generations of rabbis. The Mishnah reveals the extent to which the Hebrews sought to maintain continuity and solidarity in the face of severe trials and tribulations. And the Mishnah contains opinions about the Temple observances and the use of land, which seem to indicate that everyone expected an eventual return to the Promised Land and restoration of the Temple.

Gemara

If you look at a page of the Talmud today, you'll see the Mishnah in the center, and surrounding it you'll see chunks of text that have been added at later dates. One of those chunks is the Gemara. This is a collection of rabbinical commentary on the Mishnah from the first four centuries after the destruction of the Second Temple. In the most exhaustive version of the Talmud, the Babylonian Talmud, the Gemara section combines two different strands of rabbinical wisdom. The first strand contains various stories from the rabbis, such as accounts of their interactions with students and other rabbis over questions relating to the Torah. The other strand contains further commentary on the commandments and regulations of Judaism, the so-called *halakhah*.

Through the Talmud, the rabbis taught that God is to be experienced in every part of life. If you want to live out God's will, then everything about you has to reflect the holiness and sanctity of God—your style of clothing, choice of food, personal demeanor, and so on. Your behavior on holy days and in the marketplace must reflect this as well. What you'll find in the Talmud is nothing short of a description of the Jewish way of life. The laws and regulations, the halakhah, instruct Jews in the right manner of living so they might be a daily testimony to God's righteous involvement with humanity.

Take Heed!

A simple reading of the Talmud might leave you thinking that Jewish believers are obsessed with trivial matters such as what sorts of things can be eaten or how to prepare for the Sabbath. But this is a gross distortion. Jews believe the Talmud offers a vision of how to live in order to reflect the holiness and purity of God. And the study of the ancient conversation about the divine in the Talmud is thought to be one of the greatest acts of devotion to God.

There's a passage in the Tanak that offers some insight into why Jews follow the halakhah:

> The law of the Lord is perfect,
> reviving the soul;
> the testimony of the Lord is sure,
> making wise the simple;
> the precepts of the Lord are right,
> rejoicing the heart;
> the commandment of the Lord is pure,
> enlightening the eyes;
> the fear of the Lord is clean,
> enduring forever;
> the ordinances of the Lord are true,
> and righteous altogether. (Psalm 19:7–10)

So if you find yourself scratching your head, wondering why Jews follow intricate kosher laws or maintain strict Sabbath observance, perhaps you'll realize that this is the Jewish way of living with a greater sense of the spiritual presence of God in their midst.

Rashi's Commentaries

Think of the Talmud as an open-ended conversation about the nature of the divine and the best way to live as a follower of God, and you'll begin to appreciate the beauty and power of the text. And you'll realize why the conversation didn't stop with the Mishnah and Gemara. Rabbi Schlomo Yitzchaki (1040–1105 C.E.), or Rashi, penned a thoughtful commentary on the Torah and the earliest sections of the Talmud. In Troyes, France, he lived a life of scholarly dedication to the study of the ancient Hebrew manuscripts. His work established the authoritative version of the Talmud, and offered a complete, line-by-line elucidation of its meaning to people living in northern Europe in the Middle Ages. No other rabbi attempted such a sweeping reappraisal, and so his work has been included in subsequent editions of the Talmud as Rashi's Commentaries.

Tosafot

And in the few centuries after Rashi's Commentaries were added, rabbis continued the exchange of views characteristic of the Talmud by offering comment on Rashi's commentary on the earlier rabbis' views of the halakhah. These are collected together as the Tosafot, the Hebrew word for additions, usually included as a column of text alongside the Mishnah and Gemara and opposite the page from Rashi's Commentaries. Here, teachers such as Rabbi Jacob ben Meir of France and Rabbi Meir ben Barukh of Germany propose opinions different from those suggested by Rashi.

Divinations

The word *Talmud* is Hebrew for "study" or "learning," and indicates the importance of intensive study of the Torah and rabbinical writings in Jewish spirituality.

Interestingly, both rabbis explore tensions and contradictions in the Talmud by utilizing new concepts available in the twelfth and thirteenth centuries, trying ultimately to alleviate and resolve these tensions. Put together, the Tosafot sections reveal the determination of Jews to persist in their efforts to understand the meaning of the Torah and its application to life thousands of years and thousands of miles removed from Moses and Mt. Sinai.

Wrestling with God

The rabbis who left behind the Talmud—the collected wisdom of the sages of Judaism—engaged in a sophisticated conversation about God's law revealed to Moses, and its continued relevance for the dispersed Jewish community. The Talmud, in fact, gave the Jewish faith much of its unity and coherence as it alighted on thousands of communities in Europe, Asia, North Africa, and the Middle East. To learn the Jewish faith, children read and studied the Torah, and reflected on the layers of conversation among earlier Jewish teachers who also read and studied the Torah. In other words, becoming Jewish meant joining a centuries-long conversation on what it means to be Jewish.

In that conversation Jews discovered the importance of Sabbath observance, proper marriage arrangements, and the celebration of special festivals. They also learned how to maintain purity through proper food preparation and personal hygiene. And yet the whole of the Talmud evokes an image of a religious community in continuous development. It's a religious community in constant dialog about God, and with God. We might even be reminded of the meaning of the word *Israel*, the name given to Jacob after his visitation by God in Genesis 32:22–32. It means "Wrestler with God." As Israel, the religious community of Jews is involved in a grappling match with Yahweh, and the Talmud, the centuries-long dialog over the meaning of the Torah, is the clearest expression of this way of perceiving the divine.

The Least You Need to Know

- The Hebrews disagreed among themselves about how to respond to exile, occupation, and dispersion, leading to the creation of different sects, such as the Zealots and the Sadducees.

- Pharisees influenced Judaism through the rabbis, who stressed intense study and adaptation of the faith to changing circumstances.

- Rabbis, or teachers, committed the oral Torah to writing, which formed the core of the Talmud.

- Through the Talmud, Judaism described God as intimately involved in the details of ordinary, everyday life.

Chapter 8

God in Jewish Mysticism

In This Chapter

- Unusual ways of perceiving the divine in Judaism
- Revisiting the creation story in Genesis
- Early Jewish mystics and the rabbis
- The essence of Kabbalah
- How mystics experience God in the deep places of the mind
- *Tikkun olam*, or repairing the world

A peculiar vision came to one of the ancient priests, Ezekiel, sometime around 593 B.C.E. while the Hebrews were exiled in Babylon. He saw a cloud rimmed in light, from which came a chariot pulled by four creatures. These were fantastic beings, each with a combination of four human and animal faces and each with two pairs of wings, with a light in the form of burning coals dancing among them. In the sky above the chariot appeared a throne, upon which sat a shining figure in the shape of a person. The very Lord had appeared, instructing Ezekiel to call Israel to repentance for their rebellious ways.

Ezekiel's vision gave rise to a distinct tradition within Judaism, a set of beliefs and practices separate from—and often at odds with—the rabbinical tradition, known as *mysticism*. Eventually, mystics came to believe that human efforts to comprehend and experience God through words and concepts are ultimately unsatisfying. Because these words and concepts act as intermediaries between the divine reality and human consciousness, they fall short in capturing God's holiness, majesty, and power. Follow along, and you'll encounter a group of seekers who taught that God is more clearly perceived in the deep recesses of the mind than in spiritual language, theological concepts, or religious observances.

> **Word to the Wise**
>
> **Mysticism** has several different meanings; in the philosophical sense mysticism is the pursuit of hidden or secret knowledge, while in the religious sense it generally refers to direct experience with the divine or Absolute.

The Journey of Rabbi Akiba

There's a well-known story in the Talmud about a group of rabbis from the first century who were engaged in the study of Ezekiel's vision and the meaning of the chariot. Among them was Rabbi Akiba (40–c. 135 C.E.), perhaps the most important of the early Torah scholars. He's remembered for starting a rabbinical school at Bene Beraq and organizing the oral Torah into categories, which eventually gave structure to the Mishnah.

As the story goes, the four rabbis entered a garden, whereupon Rabbi Akiba warned, "When you arrive at the stones of pure marble, do not say: 'Water! Water!' For it is said: 'He who tells lies shall not stand before my eyes.'" (Ps. 101.7b) One of the rabbis took a look, and died on the spot. Another looked and became insane. A third lost his faith and was declared a heretic. Only Rabbi Akiba survived his journey in the garden unscathed. The Talmud notes, "Rabbi Akiba departed in peace." (Talmud, Festival Offering, 14b)

In this passage, the rabbis used the word *pardes* for garden, a conventional term identifying special methods of interpretation thought to produce mystical insights into the divine. So what you have is a cautionary tale about the dangers of the mystical path, at least for those who travel without the correct preparation and guidance. Rabbi Akiba proved equal to the challenge; his three companions clearly did not. Maybe this is why many early rabbis condemned the mystical path. Evil fates such as heresy, insanity, and even death lurked around the corner for those who treaded lightly.

Seeing God

Of course, rabbinical Judaism went an entirely different direction from the early mystical visionaries. Rabbis stressed the sanctification of everyday life through adherence to the mitzvoth. And they offered a model of devotion in their intensive study of the Torah. Yet, a few mavericks among their number came to believe that a greater insight into the divine awaits the spiritual pilgrim who is prepared to go beyond verbal constructions and sensory perceptions. These seekers embraced the Torah and the mitzvoth, but weren't ready to limit their search for heightened spiritual awareness to doctrinal and behavioral modes of religiosity.

These seekers came back time and time again to the stories of Moses' theophany and Ezekiel's vision of the throne, among others in the Tanak. They found meaning in stories that told of manifestations of the divine presence, and were excited by the possibility of human glimpses of the glory of God. Though Rabbi Johanan ben Zakkai's status as a first-century C.E. mystic is debatable, he experienced the presence of the Holy Spirit during a session in which he and his students had been discussing the chariot imagery in Ezekiel's vision. And much later, writers of the fifth and sixth centuries developed a body of work known as Throne Mysticism, derived in part from the tradition of early rabbis who contemplated the meaning of Ezekiel's vision of God.

Throne Mysticism is a highly unusual way to perceive the divine. In a fifth-century book titled *Shi'ur Qoma* (*Divine Dimensions*), the writer gives a name to the being on the throne in Ezekiel's vision: *Yotzrenu* ("Our Creator"). Amazingly, the text goes on to provide actual measurements of the figure, though the geometric values are of an uncertain and quite bizarre nature. Another fifth-century text, *Sefir Yetzira* (*Book of Creation*) picked up on the creator theme and worked out a strange scheme for ordering the beginning of all things. It blended the numbers between 1 and 10 with the 22 letters of the Hebrew alphabet and arranged them in combination, producing a sort of grid that purported to capture the flow of God's creative process. Taken together, the texts claim to reveal hidden truths by virtue of their discovery of secret knowledge about the divine.

> **CAUTION**
>
> **Take Heed!**
>
> Jewish mystics cautioned that while they caught glimpses of the glory of God in their mystical journeys, they never actually become one with God. That is where Jewish mysticism departs from Christian and Islamic mysticism and the devotionalism of Eastern religions.

During the first century C.E., Jewish mysticism developed into a spiritual discipline, a method whereby the pilgrim receives unfiltered visions of the ultimate reality. The disciplines of physical posturing and mental concentration, advocated by later mystics such as Hai ben Sherira Gaon of Babylon (939–1038 C.E.), enable seekers to focus their energies within, to ascend through the so-called seven heavens and approach the throne of God. Mystics who practice these disciplines are rewarded with visions that go beyond metaphysical abstractions. This is where the training and guidance comes into play. Believers must not mistake a vision of gardens or thrones for the actual divine being—only a novice would commit this error. In reality, what the believer gets is an inner, highly personalized experience of God's presence.

Origins of Kabbalah

The idea of a method for attaining mystical experiences, or a personal experience of the ultimate reality, is behind the Kabbalah, from the Hebrew root word for oral tradition. It is possible to speak of a tradition of Jewish mysticism by the beginning of the Middle Ages, particularly with the appearance of *Sefer ha-bahir* (*Book of Brightness*) in twelfth-century France.

The *Book of Brightness*

Believers who followed the way described in the *Book of Brightness* (or commonly *Bahir*) were not yet practicing a method so much as adopting a very peculiar view of the cosmos and God's relation to it. They perceived God as manifested through 10 *sephiroth*, or powers, that are one with God, yet also distinct and identifiable entities. The *Bahir* appears to borrow from Throne Mysticism the tendency to use Hebrew letters to elaborate the nature of the sephiroth, and it seems to loosely correspond to the Talmudic view that God created the world through 10 attributes or traits: "by wisdom and by understanding, and by reason and by strength, by rebuke and by might, by righteousness and by judgment, by loving kindness and compassion." (Talmud, Festival Offering, 12a) Importantly, the sephiroth became associated with the Tree of Life mentioned in the creation story in Genesis. This connection offered Kabbalah writers a way to interpret the nature of God and his activity in the world.

> **Pearls of Wisdom**
>
> Rabbi Simeon ben Yohai, a second-century C.E. ascetic, spoke for those who search for deeper truths when he apparently wrote this, as recorded in the *Zohar:* "Fools see only the garment of the Torah, the more intelligent see the body, the wise see the soul, its proper being."

But the writers push well beyond the Talmud and delve into the territory of mysticism by depicting the sephiroth as involved in some sort of symbiotic relationship with humanity, responding to human action with mercy or justice as the situation dictates. The text arranges these sephiroth in a complex, geometric hierarchy, with a higher and a lower power, the lowest perhaps being wisdom. It is this sephira (singular of sephiroth) that must directly contend with the material world, and it is this sephira that joins together with the people of God in a kind of marital relationship. And what God's people do in this relationship affects, and even disturbs, the very being of God.

Isaac ben Abraham

A few years after *Bahir* appeared, a Jewish mystic named Isaac ben Abraham or Isaac the Blind (c. 1160–1236) pushed in the direction of spiritual discipline and immediate experience of the divine. He understood the sephiroth as vitally connected to the material world, and the purpose of the material world as a return to the divine, forming what is known as *devequt*, or "attachment to God." Isaac believed the journey toward God was an individual effort, unlike the view of spiritual discipline expressed in the *Bahir*, which espoused collective spiritual progress. He believed the journey progressed through a personal regimen of right moral action, prayer, contemplation, and other devotional practices.

Spanish Mysticism

Kabbalah wasn't really Kabbalah until a network of mystics in the medieval Spanish town of Gerona further developed the special cosmological insights found in the *Bahir*. The Gerona mystics kept the hierarchical arrangement of sephiroth, but perceived them as the willful manifestations of a hidden, ineffable, unknowable divine, called *En Sof* ("without end"). Certain strands of thought in Kabbalah refer to En Sof as Nothingness, since it is perceived as the totality of being, rather than a being among beings. The sephiroth of En Sof are then set into a hierarchically ordered matrix; these sephiroth shed light upon the eternally dark and unfathomable En Sof, which in turn flows throughout the matrix of sephiroth and gives it unity and power (see the following figure).

Jewish Kabbalah perceived the Absolute as one unitary God, En Sof, uniting in treelike matrix the 10 Biblical manifestations of the divine, known as the sephiroth (in Hebrew, numerations).

(Courtesy of Suhrkamp Verlag)

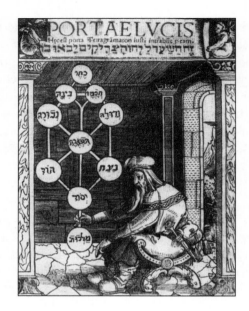

By the thirteenth century, the names of the sephiroth had been more or less established:

1. Kether Elyon: Supreme Crown

2. Chokmah: Wisdom

3. Binah: Intelligence

4. Geburah: Power

5. Chesed: Love

6. Yesod: Foundation

7. Tiphareth: Beauty

8. Netzach: Eternity

9. Hod: Majesty

10. Malkuth: Kingship (also called Shekhina, or "presence")

There are plenty of ambiguities here; keep in mind that Kabbalists were not prepared to explain this system rationally. They had trouble accounting for evil, as other thinkers did, so they began to see it a consequence of the emanation process that ultimately produced the sephiroth. To their way of thinking, the divine is consistent with the Torah and Talmudic depictions of God, and they took pains to illustrate how the sephiroth corresponded to various aspects of the *Heilsgeschichte*, or salvation history of the Jewish people. In this way, the halakhah comes into play, since Kabbalists believed that strict performance of the law was required in order to sustain the order of universe. In fact, strict performance of the law is the means by which the universe might be set aright, put back "together," as it were.

God in the *Book of Splendor*

If there's an über mystic anywhere in the Jewish mystical tradition, it's probably Moses ben Shem Tov de Léon (c. 1250–1305 C.E.), the seeker and writer who pulled together the *Sefer ha-zohar* (*Book of Splendor*). This book represents the maturation of Jewish mystical concepts and contains a compendium of creative—but nevertheless still Jewish—ideas about the divine.

In the *Zohar*, as it's commonly known, believers are encouraged to go beyond the surface language of the Torah and wrestle with its secret, hidden meanings. Believers are introduced to various levels of interpretation, from the literal sense of the words (i.e., God actually has hands and feet) to moral, allegorical and ultimately mystical meanings. In fact, there might be limitless meanings, as many as there are people willing to undertake the difficult journey of spiritual progression. On this journey, the pilgrim discovers greater and greater insights into the divine, ascending a path that En Sof created through the various emanations of the sephiroth. In the beginning En Sof chose to become apparent, coming out of the eternal Nothingness and presenting as Kether, Chokmah, and Binah. Further emanations flowed downward, reaching toward the material world, taking such forms as Tiphareth, Hod, Yesod, and Netzach. Finally, the En Sof came to be revealed through the Shekinah, or the divine presence.

The *Zohar* taught that the manifestations of the material world form a path for the spiritual pilgrim to follow. The seeker must learn that behind the visible world lay another, more profound and more truthful reality waiting to be discovered. First, the believer sees and understands the external realities of things, then proceeds to grapple with their inner essences. In later stages

Divinations

Students of Kabbalah sometimes speak of the 32 Paths of Wisdom, which are discerned in another book called *Sefer Yetzirah* from a combination of the 22 letters of the Hebrew alphabet and the 10 sephiroth.

of the journey, the pilgrim comes to perceive truth through intuition, and then acquires the knowledge that can be gained only through love (here described as the love of the Law). This ascent follows the course mapped out by the descent of the sephiroth; by strictly following the law, and using personal devotions such as hymns and prayers, the mystic acquires knowledge of God's loftier manifestations, reaching ever closer to the very source of all reality.

Tikkun Olam (Restoring the World)

Kabbalist writers perceived a problem in the conventional Jewish concept of God: the origins and nature of evil. The *Zohar* offered an explanation by associating the emanation of the final sephira, the Shekinah, with Original Sin. Adam, apparently, was instructed to appreciate the beauty of the first nine sephiroth embodied in the Tree of Life, and the beauty of the final sephira, the Shekinah, embodied in the Tree of Knowledge. But Adam came to prefer the latter over the former, triggering the onset of a cosmic imbalance and a separation of Shekinah from the other sephiroth. As Karen Armstrong writes in *A History of God* (see Appendix A), "The divine life could no longer flow uninterruptedly into the world, which was isolated from its divine Source." Now humanity had a new problem, but also a new task. The objective of humankind is to reconnect the Shekinah to the divine, and to restore equilibrium to the cosmos. God's people accomplish this task by reading the Torah and living out the mitzvoth.

The incredible vision of a newer form of Kabbalah offers further wisdom in this vein. Spain sent the Kabbalah mystics packing in the fifteenth century, and many wound up in Palestine, where a teacher named Isaac ben Solomon Luria (1534–1572 C.E.) expanded on the Kabbalah concepts of emanation and divine transcendence. He taught that the divine (defined as light) shrank to create space for the created world, which splintered some of the light into particles that descended to the material realm. This is the nature of evil, according to Lurianic Kabbalah, which is to say the encasing of divine light in earthly matter. The believer must restore (*tikkun*) this light to its original source by living in strict conformity to Jewish law, forsaking worldly attachments, and following the mystical path. In this way, the community of believers heals God, and heals the world (*olam*).

Word to the Wise

Tikkun is the Hebrew word for "restore" or "reintegrate." It comes from a tradition of thinking about the role of humanity in bringing healing to the world.

Is Mysticism Accepted in Judaism?

Kabbalah found fertile soil in medieval European Jewish communities, because it provided an imaginative and creative escape from sterile metaphysics and the regimen of Torah and Talmudic study. Kabbalah continues to be practiced in the present day, finding supporters among Orthodox Jews who appreciate the deeper insights that it promises, and among secular Jews who appreciate the social and environmental ethics of tikkun olam.

However, the rabbis found all sorts of things to dislike about Kabbalah. For example, the rabbis believed the focus on numerology and the letters of the Hebrew alphabet blurred the focus on the content of the writings. Today, rabbis complain about the Kabbalist practice of optically "scanning" the letters to induce a trancelike state. This, they believe, is nothing short of superstition. Rabbis thought, and many continue to think, that Kabbalah takes the mind of believers off high moral living and fulfillment of the law.

Other issues are more complex. Critics charge that Kabbalah traffics in eroticism in its depiction of Shekinah's exile from the divine source. Early Kabbalah literature linked Shekinah with Sophia, the goddess of wisdom. And the idea that this aspect of the divine might be female, and might be wandering around seeking reunion with her lover, seemed to push beyond the boundaries of acceptable talk about God. Critics also disliked Luria's belief that God became God through a process that included the sexual intercourse of personified, and specifically gendered, sephiroth. Its easy to see why many tradition-minded rabbis believed this sort of thinking led to error and even blasphemy.

> **CAUTION**
>
> **Take Heed!**
>
> Many rabbis consider Kabbalah to be a heresy because certain strands of Kabbalah teach the doctrine of reincarnation. This idea reflects the close association between Jewish Kabbalah and Eastern religions.

Kabbalah invited believers to seek out direct encounters with the divine, and at several points in Jewish history this led to unfortunate episodes, such as the story of Shabbetai Zevi (1626–1676 C.E.) who studied Lurianic Kabbalah, experienced mystical ecstasy, and became convinced he was the Messiah. Many others were convinced, too, and thousands of Jews across Europe and the Middle East converted to his cult. Even some influential rabbis were taken in. The whole affair ended in a mess when Shabbetai was arrested by the Ottoman Turks in Istanbul for disturbing the peace and agreed to convert to Islam to spare his own life.

In our own time, orthodox rabbis have distanced themselves from controversial Kabbalah teacher Philip Berg and his Kabbalah Centre in London, which sells special vials of water to those who seek miracle cures. In a larger sense, however, the question of whether Kabbalah is Jewish is really a matter of one's point of view. While that debate continues, it is impossible to ignore the influence of the mystical tradition within Judaism. Kabbalah reminds Jews of the ineffectiveness of human language, metaphysical concepts, and religious rituals to penetrate the deeper mysteries of the universe. Human beings seek to know the shape and composition of the spiritual realm, the nature of time and eternity, the character of the human soul, and of course the very essence of God. The appeal of mysticism reminds us that words, concepts, and religious observances continue to be unequal to this task.

The Least You Need to Know

◆ The term mysticism has different uses, such as the pursuit of hidden knowledge, or the direct encounter with the divine.

◆ Jewish mysticism grew up alongside the Talmudic tradition in Judaism.

◆ The golden age of Jewish mysticism occurred in the twelfth and thirteenth centuries with the appearance of the *Bahir* and the *Zohar*—key texts of Kabbalah.

◆ Lurianic Kabbalah produced many of the doctrines that traditionalist rabbis find objectionable.

◆ Kabbalah energized the concept of tikkun (restoration), which provides humanity with a motive for improving the world.

Chapter 9

God in Jewish Thought

In This Chapter

- Philo's influence

- Can Judaism stand on a rational foundation?

- Jewish thinkers flirt with philosophy

- Maimonides' famous list of necessary Jewish doctrines

- Judaism meets modern science

- Reading the Torah after the empirical turn

In earlier chapters we met two groups of writers who produced two distinct literary traditions within Judaism—the Talmud and the Kabbalah. These traditions offer different takes on the nature of the divine. The Talmud wrestles with the history of rabbinical commentary on the Law revealed to Moses, while the Kabbalah imagines an elaborate system by which God revealed himself to humanity, and by which believers can ascend toward God. It's time to add the voices of another first-century C.E. group to the conversation about God within the Jewish tradition: Jewish philosophers.

These thinkers offer a fascinating counterpoint to the rabbinical and mystical writers, because they freely engaged the broader current of thought about ultimate reality coursing through Western civilization. In doing so they invigorated ancient and medieval Judaism by cross-fertilizing Jewish readings of the Torah with concepts from such diverse schools of thought as Neoplatonism, Muslim falsafah, and Christian Scholasticism. Even though Judaism began to incorporate a new language, its focus nevertheless remained the God of history who selected the Jews to fulfill a special mission on Earth. Those who created this philosophical tradition within Judaism gave us a body of work that's nothing short of an intellectual feat.

Philo of Alexandria

When the Hebrew people emerged from exile and came under Greek and Roman control in the second and first centuries B.C.E., they started talking about a coming Messiah who would intervene in history and bring justice to Israel's enemies. They looked for signs of this coming "Day of the Lord," and those who joined sects, such as the Essenes and Zealots, lived as if that day might come within their own lifetimes. But another voice surfaced in this period of political crisis and otherworldly expectation within Judaism—Philo of Alexandria (20 B.C.E.–50 C.E.).

Philo sympathized with the conflicting visions of first-century Palestinian Judaism, but also with the Greco-Roman culture of the Mediterranean world. He lived in Alexandria, Egypt, which served as the cosmopolitan hub of the empire built by Alexander the Great. It also happened to be the home of the largest Jewish community outside of Palestine. Philo came from an elite Jewish family of Alexandria with political connections to Rome. He was a scholar and a teacher, but he was occasionally pressed into service by the Jewish community to speak to the authorities on their behalf—even reportedly traveling to Rome in 39 C.E. to discuss Jewish problems in Alexandria with the notorious Emperor Caligula.

Pearls of Wisdom
Have you ever heard the saying "With God, all things are possible"? This seems to have been a repeated refrain in Philo's many writings about the Torah and Greek philosophy.

Rereading the Torah

Philo spent most of his time in the study of the Torah, just like scores of other rabbis in the Jewish Diaspora. He came to believe that the Torah should be read both literally and allegorically. In other words, he believed the story in the Torah was an actual record of God's supernatural intervention in history, setting the Hebrews apart to pursue his purposes on Earth. But Philo thought the Torah suggested some deeper meanings beyond the literal words, characters, and events contained in its pages.

This allegorical reading brought Philo to associate Moses' work with the work of other ancient thinkers who pondered ultimate things, especially Plato. To the rabbis and prophets, Moses was a visionary and deliverer; to Philo he was a sage, having "learnt from the oracles of God the most numerous and important of the principles of nature." Philo thought that the God of Moses was the same as the God of the philosophers, who taught a doctrine of universal law, borne within the mind of each member of the human race. In his allegorical mode, Philo rejected the literalism of the Torah's physical descriptions of God. Philo's Yahweh doesn't appear as a being that walks and talks, or as a pillar of fire springing from a bush. Instead, his God cannot be associated with any particular property or attribute but is known only by means of the abstract revelation of God in the form of Logos, which we'll learn more about in this chapter.

Mystical Knowledge of God

Philo is among the earliest thinkers to make the clear distinction between the nature of God, which is unfathomable, and the existence of God, which can be perceived and understood. There's a bit of mysticism in Philo's approach to the question of just how people can know God through the Logos. He taught that the mind contains two different organs: sense perception and intuition. God sends signals to humanity through nature that are picked up by the senses and used to make inferences about God's ways (as in our appreciation of the intricate order of the universe and its designer), and God sends mental impressions of the divine directly into the minds of those who are properly disciplined and prepared to receive them.

This idea of a special sort of cognition puts Philo squarely in the tradition of the mystics. He talked about three levels of knowledge; most people cannot see past the material world and therefore remain at a base level of understanding, while some can perceive the divine as the supreme governor of the universe—the Logos—and thereby ascend to a middle level. But then a gifted few can reach the summit of human understanding where a direct, unmediated appreciation of God's workings awaits. Moses reached this level, and so did Plato and a few other exceptional people. Philo gave special emphasis to the spiritual and contemplative life, because the highest levels of cognition are accessible only to those who go beyond mere training and habituation and seek higher truths through purification of the mind.

The Logos

According to Philo you have inside your mind a small part of the universal Logos, and if you educate, then purify, your mind you make it suitable for God to give it direct impressions of ultimate reality. This brings us to the idea of Logos in Philo's writings, which is Philo's main departure from rabbinical thinking about God, and which helped to shape later Christian theology of God as well.

In Philo's writings you can find lots of different definitions for Logos—the creative power of God, the rational property of the mind, the glue holding the universe together, the mediator between God and humanity, wisdom itself, among other things. So it's safe to say that his understanding of Logos was pretty chaotic. And yet you can see in the various uses of Logos Philo's attempt to harmonize Greek philosophy and Jewish concepts of God.

God created the world by means of the Logos, and the world itself forms an image of the Logos. Philo perceived the Logos by which God created the world in Moses' account in Genesis as the same Logos who structured Plato's world of Forms, as the "the archetypal model, the idea of ideas." So Philo thought that Moses and Plato were really talking about the very same entity, but in very different ways. Keep in mind that the Greek translations of Hebrew scripture, the Septuagint, used the word *Logos* to identify God's audible speech to various hearers. Philo's legacy in Western philosophy and theology was to join together the idea of Logos as the unifying principle of reality and the idea of Logos as God's speech—verbalized revelation—to human listeners. When God spoke things into existence in the first chapter of Genesis, God also injected the universal, rational principle into the material world (and as we have noted, the human mind as well), thereby providing the means by which God can be known to humanity.

> **Divinations**
>
> In Philo's time, the ratio of Jews to non-Jews in the Roman Empire was about 1:9 and some accounts place the Jewish population of Alexandria—the Empire's second largest city—at 40 percent of the total. The Jews are thought to be the reason Rome adopted the seven day week and rest on the Sabbath.

Philo's effort impressed a lot of believers in the first century, especially early Christian thinkers who struggled to find ways to talk about the relationship between the person of Jesus and the God of the Torah. Philo was so influential among this crowd that one of the earliest historians of Christianity, Jerome, identified him as one of the fathers of the Christian faith.

Rabbinical Judaism: Challenges and Responses

If Philo's work influenced the shape of Judaism, it did so only indirectly. He taught the Jews that their faith was consistent with the best thinking available in the pagan world, and that seemed enough for most. The chief influence on Judaism after the first century were the rabbis who organized and propagated the Talmud from their seats of authority in the synagogues. It wasn't until the Karaites appeared in the ninth century that Judaism returned to Philo and philosophy for assistance in explaining the nature and attributes of God.

The Karaites

The Karaites were a group of Jews in Babylon led by a fellow named Anan ben David, who came to believe that the rabbis had introduced novel ideas and perhaps even corruptions into the law as it was revealed to Moses. Close at hand were the rabbis of the Sura Academy of Babylonia. The Karaites kept asking why the Jews needed further elaboration on the Torah—weren't Moses' own words good enough? The Karaites believed the meanings that rabbis attached to the Torah and recorded in the Talmud were not only unnecessary, but potentially destructive to the faith of the primitive Hebrew people.

Starting in the tenth century C.E., the Karaites openly opposed rabbinical teaching and rabbinical authority. They denied the authority of the Talmud and accepted only the Torah as being of divine origin; they studied it feverishly and interpreted it literally. Since the literal meaning of the text was the only legitimate meaning, Karaites tended to discount reason as an appropriate means to discern the nature and functions of God. Outwardly, there seemed to be little difference in the Judaism of the Karaites and the Judaism of rabbinical teaching, though Karaites tended to be a wee bit more conservative than their counterparts in the Jewish mainstream. The Karaites were more zealous in their application of Sabbath regulations, use of the lunar cycle to date holy days (unlike the fixed calendar of the rabbis), and the requirement of pilgrimage to Jerusalem on certain of these days. In addition, Karaites didn't follow rabbinical wisdom on purity laws, and so they acquired a reputation for being a little more, well, puritan on these matters.

Saadia ben Joseph

Rabbis had little patience for the Karaites, and one of the rabbis' leaders in Babylonia, Saadia ben Joseph (882–942 C.E.), took the Karaites to task. Saadia focused on the

Karaite tendency to read the Torah in its most literal sense and accordingly discount reason as a means to discern truth. Saadia found a kindred spirit in Philo. He revisited all the same territory that Philo charted in the Greco-Roman philosophical landscape, using Greek philosophical language and concepts to demonstrate the Talmud's consistency with the Torah. In the process, Saadia discovered the Greek method of discerning metaphysical truths through mental calculation, and thereby came to appreciate the value of reason. After identifying and examining four different sources of knowledge, he concluded that revelation and human reason agree.

CAUTION

Take Heed! _____

Like Philo before him and Maimonides after him, Saadia ben Joseph identified a list of core doctrines implicit in the faith of Moses as revealed in the Torah. Philo identified five, Maimonides thirteen, and Saadia eight. Though Saadia thought articles of faith were necessary to avoid what he considered to be heresies—such as Karaism— most Jews did not accept lists of doctrines as appropriate features of Judaism.

Saadia's response to the Karaites both reflected and hastened the coming of a new mood among the people of God in the Middle East and Europe, which is to say an increasing appreciation for the metaphysical insights of ancient philosophy. Saadia himself helped to translate the Hebrew scripture into Arabic, and used Arabic translations of Greek philosophical works in his dialogue with the Karaites. This sharing of information between Muslims and Jews in the tenth century was a pivotal moment in the ages-long conversation about the nature of God. Saadia's work, and the work of contemporary Muslim rationalists, is thought to be one of the reasons why medieval thinkers came to believe that reason and revelation could be integrated into one harmonious system.

Judah Halevi

So could God be discerned through reason? Yes, answered the philosophically inclined rabbis, but only imperfectly. Over in Toledo, a Spanish Jew named Judah Halevi (1075–1141) entered the exchange over the relative value of reason with his remarkable book, *The Kuzari*. It's a fictional account of Bulan, a leader among the Tartars, who one day summoned spokesmen from the major traditions to convince him of their version of the divine. Bulan quickly dismissed a philosopher with his conception of a universal Intelligence achieving oneness with humanity by means of reason. He found the Christian equally unconvincing because his concepts defied reason, and because it owed so much to Judaism. Apparently Bulan responded better to the Muslim apologist, but Islam, like Christianity, took its starting point from Jewish concepts of God. So along came the rabbi and explained to the Tartar king that God revealed himself to Moses and to the prophets, filled with promises of earthly blessings in exchange for the Hebrews' single-minded devotion and high moral living. Now Bulan had found his religion. It was a religion that wasn't contrary to reason, but nevertheless contained mysteries that reason could never wholly penetrate.

The Coming of the Faylasufs

Saadia and Halevi reflect the tensions that emerged in the Mediterranean world and the Middle East over the relationship between faith and reason. In the 800s, Muslims discovered the ancient works of Plato, Aristotle, and other Greek rationalists and pioneered a new conversation about God using Greek ideas as a stimulus. Scholars such as Yaquid ibn Ishaq al-Kindi (d. 870) put the Qu'ran into dialogue with Aristotle and came to believe that both spoke of the same eternal, universally applicable principles of the universe. He saw Allah as Aristotle's First Cause, the chief principle of the universe and ultimate source of being. Though Qu'ranic revelation offered a complete vision of ultimate reality, philosophical speculation offered support for faith and offered illustrations of faith's universalizing claims.

Islamic philosophy, or falsafah, produced several generations of thinkers, the Faylasufs, who exercised enormous influence over medieval Islam, Judaism, and Christianity. Ultimately their vision fell out of favor within Islamic circles, but it offered new inspiration for believers to ground the truths of their religions upon rational principles. Scholars such as Abu Nasr al-Farabi (d. 980) accepted Platonic and Aristotelian perspectives on ultimate reality and in fact preferred the abstractions of the philosophers to the fanciful anthropomorphisms offered by the teachers of the tradition. Avicenna (Abu Ali ibn Sina, 980–1037) read al-Farabi and decided that Islam offered a perfection of the ideas of Aristotle and Plotinus, with the Prophet Muhammad himself achieving the philosophical ideal of perfect insight into the Absolute. Avicenna worked from Aristotle's proofs of the existence of God to establish Allah at the pinnacle of existence—an unknowable, yet intelligible, being, perceived by humanity through systems of logic, but also more the fantastical visions of the prophets and mystics.

We'll learn more about falsafah and its traditionalist critics in Chapter 17. For now, you should understand how Jewish thought came to be influenced by the Faylasufs and their far-reaching engagement with concepts of Greek metaphysics. And maybe the most important of the Jewish thinkers to come under their influence was Moses ben Maimon (1135–1204), also known as Maimonides. More than anyone else, Maimonides reflects the impulse in the early Middle Ages to package faith and reason in one harmonious system, offering both as part of a seamless whole designed by God for the benefit of all humanity.

The World of Maimonides

Maimonides was born in Moorish Spain, the part of Spain controlled by Islamic caliphs until the fall of the last Muslim stronghold in Granada in 1492. He studied the Torah and Talmud under the direction of his father, but then went with his family as they fled anti-Jewish persecution in Córdoba, first to Morocco and then to Palestine and finally Egypt. Maimonides also studied medicine and eventually became court physician to the famous Muslim conqueror Saladin. Meantime, he served as a leader of the Jewish community in Fostat, a small town near Cairo. His life illustrates the conflicts among early medieval Jews, Muslims, and Christians, but also the fluidity of the boundaries among these communities of faith.

Divinations

Apparently, word of Maimonides' intellectual talents and professional expertise spread far and wide in medieval Europe. Legend has it that King Richard II of England even offered him a position in his retinue, which Maimonides declined in favor of continued service to Saladin's son and heir, al-Afdal.

With Maimonides we again arrive at the question of Biblical interpretation. He spent much of his young adulthood studying the Torah and the Talmud, and authored a much-admired and widely read commentary on the Mishnah, called *Mishneh Torah* (Torah Revealed). Here, he followed Philo's lead and reasoned that the account of creation in Genesis might be read allegorically, rather than literally. This followed from his reading of the rest of the Hebrew canon, wherein prophets used figures of speech and strange visions to capture the essence of the divine; he believed these accounts must not be interpreted literally, but as flashes of insight into an otherwise unknowable and mysterious God. Maimonides reasoned that it is best to speak of God in negatives: not as a being that knows everything, but as a being that is "not limited" in knowledge. This way of portraying God, he believed, helped us avoid the inevitable weaknesses of human concepts in describing God's ineffable nature.

Still, Maimonides embraced Aristotle's method of establishing belief in God upon a rational basis. Taking his cue from Aristotle's proofs of the existence of the Absolute, Maimonides wrote *Guide of the Perplexed* (1191), a sort of introduction to the philosophy of religion that examines the philosophical underpinnings of belief in the divine. It was written in Arabic for one of his students, but others quickly translated it into Hebrew, Latin, and a number of European languages. As such, it became a sort of early, standardized textbook for the study of the intersection between reason and revelation.

From Maimonides' vision of a rational faith came a set of principles that began to define the nature of God. Maimonides thought these principles were necessary because every being that lacked them couldn't be God, but would be something short of the supreme creator, sustainer, and governor of the universe. This list of principles served as a sort of creed for medieval Judaism, though its acceptance has waxed and waned, and varied from community to community. Maimonides' 13 necessary principles are:

1. The existence of God

2. The oneness or unity of God

3. The spirituality or incorporeality of God

4. The eternity or timelessness of God

5. The omniscience or all-knowing nature of God

6. The exclusive worship of God alone

7. The divine origin of all knowledge

8. The supremacy of Moses among the prophets

9. The timeless perfection of the Torah

10. The knowledge God possesses of man's deeds

11. The inevitable judgment of God for sins

12. The truth of an eventual Messiah

13. The certainty of resurrection of the dead

This offered a new twist on Jewish divinity. Now, Maimonides found a rational basis for belief in the Torah and the teachings of the rabbis, and then inferred that believers must ascribe to an irreducible list of doctrines, lest their faith be found hollow, incomplete, or in error. This belief is what scholars of religion call *orthodoxy*. Maimonides' version of Jewish orthodoxy came under severe criticism by Jewish thinkers, such as Hasdai Crescas in the fifteenth century and Moses Mendelssohn in the eighteenth century, because it seemed to close the conversation with God that rabbis believed had been opened with Moses and continued in the oral Torah and the Talmud. Nevertheless, Maimonides' vision energized Judaism, laying the groundwork for greater engagement between Jewish concepts of God and the rationalism of the Renaissance and Enlightenment periods.

Word to the Wise

Orthodoxy means right belief, typically in reference to religions with official doctrines that adherents are expected to support.

Jewish Thought in Modern Times

Maimonides triggered an unsurprising response from tradition-minded rabbis; Rabbi Solomon of Montpelier in France ordered *Guide to the Perplexed* burned in 1233 because of its rationalizing tendencies. Eventually, though, many found Maimonides' techniques for reading the Torah very helpful, and others were attracted to his vision of a path to God that was guided by reason. His creed was even adapted for use in Orthodox Jewish observances. But it was among the philosophers that his influence was most pronounced.

Baruch Spinoza

Maimonides influenced the concept of God in the writings of Baruch de Spinoza (1632–1677), a Jewish thinker from Amsterdam. After some study of the Talmud and various European languages, Spinoza became a serious skeptic and eventually embraced views that most considered atheistic. More properly we might call his views pantheist, as we discovered in Chapter 2. Spinoza discounted the wisdom to be gained through the revelations of various prophets and mystics, and instead spoke of natural religion and the universal law that infuses and orders all material existence. Spinoza's God was totally immanent, nearly to the point of being equated with existence itself. Not much Jewish content here. In fact, Spinoza's writings earned him an anathema from the synagogue in Amsterdam. Still, his ideas contain a faint echo of earlier Jewish rationalists such as Philo and Maimonides who viewed reason as an avenue, albeit an imperfect one, to truth.

Judische Wissenschaft

And then there were the nineteenth-century writers who created the school called Judische Wissenschaft (Science of Judaism). These German-Jewish scholars seemed to pick up where Maimonides left off, which is to say rereading the Torah to gain greater insight into the divine. And yet these thinkers, such as Leopold Zunz (1794–1886) and Solomon Formstecher (1808–1889), approached the concept of God in a more historical, progressive manner. God became clarified, according to Formstecher, as primitive pantheism and animism morphed into monotheism—at least the sort of transcendent monotheism you see in the Hebrew Torah. But God wasn't done yet. He then developed from a Temple-based deity who required physical sacrifices and legalistic observances into a more intimate being who could be perceived and experienced directly. Eventually, God would be released from external supports altogether and become the God of free individuals seeking to live the high moral life. Other Jewish writers who contributed to the Science of Judaism pushed in the direction of rationalism, away from the strange visions of the Kabbalah and the hyper-legalism of Hasidic Judaism (see Chapter 10 for more on Hasidism). The idea was to make Judaism more appealing to an increasingly humanist, secular, and in fact quite anti-Semitic culture in Northern Europe.

> **Pearls of Wisdom**
>
> In the introduction to his work *Eight Chapters*, Maimonides wrote: "One should accept the truth from whatever source it proceeds." That spirit still courses through many Jewish communities in the Middle East and throughout the world.

The Haskalah

The rationalizing tendencies of the Judische Wissenschaft culminated in a new outlook among nineteenth-century European Jews, the so-called Haskalah. European Jews confronted various challenges to their faith, namely a surging scientific outlook that denied supernatural phenomena and metaphysical realities, and a shifting set of attitudes that defined Jews in strongly negative terms. Just like their counterparts in first-century Palestine, modern Jews were induced to rethink the question of how to be Jewish amid trying circumstances. Those who advocated adaptation and assimilation to modern ways formed a movement known as Haskalah. Haskalah Jews abandoned the rabbinical schools for secular universities, wore modern clothing and spoke German or Polish (instead of Yiddish), and began to think of Judaism as a national identity or a cultural ethos, rather than a religion or disposition toward God.

Soon, the Haskalah produced a highly secular vision of Judaism, utilizing the Hebrew language and a common national heritage as points of connection, and abandoning the intensive study of the Torah and Talmud and the observance of the mitzvoth. This change wasn't the most important variant of Judaism to emerge from the nineteenth century, but it's an indication of how some Jews came to respond to the immense pressures exerted upon their community by the social, political, economic, and intellectual forces of the modern era. Hints of Haskalah can be found in contemporary Reform Judaism and secular Zionism, just two of the many variants of Judaism that form the contemporary landscape of the Jewish faith. We'll cover that ground in the next chapter.

The Least You Need to Know

- Some Jewish thinkers have had little trouble showing the rationality of Judaism.

- Philo of Alexandria was among the earliest to distinguish between God's unknowable essence and God's knowable attributes.

- You can find some important interconnections between Jewish and Muslim thinkers in the Middle Ages.

- Maimonides used Aristotle's proofs of the existence of God, which medieval Muslims and Christians found persuasive as well.

- In the modern period, some Jewish thinkers accepted the ideas of science and Enlightenment philosophy, creating a nonreligious vision of Jewish identity.

Chapter 10

God in Contemporary Judaism

In This Chapter

- ◆ Various Judaisms in the modern age: Reform, Conservative, Orthodox, and ultra-Orthodox
- ◆ Principles of Reform Judaism
- ◆ Where God fits into modern Jewish movements
- ◆ Origins of secular Judaism in the 1800s
- ◆ Differences of opinion among Jews regarding Israel

Today, we number the worldwide Jewish community somewhere between 13 and 14 million, with roughly 10 million divided equally between the United States and Israel. But to call it a community belies a great diversity of opinion about what it means to be Jewish, and about the continued relevance of the rabbinical tradition in the contemporary world. You discover right away that Judaism has flowed down different channels in recent years, as in Reform, Conservative, Orthodox, and Haredim (ultra-Orthodox) Judaism; this is to say nothing of the welter of religious parties in Israel that offer divergent views on key issues of the faith.

Among these groups, the differences can be rather pronounced. Some who claim Jewish nationality embrace Judaism's historical and ethical components, but reject the intense religious observances of the halakhah and the metaphysical architecture associated with Jewish monotheism. Others claim that you can't be Jewish unless you proclaim faith in the God of Abraham, Moses, David, and Elijah, and pledge to follow the Law of Moses as interpreted by the Talmudic scholars and local rabbis. And the movements seem to hold very different views on what "Israel" means. Is "Israel" a spiritual union among believers, a vision of collective salvation in the future, or a secular state in the Middle East? Can we speak of a shared concept of God in contemporary Judaism? Keep reading and we'll try to get to the bottom of these issues.

Looking for God in the Diaspora

In the previous chapters, we discovered a few variations in the way Jewish teachers and writers perceived God. Talmudic writers attempted to remain faithful to the picture of a perfect, all-powerful, all-knowing, transcendent God in the Torah, while mystics offered a complicated model of divinity centered on the idea of sephiroth (God's manifestations) and spiritual return to the divine source. The visions of the rabbis and the mystics spread as far as the Jewish community itself, from Palestine through Central Asia and the Middle East into North Africa and western Europe, finally reaching the New World, particularly the United States.

The Sephardim and Mizrachim

Within worldwide Judaism, culture came to give subtle inflections to the faith in different regions. In the Middle East, North Africa, and Spain, Jews were influenced by direct contact with Islam and Arabic culture, and via these contacts, the ideas of ancient Greek and Roman philosophy. These Jews are known as *Sephardim* (from the Hebrew word for Spain, Sefarad) and *Mizrachim*. They tended to mix casually with indigenous people, though at times they experienced persecution; Jews were famously expelled from Medina (in present-day Saudi Arabia) after Muhammad failed to convert them to Islam in 622 C.E., while some 200,000 Spanish Jews were expelled when the Muslim city of Granada fell to Christian forces under Ferdinand and

> **Word to the Wise**
>
> **Sephardim, Mizrachim,** and **Ashkenazim** identify different cultural groups within Judaism.

Isabella in 1492. In any event, Mediterranean Jews tended to speak Hebrew or a mix of Hebrew and Spanish, and to observe the holidays with fewer restrictions than their northern European counterparts. Their exposure to Islamic falsafah and Sufism encouraged the rationalist and mystical elements in Judaism, as you see in the work of Avicenna, Maimonides, and writers in the Kabbalah tradition.

The Ashkenazim

Another major cultural group is the *Ashkenazim* (from a Hebrew name in Genesis 10, but now commonly used in reference to Germany). The Ashkenazim popped up along the Rhine River in France and Germany, which gave their Judaism more of a northern European flavor. They adopted a German-influenced dialect of Hebrew called Yiddish, but ironically were more protective of their ancient Jewish customs than the Mediterranean Jews, mostly in response to local hostility toward their religion and folkways. Ashkenazim engaged Talmudic study with great zeal, producing among their number the great Talmudist Solomon ben Isaac (commonly known as Rashi) (1534–1572) and the writers of the Tosafot. Both sets of commentary on the rabbinical writings, Rashi's Commentaries and the Tosafot, were printed in later editions of the Talmud. Ashkenazim also maintained the tradition of Hebrew liturgical poetry from late antiquity, which seems not to have been very important among the Sephardim and Mizrachim.

Hasidism

The vast majority of the worldwide Jewish population could be numbered among the Ashkenazim, Sephardim, and Mizrachim. A little outside of this mainstream stands the Hasidic Jews of eastern Europe, centered in Poland. Israel ben Eliezer (c. 1700–1760), considered the founder of Hasidism, believed that the Talmudic and Kabbalistic versions of Judaism were a little too brainy; he once told a pupil that his explanations of Lurianic Kabbalah were correct, but his conclusions were "thoughts without any soul in them." Around the age of 36 he took the name Ba'al Shem Tov and started a career moving around as an itinerant healer and teacher.

Ba'al Shem Tov told his listeners to see God in everything. In contrast to the rabbinical vision of God's radical transcendence, he taught that God was omnipresent, as both creator and sustainer of all things. He liked to speak of all things as having an essence, which he identified as the divine spark within. This sounds a little like pantheism, but he was careful to add that the idea of a divine spark didn't imply a broken and diffuse God, but rather, a means by which believers might experience the presence of the divine. It's God's way of limiting himself so he can be known, or manifested, to humankind.

Take Heed!

Hasidic Jews may *look* serious, but in reality they preach joyfulness in the face of suffering and despair. This comes from their founder, Israel ben Eliezer, who put sadness (*atzut*) at the core of all sin, and led his followers in happy celebrations of singing, dancing, and enthusiastic prayer.

Hasidic Jews came to believe that it was possible to release these sparks from the material world and reunite them with the divine, thereby witnessing something of the glory of God. They thought this could be done through deep contemplation and ecstatic prayer; they believed that truly pious believers who forsake the world and practice the spiritual disciplines prepare themselves to be special tools used by God to reintegrate worldly things unto himself. Certain exceptional people—the Zaddik—reached an exalted plane of existence somewhere between the divine and material realms, where they serve as intermediaries between God and humankind. Hasidic Jews saw the Zaddik as exemplars of spiritual progress, and sought them out as guides for their own personal journeys. Hasidic rabbis soon became famous for rejecting worldliness, practicing intense devotionalism, and claiming ecstatic religious experiences. Numbers are sketchy, but it's thought that perhaps a quarter million Jews living today are of the Hasidic variety, with some 200,000 of those in the United States.

Signs of the Times

More pronounced disagreements within Judaism came about in the 1800s, as the Jewish community confronted two serious challenges to the traditional faith. First, European intellectuals in the 1700s started to identify God with reason, tempting Jews to abandon the old idea of a personal deity who supernaturally intervenes in history. Then came the movement for toleration, which seemed to encourage greater contact between Jews and non-Jews, and a blending of Judaism with secular culture. These forces triggered debates within Judaism (the northern European Ashkenazim in particular) over the concept of God, the relationship between God and humanity, and the special status of the Jews among the different nations of the earth. These forces also brought Jews to question the continued relevance of the halakhah within an increasingly secular environment. Over time, these debates produced the major divisions that survive to the present day: Reform, Conservative, and Orthodox Judaism.

Reform Judaism

German Jews in the eighteenth and nineteenth centuries had a front-row seat to an intellectual donnybrook the likes of which the world has never seen. Such heavyweights as Immanuel Kant, Johann Gottlieb Fichte, Friedrich Schleiermacher, and Georg Wilhelm Friedrich Hegel took on the subject of metaphysics and presented a serious challenge to Western concepts of God. You'll discover more about their ideas in Chapter 26. For now, you'll need to know about the work of Abraham Geiger (1810–1874), a German rabbi and theologian who studied the historical development of Judaism and the composition of the Hebrew scripture. His studies, along with the rationalizing and humanizing influences of Enlightenment philosophy, led Geiger to advocate positions that formed the core of Reform Judaism in Europe and elsewhere, particularly the United States.

Geiger observed that the Talmudic literature revealed a progressive adaptation of the Jewish law to changing historical circumstances. The Judaism of Moses, David, and Solomon was not the same as the Judaism of post-exhilic rabbis or the first-century Sadducees and Pharisees. If the Jewish faith ran with the times for much of its history, then it was conceivable that it should adapt itself to the modern world as well. Geiger further explained that the mitzvoth was culturally relevant in the ancient Near East, but bloody sacrifices and purification rites held no meaning in the present. To Geiger, the essence of the Jewish faith was its vision of a single, holy, perfect, all-powerful and all-knowing God who insists on ethical behavior from all people. These ideas formed the core of the faith in Moses' time and represent the parts of Judaism that were relevant for all times and places.

Geiger seemed to give Jews permission to ignore the intricate set of laws that comprised the halakhah. In fact, many had already done so in Germany, France, and Britain. When these countries extended toleration to Jews, many Jews emerged from their forced isolation and entered the cultural mainstream, becoming known as the Haskalah. As early as 1809, some European synagogues held services in the common language, permitted the mixing of men and women, and abandoned the bar mitzvah ritual for boys. The practice of wearing head coverings fell by the wayside and dietary laws were ignored. Perhaps the most telling reform came when progressive rabbis broke tradition and reinterpreted the meaning of Israel. No longer did they preach an eventual repatriation of the Jews to Palestine, or prophesy the coming of a Messiah to deliver the Jewish people. To their minds, the Diaspora was not another exile to be followed by repentance and restoration; rather, it served God's purposes in spreading ethical monotheism to the four corners of the earth.

Reform Judaism crossed the Atlantic in the nineteenth century with Ashkenazi Jews from Germany. Rabbi Isaac Mayer Wise (1819–1900), David Einhorn (1809–1879), and Samuel Hirsch (1815–1889) led rabbis in organizing Reform conferences, such as the Philadelphia meeting of 1869 that rejected the doctrine of bodily resurrection and the idea of return of the Jews to Palestine. In Pittsburgh in 1885, the Reform rabbis eliminated kosher and purity laws, regulations on dress, and the performance of religious ceremonies. But they also went a step further, soft-pedaling belief in the supernatural elements of the Torah and stressing only the moral code as obligatory, with the Ten Commandments at its core. Later meetings restored traditional ideas about Israel (1937) and Sabbath observance (1976). About 900 synagogues across North America style themselves Reform Judaism, and continue to project an ethical vision of the faith, even as they permit a range of opinion on metaphysical issues.

> **Divinations**
>
> According to the Annual Survey of American Jewish Opinion (2000), 10 percent of U.S. Jews polled called themselves Orthodox. Reform and Conservative Jews each tallied 31 percent, Reconstructionists (a modified version of Reform Judaism) 2 percent, and "Just Jewish" 25 percent.

Conservative Judaism

Whereas Reform Jews seem willing to adapt ancient religious observances to modern times, Conservative Jews hold fast to tradition. The Conservative view started out as a response to the views of Abraham Geiger, who raised the concerns of tradition-minded Jews in Germany, including Rabbi Zacharias Frankel (1801–1875). Frankel looked with favor upon Geiger's historical approach to the Torah and believed that scholarly analysis provided some insight into how the halakhah could be fitted to contemporary needs. But he insisted that halakhah contained an element of the sacred that bound Jews together as a people, and to chip away at these customs and rituals was to weaken the very bonds of national identity that sustained Jews during troubled times.

Conservative Judaism retained kosher laws and regulations covering Sabbath observance. But there's a wide variation among Conservative synagogues in how they adapt the halakhah to present-day circumstances. Some synagogues are indistinguishable from Reform Judaism, except for maybe a little more Hebrew in the liturgy and the insistence on a Jewish education for children of the congregation. Others are very traditional, and appear on the surface to be identical to Orthodox synagogues attempting to carry on pre-modern rabbinical Judaism. Several features that

Conservative Jews hold in common tell a great deal about its position on the spectrum of Jewish responses to modernity; Conservatives allow men and women to sit together, which is a nod to the Reform vision of cultural adaptation, and yet they support the state of Israel, which affirms a traditional position on the issue of whether the Jews should be reconstituted as a people in the Promised Land. There are about as many Conservative as Reform synagogues in the United States today.

Orthodox Judaism

Among the Jewish movements of the nineteenth century, Orthodox Judaism is at once the easiest and most difficult to define. First we'll take a look at the tenets of Orthodoxy that are easy to describe. Orthodox Judaism is merely a continuation of the rabbinical tradition, emphasizing the miraculous history of the Jewish people as recorded in the Torah. Like the old rabbis, the Orthodox discover in the Torah a conception of God as wholly transcendent, completely good, jealous of the loyalties of his chosen people, and perfect in his judgments. And they accept the requirements of the mitzvoth as the sacred duty of the Jewish people under their covenant with God. They pursue Talmudic study with great intensity, since it contains the oral Torah communicated to Moses and written down in the Mishnah. Finally, they believe that Palestine is for the Jews, and believe in the continued relevance of halakhah provisions for its land and sacred places.

So it's pretty easy to describe Orthodox Judaism as a continuation of the rabbinical tradition and leave it at that. But Orthodoxy is really another response to modernity, and so it must be seen in light of the other responses of contemporary Jews to modern cultural, social, and political forces. And this is where Orthodoxy starts to become more difficult to describe.

Take the issue of the Torah itself. Reform Jews followed the lead of eighteenth- and nineteenth-century scholars of ancient texts and began to read the Torah as a historical record of the human encounter with God, written by human hands. So Reformed Jews are more inclined to think of the laws regarding ritual purity and severe penalties (eye for an eye) as relevant only to ancient people. Since the Talmudic rabbis themselves reread the laws in the face of changing circumstances, Reform Jews believe they are justified in abandoning most of these laws. Like Reform Jews, Conservatives read the Torah as a historical document, but consider the laws to be necessary as an authoritative expression of Judaism. To Conservatives, the halakhah can and should evolve with the culture in which the Jews find themselves. However, Orthodoxy goes a different direction entirely. Orthodox Jews perceive the Torah as the divine word of God spoken to Moses, who put it down in writing and delivered it to the people. So it is sacred speech. That's also true for the oral Torah communicated to Moses and later committed to writing in the Mishnah. Nothing is there that God didn't intend to be followed, whether in ancient Palestine or modern Europe.

Orthodoxy is also rabbinical in the sense that its adherents understand the need to keep open the ancient rabbinical conversation between God and humanity. As issues surface, such as stem-cell research or homosexuality, Orthodoxy returns to the tradition and uses it to make determinations about the fitness of these practices for the Jewish faith. Orthodox Jews are permitted to engage in business and politics, but continue strict observance of the halakhah because of its original, divine mandate. There are fewer Orthodox than Reform or Conservative Jews in the United States, but Orthodox Jews attend synagogue more frequently. As a result, there are more Orthodox congregations in the United States than Reform or Conservative congregations.

The Haredim, or Ultra-Orthodox

Orthodox Judaism holds to a traditional concept of God in response to Reform tendencies to define God in terms of a broader "God-idea" and to consider only the ethical standards of Judaism as binding. But some Orthodox felt that even the Orthodox teachings of rabbis such as Samson Raphael Hirsch and Solomon Schechter didn't go far enough. New movements in the twentieth century, clumped together under the media-derived label ultra-Orthodox, strive to resist compromise with a changing culture, and to create separatist enclaves where the Jewish faith can be practiced in its most undiluted form. At the root of the Haredim way (Hebrew for "those who tremble") is a conviction that other Jews have compartmentalized their lives, acting Jewish in their families and congregations and non-Jewish in their professions and civic affairs. Haredim seeks to break down this perceived division and sanctify all of their activities, from diet, dress, and marriage to work, leisure, and politics.

So Haredim opposes both the assimilationist lifestyle of the Haskalah, represented by today's Reform Judaism, and also Conservative and even Orthodox Jewish compromises with modern life. Outside of Israel, where Haredim form a small minority, the results tend to be separatism and creation of an alternate Jewish world apart from the rest of society. Haredim maintain purity through strict observance of Sabbath and Jewish holidays, distinctive black clothing and head coverings, beards for men, and exclusively religious education for the young. In many places Haredim have achieved sufficient numbers to support schools, groceries, banks, medical clinics, and even community police that conform to the halakhah, normally through intense application of the Torah by Haredi rabbis. Haredim believe that creating this parallel Jewish world is the only way to ensure that all areas of life—public and private—remain sanctified to God, and the only way to demonstrate complete faithfulness to the covenants God first made with Abraham and Moses.

Secular Judaism

Haredi belief leads to a distinctive style of life, often in opposition to other Jews who have chosen a more accommodating approach to prevailing social and cultural norms. Over the last 200 years the choice between assimilation and separatism intersected with another pressing issue within Judaism, which is the meaning of Israel. Inspired by Enlightenment philosophy and the growth of nationalism, Reform Judaism taught a doctrine of loyal citizenship in the various countries of Europe and North America. Jews emerged from forced isolation to revise the mission of the Jewish people in the contemporary world as propagating the moral code of Judaism and calling their fellow countrymen to a higher ethical standard, rather than living in conformity with the law of Moses. In this view, the term Israel came to define a people destined to lead humanity in the direction of progressive social and political change, without the need for a covenant with God or hope for reestablishment of Jewish control over the Holy Lands.

This secular view of Israel resonated beautifully with the Enlightenment idea of progress, or the idea of building a more rational, more humane, more just society. And when Karl Marx began to speak of a future without economic exploitation or social injustice, some Jews responded with a doctrine of Jewish socialism, building into it an updated version of the old messianic idea of a coming order in which peace and justice reign throughout the world. In embracing a socialist doctrine, secular Jews had a way to talk about the historical destiny of the Jewish people, without accepting what they perceived as the irrational superstitions of the Talmudic and Kabbalistic rabbis. Jewish socialism came to define the word Israel as a program of progressive social, economic, and political change, hastening the onset of a perfectly just and rational society. Jewish socialists actually returned to Palestine in small teams to build agricultural settlements (the kibbutzim), intending to show the rest of the world how to accomplish this vision.

If some Jews were hopeful about the role of Judaism in establishing a just socioeconomic and political order, others were more doubtful. Jews enjoyed increased freedom with the Enlightenment, but the promise of the Enlightenment had been broken in the nineteenth century with the appearance of widespread anti-Semitism and outright persecution in Germany and Russia, among other places. Theodor Herzl (1860–1904) and other noteworthy secular Jews led a movement soon to be known as *Zionism* to build a state where Jewish people could be safe and secure. Herzl wrote *The Jewish State* (1896) and organized conferences and fund-raising drives in order to build support for the idea, which bore fruit in the Balfour Declaration (1917) where the British government pledged to use part of the land under its imperial control in Palestine to build a secular Jewish nation, at which point the word Israel took on a new meaning—the Jewish nation. When Israel finally became an independent nation with U.N. approval in 1948, political Zionism had become an accomplished fact.

Word to the Wise

Zionism refers to beliefs regarding the Jews and the land promised to Abraham, and in recent years a political movement to place control of Palestine in Jewish hands.

Political Zionism gained the support of the U.N. largely because of the experience of the Holocaust. Jewish responses to the Holocaust varied greatly; some argued it was a divine punishment for Jewish sins of watering down the concept of God and failing to observe the mitzvoth, while others interpreted it as an invitation for Jews to dialogue with God over his plan for humankind, like Abraham's protest against God's intention to destroy Sodom. Still others perceived in the Holocaust and the formation of the state of Israel a contemporary instance of the historical pattern of humiliation, exile, and redemption. This historical pattern, they argue, forms the core of Jewish identity and explains the relationship between the Jewish people and their God. The Holocaust and the formation of Israel are the single most important events to occur in the modern Jewish consciousness, and so it's natural that much thought and debate has ensued regarding the significance and meaning of these two events.

Judaism and Israel

In the Diaspora, the concept of Israel was and continues to be the subject of earnest discussion and speculation. But for many Jews the formation of the state of Israel turned a theoretical and doctrinal debate into a living experience. Within Israel there's a fairly wide difference of opinion on the subject of God and the question of the role of religion in public life. There's also the continuation of the debate about what makes a person Jewish and what the Jewish lifestyle should entail, a debate that takes on new urgency now that Jews have control over the direction of their own independent nation.

> **Divinations**
>
> One of the disagreements between American and Israeli Jews is the issue of religious pluralism. American Jews pressure Israel to accept diversity among Reform, Conservative, and Orthodox factions. Many Israeli Orthodox Jewish groups in Israel continue to lobby their government to classify only the Orthodox as Jewish.

Over half of Israeli Jews describe themselves as Jewish in a racial or cultural sense, rather than a spiritual or religious sense. They are more likely to see Israel in secular terms, as a nation among other nations that exists to provide a safe haven for any Jewish person who might wish to live there. For them, religion is a secondary concern to the more pressing issues of economic development, internal security, and peace among Israel's neighbors. But another 20 percent or so of Israelis identify themselves as *dati* or *haredi* (either Orthodox or ultra-Orthodox). These two groups formed minority political parties, such as Agudat Yisrael, Gush Emunim, Neturei Karta, and Shinui, and made coalitions with the major parties, Likkud and Labor, to pursue their goals of making Israeli public life more and more consistent with the halakhah. They lobby for stricter criteria for declaring someone Jewish, for exerting control over marriage and divorce laws, and for holding fast on restrictions on Sabbath-day activities.

Curiously, the most religious parties in Israel disagree about whether the nation of Israel itself is the legitimate heir to the covenants God originally made with Abraham and Moses. Israel is mostly Jewish, and it is positioned in the area of the Promised Land, and yet some traditionalists do not believe the modern state of Israel is the historical continuation of the Israel of the Torah. One party, the Neturei Karta, is composed of Haredi immigrants from eastern Europe who reject the political Zionism of Herzl and the architects of Israeli statehood. The Haredi hold the view that since Israel admits nonobservant Jews into citizenship, and since the state was founded without the aid of a supernatural Messiah, it is therefore not the same Israel that God selected for a special destiny. In their eyes, the only true Israel is the people of Israel, comprised of those who love God and demonstrate their faithfulness to him by carrying out the mitzvoth, studying the Torah, and consecrating every aspect of their lives to God.

The Least You Need to Know

- ◆ The Reform, Conservative, and Orthodox divisions appeared when Jews disagreed over how to respond to the philosophical and political climate of the 1800s.

- ◆ Reform Judaism stresses the ethical components of the Jewish tradition over metaphysics and religious observances.

- ◆ Both Conservative and Orthodox Judaism maintain the commandments, metaphysical beliefs, and religious observances of the Torah but disagree over adjustments to the halakhah.

- ◆ The Haredim, or ultra-Orthodox, formed a block in protest against compromises evident in Reform, Conservative, and Orthodox Judaism.

- ◆ Israel is a much-discussed topic within the Jewish community, since opinions differ on whether it is continuous with the Israel of Hebrew scripture.

Part 3

The Concept of God in Christianity

The appearance of Jesus of Nazareth in first-century Palestine gave birth to a new vision of the divine in Western civilization. His followers, drawn from the Jewish messianic sects and later from among Gentile populations in central Asia, North Africa, Asia Minor, and Southern Europe, clothed Hebrew monotheism in new garments, perceiving Jesus as a distinct "person" in a Trinity comprised of God as Father, Son, and Holy Spirit. Christians offered various explanations for how three could be one in a united godhead, and various accounts for how an immortal God could assume the form of a mortal human being. These differences helped to give shape to divergent Orthodox and Roman Catholic communities; in time, Protestants would depart from their Catholic cousins on the vital question of how humanity obtains salvation through the work of Jesus Christ. And in these chapters, you'll encounter contemporary voices that have differed over how Christians might respond to modern intellectual and cultural movements.

11

God in the Bible

In This Chapter

- ◆ Predictions of a Messiah fulfilled
- ◆ The prophetic message of Jesus of Nazareth
- ◆ Lots and lots of miracles
- ◆ Meet the Apostle Paul and learn what he had to say about Jesus
- ◆ Apocalypse soon

In the Christian tradition, God took the form of a human being and appeared in Palestine during the reign of Emperor Augustus. Christians believe that God chose to do this to fulfill his purposes, foretold in ancient Hebrew scripture, of creating a new covenant with the human race and establishing the kingdom of heaven on Earth. This person, Jesus of Nazareth, received a traditional Jewish education and at the age of 30 began a remarkable career of teaching, exhorting, and healing, only to be captured by the Roman garrison in Jerusalem, tried by the governor Pontius Pilate, and crucified as a common criminal.

But his closest followers told of a miraculous event that soon followed. Jesus' lifeless body lay in a tomb for several days, but then he rose from the dead, appeared to dozens of people throughout the area, and ascended into heaven. This was enough to convince his disciples that Jesus was truly the Messiah, and they began to preach the good news of his appearing on Earth. But their letters described Jesus not as a warrior God sent to free the Jews from Roman occupation, but as a spiritual deliverer, an agent of salvation sent to Earth to die as an atoning sacrifice for the sins of all people. It was, in the words captured in the title of a famous book about Jesus, the Greatest Story Ever Told.

Jesus the Messenger

Like Socrates, Jesus didn't leave behind any written work, but relied on his chief pupils to document and disseminate his ideas. Their testimony is contained in the Gospels (Greek for good news), which are essentially anthologies of Jesus' sermons, coupled with biographical material interspersed throughout to form historical narratives of his life. Four of these gospels (the writings of Matthew, Mark, Luke, and John) were deemed authoritative by early councils of Christian leaders and are included in the Christian scripture. The Christian canon, known as the New Testament, also contains a history of the early community of Christians, and numerous letters written by Jesus' followers to explain his teachings and the meaning of his life.

> **Pearls of Wisdom**
>
> The Jewish historian Josephus confirmed the Gospels' accounts of Jesus of Nazareth: "About this time arose Jesus, a wise man, if indeed it be lawful to call him a man. For he was a doer of wonderful deeds, and a teacher of men who gladly receive truth." (*Antiquities of the Jews*, xviii)

Rethinking the Law of Moses

Jesus' message, as recorded in the four canonical Gospels, has a few core themes. Chief among them is Jesus' perspective on the meaning of the halakhah. Right out of the gate, Jesus made it clear that he found the practice of religion in his own time repugnant. In Jesus' crosshairs sat the Pharisees themselves, rabbis who were the most knowledgeable about the Torah and Tanak, and who ensured the proper performance of the mitzvoth in the synagogues of the region. Jesus summoned the rage of the greatest Jewish prophet in castigating their hollow faith, "Well did Isaiah prophesy of you, when he said: 'This people honors me with their lips, but their heart is far from me.'" (Matthew 15:7–8) Later, Jesus' words bit even harder: "Woe to you scribes and Pharisees, hypocrites! … You also outwardly appear righteous to men, but within you are full of hypocrisy and iniquity." (Matthew 23:28) And he threw in an epithet or two for good measure, calling them a brood of vipers and whitewashed tombs, neat and clean on the outside, and dead as dust on the inside.

Jesus' message was simple: The law was intended to promote holiness and devotion to God, not legalistic hairsplitting, religious exhibitionism, and self-righteous posturing. When the Jewish teachers challenged Jesus for letting his followers eat with unwashed hands, asking, "Why do your disciples transgress the tradition of the elders?" Jesus replied, "Why do you transgress the commandment of God for the sake of your tradition?" Jesus interpreted the law for them: "Not what goes into the mouth defiles a man, but what comes out of the mouth, this defiles a man." Finishing his point, he concluded, "What comes out of the mouth proceeds from the heart, and this defiles a man. For out of the heart come evil thoughts, murder, adultery, fornication, theft, false witness, slander. These are what defile a man; but to eat with unwashed hands does not defile a man." (Matthew 15)

It's What's Inside That Counts

Jesus' comments evoked the spirit of Jewish prophets such as Micah, who was appalled at the sham religiosity of the age and called Israel to inner purity. Micah even posed the question, "Will the Lord be pleased with thousands of rams, with ten thousands of rivers of oil?" Obviously not: "What does the Lord require of you but to do justice, and to love kindness, and to walk humbly with your God?" (Micah 6:7–8) Following his cue, Jesus called for a clean heart and pure motives, a kind of internalizing of the law so that the performance of rituals flowed from a heartfelt desire to please God.

The Sermon on the Mount is a perfect example of Jesus' prophetic voice: "You have heard that it was said, 'You shall not commit adultery.' But I say to you that every one who looks at a woman lustfully has already committed adultery with her in his heart." (Matthew 5:27) Like the Jewish prophets, Jesus believed that true religion must come from within. Later he summarized his interpretation of the law, remarking when asked which was the greatest commandment, "Love the Lord your God with all your hearts, and with all your soul, and with all your mind." Then he added, "Love your neighbor as yourself. On these two commandments depend all the law and the prophets." (Matthew 22:37–40)

> **CAUTION**
>
> **Take Heed!**
>
> Like Judaism, Christianity is a textual religion that generates differences of opinion regarding the meaning of scripture. Agreement about the Christian canon itself wasn't secured until several hundred years after Jesus. One scholar found 16 different books or book fragments that told the message of Jesus, but failed to win acceptance. And you thought four Gospels were too many?

The Kingdom of God

So Jesus fulfilled the law, in part, by encouraging his hearers to purify their desires, thoughts, and motives. What gave this message greater urgency was Jesus' call to "Repent, for the kingdom of heaven is at hand." (Matthew 4:17) It's hard to know what Jesus meant here, but it appears that he believed the God of the Hebrew Tanak had developed a new plan for redeeming a sin-ridden world, cut off from communion with the divine.

In some places Jesus uses strange language to describe the kingdom. For example: It's like a mustard seed that starts small and grows into a giant plant; it's like a treasure hidden in a field that when found, brings joy; it's like a sower who casts out seed into various types of soil; it's like a net cast out into the sea, pulling in both good and bad. At times Jesus' comments described a fellowship of believers who possessed special knowledge of ultimate truth: "To you it has been given to know the secrets of the kingdom of heaven, but to them it has not been given." (Matthew 13:11) Jesus' parables embedded truth in allegorical and figurative language, which evoked the mysterious nature of the divine realm and invited his audience to struggle with the parables' meaning to discover the deeper insights contained within.

If it seemed as though Jesus spoke of the kingdom as a sort of mystical knowledge of the divine, elsewhere the kingdom shows up as a spiritual force ready to come to the aid of those who follow God's will. After an exorcism, Jesus remarked, "If it is by the finger of God that I cast out demons, then the kingdom of God has come upon you." (Luke 11:20) When the Pharisees demanded to know when the kingdom was to arrive, he said, rather cryptically, "The kingdom of God is not coming with signs to be observed … for behold, the kingdom of God is in the midst of you." (Luke 17:21) This made the kingdom of God seem more like a potent force or inner power; and still other passages describe the kingdom in ways that sound rather like a conventional afterlife.

Sin and Repentance

Some might have assumed that Jesus was talking about restoring the Israelite kingdom in Palestine. The perceived threat of restoration is why Roman troops were killing Zealots at the time, and why King Herod and the rest of Jerusalem were shocked when Persian wise men came out of the east asking about the king of the Jews born in Bethlehem in fulfillment of Micah's prophecy. Given Micah's prophecy and the political struggles of the Maccabees and the Zealots, you can forgive the Jews their confusion when Jesus spoke of the kingdom of God. But if you listened closely, you could tell Jesus wasn't talking about defeating the Romans and delivering the Israelites from subjugation, but rescuing souls from the spiritual oppression inflicted upon humankind by God's enemy, Satan.

In a number of sermons and conversations, Jesus explained that he was sent by his Father to accomplish a special mission: saving people from the consequences of their sinful thoughts and actions. Jesus explained this most clearly in an encounter with Nicodemus, an important Pharisee. He told Nicodemus that unless one is born of both water and spirit, he cannot enter the kingdom of heaven. Nicodemus took the bait and asked what he meant by spiritual birth. Jesus offered his famous reply: "For God so loved the world that he gave his only Son, that whoever believes in him should not perish but have eternal life." (John 3:16) What's required, though, is a total moral commitment to God; after all, as Jesus said in the Sermon on the Mount, "No one can serve two masters; for either he will hate the one and love the other, or he will be devoted to the one and despise the other." (Matthew 6:24)

> **Divinations**
>
> Other religions contain the motif of a God who dies and is revived, such as the Babylonian god of agriculture Tammuz. Apparently his lover, fertility goddess Ishtar, was distraught over his death and went into the underworld to rescue him. Worship of Tammuz commemorated the annual death and rebirth of plant life.

The Message of Love

Jesus preached a message of salvation through repentance from sin and devotion to God. This message was couched in an idiom that was quite new for listeners who were used to hearing God spoken about in sterile philosophical concepts or rabbinical legalese. In neighboring cultures the gods were feared, honored, invoked, appeased, and so forth; if the gods liked you or your sacrifices, then you might prosper. Jesus invited hearers to think about God in a very new way, as a God who seeks a bond of affection between himself and his people. As Jesus said in his last words to his friends, "As the Father has loved me, so I loved you; abide in my love." (John 15:9)

Jesus had been talking about love for several years, and demonstrating it in acts of charity throughout Palestine. Luke records a story Jesus told to illustrate his point about loving your neighbor as yourself (remember, he taught that this was the essence of the Law of Moses). A man headed to Jericho was robbed and left for dead. After several Jewish leaders passed him by, a kindhearted Samaritan took the trouble to patch him up and paid his bill at a local inn so he could recuperate. (Luke 10:29–37) To make the point crystal clear, Jesus left as a final command to his disciples on the eve of his capture: "This is my commandment, that you love one another as I have loved you." (John 15:12)

Jesus the Minister

When thinking about the person of Jesus, observers tend to distinguish between what Jesus said and what Jesus did. But that's an artificial distinction. Jesus practiced what he preached. In fact, Jesus' biggest complaint against the religious leaders of his day was their hypocrisy in word and deed. When Jesus reminded his disciples that he loved them, they could conjure up a picture of what that looked like, because he demonstrated this love time and time again during the short time he spent with them.

Jews and Everyone Else

The Gospel writers took pains to show that Jesus' love knew no boundaries at a time when racial and cultural boundaries were an important part of everyday existence. Jesus made enemies among the ritually purified crowd for cavorting with tax collectors and sinners and rubbing elbows with lepers and prostitutes. Although Jesus was known to say things such as "I was sent only to the lost sheep of the house of Israel" (Mt. 15:24), he made it clear that the new order would begin with the Jewish people and eventually grow to embrace all humanity. In Luke's Gospel, Jesus is described as "a light for revelation to the Gentiles" and through his work, "all flesh shall see the salvation of God." (Luke 2:32; 3:6) And just before Jesus ascended to heaven, he instructed his astonished disciples that "repentance and forgiveness of sins should be preached in his name to all nations, beginning from Jerusalem." (Luke 24:47)

Especially noteworthy is Jesus' effort to build a ministry that included women, both as recipients of help and partners in his work. Luke tells of the importance of Mary, Joanna, and Susanna in providing for Jesus and the disciples (Luke 8:3). There's also the tender story of Jesus and the Samaritan woman who was shocked that a Jew would even speak to her, and eventually realizes Jesus is the Messiah and receives forgiveness for her sins. (John 4:7–42) You might recall the role of Mary Magdalene; Jesus exorcized seven demons from her, a service she repaid by attending him at his death and preparing his body for burial. Jesus then favored Mary by appearing to her first after his resurrection. More broadly, the Gospels carefully document the faithfulness of Jesus' mother, Mary, as well as the faithfulness of John the Baptist's mother, Elizabeth. The heightened profile of women in the Gospels tells of the universal nature of the kingdom Jesus came to establish.

Pearls of Wisdom

Jesus was fond of capturing truths in simple language:

- ◆ Judge not that ye be not judged. (Matthew 7:1)
- ◆ A house divided against itself cannot stand. (Matthew 12:25)
- ◆ A city that is set on a hill cannot be hid. (Matthew 5:14}
- ◆ Where your treasure is, there will your heart be also. (Matthew 6:21)
- ◆ Do not be anxious for tomorrow, for tomorrow will be anxious for itself. (Matthew 6:34)
- ◆ Why do you see the speck in your brother's eye, but not the log in your own? (Matthew 7:3)

A Gentle Healer

You can't get very far in the Gospels before you start hearing of the dozens of miracles Jesus performed during his ministry on Earth. As an embodiment of the divine, Jesus possessed divine power, which he used to walk on water, convert water into wine, multiply loaves of bread and fishes, and calm the stormy seas. These demonstrations of supernatural power over nature took second place to his compassionate healing of the sick, the lame, and the blind. He even raised several people from the dead: the daughter of Jarius, leader of a synagogue near Galilee, and Lazarus, the brother of one of Jesus' followers, Martha.

The point of Jesus' healing was to communicate the dual message of forgiveness of sins and the unity of all humankind. He touched and healed unclean lepers to prod the Pharisees to reconsider the real meaning of the purity laws of the halakhah. Healing lepers reinforced the idea that strict attendance to cleanliness violates the spirit of the law if it gets in the way of compassion. In another instance, a crowd lowered a paralyzed man into a room full of people gathered to hear Jesus' teaching. Instead of healing the man, Jesus told him that his sins were forgiven. This scandalized the Pharisees, and Jesus used their indignation as an opportunity to explain that the Son of man had power not only to heal, but to forgive sins as well. Of course Jesus then miraculously cured the paralyzed man to make the point complete.

Spiritual Warfare

Today we have trouble imagining a world teeming with spirits, both good and evil, and yet the people of Jesus' time spoke of this as an integral part of their world. Matthew's Gospel records dozens of healings and exorcisms in order to show that Isaiah's prophecy was fulfilled, that he "took our infirmities and bore our diseases." (Matthew 8:17) Exorcisms also offered an occasion for Jesus to cross boundaries, as when he cast out a demon from the daughter of a Syrophoenician woman. In Gerasenes, Jesus conversed with a malignant spirit called Legion, who recognized Jesus as the Son of God and understood his (Legion's) subordinate position in the spiritual hierarchy. Legion's submission gave the Gospel writers the chance to explain what sort of Messiah they had in Jesus—a spiritual warrior and ultimate hero in the battle between good and evil.

Passing It On

Surviving accounts of Jesus' life are populated with a supporting cast of paralytics and lepers, hordes of starving seekers, villains like Judas, and of course the disciples. Jesus called the disciples and "gave them authority over unclean spirits, to cast them out, and heal every disease and every infirmity." (Matthew 10:1) The disciples were told to preach the gospel of repentance and salvation, saying "the kingdom of heaven is at hand." As you can see, the disciples were fully integrated into Jesus' healing ministry and partners in the work of spreading his message.

The disciples' affection for Jesus and his affection for them is unmistakable. When told that they couldn't follow Jesus anymore, Peter asked "why cannot I follow you now? I will lay down my life for you." (John 13:37) But they were pretty feckless at times; Jesus followed Peter's comment with a prediction, soon to come true, that Peter would deny ever knowing him when the chips were down. They fell asleep when Jesus asked them to stand vigil in the Garden of Gethsemane, and one of them even betrayed him. Thomas doubted that Jesus rose from the dead until he could feel for himself the crucifixion wounds in Jesus' hands.

Still, Jesus spent a great deal of time training and exhorting the disciples, preparing them for the difficult task of explaining the gospel message to a receptive but skeptical world. A good number of disciples would be stoned or crucified for preaching the message of Jesus. Their reward was intimate communion with the divine. Jesus once told them privately, "Blessed are the eyes which see what you see! For I tell you that many prophets and kings desired to see what you see, and did not see it, and to hear what you hear, and did not hear it." (Luke 10:23–24) Jesus' disciples caught a glimpse of the ultimate truth, going beyond the written Torah and even the spiritual heights of the Jewish and pagan mystics.

Jesus the Messiah

What we know of Jesus we know through the eyes of his followers, particularly writings attributed to Matthew, Mark, Luke, and John, but also Peter and a later convert, Paul. Much of the Christian concept of God was the product of their reflections on the meaning of Jesus' life, written some years after his death and resurrection. The benefit of historical perspective—a little hindsight—enabled the disciples to craft a compelling vision of the relationship between Jesus of Nazareth and the God of Moses. So we turn to the question, was Jesus divine?

Jesus Foretold

The question of Jesus' divinity is complicated, and it overlaps the question of whether Jesus was the *Messiah*. Observers perceived that certain details of the life of Jesus of Nazareth called to mind a number of references to the coming Messiah in the Tanak.

Isaiah predicted that a young woman would bear a son called Emmanuel (God with us): Mary bore in a miraculous way the very Son of God. Micah foretold that the coming "ruler of Israel" would be born in Bethlehem: sure enough, Jesus of Nazareth was born there. Many aspects of Jesus' death seemed to evoke the description of Isaiah's suffering servant who "makes himself an offering for sin" and "bore the sin of many." (Isaiah 53:10–12)

> **Word to the Wise**
>
> **Messiah** means anointed one in Hebrew. The equivalent word in Greek is *Christ*, hence the title Jesus Christ in many early Greek Christian texts.

We can find several accounts in the Gospels of people perceiving Jesus as the Messiah, such as Peter who, when asked by Jesus "Who am I?" responded, "You are the Christ, the Son of the living God." (Matthew 16:16) Jesus was happy with Peter's answer, but told the disciples not to tell anyone because public acclaim would compromise his plans. In the last account to be written, the Gospel of John, Jesus more clearly establishes a Messianic claim. When the Samaritan woman at the well said "I know that Messiah is coming (he who is called Christ)," Jesus replied, "I who speak to you am he." (John 4:26) Others debated whether Jesus was really the Messiah, and the Jewish leaders seemed to follow the lead of the high priest Caiaphas in denying claims—like Peter's—that Jesus was the anointed one.

Early Types of Christ

But Jesus' disciples became convinced that even denials were part of the fabric of biblical prophecy, and the disciples remembered Jesus citing a passage from Psalms to the effect that "the stone which the builders rejected has become the head of the corner." (Matthew 21:42; Psalms 118:22) The disciples went quickly to work on their biographies of Jesus and on their letters to Jesus' followers, trying to situate the life of Jesus into the context of the Tanak. They likened Jesus to Adam, because Jesus called himself Son of God (like Adam, who had divine provenance) and came to Earth to establish a new order. They perceived him as a type of Melchizedek, the priest in Genesis who blessed Abraham, because Jesus appeared to sanctify the new covenant between God and humanity. Other comparisons followed: Jesus was compared to Isaac for Isaac's miraculous birth and experience as potential human sacrifice, and to Moses for leading the Hebrew people out of bondage into freedom. These early portents of Jesus' life convinced the disciples that God had been preparing the Jewish people for the appearance of Jesus, and that his Messiahship was indisputable.

The Incarnation of God

During Jesus' life, people struggled with the idea that Jesus was divine. Later people had no doubt that he was divine, but began to doubt his humanity. So was Jesus God's son, a manifestation of God, a part of God, or actually just God himself? This question vexed Jesus' followers and triggered intense debates over the next three centuries. We'll discuss some of the positions that these thinkers adopted in the next chapter.

For now you should keep in mind that some of the words attributed to Jesus and to his contemporaries revealed an assumption that he was divine in some sense. At his baptism, observers claimed to see the Spirit of God descend upon Jesus, declaring "This is my beloved Son, with whom I am well pleased." (Matthew 3:17) The Son of God label followed Jesus into his public ministry, and the Apostle John's Gospel attempted to use some of Jesus' comments to find an answer to the riddle of Jesus' relation to God. But Jesus' comments are pretty mysterious and paradoxical: "I proceeded and came forth from God," but then "I and the Father are one." (John 8:42; 10:30)

Peter, Matthew, and other early followers kept the focus on Jesus' humanity, demurring on the question of whether Jesus was actually an incarnation of God. In a sermon after Jesus' ascension, Peter spoke of how God anointed Jesus, and was with Jesus in his fight against demonic forces. Peter also identified Jesus as the one ordained by God to judge the living and the dead, through whom all receive forgiveness of sins. (Acts 10:34–42) This dovetailed nicely with Messianic thinking in first-century Judaism. It wasn't until a thoroughly Hellenized Jew, the Apostle Paul, came around did anyone attempt to reconcile the paradoxes of Jesus' claims of divinity. Speaking to an audience of Greeks, Paul naturally used Platonic language, presenting Jesus as being in the "form of God" and equal to God, a divine being who "emptied himself" and became "born in the likeness of men." Jesus then died a human death, whereupon God "highly exalted him." (Philippians 2)

John's Gospel also utilized Greek concepts, specifically the idea of Logos we discovered earlier (see Chapter 9) in the work of Philo, to describe Jesus' eternal coexistence with God: "In the beginning was the Word (Logos), and the Word (Logos) was with God and the Word (Logos) was God. He was in the beginning with God" (John 1:2) Logos enabled John to equate Jesus with God in essence, while also identifying him with God's powers or attributes: "All things were made through him, and without him was not anything made that was made. In him was life, and the life was the light of men." (John 1:3)

> **CAUTION**
>
> **Take Heed!**
>
> It's a mistake to see Jesus as an avatar of God in the way that Krishna is a personification of Vishnu in Hinduism. It's also a mistake to see Jesus as a sort of divine presence, like the Shekhina of En Sof in Jewish Kabbalah. Christians insist that Jesus was both fully God and fully human.

The Meaning of Atonement

This "bothness" of Jesus is critical because of the view among his followers, and accepted throughout history, that Jesus was sent to Earth as an atoning sacrifice for the sins of all humanity. Cloaked in mysterious language, Jesus said "the Son of man came not to be served but to serve, and to give his life as a ransom for many." (Matthew 20:28) Jesus would become a kind of atoning sacrifice to reverse the effects of the fall of Adam, to replace the sacrificial system of the Torah, and to bridge the gulf between God and humanity. John the Baptist had these aims in mind when he proclaimed, "Behold the Lamb of God who takes away the sin of the world!" (John 1:29)

The doctrine of atonement, just like the doctrine of Jesus' divinity, soon became the subject of much discussion and debate among Christians. In their earliest texts, such as the Letter to the Hebrews, the disciples interpreted Jesus' sacrificial death in the kind of language that ancient Jews would understand: "He is the mediator of a new covenant, so that those who are called may receive the promised eternal inheritance, since a death has occurred which redeems them from the transgressions under the first covenant." (Hebrews 9:15) In other words, being fully God and fully human, Jesus sacrificed himself for humanity's sake to offer the spiritual purification that God required to become reconciled to a sinful and wicked world.

And so the disciples believed they had discovered the meaning of the prediction in Jeremiah of a new covenant: "Behold, the days are coming, says the Lord, when I will make a new covenant with the house of Israel ... and I will put my law within them, and I will write it upon their hearts ... and I will remember their sin no more." (Jeremiah 31:31–34) As Paul explained to the Greek Christians at Galatia, "before faith came, we were confined under the law," and "the law was our custodian until Christ came, that we might be justified by faith." He concluded: "In Christ Jesus you are all sons of God, through faith." (Galatians 3:23–26) Paul bequeathed to Christianity the idea that confession of sins, coupled with ritual assimilation to Christ through baptism, was sufficient to make a person party to the new covenant established by Jesus' sacrifice, regardless of whether you are Jew or Greek, slave or free, or male or female.

He's Gone: What's Next?

Jesus predicted his own death and resurrection, though it seems the disciples were not so ready for it. It took them a number of decades to fully understand the nature of his Messianic office and to appreciate the atoning aspect of his death. They also heard him say repeatedly that he would return to Earth a second time to establish his kingdom on Earth. Now the kingdom had still another meaning. It was not only a kingdom in the present, but a kingdom to come. And the disciples were expecting him to return very soon, because Jesus said, "there are some standing here who will not taste death before they see that the kingdom of God has come with power." (Mark 9:1)

The disciples peppered Jesus with questions about what sort of signs they should look for when his return was imminent, and Jesus obliged them with stories of a desolating sacrilege of wars, famines, earthquakes, pestilence, and so on. In the Apocalypse of John, called the Book of Revelation, we are treated to the writer's vision of the end of time, which tells of grievous woes such as rivers of blood and plagues of locusts and boils. Jesus told the disciples they would survive to the end with the assistance of a Comforter, the Holy Spirit, who would give them the strength necessary to overcome these challenges and would guide them into "all the truth." (John 16:13) The disciples received the Holy Spirit on the day of Pentecost, which they experienced as a rush of wind, a vision of tongues of fire, and a sensation of the divine presence within. The Spirit gave Christians the comforting notion of intimacy with a loving, immanent God, but also lots more to sort out in order to sustain the Judaic concept of the oneness of God.

The Least You Need to Know

◆ Jesus taught that he came to fulfill the law of Moses, not create a new religion.

◆ The message of Jesus was prophetic in the sense of calling Israel to a higher ethic of inner purity.

◆ The central message of Jesus was love—the love of God for humanity, the love of humanity for God, and the love of human beings for each other.

◆ Debates raged over the claims that Jesus was the Messiah foretold by the prophets, which was proved to the satisfaction of his most loyal followers.

◆ The Holy Spirit gave Christians a way to perceive the immanence of God, but presented a challenge to conventional Jewish monotheism.

12

God in Early Christian Theology

In This Chapter

- ◆ Christianity disentangles itself from Judaism
- ◆ A glimpse of the complexity of Christian divinity
- ◆ How three can be one, and one can be three
- ◆ Jesus Christ: both God and man at once
- ◆ Greatest hits of the Cappadocian Fathers
- ◆ Augustine's ideas about God

Jesus' departure left his followers with a few puzzles to solve. If Jesus was God, and the Father was God, too, how could you consider them both divine and still have only one God? That question was further complicated by Jesus' talk about sending a comforter, the Holy Spirit. Didn't that make three gods? How can three be one at the same time? People also began to wonder how Jesus could be fully God and fully human at the same time. Did one destroy the other? How could something be both matter and spirit? And didn't the divine spirit lose its purity when mixed with corrupt and finite matter?

These questions were the starting points of a very technical and intricate conversation about God among Christians in the five centuries after Jesus' death and resurrection. Once the Jesus movement skipped outside the boundaries of Judaism and became the faith of non-Jews throughout the Mediterranean world (Gentiles), Christians found it quite natural to discuss the nature of their God using Greek philosophical and religious concepts. This cross-fertilization shaped Christian thinking about the divine. In the wake of the Trinitarian and Christological controversies, Christians today speak of a Trinity of Father, Son, and Holy Spirit that is nevertheless monotheistic, and they perceive the man Jesus of Nazareth as the incarnation of God, who is nevertheless one with God. These are mysteries of the faith, and you'll find out in this chapter how Christians were prepared to explain and defend them.

Christianity Meets Greek Culture

In the New Testament you already see the break between Christianity and Judaism. At the end of the Book of Acts, Paul spent a very long and frustrating day with the Jews of Rome, "trying to convince them about Jesus both from the law of Moses and from the prophets." Paul ran out of patience and saw them off, saying "let it be known to you then that this salvation of God has been sent to the Gentiles; they will listen." (Acts 28: 28) This was a pivotal moment in the history of God, since from this point forward Christians began to use language more familiar to Gentiles to explain how the God of the Torah took the form of a man, lived in Palestine, and eventually died and rose again to save people from their sins.

Paul in Ephesus

If you lived in the ancient Mediterranean world, you had lots of options if you were shopping for a religion. The story of Paul's visit to Ephesus on the Aegean coast in Asia Minor offers a good window on this diversity. Upon his arrival, Paul found some people who had been drawn to Christianity but hadn't been taught or baptized properly. So Paul taught them about repentance and about the person of Jesus Christ, and then performed the proper baptism ritual. He then spoke for about three months in the Jewish synagogue and performed acts of healing and exorcism. Some Jewish exorcists tried to use Jesus' name to cast out demons and were themselves possessed and fled "naked and wounded."

Divinations

Among the more noteworthy conversions to Christianity among the Gentiles was Pomponia Graecina, wife of Aulus Plautius, conqueror of Britain, who was charged for allegedly embracing a "foreign superstition."

In response, some who followed the mystery religions converted to Christianity and burned magic books worth a total of 50,000 pieces of silver. These events disturbed the purveyors of religion in Ephesus, such as Demetrius, who apparently made silver shrines for the local cult of Artemis (daughter of Zeus and Leto and one of the fertility goddesses in Greek religion). So Demetrius warned the silversmiths of the danger to their local customs (and their bottom line), driving the people into a frenzy with shouts of "Great is Artemis of the Ephesians!"

Although Paul's missionary companions were subjected to a little mob justice, cooler heads prevailed and Paul's group was sent on its way. In this one town, Paul witnessed the wide religious diversity of the Roman Empire. You could convert to Judaism, worship Artemis or any of the gods of the Greco-Roman pantheon, or participate in the magical practices of the cults of Mithras, Isis, or any of the exotic mystery religions of the Near East. The Temple of Artemis in Ephesus even supported worship of the Roman Emperor and his family in the so-called imperial cults. It's no surprise that Paul and the other disciples used language, concepts, and allusions that would be familiar to these cosmopolitan people in order to make their appeal.

Neoplatonism

This brings us to Neoplatonism once again. Plato left a huge imprint in the Mediterranean world with his notion of perfect, unchanging, universal forms that exist apart from the material world. To Plato, this world of forms contained the divine element, which imprinted itself on the minds of human beings before they left the realm of spirit and took on bodily form. These mental imprints enabled people to sense the world of forms and recognize the divine. Later, Stoics seized on the idea of a universal divine element in every human mind and called it reason, or Logos. And of course during the lifetime of Jesus of Nazareth, Philo of Alexandria used Neoplatonic concepts of Logos as a way to describe the creative power of God or the manner in which God relates to humanity. Philo made a strong distinction between the unknowable essence of God and his discernable powers or attributes, and thereby perceived Logos as the means by which God reveals himself to humanity.

Jesus' followers used this language of Logos, most famously in the first chapter of the Gospel of John, which we encountered in Chapter 11. This tendency shows up in the writings of Justin Martyr and Irenaeus, both influenced by Greek philosophy. In the third century, Plotinus—perhaps the chief Neoplatonic thinker of the age—picked up the tendency from Plato to Philo through the Christian Gospels and arrived at his unique conception of the divine. He spoke of a unified One as the ultimate reality.

Following Philo, he refused to name it or describe it, because he believed it was beyond the normal descriptors that humans used to account for things in the material world (measures of size, shape, color, brightness, density, and so forth). Plotinus thought that the One is unknowable, and yet Plato taught that the ultimate reality could be discerned. So Plotinus taught a doctrine of emanation: The One begat Mind, which provides us with intuition, and Mind begat Soul, which engenders the human sense perception. And Soul begat the rest of existence, including the spiritual and material world with all its seeming fragmentation and disconnectedness. Plotinus taught that you can put an end to your fractured existence by working backward, through cognition to intuition to ultimate communion with the divine.

Gnosticism

Plotinus's system satisfied the need for philosophical rigor in a highly urbane culture. And his three-in-one scheme of One, Mind, and Soul bore a faint resemblance to the Christian doctrine of Father, Son, and Holy Spirit, so it could be said that he found another, more rational path to the ultimate reality that Christians discovered, but without requiring belief in divine incarnations, human sacrifices, or resurrection of the dead. And yet Plotinus's divinity was pretty cold and sterile. It certainly lacked the affective appeal of God's love or Jesus' passion or the Spirit's consolations. What Plotinus's scheme lacked, Christianity seemed to supply.

It's a good idea to bring up Gnosticism in this discussion. Gnosticism contained lots of Neoplatonic elements but brought in the message of Jesus; later it was branded a heresy because it tended to push the disciples' teachings about Christ too far in the direction of pagan philosophy. Gnosticism (from Greek *gnosis*, meaning "knowledge") worked from Platonic dualism to argue that spirit is good, and matter is evil. The goal of humanity is to escape the prison of evil matter and enter the realm of pure spirit, which some Gnostics taught could be accomplished through faith and devotion to Jesus Christ. As they deepened their commitment, Jesus provided special insights into the ultimate reality, enabling their escape from the flesh and eventual union with the divine.

> **CAUTION**
>
> **Take Heed!**
>
> Gnosticism is very difficult to pin down because of its tendency to combine different forms of belief and practices. It had elements of philosophy, Greek mysticism, Christianity, Near Eastern mystery religions, and even magic and divination.

The Gnostics offered a scheme that promised mystical knowledge of the ultimate reality, but only for a chosen few. Along the way, the Gnostics developed a cosmology for understanding the origins of the universe and the problem of evil. In some of the Gnostic schemes, an eternal "All-Father" or first principle created other beings, called aeons, which together with the All-Father formed the "fullness" that some of Jesus' disciples talked about (known as the Pleroma in Greek Gnostic thought). One of the aeons was motivated by pride to replicate the creative work of the All-Father and proceeded to create the material world. Here you can see why Gnostics thought that the matter was corrupt and sinful for having been created through pride and ambition. This aeon was identified as both the Demiurge from Platonic philosophy and Yahweh of the Jewish Torah. His angry, jealous, bloody reign over the world was challenged by another deity, Jesus Christ, who brought a message of peace, love, and redemption and at the end of time would establish his kingdom on Earth.

Three Is One

The Gnostics represented yet one more example of the Hellenistic tendency to combine beliefs, and early Christian leaders worried that the Gnostics might dilute the message of Christ by blending it with other philosophical and religious traditions. The conversation among Philo, Gnostic teachers, Plotinus, and early followers of Jesus convinced the bishops of the church that getting the doctrine of the *Trinity* right was essential to the survival of the Christian faith.

> **Word to the Wise**
>
> **Trinity** is a concept in Christian theology that conceives of God as one substance or essence in three persons or aspects.

Initial Questions

The most dangerous quasi-Gnostic in the early Christian movement was Marcion (100–165 C.E.), who accepted the Gnostic idea that the God of the Torah was the Demiurge of Platonic philosophy, and this God was responsible for creating the world with its corrupt matter and making impossible demands of obedience from human beings. Marcion taught that a second God appeared in the form of Jesus Christ to bring freedom and love to humanity, and asks only faith and love in return. Marcion was marched out of the church by the early bishops for teaching a doctrine of two gods, and teaching that Jesus wasn't really human, but only appeared in the form of a man. In Marcion's view, Jesus was, so to speak, an apparition. This is called *docetism* (from the Greek for "to appear"), which is a fairly common way of thinking about the presence of God in the material world in the history of religion.

Christian teachers responded to Gnostic polytheism and the Marcionite conception of two gods with forceful statements of God's oneness and unity. A diverse group of Christian thinkers emerged to defend the idea of God's oneness, and it's tough to make generalizations about them, but all seem to agree that God was unified and that Father, Son, and Holy Spirit were more or less modalities of the unified being. Experts group these thinkers together under the umbrella of Monarchianism. Some believed Monarchianism made Jesus seem less than fully human, or less than fully God, and believed that Monarchianism tended to deny that the distinctions between Father, Son, and Holy Spirit were permanent and eternal. This is true, for example, in the writings of Sabellius, who taught that God was one, and revealed himself in three different modes: the Father in creation, the Son in redemption, and Spirit in life-giving power. When Sabellius defined God as one with three qualities or modes, he could be interpreted as saying that God was one but three just as the sun is bright, hot, and round.

The tradition of thinking about Father, Son, and Holy Spirit had brought Christianity to crisis in the third and fourth centuries. Lots of different options were left on the table. Was Jesus a shadow or apparition of the divine? Was God a shape-shifter, morphing into Jesus Christ and then morphing back into the Supreme Being? Did this human being, Jesus of Nazareth, merely receive the powers of God upon baptism? Were Father, Son, and Holy Spirit just particular qualities of the one God of the universe?

Warring Camps

An important Christian teacher in Carthage, Tertullian (c. 160–220), pointed in the direction of the eventual formula later adopted to resolve questions about the Trinity.

> **CAUTION**
> **Take Heed!**
>
> Christians are not polytheists. They say that God is one in nature and essence, and when God permits himself to be known, he is perceived in three persons. None can subsist without the other: the Son revealed the Father, and the indwelling Spirit makes known to us the Son.

He used the Latin word *substantia*, meaning "status" or "being," to identify the singleness of God's substance. And he used the Latin word *personae*, meaning "person" or "party to a contract," to identify the multiplicity in God's form or aspect. Latin would eventually help to resolve some of the ambiguities built into Christian theology because of the sublime quality of the Greek language.

The church didn't discover the power of Tertullian's vision until well after the Arian Controversy of the late second century, which was begun by Arius (c. 250–336), an elder in the church in Alexandria.

He accused his bishop, Alexander, of teaching a kind of Sabellianism that threatened to blend God and Jesus together. Arius taught that Jesus Christ was distinct from God the Father, and that there was a time in the distant past when Jesus was not in existence. The Father had given Jesus his divinity because he was perfectly obedient unto death and morally pure throughout life. Alexander and his talented student of theology, Athanasius, went to work on Arius and his supporters, condemning them for making Jesus a secondary and subordinate deity.

The Nicene Vision

The dispute in the Alexandrian church spread quickly throughout the Roman Empire, given the relative diversity of opinion on the subject of the Trinity, and given the importance of the question to the integrity of the Christian faith. Emperor Constantine summoned all the bishops to a meeting at Nicaea (325 C.E.), across the Sea of Marmara from Istanbul in present-day Turkey, and gave them a mandate to resolve the issue. The Nicene bishops worked through a document known as the Creed of Caesarea, which was pretty vague on the question of how Jesus came about, and put in language that tried to clarify how Father, Son, and Holy Spirit relate together in a Trinity.

The Creed of Nicaea added clauses stipulating that Jesus was "begotten of the Father, only begotten, that is, of the substance of the Father," and that Jesus was "true God of true God, begotten not made, of one substance with the Father." These clauses were added to existing language about the Father creating the world through Jesus, becoming flesh, and dying for the sins of humanity. The bishops condemned any who taught such things as "there was when he was not," or "before he was begotten he was not," or "he came into being from what-is-not." They also rejected any position that held that Jesus was of another substance or essence from God, or was created, changeable, or alterable.

The Nicene vision of Father and Son being of the same substance and coexisting through eternity received official endorsement from the Roman Emperor and was probably the majority view in the church. From this point it became harder to propagate the notion that the Son of God was an aeon from the Pleroma, a human being elevated to the status of divinity, or a mode of the Supreme Being among other modes. It's possible to date the advent of formal Trinitarianism in Christian thought from the Council of Nicaea.

Irreconcilable Differences?

Branding Arianism a heresy didn't make it go away. Arianism appealed to Christians because it perceived Jesus Christ in strongly human terms and offered a way to understand the nature of our own challenges and possibilities as human beings separated from God. Just as Jesus suffered, so we, too, suffer; just as Jesus died, so we, too, must die. But Jesus conquered death and ascended into heaven. Could we not also conquer death and become Sons of God as well? In some sense, Jesus' moral perfection and timeless wisdom become more impressive if we assume he achieved them without having the benefit of being divine.

In the decades following the Council of Nicaea, Arianism continued to have appeal, particularly in the eastern portion of the Roman Empire in Asia Minor, Palestine, and North Africa. When the Empire was split into two halves after the death of the pro-Nicene Constantine, the eastern half with its capital in Constantinople drifted even closer to Arianism. For a short time in the fourth century, Constantine's son Constantius, an Arian through and through, united the Empire and tried to force out the Nicene proponents; one of the Nicene leaders, Hosius, was beaten and tortured until he agreed to sign a pro-Arian creed. It became proper to refer to Jesus not as one substance with the Father, but similar to the Father, using the Greek term *homois*.

> **Pearls of Wisdom**
>
> To Synesius of Cyrene (d. 414), the Trinity had great devotional value, as in this stanza:
>
> Send, O Christ, the Spirit, send the Father to my soul;
> Steep my dry heart in this dew, the best of all thy gifts.
> (Hymn 3.5)

Finding Words for God

Unfortunately, the dispute between the Nicene and Anti-Nicene fathers came down to rather technical issues of language. Priests, prophets, and philosophers generally perceived the divine to be unfathomable, and considered words and concepts to be an imperfect vehicle for expressing the nature of the ultimate reality. And yet stormy debates ensued among the bishops of the church over whether Father and Son were *homoousian* (in Greek, commonly used to denote sameness), or *homoiousion* (commonly, likeness). To an outsider, the question of sameness versus likeness might seem bothersome, but to insiders, the precise term here is quite important because it serves as a balance point in the doctrine of God; a tilt too far in one direction results in polytheism and a tilt too far in the other denies the divinity of Christ.

Something of a resolution was attempted in the writings of the Cappadocian Fathers, whose name derived from their home region in the eastern borderlands of Asia Minor. Toward the end of the fourth century, Gregory of Nazianzus, Basil of Caesarea, and Gregory of Nyssa returned to an idea we encountered a little earlier in the work of Tertullian, the idea of *substantia* and *personae*. In their view, the Nicene Creed was right to hold that Father and Son were of one essence (*ousia*), but they added that Father, Son, and Holy Spirit are also three countenances or visible expressions (*hypostases*). The Cappadocians taught that in His essence, God is the ineffable One, shrouded in mystery, but since God also wants to be known, He permits human discernment by means of three countenances. Keep in mind here that the Cappadocians carefully warned their readers not to think of the Trinity as a set of logical propositions, but as statements about a symbol that encodes the mysterious nature of ultimate reality. As Gregory of Nyssa wrote, "there is between the three a sharing and a differentiation that are beyond words and understanding.… Using riddles, as it were, we envisage a strange and paradoxical diversity-in-unity and unity-in-diversity."

Who, Exactly, Is Jesus?

Of course the Cappadocian Fathers couldn't give an expression to the idea of the Trinity that would please everyone in the Mediterranean world. Words and concepts have always been imperfect mediums for containing the infinite and ineffable God, then as now. With the Nicene Creed, in fact, new disagreements surfaced over the relationship between the divine and human natures of Jesus Christ. Was Jesus sort of schizophrenic, with divine and human personalities alternating control of a single being? Might he have been composed of a mortal body, a human soul, but a divine mind (Logos comes up here again)? Or perhaps Jesus was a *tertium quid*, a blend of divine and human that once combined, was neither of the two, but a third thing altogether?

The church had been on the alert for this sort of thinking from the start. The Apostle Paul warned the Colossians to "see to it that no one makes a prey of you by philosophy and empty deceit, according to human tradition, according to the elemental spirits of the universe, and not according to Christ. For in him the whole fullness of deity dwells bodily." (Colossians 2:8–9) Struggling over the meaning of "whole fullness" and the Nicene vision of one substance, Appolinarius couldn't handle the idea that the infinite and the finite, or the spiritual and the material, could come together to form one being. He construed Jesus' rational element as the divine Logos. But to his critics, this doled out to Jesus the divine and the human by half measures.

Appolinarius's writings shook loose other variant interpretations of Jesus' divinity and humanity. Jesus was "man" only in the generic sense, not a flesh-and-blood person. Jesus was God and man bound together in some mysterious kind of moral union. Still other ideas came to light. A third major council of the bishops gathered in Ephesus in 431 C.E. (the first two being in the previous century in order to combat Arianism), and they found the language of "natures" to be helpful in sorting through the issues at hand. Jesus had two complete natures, divine and human, but was of one substance, and in one person.

Works of Augustine

The Trinity and incarnation remained mysteries of the faith, and remain so to the present day. They are ways to symbolize the seeming paradoxes of infinite God becoming finite man, or one Absolute appearing in the form of three distinct entities. The church in Greece, Asia Minor, Palestine, and North Africa followed the Cappadocian Fathers in their appreciation of the mysteries of the Godhead, valuing the devotional possibilities inherent in the Trinity over contentious speculation. Roman Christians, however, continued to pursue metaphysical questions, especially after they were blamed for eroding Roman culture, thereby leaving the Empire too weak and divided to withstand the pillaging Gothic horde under Aleric who sacked Rome in 410 C.E.

Confessions

Christianity's great defender in the west was Augustine, Bishop of Hippo in North Africa. During his lifetime (354–430 C.E.) Christianity endured the Christological debates that led to the Council of Ephesus, but also the appearance of Manichaeism and Pelagianism, two movements with different perspectives on the nature of sin and redemption. Augustine wrote in *Confessions*, his spiritual autobiography, of spending his young adulthood under the influence of Manichaeism, and being taught that two principles, good and evil, were separate and co-eternal, and that both were present in all kinds of matter in greater or lesser degree. The good in matter struggled to escape the bad, and flesh of all sorts contained a preponderance of the bad. Manichaeism instructed its adherents to avoid eating meat and having sex, since these were thought to further contaminate whatever good people had inside.

Augustine wrote in *Confessions* that Manichaeism failed him because its theory of evil couldn't bear the least amount of scrutiny and provided no escape from sin. He came to realize that sin lay not in externals such as eating flesh but in an inner deficiency of the human will to choose God. He would discover about God that "all that you asked of me was to deny my own will and accept yours." This also brought him to reject Pelagianism, a doctrine that rejected original sin and held out the possibility of sinless perfection. Augustine rejected the idea of spiritual regeneration through outward purity or moral action: "If I am to reach him, it must be though my soul." He concluded, "You were within me, and I was in the world outside myself. I searched for you outside myself and, disfigured as I was, I fell upon the lovely things of your creation. You were with me, but I was not with you." (*Confessions*, 10:27)

The City of God

Augustine's ideas about God and the inner life profoundly influenced Christian belief and practice. In his other great book, *The City of God*, Augustine engaged in a lengthy defense of the Christian faith, and in the process neatly captured the entire Christian story from the fall of Satan and the creation of the world through the incarnation, death, and resurrection of Jesus and finally to the future judgment of humanity and onset of the eternal realm. Augustine used Roman history to demonstrate the folly of pagans who attributed temporal blessings of safety, prosperity, and happiness to the gods of the pantheon. The gods didn't prevent the fall of Troy, or Saguntum, or the Roman Republic before Christ appeared.

According to Augustine, Christians have much broader vision because they seek a heavenly reward. Because "some live according to the flesh and others according to the spirit," two conflicting cities emerged. (*The City of God*, 14:4) God wants all humanity to live according to the principles of his spiritual city, and speaks to us "by the truth itself, if any one is prepared to hear with the mind rather then with the body." And yet "the mind ... is disabled by besotting and inveterate vices not merely from delighting and abiding in, but even from tolerating his unchangeable light, until it has been gradually healed, and renewed, and made capable of such felicity, it had, in the first place, to be impregnated with faith, and so purified." (*The City of God*, 11:2) In *The City of God*, obedience to God's voice is the mother and guardian of all virtues, and ensures the passage of the soul to the celestial paradise so vividly described in the closing passages of the book.

The Least You Need to Know

- When Christianity left Judaism, it grew more responsive to Greek metaphysical speculation.

- The Trinity emerged in response to thinkers who would make Jesus a second and subordinate god.

- Christianity holds the view that three distinct persons, Father, Son, and Holy Spirit, are a single, unified God.

- Christians believe Jesus was fully God and fully man, two complete natures, of one substance and in one person.

- Augustine is hailed for developing a Christian philosophy of history and for his deeply interior and spiritualized perspective on the faith.

13

God in Christian Experience

In This Chapter

- ◆ Encountering God through the sacraments

- ◆ Becoming holy the Christian way

- ◆ Icons: God in pictures

- ◆ How Christian mystics achieve union with God

- ◆ What does it mean to be filled with the Holy Spirit?

- ◆ Other practices and objects used to achieve closer communion with the divine

The Christian doctrines of the Trinity and incarnation present God as simultaneously transcendent and immanent. God is not us, and God is not equivalent to the world around us, therefore God is transcendent. At the same time, God took the form of man and lived a natural life, later sending the Spirit to dwell in the hearts of all believers. This brought God a lot closer to humanity and illustrates God's immanent quality. If the dual transcendence and immanence of God is an important part of Christian belief, it's an important part of Christian practice as well.

Christians do a lot of things to facilitate communion with the divine. Their prayers, songs, meditations, fasting, and rituals put them in touch with a deity whose power and reach is perceived as beyond measure. Their sacred places, shrines, relics, iconography, and other tangibles activate the senses and pave the way for a total mental, emotional, and physical experience of the Supreme Being of the universe. In this chapter, you'll discover that as you go from Orthodoxy to Catholicism to Protestantism, you find slight variations in the way God is thought to manifest himself to humanity and how believers are taught to seek the divine presence.

The Way to God

Christians in the early church disagreed about what kind of lifestyle was required of those who seek God. Remember, Christianity grew out of Judaism, and the first-century rabbis taught that God demanded complete purity of life from dress and diet to interpersonal demeanor. Every aspect of life was to be ritually purified and made holy in conformity to the halakhah, or God's law delivered to Moses. When Jesus came, however, a new covenant was to be established: "When Christ appeared … he entered once for all into the Holy Place, taking not the blood of goats and calves but his own blood, thus securing an eternal redemption." (Hebrews 9:11–12)

Jesus and the disciples spoke of a spiritual covenant sealed with Christ's blood and written on the hearts of men. Did this mean that Christians were free to sin? Heaven forbid, the Apostle Paul famously replied. Belief in Christ necessitated a complete outer and inner transformation: "I appeal to you therefore brethren, by the mercies of God, to present your bodies a living sacrifice, holy and acceptable to God, which is your spiritual worship. Do not be conformed to this world, but be transformed by the renewal of your mind, that you may prove what is the will of God, what is good and acceptable and perfect." (Romans 12:1–2)

As you can imagine, Paul's entreaty raised a rather thorny issue for early converts to Christianity. What does a transformed life look like? When some Gentiles espoused faith in Christ, believers reared under the teachings of the Pharisees said "it is necessary to circumcise them, and to charge them to keep the law of Moses." (Acts 15:5) A council of early Christian leaders decided on a compromise; Gentile converts wouldn't have to undergo circumcision, but had to give up food offered to idols, meat from strangled animals, and anything that still contained blood. Oh, and unchastity. It seems living for God in the new covenant still entailed some elements of the old.

Asceticism

When Paul instructed the believers in Rome that they were not to be conformed to the world, this left quite a bit open for interpretation. Paul and the other apostles prodded early Christians to demonstrate virtues such as love, hope, patience, and kindness, and to exercise their talents to develop the so-called "body of Christ," which was interpreted to mean the church composed of all Jesus' followers. Jesus and the Apostle James, on the other hand, preached against worldliness, including the pursuit of material wealth and prosperity. Jesus' claim that it would be easier for a camel to go through the eye of a needle than for a rich man to enter the kingdom of God was taken up by James, who wrote, "Come now, you rich, weep and howl for the miseries that are coming upon you." (James 5:1)

It's hard to believe that Jesus and James had in mind the example of John the Baptist, who lived in the wilderness, wore a garment of camel's hair with a leather girdle, and ate locusts and honey. That would be a rather extreme example of *asceticism*.

But nevertheless some believers pursued a lifestyle with few or no material comforts. Early Christians in the Book of Acts sold their goods and gave to those in need, and in a famous case Ananias and Sapphira fell down dead when Peter exposed their lie about keeping some of the profit from the sale of property. However, these cases were not about asceticism, but rather about the sharing of wealth to promote Christian community.

> **Word to the Wise**
>
> **Asceticism** comes from the Greek word for exercise or athletic training, and usually refers to the denial of bodily pleasures in order to develop religious virtues.

In some instances the impulse to lead a purified life came from the larger culture of Hellenistic Greek religion and philosophy, as in the case of the Gnostic and Manichaean idea of forgoing physical pleasures because the material world, in their view, was corrupt. But Christianity was cutting new channels. The Montanists, for example, emerged in the second century with new revelations about Jesus' expected return. They sparked a movement to sell possessions, and even houses and property, and Montanists seem to have cultivated certain practices that were to become traditions in the church: fasting and celibacy.

Early persecutions hardened the Christian community, producing heroes courting martyrdom and hermits fleeing into the wilderness. The story of Anthony (c. 250–356 C.E.) of Egypt intersects with these developments. He was born amid the Decian persecutions (named for Roman Emperor Decius) of 249–251 C.E., and his parents left him a huge inheritance. Apparently he sold all his property and gave it to his fellow villagers, choosing to live a life of extreme poverty among the other desert hermits nearby. Eventually Anthony withdrew to a deserted fort atop a mountain and brought other hermits into the facility, thereby creating a kind of blueprint for the monastic communities of late antiquity and beyond. Anthony's asceticism was legendary; he consumed a small amount of bread, salt, and water after sunset each day, and often went without for three or four days. He slept on the ground, gave up bathing, and wore his animal skins with the hair toward his body so as to increase the discomfort. All of this he did in order to resist worldliness and devote all his thoughts and actions to God.

Monasticism

The ascetics of Egypt, Palestine, and Asia Minor helped give rise to a more systematic method of observing spiritual disciplines and achieving communion with God. Pachomius (c. 285–356 C.E.), an Egyptian soldier, converted to Christianity and was tutored in the faith by an ascetic Christian. He later began a sort of commune, rather like the Jewish Essenes in Chapter 7, for those who sought to live an austere life. Members of the community read and memorized scripture, and prayed at regular times during the day. Twice a week the Pachomian monks fasted and observed the Eucharistic rite. They denied themselves bodily pleasures through a restricted diet, limited sleep, and simplified dress. Apparently Pachomius's format impressed one of the Cappadocian Fathers, Basil of Caesarea, who devoted himself to the monastic life for part of his adulthood, then developed rules for communal living that helped to shape the monastic tradition in Christianity.

The whole point of Basil's rules, later picked up and developed in the Rule of St. Benedict during the sixth century, was to systematically practice Christian virtue with built-in accountability from other seekers. Here we're back in the rabbinical mode, with every area of life seemingly governed by regulations. In the Rule of St. Benedict, the monk's life is lived according to a strict schedule with every hour accounted for, with allotted times for eating,

Divinations

Basil and Benedict hoped to create disciplined, orderly lives, not the sort of ascetic exhibitionism you see in the famous "pillar saints" of the ancient Middle East. For example, Simeon Stylites (d. 459) lived atop a pillar in Antioch for 36 years without possessions, teaching and healing pilgrims who came to visit. He once touched his forehead to his foot 1,244 times in succession.

sleeping, and working, and of course individual prayer, study, and meditation. The schedule also included times for community worship, prayer, and singing. Benedict even identified times when silence and a somber frame of mind were appropriate. These rules intended to discipline the believer to live in conformity with Jesus' teaching, and to serve the community outside the walls of the monastery with prayer, healing, and acts of charity.

Sacramentalism

The monastic life didn't appeal to everyone. Paul himself said that some people would be apostles and prophets, and others would serve God in other ways, as teachers, healers, helpers, administrators, and "speakers in various kinds of tongues." (I Corinthians 12:28) (More on the speaking in tongues later in this chapter.) These Christians who served God in everyday life might even find themselves mixed together with pagans in their neighborhoods and professions, and therefore lack the spiritual advantages of men and women living the monastic life of complete surrender to God.

Nevertheless, all believers were expected to live a purified life, following Paul's instruction to the churches of Galatia in Asia Minor to "walk by the Spirit, and do not gratify the desires of the flesh." (Galatians 5:16) Christians were exhorted to experience God in the context of community worship and the practice of the sacraments. Jesus taught the disciples to initiate members into the fellowship through water baptism, a Jewish purification rite that survived Christianity's conversion into a Gentile faith. He also instructed them to observe the Lord's Supper; together baptism and the Eucharist (also called communion) entered church history as special observances mandated by Jesus Christ himself and associated with the immanent presence of the Spirit.

Of course, the precise meaning of the Eucharist has been the source of much contention in the church; as early as the beginning of the second century, during the ministry of Ignatius as Bishop of Antioch, we hear of Christians who abstained because "they do not admit that the Eucharist is the flesh of our savior Jesus Christ." Later, stormy debates would arise over whether the Eucharistic elements of bread and wine actually transformed into the body and blood of Christ, or whether the Eucharist was purely symbolic. Ironically, what was intended to be a unifying practice became a point of serious disunity in the church.

In the Roman Catholic tradition, the Eucharist lies at the center of the Mass because, in the words of the participants of the Second Vatican Council, it is "the source and summit of the whole of the Church's worship and of the Christian life." (*Eucharisticum Mysterium*, 1967) It's not so hard to imagine why when you take in the explanation of Hugo of St. Victor (1096–1141), who described the sacrament as a "physical or material element presented clearly to the senses, by similitude representing, by institution signifying, and by consecration containing an invisible and spiritual grace." (*De Sacramentis Fidei Christianae*) In other words, Roman Catholics came to believe that the sacraments provide the very conduit through which the grace of God enters the church and fills the individual believer.

The Roman Catholic Church has a robust theology behind its understanding of the sacraments, which is fitting given the central position the sacraments are given in Roman Catholic belief and practice. By the Middle Ages the church had identified seven sacraments as vehicles for uniting the believer with God: baptism, Eucharist, confirmation, marriage, ordination, confession, and extreme unction. When you look at them from a distance, the sacraments embraced the entire arc of the average person's life—baptism at birth, confirmation and first communion in adolescence, marriage marking the attainment of adulthood, and later, confession and Eucharist at regular intervals until sickness and death made extreme unction (anointing the sick with oil) a necessity. So if you couldn't live like the monks, at least you could anticipate the grace of God to enter your life at predictable and sometimes pivotal moments, providing a direct sensory experience of the very presence of the divine.

Mysticism

Following Hugo, the church taught that the sacraments contained "an invisible and spiritual grace" made available by means of the senses. If most Christians in the Roman Catholic tradition would experience the divine through the practice of the sacraments, a select few would nevertheless claim a much more direct, unmediated communication with God. The earliest writers in the Christian tradition urged the contemplative life, and like their counterparts in Hinduism and Buddhism, Christian contemplatives sought an inner, subjective experience of the Absolute, unfiltered by the medium of religious language or philosophical abstractions.

The Christian idea of incarnation permitted full-bodied anthropomorphic representations of the divine, as in this icon from St. Catherine's Monastery in Egypt.

(Courtesy of St. Catherine's Monastery)

Augustine's Vision of God

Christians have long been inspired by the example of Augustine, who spoke of an inner journey that led to direct comprehension of divine power. "Under your guidance I entered into the depths of my soul, and this I was able to do because your aid befriended me. I entered, and with the eye of my soul, such as it was, I saw the Light that never changes casting its rays over the same eye of my soul, over my mind." This was a kind of divine illumination that sensory perception and even logic could not obtain, for "it shone above my mind," and "all who know the Truth know this Light, and all who know this Light know eternity." (*Confessions*, 7.10)

Augustine's process here is quite revealing. He lamented that the soul was weighted down with the body, and this physical and material existence limited the soul's ability to perceive God. But through contemplation the material world could be overcome. "I realized that above my own mind, which was liable to change, there was the never changing, true eternity of truth." He sought to transcend his own mind, and thereby embarked upon an inner journey: "Step by step, my thoughts move on from the consideration of material things to the soul, which perceives things through the senses of the body, and then to the soul's inner power, to which the bodily senses communicate external facts." Next came the power of reason, which "led me on to consider the source of its own understanding."

> **Pearls of Wisdom**
>
> Thomas Merton (1915–1968), a Trappist monk, believed insights gained from contemplation were superior to theological concepts: "So much depends on our idea of God! Yet no idea of him, however pure and perfect, is adequate to express him as he really is. Our idea of God tells us more about ourselves than about him." (*New Seeds of Contemplation*, 1961)

Pushing deeper, Augustine "withdrew my thoughts from their normal course and drew back from the confusion of images," and "in an instant of awe, my mind attained to the sight of God who IS." He had attained the kind of spiritual vision reserved for only the truly gifted. Indeed, his inner journey reached the ultimate destination: "Then, at last, I caught sight of your invisible nature, as it is known through your creatures." (*Confessions*, 7.17) But the weight of his flesh drew him back once again, to the world of sensuous pleasures where people are content to understand God through the agency of pedestrian language.

Theresa's Interior Castle

Augustine's mysticism was visionary, because he believed he observed the divine Light within by means of the "eye" of his soul. In this sense, Augustine's mysticism resonates with the mysticism of Jewish and even pagan traditions. But other strands of Christian mysticism speak not of visions, but achieving union with God.

St. Teresa of Avila (1515–1582), a Spanish Carmelite nun, read Augustine's *Confessions* and experienced a crisis when she got to the part when Augustine heard the voice of God in a garden and converted to the faith. The garden image struck her deeply; convinced that she lacked a talent for words, Teresa spoke through images and figures, such as the image of a garden or interior castle that the divine presence inhabits within the very soul of the believer. The preference for symbols, images, and metaphors distinguish mystical expressions of the divine from theological and philosophical expressions, because words and concepts, the thinking goes, distort the meaning of truths that can be grasped only intuitively.

Teresa believed that prayer and contemplation could lead to deeper insights and ultimately union with God: "The believer must think of himself as one setting out to make a garden in which the Lord is to take his delight." You could water this garden four ways, with buckets, a windmill, a stream, or heavy rain. These methods correspond to degrees of effort in prayer; the first stages require enormous concentration, but the believer is rewarded with divine favor, enabling higher, and less effort-filled prayer. The heavy rain comes in the Prayer of Union, in which the mind ceases to form images or words, and the soul experiences something like a swoon. Teresa felt this experience "cannot be understood, less still described," and the best image she could muster was of a hot sun appearing within, shining upon the soul and melting it away. "It seemed almost certain that I had been conscious of his very presence." (*Autobiography*, xviii)

Gifts of the Spirit

Christian mystics such as Teresa didn't speak of evaporating into God or the Absolute, but rather, achieving a sort of union whereby the divine bypasses the intellect and imagination and provides a sense of his presence within. Believers find it difficult to find language that satisfies our sense of God's unfathomable essence or God's limitless power, which is why mystics have offered such a compelling vision of the ultimate reality. In the same way, believers who receive the gifts of the spirit—speaking in tongues, prophetic utterances, and the power of healing—can't rationally explain what the Spirit is doing in them and through them. Still, many believe the gifts of the Spirit are an important way that God reveals himself to humanity.

Those who claim to be "filled with the Holy Spirit" and empowered to speak in tongues, heal, and prophesy are drawing from a very long tradition, beginning with Jesus himself, who said that his disciples would be given power to cast out demons and heal the sick. In Acts, the Holy Spirit descended upon the first Christians and they began to speak in foreign languages. Paul gave instructions to the church in Corinth for the use of these supernatural gifts, and Montanus of Phrygia in Asia Minor, leader of the so-called Montanists we discovered earlier, claimed to have an experience of being filled with the Spirit, complete with an ecstatic trance, speaking in tongues, and prophetic declarations. Luminaries of the church, such as Tertullian, Cyprian, St. Francis of Assisi, and even Martin Luther, offered support for the spirit-filled experience.

Modern Pentecostals and Charismatics affirm the gifts of the Spirit, which they variously call *baptism of the Holy Spirit* and fire-baptism. From an initial outbreak of glossolalia (speaking in tongues) in Los Angeles's Azuza Street Revival in 1906, the Pentecostal-Charismatic movement has grown to gargantuan proportions, particularly in Latin America, East Asia, and Southeast Asia. Today there are perhaps half a billion worldwide who believe in the doctrine of spirit baptism, which is perhaps one fifth of the global population of Christians. That's an impressive number of believers who perceive God's immanence through the activity of the Holy Spirit.

> **Word to the Wise**
>
> **Baptism of the Holy Spirit** refers to the belief that the Holy Spirit fills believers with the divine presence, empowering them to perform supernatural healing, prophesy, or speak in tongues.

Portraits of Jesus

Spirit baptism isn't quite comprehensible, and in fact that's the whole point—God confounds reason and breaks the ordinary routines of everyday life with a divine visitation. Spirit baptism is yet another example of believers teaching that God is beyond words, concepts, or images. On that last point, Jesus of Nazareth gave believers a new opportunity to visualize God, in this case as a human being, whether in a manger in Bethlehem or on a cross in Jerusalem. Between the crèche and the crucifix, Christians seem to have had no trouble with anthropomorphic depictions of God in the person of Jesus Christ.

The Byzantine church, centered in Asia Minor, the Balkans, and Greece, maintained a long tradition of using icons to stimulate devotional responses. Icons are pictures of Jesus or any other person believed to possess spiritual virtues. Emperor Leo III triggered a debate in 726 C.E. when he banned the use of visual depictions of Jesus and the saints on the grounds that they promoted idolatry. Defenders, mostly priests and monks, came to the rescue of Christians who had become fond of these images, arguing that to forbid graphic depictions of Jesus was to deny his humanity. Another Ecumenical Council (the seventh) ruled in favor of limited use of icons, affirming their devotional value and noting that "the honor paid to the image passes to the original, and he that adores the image adores in it the person depicted thereby." (Second Council of Nicaea, 787)

In the Byzantine church and in the Eastern Orthodox tradition that came out of it, icons packaged the mysterious and supernatural message of the incarnation of God, putting the believer in touch with truths about the immanent God in a way that philosophical abstractions or church doctrines could never fully accomplish. This is because icons, like other forms of art, engender a subjective experience that brings the believer closer to understanding the mysterious reality of divine immanence than can be accomplished from reason or logic. Where Roman Catholicism uses the concept of sacramentalism to describe the infusion of God into the material world, Eastern Orthodoxy uses the concept of icon—everything in the material world contains and reflects the divine. Even people are icons, bearing the image of the creator on our faces, but also in our minds and hearts.

Take Heed!

Eastern Orthodox Christians don't worship icons. They believe that images generate feelings of devotion to God in a way that words and doctrines simply cannot. They work from the basic idea expressed by John Scotus Eriugena (810–877): "Every visible or invisible creature is a theophany or appearance of God."

People, Places, and Things

The Christian experience of God includes more than ascetic living and speaking in tongues. There's a welter of practices and objects that are thought to bring the believer into closer communion with the divine.

Sacred Liturgy, Sacred Space

Of course, the Mass includes the Eucharist, which in certain strands of Christianity is thought to be the conduit through which the grace of God flows into the congregation. The liturgy is a complete sensory experience, from the visual splendor of stained glass, soaring cathedral ceilings, and colorful vestments in Catholic and Anglican churches to the olfactory sensations of burning candles and incense in Eastern Orthodox observances. Organ music and gospel choirs offer an auditory stimulus in Protestant worship. The liturgy, or order of worship in the Christian tradition, contains all the elements necessary to put believers into communication with God, and offers an opportunity for them to respond with praise, gifts, and prayers of commitment.

Devotionals

Christians do not limit their experience of God to public services on Sabbath and holy days. Christians consider the Bible to be the very word of God, and many, if not most, Christians take time to read the scripture on a daily basis. The Gallup Poll put the number of weekly readers of the Bible at 40 percent in the United States in 1999. Unlike Hindus and Muslims, Christians do not have a sacred language, but they tend to agree with Paul in his letter to Timothy, that "all scripture is inspired by God and profitable for teaching, for reproof, for correction, for training in righteousness." (1 Timothy 3:16) Of course, Christians pray, burn candles and incense, read devotional literature, and perform dozens of other spiritual exercises designed to open up a private dialogue with God.

Pilgrimage

Where Hindus and Muslims feature pilgrimage as a way to demonstrate their devotion and to enhance their spiritual experience, Christians have no obligation to make pilgrimage. And yet millions of Christians visit sacred places every year, for a wide variety of reasons. Roman Catholics pilgrimage to Rome to visit the tombs of early

Christian martyrs and the site of St. Peter's execution, believed to be located at the large obelisk in St. Peter's Square. Or they might travel to Lourdes in France where the Virgin Mary appeared to Bernadette Soubirous in 1858; the six million who visit each year believe the waters of Lourdes can heal the sick and disabled. Christians of every variety visit the so-called "Holy Lands" in Israel in order to walk the path of Jesus during his earthly ministry. The believers' encounter with sacred space is yet another way to experience the divine through other means than doctrines or theological constructions.

Material Culture

It is impossible to imagine Christianity without the bevy of religious materials that you can find in the local church or Christian bookstore. Historically, Christians have made use of candles, incense, shrines, religious art, altarpieces, crucifixes, and hundreds of other objects as a way to enhance the quality of their devotional life and communal worship. From time to time, Christians have argued about whether these spiritual aids strengthen or weaken commitment to the God who cannot be pictured or described in any craft or language known to men. You see this impulse in the Iconoclastic Controversy of the eighteenth century—an attempt to rid the church of pictorial representations of Christ—and in the English Puritan movement of the seventeenth century—an attempt to get rid of most religious objects and ceremonial rituals of the church. These episodes remind us that Christianity has the same difficulty as other major religions in giving material expression to the ineffable, mysterious, unknowable God of the universe.

The Least You Need to Know

- Historically, one of Christianity's ideals was self-denial of worldly pleasures and luxuries, which in the extreme form is known as asceticism.

- Sacramentalism is practiced in the Christian tradition as a means to facilitate communion between God and his people.

- Great Christian mystics followed the inward path to deeper spiritual truths, and even union with God.

- Christianity warns against idolatry, but believers use crucifixes and icons to help them focus on the divine reality beyond the image.

God in Christian Thought

In This Chapter

- ◆ The "A Team" of medieval Scholasticism: Anselm, Abelard, Aquinas

- ◆ Finding common ground between faith and reason

- ◆ Proof that God exists, ontologically speaking

- ◆ The many faces of Protestantism

- ◆ Inner light: encountering an immanent God

- ◆ The idea of a God of nature and nature's God

Many believers think that God is better experienced than explained. In the last chapter we read about Christians who used icons because they believed portraits of Christ did a better job than words or doctrines in activating the imagination and conveying the mysteries of the ultimate reality. Gregory of Nyssa taught that "anyone who tries to describe the ineffable Light in language is truly a liar—not because he hates the truth, but because of the inadequacy of his description." Gregory was reacting to the fourth-century obsession of trying to work out in language the mystery of the Trinity. You can bet the Nicene Fathers and later church councils didn't remove mystery from Christianity by formalizing the doctrines of the Trinity and incarnation in the language of the historic creeds of Christianity.

Still, the impulse to explain the faith—to make it appear orderly and rational—continued within the Christian tradition. Medieval thinkers hoped to prevent doubters from concluding that God, who worked in ways that lay beyond reason, might in fact be a logical impossibility. Ultimately these thinkers cared more about sin and salvation, but along the way, they became convinced that Christianity was defensible on intellectual, rather than merely experiential, grounds. Here you'll learn what medieval Christians meant when they said that faith and reason are paths to the same unchanging, eternal, and absolute truth. And you'll learn that since the time of Thomas Aquinas in the thirteenth century, Christians have gone back and forth between the reasonableness and the mysteriousness of the faith.

Faith and Reason

All religions have their philosophers, but Christianity is distinct for having been shown to be compatible with Greek metaphysical and epistemological concepts. The Greeks bequeathed to Mediterranean Christians a framework that enabled them to speculate about the ultimate nature of existence, or what we call metaphysics, and to think about the sources of knowledge, or epistemology. The Christian philosophical impulse lay dormant for hundreds of years after the Iconoclastic Controversy of the eighth century, nursed along by monks inhabiting an arc of monasteries extending from Asia Minor through Northern Europe and into England and Ireland. But these impulses broke out into the open once again when Christians came into more direct contact with Judaism and Islam in the Crusades of the eleventh and twelfth centuries.

Stimulated by the work of Jewish and Muslim teachers such as Maimonides and ibn Sina (Avicenna), Christian monks came to wrestle with Greek metaphysics and epistemology in an effort to demonstrate the reasonableness of Christian doctrines. St. Anselm (1033–1109), for example, thought he proved the existence of God in *Monologium* (Soliloquy) and *Proslogium* (Discourse). He reasoned that the human mind can conceive of a perfect Being that has no limits or defects. Such a Being must exist not only in the imagination, but in actuality, because a perfect Being that lacks actuality is obviously limited and defective, and therefore imperfect. This logical contradiction convinced Anselm that God is a perfect Being, and that God must therefore exist.

Anselm also reasoned through the doctrine of the atonement, claiming that Jesus was necessary because God is perfectly moral, and to overlook man's sin without judgment and punishment is immoral. Since God can't be perfectly moral and commit an immoral act, Jesus' atoning sacrifice was necessary to compensate for the sins of humanity. Here again, Anselm worked from reason and logic to arrive at Christian precepts, rather than using scripture and creed.

Peter Abelard (1079–1142), another architect of this movement known as Scholasticism, left a small imprint on the development of the faith-learning matrix, but was best known for his method. One of his books, *Sic et Non* (Yes and No), took a set of theological topics and aligned quotes from scripture with quotes from the early church Fathers that appeared to take opposite positions. This wasn't meant to expose Christianity as self contradictory, but to illustrate how truth could be attained through a dialectical process of logic and reasoning. According to Abelard, faith and reason aren't enemies, but partners in the pursuit of ultimate truth.

Divinations

Abelard lived a colorful life in twelfth-century Paris. He fell in love with a pupil, Heloise, who bore him a son. They secretly married, but when Heloise denied the marriage, she was sent to a convent, and Abelard was castrated and banished to the monastery at Saint Denis. They later carried on a passionate correspondence that has gone down as the greatest set of love letters in history.

Thomas Aquinas

Perhaps Abelard was misunderstood, or perhaps he pushed too far. But it's clear that he made the wrong enemies. He locked horns with Bernard of Clairvaux, who turned church authorities against him. Tragically, Abelard lived to see his *Treatise on the Unity and Trinity of God* burned, and the Pope issue a ruling of condemnation and excommunication against him. Even so, the tide was turning in the direction of the Scholastics amid increasing contact with Muslim and Jewish falsafah (philosophy) and widespread circulation of Greco-Roman philosophical texts. By the early thirteenth century, Scholastics discovered Aristotle, whom they simply called "The Philosopher," and the greatest student of Aristotle in the Middle Ages was Thomas Aquinas (c. 1225–1274). Aquinas was born into a respected Italian family, but gave up a life in politics to devote himself to the service of the church. He studied at the University of Naples, joined the Dominican order of priests, and became a professor at the University of Paris, where he spent much of his highly productive and influential career.

Thomism

Aquinas developed a distinct approach to ultimate questions, later called Thomism. Aquinas started with Aristotle's departure from Plato. Plato taught that ultimate reality was located in perfect forms or ideas in some nonmaterial realm, and that we possess mental imprints of these ideas that enable us to glimpse the ultimate reality. Aristotle, on the other hand, taught a different metaphysics and a different epistemology. He held that the world is a world of senses and sense perceptions, and the senses supply the mind with raw data that is processed and rendered meaningful through the exercise of reason.

Aquinas distinguished among three sources of knowledge in his intricate investigation into the fields of metaphysics and epistemology. He identified one source of knowledge about God as the workings of human reason. Logic might lead us to an understanding of God's nature or methods of operation. But this would still leave us coming up short in our quest for God, as numerous thinkers had already shown, so Aquinas identified a second source of knowledge, supernatural revelation, like the Torah of Judaism or the Gospels of Christianity. Of course, revelation occasionally defies reason, so Aquinas perceived a third source of knowledge about God, the knowledge we obtain when reason clarifies revelation. With this threefold distinction, Aquinas gave Christians a way to think about the different roles that faith and reason play in transforming knowledge into beliefs about God.

> **Pearls of Wisdom**
>
> Christian thinkers such as Aquinas, who hoped to render God comprehensible in words and doctrines, worked against inertia in the other direction, as expressed by Evagrius of Pontus (345–399): "God cannot be grasped by the mind. If he could be grasped, he would not be God."

Summa Theologiae

As he wrote in the *Summa Theologiae* (completed in 1273), his most well-known work, "faith presupposes natural knowledge." In this way, the Book of Nature and the Book of Revelation form a unified whole, with God as the author of both. This perspective led Aquinas to value and even celebrate the fruits of reason, because they could support the knowledge we gain about God through faith.

The *Summa* is over 3,000 pages long, containing a thick exposition of the church's kerygmatic teachings, revealed in scripture and affirmed in ecumenical councils. What comes through these pages is a conviction that faith and reason could never contradict, provided both are rightly used. One example of how Aquinas utilized the methods of Aristotle and the Scholastics to focus reason in the right direction is his cosmological argument for the existence of God. He framed this argument using a system of logic that had four essential ingredients. Beginning with common experience and observation, the first ingredient, we then generate all the possible explanations available to humankind through reason and revelation, thus adding a second ingredient. These two elements get us ready for the crucial third component, the process of eliminating those explanations that contradict reason, revelation, and revelation as clarified by reason. The fourth ingredient is the result of the first three; following the elimination of unworkable explanations, what you have left is the equivalent of God, either in nature or method of operation.

Proofs of God's Existence

Aquinas's system offered a measure of comfort for those plagued by the question, "can I be sure that God exists and that my faith is justified?" In fact, a very small portion of the *Summa* uses his system of logic to update Aristotle's proofs for the existence of God. Perhaps a couple of illustrations from this section can provide some insight into Aquinas's thinking. Aristotle spoke of a Prime Mover, without which the things in motion (like planets or stars) could not be in motion. Aquinas reasoned, "whatever is moved must be moved by another." At this point the law of infinite regression kicks in: "This cannot go on to infinity, because there would be no first mover." As Aquinas concludes, "Therefore it is necessary to arrive at a first mover, moved by no other; and this everyone understands to be God." (*Summa*, 1.2)

The imprint of Aristotle can also be seen in the concept of a Necessary Being. If we didn't have a being from which other beings proceeded, "even now there would be nothing in existence, because that which does not exist begins to exist only through something already existing." Logic tells us "if at one time nothing was in existence, it would have been impossible for anything to have begun to exist; and thus even now nothing would be in existence." Since things exist, "we cannot but admit the existence of some being having of itself its own necessity, and not receiving it from another." And what is this being? Aquinas answers: "This all men speak of as God."

> **Take Heed!**
>
> Rational arguments persuaded people living in the Middle Ages because they confirmed what they already knew through divine revelation, which they accepted on faith. Much later, people in the West discarded ontological arguments after Immanuel Kant identified their weaknesses in *Critique of Pure Reason* (1781).

Questioning Faith and Reason

Aquinas's so-called cosmological argument for God's existence was a small part of the *Summa;* its main thrust was a systematic exposition of Christian doctrine, identifying God's limitless grace as the source of everything, including creation, the moral law, the redemptive work of Jesus, and regeneration of the human soul. And he showed how God continued to supply grace by means of the sacraments, which unite believers together in oneness as the body of Christ.

But Aquinas's work threw a scare into the church. If God can be proved through reason, perhaps God can be disproved as well. Though Aquinas, as the Bishop of Paris, was careful to affirm the importance of faith to belief in God, he nevertheless anathematized 219 propositions taught at the University of Paris by those under Aquinas's influence. Shortly after Aquinas's death, John Duns Scotus of Oxford (1265–1308) and William of Ockham (1280–1349) went to work on Aquinas's faith-reason synthesis. Duns Scotus rejected the idea that God's actions must conform to human reason, which was Anselm's claim about the rationality of the doctrine of atonement. Remember, Anselm claimed that God required a sacrifice in order to save people from their sins, and the only acceptable sacrifice for all humanity was the perfect man, Jesus Christ. Duns Scotus came along and argued that Anselm's idea of atonement placed limits on the divine; perhaps God wasn't required by some law of necessity to demand the sacrifice of his son, but just decided to act in this particular way.

Likewise, William of Ockham was convinced that the major doctrines of the church couldn't be proven through reason, and instead must be accepted on faith. The existence of God might seem reasonable, but this fell far short of certainty, using the standards of proof applied at the time. All you could say was that God's existence was probable. This is to say nothing of the core doctrines of Christianity, such as the Trinity, the incarnation, the atonement, the immortality of the soul, and so on. Ockham believed these core doctrines were true because they are found in scripture and taught by the church, not because they could be proven through reason. Along with Ockham, Western thinkers came to see reason and faith not as partners in the pursuit of truth, but potentially antagonistic.

Resurgence of Mystery

Duns Scotus and Ockham didn't doubt God; they argued instead that God's essence is utterly incomprehensible, and that human reason couldn't make it less so. They tended to stress the width of the chasm that lay between God and humanity, which no system of logic or process of reasoning could span. And where the Scholastics picked up on the ancient metaphysical interest in the attributes of God, the writers of the fourteenth and fifteenth centuries tended to view the ultimate reality as shrouded in mystery.

An indication of the turn from reason to mystery was seen in the increase of reports of mystical visions, miraculous events, and demonic activity. Some of the great mystics and visionaries of the Christian tradition lived in the fourteenth and fifteenth centuries, such as Joan of Arc, Nicholas of Cusa, and Thomas à Kempis. Catherine of Siena (1347–1380) is as good an illustration as any. At the age of seven she reported a vision of Jesus and responded by pledging her exclusive love to him. She devoted the rest of her short life to prayer and mystical visions, with occasional breaks to miraculously heal the sick and to instruct Pope Gregory XI on matters of policy and statecraft. Reports of her fabulous visions and healing powers swept across Europe and she became the object of much discussion and debate.

When you take them together, the heroes of the faith in the late Middle Ages confounded reason with their tales of direct, unmediated communion with God. And where the Scholastics struggled with the relationship between faith and reason, these believers fought the inner struggle of sin and guilt, and embarked on a quest for salvation along the narrow path of commitment to God. Moreover, their struggle took on a larger meaning because of the spiritual excitements of the age. Christians couldn't rest easy with Muslims advancing to the borders of central Europe and Christian Spain. Religious hostilities became entwined with spiritual warfare amid widespread reports of witchcraft activity in the last decades of the fifteenth century. These reports triggered a 200-year period of heightened awareness of Satan's presence on Earth, which continued through the Salem witchcraft trials of the 1690s and into the early eighteenth century.

Toward a Reformation

The Protestant Reformation came right on the heels of shattering spiritual convulsions in western Europe; the abounding philosophical arguments explain why reformers nurtured divergent impulses. They followed the Scholastics, who believed that the divine could be described in the precise language of doctrines and creeds, but they also marveled at the inscrutable power and majesty of God.

Luther's Work

Martin Luther (1483–1546) became a world-class scholar while shaking with fear over the devils in the room beside him. In fact, the whole Protestant Reformation might be said to have hinged on Luther's sense of the vulnerability of his soul to the preying hands of Satan. As a young Augustinian monk, Luther was plagued with spiritual terrors, convinced that the sacramental path to God could do nothing to help him escape the damnation awaiting him as a result of his sins. He perceived an unbridgeable chasm between himself and God. As he reflected later: "Although I lived a blameless life as a monk, I felt that I was a sinner with an uneasy conscience before God. I also could not believe that I had pleased him with my works."

> ### Pearls of Wisdom
>
> A common thread that runs through 2,000 years of Christian thought is a concern for sin, estrangement from God, and the eternal destiny of the soul. As Danish philosopher and theologian Søren Kierkegaard would write much later: "Christianity is the frightful earnestness that your eternity is decided in this life." (*Journal*, 1854)

After contemplating Romans 1:17, which read "the just shall live by faith," Luther caught a glimpse of God's immeasurable grace. "This immediately made me feel as though I had been born again, and as though I had entered through open gates into paradise itself." To Luther, God supplied the righteousness necessary to bridge the divine-human chasm through the Son of God, Jesus Christ. Jesus was, literally, the Savior. No rational process could account for how the Savior's suffering and death covered all the sins of humanity, and yet this is precisely what Luther came to believe. Try as you might, you couldn't prove this through logic or scientific deduction; it must be accepted on faith.

In his voluminous writings, Luther taught that in response to a little faith, God responds with a flood of grace and mercy, taking the sacrifice of Jesus Christ as a remission for sins. Soon, Luther embarked on a career of teaching the idea of justification by faith and the sufficiency of grace for salvation. He said as much in his famous critique of the Roman Catholic practice of indulgences: "Those who believe that they can be certain of their salvation because they have indulgence letters will be eternally damned, together with their teachers." (Ninety-Five Theses, 1517) God's plan of salvation didn't require a priest-administered system of confession, penance, and indulgences; it was accessible to every believer through faith in Christ, and explained in black and white in the pages of scripture. Pursuing God through scripture, away from the doctrines of the Roman Catholic Church, soon became the central preoccupation of the reformers of the sixteenth century.

Theologians and Mystics

With perfect zeal, the reformers attacked conventional ideas about sin and forgiveness, which produced a mountain of pamphlets and books on such perplexing subjects as human depravity, human freedom, predestination and election, divine foreknowledge, justification and sanctification, and the list goes on. This theological slicing and dicing reached its apogee in John Calvin's *Institutes of the Christian Religion* (1535) a systematic dissertation on the nature of God, the pathologies of original sin, the redemptive work of Christ, the role of the Holy Spirit in sparking faith, and the purpose of the church. In one sense Calvin took a page from the Nicene Fathers, who turned to language to express the nature of the divine and God's relation to humankind. In another sense, Calvin reacquainted believers with mysteries that were as old as Augustine and older, such as *predestination* and human choice. Calvin spoke of but could never fully resolve the question, how can God plan our futures and yet give us freedom to choose?

> **Word to the Wise**
>
> **Predestination** is the belief that God has chosen some souls for salvation, and others for damnation. In the *Institutes*, Calvin defines it as the "eternal decree of God, by which he determined what he wished to make of every individual. For he does not create all in the same condition, but ordains eternal life for some and eternal damnation for others."

Perhaps the reformers might have taken a page from the church fathers in the eastern portion of Christendom, who encouraged silence on unanswerable questions. This could have saved them from vexatious disputes over grace and the sacraments, which ultimately produced a schism within their ranks, leading to separate Lutheran, Reformed (Calvinist), and Anabaptist traditions. Lutherans taught that the real presence of Christ was in the sacraments, while Reformed theologians spoke of the sacraments as conveying the grace of God to believers, uniting them as bride to their groom, Jesus Christ. Anabaptists came to believe that the Eucharist lacked a supernatural dimension; they performed the rite as per Jesus' instruction as a commemoration of his suffering and death.

Disputes over the way in which God worked through the sacraments gave some ex-Catholics a headache, which was compounded by raging debates on a litany of other doctrinal matters. Soon Protestantism spawned its own mystics, such as Caspar Schwenkfeld (1487–1541) and Jacob Boehme (1575–1624), who parted ways with

Lutheranism because they felt spiritually impoverished by its dry theological ruminations. Instead, they spoke of an inner light, an element of the divine within each person that generated knowledge of salvation and prompted the sinner to repentance and faith. This inner presence empowered the saints for miraculous work in building the kingdom of God, and even provided some with direct comprehensions of the Absolute, or prophetic visions of things to come.

Disquisition and Ecstasy

Of course, Protestant theologians and clergy continually policed their ranks for spiritual enthusiasts, and normally marched them out of the church. Nonetheless, Protestant Christianity offered something for everyone, wherever they landed on the spectrum between the cognitive and affective extremes of the faith. The English Reformation in particular seemed to draw out these theological and mystical impulses in Christianity.

Henry VIII's decision to sever ties between the Church of England and Rome (1535) invited reformers to go to work on the theological infrastructure of the church, producing lists of doctrines such as the Forty-Two Articles (1553), the Thirty-Nine Articles (1571), and the Westminster Confession of Faith (1646). Puritan theologians responsible for these monuments of theological doctrine embraced the scholastic tradition, and here Puritan evangelist Richard Baxter (1615–1691) offers some testimony:

> No books so suited with my disposition as Aquinas, Scotus, Durandus, Ockham and their disciples; because I thought they narrowly searched after truth and brought things out of the darkness of confusion. … I never thought I understood any thing till I could anatomise it and see the parts distinctly, and the conjunction of the parts as they make up the whole. (*Autobiography*)

The sheer density of Puritan theology thwarts any effort to make meaningful generalizations about it. Much of it was devoted to thick exposition of covenant theology, which perceived God in a successive array of agreements (with Adam, Israel, the human race, and the church, for example) promising salvation in exchange for fulfillment of the covenant. Sacraments were then reconstructed as signs of the new covenant between God and believers.

Puritanism capped off a great resurgence of doctrinal and theological systematization in the Reformation. And yet, if Puritans perceived God as wholly transcendent, a distant being who orders affairs through a system of covenants, they nevertheless testified to having intense encounters with the indwelling Spirit. In the 1650s, some Puritans affirmed the presence of an inner light and shocked England with reports of spirit-induced shaking, trembling, moaning, and shrieking. The Children of the Light, soon to be known as the Society of Friends, or Quakers, became a foil for starchy Puritan pamphleteers, but taken together, they illustrate something profound about English Protestantism: It produced hair-splitting logicians and tremulous ecstatics, each affirming in their own way the dual nature of God as transcendent and immanent.

Enlightened Christianity

The Puritan extension of the Reformation got quite technical in its exploration of Protestant concepts of salvation, and yet taught believers to stand in awe of the utterly incomprehensible majesty and power of God. Puritans ascribed natural catastrophes to God's divine wrath and special blessings such as drought-breaking storms to God's miraculous providence. As late as the 1690s, Puritans could accept reports of bewitchment in Salem and believe God permitted Satan to break loose for a season in response to the failure of the New England churches to fulfill their end of the covenant.

By 1700, though, a new skepticism born of the scientific turn in Western intellectual life questioned the mysteries and miracles of traditional Christianity. John Toland (1670–1722), a Roman Catholic Irishman, published *Christianity Not Mysterious* in 1696, which argued that God could not act in nonrational ways, and any confusion we have at present about the ineffable mysteries of God would eventually be dispelled through the advance of knowledge. It was the starting point for a century of critical assessments of Roman Catholic and Protestant theology and ritualism in Europe and the American colonies. The work of Enlightenment skeptics merged with metaphysical speculations of Baruch Spinoza and Abraham Cardazo and produced Deism, a system of belief that perceives God as a Supreme Being responsible for the laws of nature and the ordered universe, but who nevertheless receded from creation and permits it to run according to its own inner design. Deists rejected Roman Catholic and Anglican sacramentalism as contrary to reason, and of course the same was true for traditional ideas such as the Trinity and incarnation, and the Protestant emphasis on predestination and the inspiration of scripture.

Maybe the most well-known Deist was Thomas Paine, a Quaker's son whose book *Common Sense* (1776) is credited with pushing colonial American public opinion from resistance to revolution. His *Age of Reason* (1794) denied the doctrines of virgin birth, original sin, atonement and redemption, angels and devils, and the resurrection of the dead. He rejected the Trinity and the incarnation, twin pillars of Christian orthodoxy from late antiquity through the Reformation, and claimed "the only idea man can affix to the name of God is that of a first cause." (*Age of Reason*, 41) To Paine, God isn't ineffable, shrouded in mystery; God's wisdom, immensity, munificence, and mercy were quite comprehensible, so long as believers avoid the Bible and search "the scripture called the Creation." Paine's God was the "Almighty Lecturer" who was manifest only through the workings of the universe and known to humanity through scientific investigation.

> **Pearls of Wisdom**
>
> Thomas Paine spoke for the scientifically inclined Deists when he said, "The Word of God is the creation we behold: and it is in this word, which no human invention can counterfeit or alter, that God speaketh universally to man." (*Age of Reason*, 1794)

Paine claimed to be a believer, even if he limited his vision of the divine to the natural order and the first cause that lay behind it. Very quickly, Deism produced reactionaries among the orthodox who reasserted the primacy of divine revelation over human reason, and preached traditional doctrines of sin and salvation. In many ways the exchange between reason and revelation continues to the present day, even if it has employed a language more suited to the contemporary world.

The Least You Need to Know

- Medieval Scholastics saw no inherent tension between faith and reason: both were avenues to the ultimate truth.

- Thomas Aquinas thought reason would ultimately come up short, and some beliefs would have to be accepted on faith.

- Aquinas's proofs for the existence of God illustrate the rational impulse in Christianity, though they have been subsequently abandoned.

- Protestantism nurtures competing impulses to expound upon doctrines and to marvel at God's ineffable nature.

- Enlightenment rationalism of the Deists limited God's role to that of wise creator, with no continuing involvement in nature or human affairs.

God in Modern Christian Theology

In This Chapter

- ◆ Coming to faith the existentialist way
- ◆ Meet the Fundamentalists
- ◆ Christianity discovers Marxism, and births liberation theology
- ◆ Process theology: God suffers with the world
- ◆ Does God have a gender?

The Protestant Reformers and Deists shared a common desire to scrape away all the supposed barnacles that attached to the hull of Christianity during its centuries-long voyage from antiquity to the modern age. Of course they disagreed about what, precisely, was added onto the message of Jesus. Reformers Martin Luther and John Calvin disliked much of the church's teaching since the time of the early Fathers, while Thomas Paine, a Diest, would go further, discarding even the apostles' testimonials about Jesus' virgin birth, miracles, and resurrection in the New Testament. Nevertheless, their sermons, lectures, and books cut Christian belief from its orthodox Roman Catholic moorings, producing along the way several important re-imaginings of the God of the Bible.

Many Christian thinkers in the nineteenth and twentieth centuries struggled to justify continued belief in God in the face of rampant secularism and materialism. I'll discuss their efforts a little more in Chapter 26. For now, let's tour through some of Christianity's creative responses to Enlightenment speculation about ultimate reality, and modernist approaches to human nature, ethics, history, religion, and culture. Our tour won't exhaust the wide variety of theological cogitations hammered out in the last century, but will give you a sampling of what creative minds have done to update traditions they've inherited in light of the changing times.

Christian Existentialism

One creative strand of thought that emerged from Christianity's encounter with modern ideas is what's been called Christian existentialism, beginning with Søren Kierkegaard (1813–1855) and continuing through the work of Martin Heidegger and Paul Tillich in the mid-twentieth century.

The Modern Temper

During Kierkegaard's time, Christianity faced a growing challenge from Enlightenment thinkers who questioned core doctrines that dated back to the first millennium of the faith. Western European and North American intellectuals grew disinterested in metaphysics and left precious little ground for spirituality, at least spirituality focused upon a transcendent Other who sustains and directs nature and human affairs. In response, writers and poets of Romanticism rebelled by seeking inspiration through nature, and a few, like the Transcendentalists, believed truth could be gained through an inner journey, progressing beyond human reason to quasi-mystical apprehensions of the Absolute.

Kierkegaard's Big Questions

None of this eased Kierkegaard's feelings of alienation and angst, as revealed in the now classic existential questions: "Where am I? What is this thing called the world? Who is it who has lured me into the thing, and now leaves me here? Who am I? How did I come into the world? Why was I not consulted?" To his mind, the rational explanations of the philosophers and the sophisticated doctrines of the churchmen were equally barren. He thought their work reduced the Christian faith to a simple matter of consenting to a list of propositions about God. He believed that the proper response to the existential questions vexing the human mind wasn't intellectual assent, but personal commitment to live in faith and to assume individual responsibility over the truth. Christian faith, in this regard, had less to do with how one thinks and more to do with how one chooses to live.

From Heidegger to Tillich

Kierkegaard's writings appealed to many others who were impatient with the sophistry of doctrinaire Christianity, and who came to believe that Enlightenment rationalism and the growing empiricism provided no essential reason for human beings to do good. For example, Heidegger (1889–1976) picked up on Kierkegaard's themes of existence and choice, fashioning a philosophy of authentic living, of choosing a positive course of life within the parameters that define one's material existence.

And here is where Tillich (1886–1965) entered the picture. Whoever speaks of God, he reasoned, must correlate the eternal truths of faith with one's particular experience of time and place. Concepts of God are, so to speak, situated concepts. That's why Tillich argued that the old concept of God, of an all-powerful creator and sustainer, "worked" for premodern people, but perhaps not today. He wanted to get away from thinking of God as a thing, or even a first cause: "The God who is a being is transcended by the God who is Being itself, the ground and abyss of every being." (*Biblical Religion and the Search for Ultimate Reality*, 1955) He taught that it wasn't right to say that God exists or doesn't exist, since God transcends existence. Put simply, God is Being itself. And you can escape the apparent meaninglessness of existence and separation from God by participating in Being through the New Being, Jesus "the Christ."

> **Pearls of Wisdom**
>
> The question of the existence of God can be neither asked nor answered. If asked, it is a question about that which by its very nature is above existence, and therefore the answer—whether negative or affirmative—implicitly denies the nature of God.
>
> —Tillich, *Systematic Theology,* 1.237

The New Theology

It's hard to get your mind around existentialism, since it uses a lot of abstractions to give voice to its perception of the Absolute. Others truth-seekers who engaged modern thinking weren't so difficult to comprehend. Instead, they wanted the Christian concept of God to be more responsive to developing problems in the human experience. Theodore Munger (1830–1910), a Congregationalist minister in Connecticut, wrestled with the same intellectual movements as Kierkegaard did, and advocated a New Theology that could go beyond logic and doctrines to include "intuitions, the conscience, the susceptibilities, and the judgment, i.e., man's whole inner being." (*Freedom of Faith*, 1883) This theology would grow and develop, seeing revelation "as under a process still enacting, and not as under a finality."

Munger put this approach to work when he played off the era's concern for the social life of humankind, seen in the writings of Karl Marx and Charles Dickens, among others. He believed that individuals possess unity in Adam's fall, but also possess unity in Christ's regenerating power. So "humanity is charged with redemptive forces, wrought into the soul and into the divine institutions of the family, and whatever other relation binds man to man." Munger's vision rang a familiar tone, rather akin to the Lurianic Kabbalah's idea of *tikkun olam*, though without the notion of healing God. Redeeming society shows up in the theology of the *Social Gospel*, particularly in the work of Walter Rauschenbusch (1861–1918) and Washington Gladden (1836–1818), urban ministers in the United States who, in the words of Rauschenbusch, perceived the Kingdom of God as the "Christian transfiguration of the social order." (*Theology for the Social Gospel*, 1917)

> ### Word to the Wise
> **Social Gospel** refers to a movement in Christianity that promotes social and political activism on behalf of the poor and disadvantaged, and broke on the scene at the beginning of the twentieth century in the United States.

Fundamentalism

By the late nineteenth century, the Social Gospel came under attack for supposedly reducing much of the Christian faith to social ethics. Christians also witnessed the advent of scholarship on the subjects of comparative religion and sacred texts. Academics encouraged people to think of religion as essentially a human contrivance that evolved in response to human needs—no supernatural forces at work here. Then, too, scholars such as Sigmund Freud and William James sparked interest in the psychological dimensions of religious sentiment, which had the effect of making belief appear as a type of human consciousness or even self-delusion.

Darwin and His Critics

Of course, there's the whole question of Darwinism, which taught people in the late nineteenth century that all existing species are the result of a long process of adaptation; this process was governed by the principle of natural selection and driven by competition for scarce resources that only the fittest members of the species would survive. In Darwinism, you now had an explanation for how creation reached its present state with what looked like a designed order that didn't presume the active involvement of a Supreme Being. This was the golden age of historical theories. The century began with G. W. F. Hegel and his dialectical scheme for the development of ideas, moved through Auguste Comte and his law of three stages (from theological to metaphysical to scientific stages of history), and eventually produced Karl Marx and his dogmas of class conflict and historical materialism. By the end of the nineteenth century you had plenty of theories explaining how the world got to be the way it was, without invoking God.

Divinations

To the traditionalists, no compromise with modern intellectual movements was permissible. For example, Pope Pius IX's *Syllabus of Errors* (1864) identified 80 contemporary ideas he believed were corrosive to the Christian faith, and which no Catholic was permitted to accept. A council six years later declared the Pope infallible on questions of doctrine, which gave traditionalists a tool to combat internal heresy.

These theories were the point of departure for a movement known as Fundamentalism. Fundamentalists offered a tradition-minded response to the emerging theories of historical and cultural development, and yet produced some creative innovations in Protestant thinking as well. In *The Fundamentals: Testimony to the Truth*, a series of 12 books published between 1910 and 1915, conservative teachers from schools in the United States, such as Moody Bible Institute and Princeton Theological Seminary, came to the defense of the authority of scripture and conventional belief in the supernatural.

Doctrines: Inerrancy and Dispensationalism

The Fundamentals directed much of the writers' ire toward critics such as F. C. Bauer, D. F. Strauss, J. E. Renan, and other European scholars of Hebrew and Christian scripture. These critics read biblical manuscripts in light of other contemporary documents, and fashioned theories of authorship that called into question the documents'

Word to the Wise

Inerrancy refers to a doctrine of biblical interpretation, in which the scripture is understood to be verbally inspired—breathed by God—and inerrant in the original form before copying and translation. In its earliest formulation, inerrancy considered these original autographs, though never found, to contain the very speech of God.

provenance. In response, *The Fundamentals* popularized the concept in Biblical interpretation known as *inerrancy*. At the time, this was taken to mean that the original manuscripts were verbally inspired by God and were without error in every way. Any mistakes you can find are the result of poor copyediting of the originals, which we no longer possess. Many thought this concept implied that the Bible should be read as literally as possible, rather like a scientist who draws conclusions through the inductive method. In this way, the Bible becomes a running account of historical change, complete with a literal seven-day creation, an actual Garden of Eden with a real flesh-and-blood Adam and Eve, and a physical expulsion from paradise.

The doctrine of inerrancy was a direct rebuke of modernist biblical interpretation, which according to Theodore Munger approached the Bible as a "living book" that must "be constantly and freshly interpreted." In the same way, fundamentalists disliked the historical theories of the nineteenth century that seemed to shrink the domain in which God was thought to operate. As an alternative, fundamentalists offered "dispensational" theology, which discerned a general pattern of progressive development in the Bible. Dispensationalists perceive God interacting with humanity in ordered ways through a succession of agreements, first with Adam and then with Abraham, Noah, Moses, Jesus Christ, and finally the church. Dispensational theology also includes the motif of God breaking into the normal course of human affairs in a supernatural way (expulsion, flood, exodus, incarnation, etc.), cutting off previous dispensations, and ushering in new ones.

The Living Spirit

The teachers and theologians who devised doctrinal responses to scientific naturalism (the belief that no Supreme Being is required to start and sustain the operations of nature) as a way to recapture a sense of divine activity in the world had much in common with revivalists in the nineteenth century who believed the church had shortchanged the Holy Spirit. The revivalists came from a variety of backgrounds, but mostly from Methodist and Wesleyan churches in England and North America. They taught that penitent sinners who asked for forgiveness receive the blessing of God's grace, but if they truly commit to Christ, they receive a second blessing that enables them to resist sin and live in a state of Christian perfection. This baptism of the Holy Spirit prepares the believer for a consecrated life of holiness and Christian service.

And many of these revivalists moved on in the 1890s and 1900s to perceive the possibility of a third blessing, a baptism of fire, accompanied by gifts of the spirit such as speaking in tongues, healing, and prophecy. Often fire-baptism induced uncontrollable shaking, laughing, and even trances. These physical manifestations of the indwelling Spirit were enough to convince believers that God could act outside the confines of natural law by sending heavenly visitations to those spiritually prepared to receive the blessing. The beliefs and practices of the Holiness-Pentecostal movement illustrate how the principle of divine immanence received a makeover in the early twentieth century in response to a rise in scientific and materialistic thinking.

Process Theology

Perhaps you also noticed that Protestant fundamentalism contained within it both doctrinal and experiential components. It obsessed over language, texts, and interpretive methods, while cherishing tangible evidence of God's supernatural work in the lives of believers. In an age of militant ideologies, fundamentalism moved forward with confidence in the objective facts of scripture (interpreted in its most literal sense) and what it perceived to be non-negotiable doctrines of the faith, such as biblical inerrancy, the concept of substitutionary atonement (Jesus dying for our sins), and the bodily resurrection of Christ.

But the certainties of Fundamentalism seemed to belie Christianity's historic recognition of the limits of human understanding and the ultimate failure of language and concepts to capture the essence of the divine. For example, you can hear a more provisional tone in the advocates of what is known as process theology, particularly the comment of process theologian Daniel Day Williams in "The New Theological Situation" (*Theology Today*, January 1968): "Doctrines are not infallible. They are the expression of meanings which lie forever beyond complete rationalization." Williams joined a tradition reaching back to the early metaphysical speculations of British mathematician Alfred North Whitehead (1861–1947) and American philosopher Charles Hartshorne (1897–2000), and continuing in the writings of theologian John Cobb Jr. (1925–).

Whitehead's thinking might be a useful starting point here. He was influenced by modern physics, particularly the idea of fundamental forces and elemental particles.

He sought an understanding of the first principles of existence, and perceived God not as a Being, or even Being itself, but rather as "Becoming." In an age when sensitive observers were keen to perceive change and development, Whitehead gave them a concept of ultimate reality with dynamic, rather than static, qualities.

This gets tricky, but Whitehead perceived all reality in a state of flux, or in development. All the things that make up reality are not stable entities, but are essentially a combination of their points of development from the past through the present moment and into the future. God is a part of this reality: God is the direction finder for the entities that are in a process of Becoming, and the final resting place for them once they have achieved their ultimate aims. God brings all these entities into a unity, and benefits from the experiences of Becoming that these entities have attained. For God there is no fixed future, only a perpetually receding array of possibilities created by the interplay of the divine with present actualities. God, according to Whitehead, is "the great companion—the fellow-sufferer" of the world, and as such, he eternally becomes.

We'll soon discover that process theology bears some similarities to Hindu and Taoist conceptions of unity. For example, some process theologians taught that the destiny of human beings is not to become physically resurrected and taken into heaven, but "taken up into God's life" as a part of the divine memory. If you recall, we identified this as panentheism or panpsychism in Chapter 2, which is the idea that God and the world are a unity and that the world participates along with God in the formation of an all-encompassing reality.

Liberation Theology

If Whitehead, Hartshorne, and Cobb helped to restore some shimmering luster to metaphysics amid the grinding materialism of twentieth-century thought, we nevertheless returned to material concerns in the work of the Roman Catholic priests who gave us liberation theology in the 1960s. By then the Christian social conscience was well established, with Jesus as the beacon of compassion: Jesus paid special attention to disadvantaged, downtrodden, racially oppressed outcasts in first-century Palestine. Great benevolent societies in the nineteenth century carried Jesus' commitment into the modern era (think Salvation Army). And of course the Social Gospel preached social obligation in the face of urban problems of poverty, illiteracy, poor health, and so on.

But liberation theology was different for two important reasons: its geographical location and its debt to secular ideologies. On the first account, liberation theology sprang up among Roman Catholic priests in Colombia, Brazil, Peru, and elsewhere in Latin America, making it a truly unique product of Christianity's contact with local conditions outside Europe and North America. Liberation theology is a near perfect example of what Paul Tillich spoke of when he said we must correlate the eternal truths of faith with our particular experiences of time and place. Architects of liberation theology, such as Gustavo Gutierrez (1928–) and Paulo Freire (1921–1997), responded to the clear deprivation and poverty they witnessed in Latin America in the 1960s and 1970s, and began to teach a message of liberation from suffering and oppression.

This gets us to liberation theology's debt to secular ideologies, the second important difference between liberation theology and its forebears. Marxism gave Liberation theology priests a vision that helped to explain the systemic poverty of the Colombian and Peruvian people. Marx taught that the common people were oppressed by the owners of the means of production—capitalists—who used their economic muscle to keep their friends in government and buy off potential critics in the media and the church. Taking Marx's cue, liberation theologians associated sinfulness not with individual human actions, but with advanced capitalist systems and patterns of colonial dominance and control. Because Jesus aligned himself with the poor and oppressed, the church today should follow suit, contributing to the people's eventual salvation by liberating them from economic exploitation, social injustice, and political oppression.

Feminist Theology

Liberation theology grew out of the political ferment of the 1960s, which also included an intensification of the struggle for women's rights. The women's liberation movement produced a corresponding discussion about gender and divinity within theological circles. Of course, this discussion isn't exactly new. Greek pantheists had no trouble working the feminine into their concept of God, nor did several of the other Near Eastern polytheisms. Judaism perceived feminine aspects in God within the Kabbalah tradition; early Hebrew writers associated the Shekinah, the estranged presence of God who wanders around the world, with the Greek goddess Sophia.

Divinations

An easy way to get to the bottom of the differences among the theological camps in contemporary Christianity is to ask the simple question, "Who is Jesus?" For example, fundamentalists answer that he was the sacrificial Lamb of God whose blood redeemed the elect; process theologians answer that he's the primordial aim for humanity incarnate, who made possible new avenues of human transformation.

Even Christians themselves added gendered aspects to the ultimate, particularly veneration of the Virgin Mary, who acts as an intercessor on behalf of Roman Catholic penitents.

But with the advent of liberation theology, believers predisposed to view the divine in its feminine aspects gained a new and powerful language. Colombian peasants, black Mississippi sharecroppers, and now women could be construed as sharing a common experience of subjugation and oppression. Theologians such as Rosemary Radford Ruether (1936–) argued that women should work up a more satisfying concept of God than the patriarchal vision they inherited from the early church Fathers. The feminist concept of God would derive from women's personal experiences, and result in the attainment of full humanity for oppressed women under male domination.

One strand of feminist theology involves recentering, in this case getting the male image off center stage (think Adam, the Patriarchs, God the Father, etc.) and beginning to think in less hierarchically ordered ways. Ruether perceived that the hierarchies and dualisms of Christian philosophy were artificial and in fact distortions of the ultimate reality that led to male domination and female oppression. As an alternative, she advanced the idea of an organic unity between male and female in God, which she came to call "God/ess." In this she was aided by Tillich's concept of God not as a being (which might then be gendered) but as the Ground of Being, the source from which beings derive their existence. In God/ess, there's no hierarchy or oppression, only unity. What about Jesus? Wasn't he a man? Ruether had an answer: Jesus of Nazareth was a man, but his identity as Christ transcends his manhood and is associated with the Ground of Being, hence it would be inappropriate to speak of his "Christness" as essentially male. In fact, Christ survived Jesus of Nazareth's death and today is associated with the unity of all believers.

As you can probably tell, modern Christian thinkers have different understandings of God, the incarnation of Christ, the nature of sin and evil, the means of redemption and salvation, and the ultimate destiny of humanity. Disagreements among thinkers show us why many Christians want to escape the thickets of theological discussion altogether. There's a hint of this sentiment in Clare Booth Luce's account of her initial experience of the divine, which eventually led to her conversion to Roman Catholicism. She wrote: "And now—as then—I find it difficult to explain what did happen. I expect that the easiest thing is to say that suddenly *something was*." As she continued, "I didn't know with any 'faculty.' It was not in my mind or heart or blood stream. But whatever it was I knew, it was something that made *enormous sense*." (*Road to Damasacus*, 1949) Luce couldn't accurately express in words or concepts her encounter with God, which places her in good company among the many who have spoken of God as something more properly experienced than known or understood.

The Least You Need to Know

◆ Modern intellectual, social, and economic developments inspired some Christians to make creative adjustments in their concept of God.

◆ Paul Tillich's concept of God not as a being, but Being itself, the ground and abyss of every being, illustrates the emerging theological creativity of modern Christianity.

◆ Fundamentalists created the doctrines of Biblical inerrancy and dispensationalism to limit the range of theological speculation and biblical interpretation.

◆ Process theology perceives God not as Being but Becoming, whereby God and humanity participate together in the co-creation of all reality.

◆ Liberation and feminist theologies drew from the work of Paul Tillich, and fashioned doctrines of social justice for oppressed groups.

Part 4

The Concept of God in Islam

It's hard to read the front page of the newspaper or watch a half hour of television news without coming across a story with a Middle Eastern byline. Despite Islam's obvious importance in current affairs, few Westerners know much about the faith of Muhammad and the Muslim ummah (community of faith). These chapters will get you started on understanding the life of the Prophet Muhammad, the content and meaning of the Qur'an, the disputes that resulted in the division of Islam into Sunni and Shi'ite sects, and the rich tradition of philosophical reflection within the Muslim community. But there's more. These chapters also detail the origins and progress of revitalization movements within Islam, such as Wahabbism and Madiyya, which together helped shape the movement Westerners know as Islamic fundamentalism. As today's Muslim leaders struggle over the meaning of the Qur'an and the shari'ah (Islamic law) in contemporary life, you'll want to listen in; it just might be one of the most important discussions about God going on in the world today.

Chapter 16

God in the Qur'an

In This Chapter

- ◆ God's messenger, Muhammad of Mecca
- ◆ Points of departure: Islam, Judaism, Christianity
- ◆ What's in the Qur'an, anyway?
- ◆ The importance of Arabic language to the Qur'an
- ◆ Discover how to walk the straight path

Lately, it seems you can't get through a week without hearing some breaking news on television from the Middle East, or reading a front-page story in the papers that somehow involves Islam. And yet few people are very familiar with the Islamic concept of God. You can perhaps conjure up an image of white-cloaked pilgrims swarming around the Ka'bah in Mecca, or Muslim men kneeling for prayers in the local mosque, but few of us can say with confidence that we really understand what Muslims have in mind when they recite the *Shahadah:* "There is no God but God, and Muhammad is his Prophet." The time has come to address a huge gap in your understanding of one of the driving forces in human affairs today.

A good place to begin is the sacred text of Islam, the Qur'an (or Koran). It is the focal point of Islamic devotion and public worship, and the unifying element of a religion that embraces hundreds of millions of adherents in scores of countries across the globe. When you start to turn the pages of the Qur'an, you encounter a God that bears a striking resemblance to the God of Judaism and Christianity. God appears as the one transcendent, all-powerful, all-knowing, and perfectly good being, creator and sustainer of the universe and judge of all humanity. But dig a little deeper and some important differences come to light. You discover in the process some reasons why the three major monotheistic religions with roots in the Middle East haven't merged together into one faith.

An Arab Prophet to the World

According to Muslims, their sacred book was directly revealed to Muhammad ibn Abdallah (c. 570–632 C.E.) over the course of 23 years, starting around 610 C.E. To their way of thinking, Allah gave Muhammad a revelation that belongs not just to Arabs, but to all humanity. Yet in the beginning, Muhammad belonged, in a more narrow sense, to a well-established Bedouin tribe of Arabia, the Quraysh, which had only recently moved from the desert into the city of Mecca. There they became rich through trading and supervising worship at the Ka'bah. This was a holy place to the Bedouin tribes of Arabia, who traveled from the surrounding region to worship the Ka'bah's Black Stone—a symbol of divine power—and some 360 idols of various deities. Muhammad's father died just before his birth and his mother died when he was six, and so Muhammad grew up in his uncle's household, where he tended the flocks and won credit for his dedication and good character. Reaching adulthood, he managed trading caravans for a wealthy widow, Khadija, whom he eventually married.

> **Divinations**
>
> Before Muhammad, Arabian religion was a combination of animism and polytheism. Bedouin tribes worshipped gods linked to celestial bodies, forces of nature, and geological features such as mountains and rivers. A few, the *hanifs* ("believers"), worshipped a single god. Interestingly, Arabians stood guard against the *jinn,* or numinous desert sprites that were believed to harass vulnerable travelers.

Visitor on Mt. Hira

In Mecca, Muhammad and his wife Khadija prospered and had three sons (all of whom died in infancy) and four daughters. His reputation for honesty and fidelity in business grew, but he had become disgusted by the violence, selfishness, and immorality of Meccan society. It seems that sometime between the age of 25 and 40, Muhammad joined with the *hanifs* ("believers"), or those who sought a monotheism purified of imported deities from Egypt, Greece, or Persia, and together they began a practice of retreating into the wilderness to escape the iniquities of the city and to contemplate the mysteries of the spiritual realm. During one of his night-long vigils in a cave on Mt. Hira, on the so-called Night of Power, Muhammad received a visitor. It was the angel Gabriel, who said:

> Recite with the name of your Lord Who created,
> Who created human being [sic] from a clot of blood.
> Proclaim, for your Lord is the Most Benignant;
> Who taught knowledge by means of the pen,
> He taught human being [sic] what he did not know. (Surah 96.1–5)

This revelation is recorded in the Qur'an, and Muslims understand this to be first of a series of revelations to Muhammad, who was chosen by God to be the vehicle for receiving a new dispensation to humanity.

A Recitation

Muhammad submitted to the voice of God, whom he perceived as al-Lah, or "*the* God." With each visitation, Muhammad's faithfulness was rewarded with weightier revelations, culminating in the book we know as the Qur'an, which in Arabic means "recitation." Muhammad believed, and Muslims continue to believe, that the Qur'an is the very utterance of Allah. In a new twist on Semitic religion, Muslims came to believe that the words and phrases of the text are holy in themselves, not just the underlying truths that the language of the Qur'an encodes and expresses. Muhammad didn't create the words, or will them into existence, but instead he received them while under the power of a supernatural force, often in a trancelike state. There's even some debate about whether he wrote the words himself or dictated them to a scribe. Nonetheless, Allah's revelations were so powerful that Muhammad felt them as a heavy weight bearing down on his frame. In terms of content, the recitation offered a complete vision of the divine, together with a comprehensive account of the whole duty of humankind before Allah. We'll take a fuller measure of the Qur'an's contents a bit later in the chapter.

Flight to Medina

Initially, Muhammad sensed the power of Allah's revelations, but was hesitant to teach them to others in Mecca. Encouraged by his wife and her cousin, one of the hanifs of Arabia, Muhammad listened to the voice of Allah, which said, "O you who have been endowed with excellent capabilities! Arise (with the Divine Message) and warn." (Surah 74.1–2) He began to teach the Meccans to put away idols and worship Allah alone, to live morally upright lives, and to strive for a more just socioeconomic order. Of course, Muhammad's teachings cut against the prevailing Arab temper and damaged the business interests of Muhammad's own tribe, which profited from the pilgrims visiting the shrines in and around the Ka'bah. The Meccan tribes rejected his message and conspired to kill him, so Muhammad fled into the desert and later accepted an invitation to preach Allah to the people of Medina, some 200 miles north. He and a group of ardent followers traveled to Medina in a migration known as the Hijrah in 622 C.E. Today, this event marks year one in the Muslim calendar.

Back to Mecca

The Qur'an says, "Verily, Allah has bestowed a favor on the believers when he has raised amongst them a great Messenger from amongst themselves who recited to them his Messages, and purifies them and teaches them the Book and the wisdom; although before this, they were steeped in flagrant error." (Surah 3.164) It was during his time in Medina that Muhammad became the great spiritual, political, and military leader of the Arab people, developing a remarkable core of leadership that would spread Islam to Persia, Asia Minor, and North Africa. Muhammad brought together emigrant Meccans and local Medinans into the *ummah*, or community of faith, that transcended boundaries of tribe and clan. The ummah purged Medina of dissident elements, including the local Jewish community, then began raiding Meccan caravans in a spiraling conflict that brought the Muslims into an open war with a coalition of Meccan tribes. Muhammad proved his mettle as a military commander, and achieved decisive victories, such as the Battle of Badr (624) and the Battle of the Ditch (627).

> **CAUTION**
>
> **Take Heed!**
>
> Given Muhammad's role as a military commander, there's a common misconception that Islam is inherently warlike and that the Qur'an promotes violence. Actually, the Qur'an teaches that you can fight to defend yourself, your people, and your land, and you can fight to restore law and order, but you can't instigate hostilities. As the Qur'an says, "Allah does not love the aggressors." (Surah 2.190)

Muhammad's victories were interpreted as signs of Allah's power and divine favor, and soon popular support for the Meccan forces evaporated. In 630, Muhammad returned to the city of Mecca, his boyhood home, with a divine mandate to rid the city of polytheism and institute the worship of "*the* God," Allah. Muhammad extended the ummah by including the Meccan tribes, then cleansed the Ka'bah of idols, and in March 632, conducted the first religious pilgrimage to the holy sites of Mecca and vicinity, a pilgrimage Muslims have endeavored to repeat annually ever since. Within three months the Prophet fell ill and died, leaving in his wake a new religion for the Arab people and for all humanity.

Allah in the Qur'an

So that's the story of Allah's Prophet, Muhammad. But what did Allah reveal? In the Qur'an, traditional monotheists such as Jews and Christians will find much that's familiar to them. But the differences are pretty profound, too. These differences owe to the reluctance of Allah to become known in anthropomorphic terms, as the walking, talking Yahweh of the Torah or the incarnation of God in Jesus Christ in the Gospels are known. But that's only the beginning.

Sacred Language

The Qur'an is a holy book, no doubt, but Muslims go beyond Jewish and Christian positions on their sacred texts. For example, in the previous chapter of this book we encountered a group of Christians who consider the Bible to be the inspired, inerrant Word of God. The writers of the original biblical manuscripts were filled with the Spirit and penned words that reflected the perfect will of the Absolute. Muslims, on the other hand, believe that to read or hear the Qur'an is to have a direct experience of the divine. Allah revealed himself to Muhammad in words that are perfect in themselves. Its perfection is proof of its divine origin: "And if you have any doubt as to which we have revealed to Our servant from time to time, produce a single Surah like this, summoning all your helpers besides Allah, if you are truthful." (Surah 2.23)

In a loose sense the Qur'an is to Muslims what Jesus Christ is to Christians; the Logos, or eternal divine Word of God. Its perfection lies partly in its structure and content, and partly in its diction. On that last point, you should know that according to Muslims, Allah intended the Qur'an to be read aloud. Muslim devotion and worship include oral recitation of the Qur'an, and Muslims report experiences of spiritual transcendence when hearing the cadences and rhythms of Qur'anic language. This is a departure from Hebrew and Christian scripture, which play different roles in their respective traditions.

One God for Everyone

Here's where the serious departures from Judaism and Christianity can be found in Islam. The Qur'an makes the claim that it is the final revelation to humanity within a sequence of revelations that began with Abraham and continued through Moses and Jesus, reaching its perfection in the revelation to Muhammad in the seventh century. Consider this: "He has ordained for you the same course of faith as he enjoined on Noah, and which we have revealed to you, and it is that which we enjoined on Abraham, Moses, Jesus, so keep the faith and do not differ in it." (Surah 42.13) Where the Hebrews and Christians erred, according to the Qur'an, was assuming that God played favorites with them. It reads: "And they say, 'None shall ever enter Paradise unless he be a Jew or a Christian.' These are their wishful beliefs .... The truth of the matter is, whosoever submits himself entirely to Allah and he is a doer of good to others shall have his reward with his Lord." (Surah 2.111–112)

The Qur'an emphasizes the singleness of Allah, which is another point of separation between Muslims and Christians. The Qur'an commands belief in the revelation to all the prophets sent to all the nations, and so it teaches that all Muslims should honor Jesus. But the Qur'an plainly denies Jesus' divinity: "Some say, 'The Most Gracious has taken to himself a son.' ... 'You have indeed uttered something exceedingly abominable and hideous.'" (Surah 19.88–89) There's a cherished Arabic word in Islam for the unity and oneness of the Absolute: *Tawhid*. Needless to say, Tawhid forbids even the faintest suggestion that God might have a plurality of essence, form, mode, substance, or personality.

Word to the Wise

Tawhid, which means unity in reference to the singleness of God, is one of the core concepts of Islam. It rejects the idea that God could have emanations, avatars, offspring, or distinct persons within the divine being.

Ninety-Nine Beautiful Names

What you get in the Qur'an, then, is a deity of limitless power, wisdom, and goodness, with no beginning or end, and with no spiritual or earthly equal. Again, the Qur'an observes, "Allah is he. There is no other, cannot be and will never be One worthy of worship but he. He is the Living, the Self-Subsisting, and All-Sustaining." (Surah 3.2) Like other religious traditions, Islam perceives the divine as ineffable—incapable of being described in ordinary language—at least in essence. But Allah wanted to be known, and chose to become known to humanity through various attributes. So the Qur'an refers to Allah in a number of different ways, such as the "All-Hearing," the "All-Knowing," the "Great Protector," and the "All-Mighty." These are various attributes of Allah that the human mind can discern and account for in words.

In Surah 7.180, the Qur'an says, "And to Allah alone belong all the fairest and most perfect attributes, so call on him by these, and leave alone those who deviate from the right way with respect to his attributes. They shall be repaid with punishment for their deeds." Muslims discover in the Qur'an scores of names for Allah, 99 of which have been identified as the most beautiful names, which have particular resonance for spiritual seekers. It's important to keep in mind that these are not separate divinities or modes of God, but qualities that the one true God, Allah, is said to possess; by knowing them and contemplating them, one's spiritual experience can be extended and deepened. Allah's names reveal a creator and sustainer of all things, who is perfectly good and who gives humans the freedom to choose between good and evil. Allah judges people for the choices they make, rewarding them with heaven or hell as the circumstances merit.

The Straight Path

So how do you get to heaven? The Qur'an is perhaps the most direct of all the world's sacred texts on this particular subject. In fact, how one gets to heaven is one of the complaints Muslims have against Judaism and Christianity. Muslims consider revelations given to Hebrew prophets and to Jesus to be incomplete in the sense that the revelations didn't show people how to follow the will of God and achieve divine merit. So Muslims believe the Qur'an completes these earlier revelations. In his book *The World's Religions: Our Great Wisdom Traditions* (HarperSanFrancisco, 1991), Huston Smith offers a telling quote by Muhammad Iqbal, a writer and leader of the movement that led to the creation of Pakistan, describing the Qur'an as "a book which emphasizes deed rather than idea." That tells you a great deal about its emphasis—right out of the gate the Qur'an hits you with a prayer to Allah to "lead us on the straight path till we reach the goal." (Surah 1.6)

Divinations

One of the places where Muslims depart from Christians is the issue of sin. Most Christians teach the idea of original sin, which views human nature as inherently sinful and vulnerable to the temptations of Satan. Muslims view sin as disobedience to the will of Allah.

Meaning of Islam

Muslims read in the Qur'an, "the only response of the believers, when they are summoned before Allah and his Messenger so that he may judge between them, is that they say, 'We hear and we obey.' It is they who will attain their goal." (Surah 24.51) The Qur'an offers clear direction to humanity for how this obedience is to be expressed. It states time and time again that it is the "perfect Book explaining every thing and a guidance and a mercy, and [gives] good tidings to those who submit." (Surah 16.89) In that Qur'anic verse, the word *submit* is significant, since it identifies exactly what sort of attitude the believer must adopt in order to conform to Allah's will.

In fact, the name of the religion, Islam, contains important clues to its design and ultimate ends. The word Islam contains the Arabic root *s-l-m*, which means "peace." Being a root word, however, it also contains other connotations, one of which is "surrender." Taken together, Islam is understood to be the sense of inner peace you get when you surrender yourself, in this case to Allah. Here some comparison might be helpful. Buddhists speak of following the middle path, where one becomes aware of one's self—the desires and attachments that induce suffering—and takes measures to extinguish these desires. To the Muslim, the straight path is not interior, but exterior to the self. It entails surrender to a divine Other whose majesty fills one with awe and provokes a self-abasing response.

Way of the Prophet

Muslims (a word that also contains the root s-l-m) have a ready example of surrender in the figure of Muhammad. In Islam, Muhammad isn't considered a Messiah or Savior, like Jesus Christ in Christianity, or an avatar of the Absolute as Vishnu is to Brahman in South Asian religious traditions. Muhammad is exalted because Allah selected him to receive the recitation, but also because he chose to surrender to Allah, becoming an example for others to follow as they make their way along the straight path. And he did many other things that were in keeping with Allah's wishes, despite the heavy persecution he faced in Mecca, as recorded in the Qur'an.

The Qur'an praises Muhammad because he "neither deviated nor has he erred," and because Allah's powers became manifest in him "with the result that he attained perfection and fullest vigor." (Surah 53.2,6) Muhammad's surrender and exaltation inspires Muslims to follow suit, hoping to experience the divine presence just as their Prophet did long ago. Muhammad's sayings, called *hadiths*, were considered of such value that they were recorded by his followers and used by later Muslims. And the Muslim community, or the ummah, also found Muhammad's deeds, called *sunnah*, of sufficient importance to record them for posterity. In the years following Muhammad's death, the words and deeds of the Prophet were the subject of much curiosity and even contention, resulting in the emergence of conflicting schools of interpretation. We'll encounter some of these disagreements in the next two chapters, though you should keep in mind that all Muslims revere and endeavor to imitate the Prophet of Allah.

> **Word to the Wise**
>
> **Hadiths** and **sunnah** refer to the sayings and deeds of the Prophet Muhammad, as documented in texts that supplement the sacred Qur'an.

Five Pillars of Faith

According to Muslims, the Qur'an outlines Allah's plan to bring all people together in one all-encompassing faith. The path is a straight one, within the grasp of each and every person regardless of family pedigree, economic status, level of education, or intellectual ability. No special powers of spiritual discernment or mystical insight are required. All you must do is surrender to Allah and follow his instructions as revealed in the Qur'an. These duties are encapsulated in the Five Pillars of Faith, understood as the minimum set of observances among the faithful within the Muslim ummah:

1. **Confession of faith.** Muslims are required to proclaim their faith in Allah. This proclamation, called the Shahadah, is the closest thing you can find in Islam to an official creed. The Shahadah, which reads "There is no God but Allah, and Muhammad is his Prophet," is meant to be spoken aloud. It testifies to the believer's commitment to the Qur'an's uncompromising monotheism.

2. **Prayer.** Muslims tell a story about Muhammad approaching Allah and receiving an instruction to tell his people to pray 50 times a day. After receiving his instructions, he encountered Moses on the way back to Mecca, and Moses told Muhammad to bargain with Allah for a reduction. Muhammad bargained God down to 40, then 30, 20, 10, and finally agreed to submit to 5 prayers a day. Muslims pray toward Mecca in the morning, at noon, mid-afternoon, dusk, and bedtime. They assume postures that indicate both a spiritual and physical surrender to Allah, preferably in a communal setting such as a mosque where Muslims can experience a sense of the unity of humankind in submission before the divine.

3. **Fasting.** During the holy month of Ramadan, Muslims fast to commemorate the two key events in the life of the Prophet—the Night of Power when he received his first revelation, and his flight from Mecca to Medina. Both events occurred during the same month in the Islamic calendar. Fasting during the daytime (Muslims are allowed to eat and drink sparingly after nightfall) reminds them of their absolute dependence on Allah for everything necessary for human existence.

4. **Charity.** Part of Allah's revelation to Muhammad entailed a command to give alms to the poor and to orphans, debtors, wayfarers, and others in need. Muslims believe Allah meant for them to prosper and enjoy material blessings, but only after their wealth had been purified by ritual observance of the zakat. By tradition, the zakat was set at 2.5 percent and was collected and administered by the caliphate, or Islamic state, which reinforced the Muslim vision of ummah.

> **Word to the Wise**
>
> The **Hajj** is one of the highlights of a Muslim's spiritual journey, which involves a once-in-a-lifetime pilgrimage to Mecca to visit the Ka'bah with stops at other holy sites in Saudi Arabia.

5. **Pilgrimage.** In 632, Muhammad made a final pilgrimage to Mecca to visit the Ka'bah and other holy sites. Muslims today are enjoined to follow the Prophet's example and make a spiritual journey to Mecca, a pilgrimage known as the *Hajj*, provided they are financially and physically able. Unlike the other four pillars, it is considered sufficient for observant Muslims to perform the Hajj once in a lifetime.

A Social Vision

The Qur'an strives for clarity on the duties of people before Allah, and so you get the Five Pillars of Faith. And remember, too, that Muhammad sought refuge in his cave on Mt. Hira because the iniquities of Mecca drove him to ponder the nature of good and evil. Bandits ravaged Arabian trade routes, and honor killings plunged Mecca into a swirl of chaos. Along came the Qur'an with its ubiquitous motif of order. Allah is associated with the principle of order and orderliness, and Allah revealed the moral law for all humanity. Muhammad took as his mission the institution of moral order in the social, economic, and political affairs of his people.

> **Pearls of Wisdom**
>
> The Qur'an on freedom of choice: "There is no compulsion of any sort in religion [because] the right way does stand obviously distinguished from the way of error." (Surah 2.256)

You'll find regulations about marriage, workplace relations, food and beverage, and many other aspects of daily life in the Qur'an. Among other things, gambling, intoxicants, homosexuality, and infanticide are forbidden. The Qur'an even outlaws usury, or lending money at interest, though later Qur'anic interpretation permitted lending through profit-sharing arrangements. In a passage on divorce, the Qur'an reveals the mind of Allah: "These are the limits imposed by Allah and he that violates the limits imposed by Allah, indeed does injustice to himself." The notion of limits was well established in Semitic monotheism, but its application to the rest of humanity is the Qur'an's contribution to religion.

Throughout the Qur'an you discover a vision for a just and equitable society, not unlike the message of social justice we encountered from the prophets Jeremiah, Hosea, and Amos (see Chapter 6), and in the message of Jesus of Nazareth (see Chapter 11). Here you'll find a running theme of human dignity and the preciousness of each and every human soul. The tone of Surah 90, for example, has a familiar ring when it explains the "uphill path," which includes "the freeing of a captive, or feeding in the time of famine an orphan, near of kin, or a downtrodden poor person." (12–16) And those who follow this uphill path? "These are the blessed ones."

The Least You Need to Know

- The word Qur'an literally means "recitation," and is thought to be divine speech revealed to Muhammad.

- Islam teaches that Allah's revelation to Muhammad didn't replace the revelations in other religions, but perfected and completed them.

- Muslims recite the Qur'an because its power lies in the sounds, cadences, and rhythms of the Arabic language.

- To Muslims, Muhammad is an instrument of divine revelation and a moral example, not a deity or avatar of God.

- The Qur'an tells you what's required to achieve divine favor, which is reflected partly in the Five Pillars: confession of faith, prayer, fasting, charity, and pilgrimage.

Chapter 17

God in the Sunni Tradition

In This Chapter

- ◆ Disagreement over who continues the tradition
- ◆ The Qur'an: created or uncreated?
- ◆ Islam meets Greek philosophy
- ◆ Meet the Islamic intellectuals of Baghdad
- ◆ Freedom and determinism in Islamic theology
- ◆ Shari'ah, or finding God in Islamic law

In the previous chapter, we learned about the concept of God in Islam as revealed in the Qur'an. With the Prophet Muhammad's passing, the ummah, or Muslim community, stumbled upon a brand new question: Who has the authority to interpret and apply Allah's words in light of changing circumstances? Muhammad's teachings continued to instruct through the hadiths, or records of his sayings, but even these were subject to interpretation. In response to changing times and circumstances, Muslims divided into different schools of thought, and eventually into conflicting sects. Here, you'll discover that many of the axes that cut through Islam today are the result of differences of opinion that reach way back to the infancy of the faith.

Exchanges among Muslim leaders about issues of leadership and the meaning of the Qur'an brought to light certain ideas about God that seemed rather unorthodox. As a consequence of these exchanges, Muslims struggled to ensure that nothing created could be considered divine, and that God could not be perceived as plural in either form or substance. The possibility of contamination by unorthodox ideas injected even greater urgency into the question of leadership and authority. Disagreements about leadership eventually divided Islam into sects, Sunni and Shi'ite, which continue to the present day. Within the broad traditions of Sunni and Shi'a Islam, you'll find slight inflections in the way Allah is perceived, though a much broader consensus on the faith's core elements. We'll focus on the Sunnis in this chapter and the Shi'ites in the next chapter.

Preserving Tradition

Among Muslims, there's some disagreement over which early leaders ought to be considered the proper stewards of the tradition after Muhammad's death. Sunnis point to one line of descent from the Prophet Muhammad, Shi'ites point to another. The question of leadership is an urgent one, since it involves the exercise of authority in matters of interpretation of the Qur'an and Muhammad's sayings.

This issue has divided Muslims for centuries, and it won't be resolved here. But it is important to bear in mind that asking who is the standard-bearer is a basic question in most religions, since keeping the faith typically spawns debates over which person or persons is best suited to make determinations about doctrine or proper ritual observance. By one scholar's count there are more than 70 sects within the global Muslim ummah, which is quite a number of potential claimants to role of preserver and defender of the Islamic tradition. To get a sense of how these claims are established, you have to go all the way back to the first couple of years after the death of Muhammad.

Problems of Succession

By uniting the Arab tribes into the Muslim ummah, Muhammad became the founder of not only a religion, but also a nation. Thus, his role was spiritual and political at the same time. When Muhammad died, Muslims were left with the problem of succession to the high offices that Muhammad himself had created. Muslims refer to the heirs of Muhammad as caliphs (successor in Arabic), and nobody at the time seems to have had trouble with the appointment of the first two caliphs, Abu Bakr, one of

Muhammad's earliest converts and closest advisors, and then Umar, who was related to Muhammad by marriage. Unfortunately, the third caliph, Uthman (also related to Muhammad by marriage) wasn't a popular choice among the Medina Muslims owing to his Meccan origins and tribal affiliation (he was from the Umayyad clan of the Quraysh tribe).

Uthman was murdered in 656 C.E. and two rivals for the caliphate surfaced, Ali and Mu'awiyah. The details of the controversy that followed are subject to debate, but it appears that Ali was chosen caliph, and Mu'awiyah—the

> **Divinations**
>
> Caliph Abu Bakr, who ruled from 632–634, illustrates the importance of filial connections in early Islamic leadership, which isn't surprising given the importance of tribe and clan to Bedouin culture. To give you a flavor, Abu Bakr was Muhammad's father-in-law, while Uthman was his son-in-law; Ali was both cousin and son-in-law to the Prophet.

Muslim governor of Syria and an Ummayad like Uthman—refused to acknowledge Ali's selection, instead claiming the title for himself. Both agreed to arbitration, but this prompted a group of diehards to pull away from Ali's camp, perhaps because they felt Ali had not pressed his claim hard enough. These seceders, called Kharijites, assassinated Ali and left Mu'awiyah in sole possession of the caliphate. When Ali's son Husayn began to organize a revolt against the Umayyads with an eye to establishing a caliphate, an army of Iraqis allied with the Umayyads in Mecca confronted and killed Husayn in 680 C.E.

Shi'a Challenge

Muslims who favored the claims of Ali and his sons Hasan and Husayn became known as *Shi'a*, which means "party." They refused to recognize the spiritual leadership of the Umayyads in Mecca, and instead looked toward the line of Ali, giving his heirs absolute control in resolving doctrinal disputes and matters of Qur'anic interpretation. Shi'ites disagree among themselves as to whether there were 7 or 12 true imams (chief leaders), but they all agree that the imams were invested with supernatural insight, and in fact were morally perfect and without error. Some Shi'ite groups believe the twelfth imam vanished from the earth but persists in a sort of spiritual state, guiding Islamic teachers through visions and dreams. We'll discuss the astonishing Shi'ite notion of a hidden imam and the equally astonishing expectation of his bodily return as the Mahdi when we turn to Shi'ite Islam in the next chapter.

The Umayyads

Shi'ites were, and continue to be, a minority party within Islam. Some 85 percent of the 1.3 billion Muslims worldwide belong to the Sunni sect, and they are the majority in every Muslim country except Iran and Iraq. Their sense of the tradition differs from the majority party, the Sunni. Sunnis accepted the Mu'awiyah succession, thereby denying the claims of Ali and his heirs. Furthermore, they limited the imam's role to that of supervisor of religious observances in local mosques. In other words, Sunnis denied that imams were perfect, infallible, and gifted with supernatural insight into the meaning of the Qur'an and hadiths of Muhammad.

To the Sunni majority, the caliphs were key to sustaining Muhammad's vision of a united ummah, practicing Islam in an orderly fashion consistent with the Qur'an's instructions. To this end, they supported the caliphs' remarkable military conquests of North Africa, Spain, and parts of Central Asia and India; Egypt, Palestine, Arabia, and Persia had already fallen under Muslim control by the end of the second decade after the Prophet's death. Sunni imams were disappointed when the Umayyad caliphs failed to measure up to the lofty moral standards of the Qur'an, but they found the alternative of Kharijite or Shi'ite belief more troubling.

The Abbasids

In 750 C.E., Muslims were fed up with Umayyad control and helped a new dynasty of rulers take over the caliphate: the Abbasids, named for their descent from Muhammad's uncle 'Abd Allah ibn al-'Abbas. The Abbasids controlled the ummah from their headquarters in Baghdad for 500 years, until the Mongols sacked Abbasid lands in the thirteenth century. But until then, the Abbasids' longevity ensured the preservation of traditional ideas about the Qur'an and the Prophet's teachings.

Early tradition-minded scholars laid the foundation of Sunni theology. Men such as Muhammad ibn Ismail al-Bukhari (810–870) and Muslim ibn al-Hijjaj al-Qushayri (c. 817–875) compiled reports of the Prophet's sayings into the hadiths; al-Bukhari reportedly gathered some 600,000 sayings and authenticated 7,275, which he published as *Al-Jami' as-Sahih* (Authentic Collection). Muslim jurists such as Muhammad ibn-Idris al-Shafi'i (767–820) utilized the Qur'an, the hadiths, human reason, and the consensus of the ummah to build a tradition of Islamic legal interpretation, called *fiqh*. We'll discuss fiqh in a bit more detail later in this chapter.

> **Word to the Wise**
>
> **Fiqh** means jurisprudence in Arabic, and refers to the practice of legal reasoning in relation to the religious laws of Islam.

Generally, the architects of Sunni thought maintained the idea that the Qur'an was divine in source and content. They spoke of the recitation given to Muhammad as the uncreated manifestation of the eternal Word of Allah. This means, in their view, that there was never a time when the words of the Qur'an were not in existence. They interpreted the Qur'an in a rather strict fashion and applied it to present situations in as direct a manner as possible. And because of the Prophet's special status, they urged Muslims to follow his example in every area of life, with the instrument of Islamic law providing the proper array of incentives. They thought that the closer you get to living like the Prophet, the more likely the chance that Allah will favor you with a sense of divine presence. But this traditional formulation grew up alongside, and in response to, a more philosophical version of Islam, which was evident in the work of the Mu'tazilites.

Islam and Greek Philosophy

The tide of Muslim advance in the seventh and eighth centuries enveloped territory where Greek philosophy had already taken root, namely Palestine, Syria, Egypt, and Iraq. Hellenistic ideas and methods influenced a student in Basra named Wasil Ibn 'Atta' (c. 700–748), who reportedly grew dissatisfied with what he was learning and walked out on his teacher, giving a new movement in Islamic theology its name, *Mu'tazili* (Arabic for "leave" or "withdraw"). The Mu'tazilites were convinced that Islamic doctrines could be reconciled with Greek metaphysical concepts, and perhaps even established through dialectical reasoning.

Mu'tazilites worried about strict interpretations of the Qur'an, especially in light of passages that spoke of Allah's face and hands and other human attributes. They reasoned that the Oneness of Allah, or tawhid, prohibited any reading of the Qur'an whereby his essence could be distinguished from his attributes (as in all-knowing, all-powerful, all-wise). They denied that Allah could be conceived of as plural in either form or essence. These ideas led them to interpret the Qur'an figuratively and allegorically, with Allah's hands and face merely symbolizing the presence or power of God. They interpreted the anthropomorphic

> **Pearls of Wisdom**
>
> The nineteenth-century Islamic mystic Amir 'Abd al-Kader warned: "No one knows him in all his aspects; no one is ignorant of him in all his aspects. Those who are among the most knowing regarding him have said: 'Glory to Thee. We have no knowledge except what You have taught us. (Qur'an 2.32)'" *Spiritual Writings* (State University of New York Press, 1995)

passages in light of ringing statements about the unity of Allah, such as Surah 112: "He is Allah, the One and Alone in his Being." (v.1)

Mu'tazilites also worried about the traditional view of the Qur'an as an eternal, uncreated thing. They reasoned that to make the Qur'an to be the uncreated Word of Allah was to equate it with God or make it part of God. To their way of thinking, the Qur'an came into being at some point during the course of historical time. This was a demonstrable fact. Drawing upon logical reasoning, the Mu'tazilites concluded that an eternal Qur'an compromised the unity of God; conversely, a created Qur'an couldn't be considered divine since nothing created could be considered God. So here you see where Islamic thinkers owed something to their contact with Hellenistic Greek ideas. With the school of thought developed by the Mu'tazilites, Islam began to echo the rational tendencies in both Jewish and Christian traditions.

The Saga of al-Ash'ari

Not everyone appreciated the theories of the Mu'tazilites, even though the Abbasid caliphs in Baghdad enforced their doctrines with ruthless zeal in an episode called the *mihnah*, or inquisition. For 20 years beginning in 827 C.E., Muslims were required to accept these rational variations on traditional Sunni beliefs, with torture and even execution awaiting those who refused. One jurist, Ahmad Ibn Nasr al-Khuza'i, was crucified when he refused to give up the idea that the Qur'an is eternal and uncreated.

Sunni writers soon took up the challenge posed by the Mu'tazilites. Chief among their number was Abu al-Hasan ibn Ismail al-Ash'ari (878–941), a Mu'tazili student who during a dream one night experienced a visitation from Muhammad telling him to read the hadiths. Through his reading, he discovered a God of mystery and wonder and eventually became an uncompromising critic of the Mu'tazilites. But then al-Ash'ari had a second dream in which Muhammad rebuked him for his hard-headedness, and instructed him to use his god-given reason to pursue truth. Al-Ash'ari followed this advice and discovered a third way, somewhere in the middle between the metaphysical gymnastics of the Mu'tazilites and the unquestioning dogmatism of their ardent critics.

On the subject of Allah's attributes and his essence, al-Ash'ari taught that the attributes were real because the Qur'an said they were real. And not only were the attributes real, they were as eternal as Allah himself, and could not be otherwise. Al-Ash'ari pointed out the senselessness of using human analogies to account for

Allah's hands and feet and showing how they relate to the divine essence. Al-Ash'ari taught that human efforts to explain the divine essence and the timelessness of divine attributes would ultimately fail; such things were plainly beyond human reason and must be accepted on faith.

This raised the question of how Muslims should think about the Qur'an. Sunni theologians followed al-Ash'ari's lead and spoke of the Qur'an as being divine in its language and meaning, but not in the verbal intonations of the reciter or the physical pages of the book. So Sunnis believed that part of the Qur'an was, in fact, created, but the words themselves—the part that's important to salvation—are uncreated and eternal. Al-Ash'ari' allowed for interpretive approaches to the Qur'an, but rejected the idea the Qur'an must square with human reason.

Emergence of Kalam, or Theology

Al-Ash'ari is considered the founder of Sunni theology, called *kalam* (Arabic for "reason" or "discuss"). His successors continued to examine the question of Allah's being and his attributes, picking up where the ancient Greek metaphysicians and even the Mu'tazilites had left off. Al-Ash'ari had forged a third way, accepting both human reason and mystery, a partly created and partly uncreated Qur'an, and an Absolute with knowable attributes and an ineffable essence. Abu Bakr al-Baqillani (d. 1013) continued al-Ash'ari's work on the nature of God, and in *al-Tawhid*, he showed that Allah's existence could be proven through human reason, but other realities associated with the divine are known only through nonrational means, such as the Qur'anic revelation.

On another front, Sunni theologians tackled the thorny issue of predestination and free will, a classic issue in most theistic systems. If God is all-powerful and all-knowing, does that mean that human beings can't affect their eternal destiny? Does an omnipotent and omniscient God preclude human action and human choice? The Mu'tazilites and al-Ash'ari arrived at this question somewhat earlier because of their preoccupation with Allah's attributes. The Mu'tazilites came out in favor of human freedom: We can choose to follow Allah or not, and Allah judges us accordingly. For al-Ash'ari, this position

> **CAUTION**
>
> **Take Heed!** _____
>
> Muslims caution against putting your own personal spin on the Qur'an, following the Prophet's warning: "He who interprets the Qur'an on the basis of his opinion is in error, even if he should put forward a commentary which he considers right."

diminished Allah's omniscience and omnipotence. He argued instead that our actions are determined. What lies in the domain of freedom is the goodwill we earn or spurn because of these actions. This is hard to grasp, but then again, al-Ash'ari kept trying to remind everyone that some things defy human reason and must be accepted on faith.

Later writers picked up the question of good and evil, which grew out of the problem of human freedom and predestination. If Allah is in complete control, does that mean he is the author of evil? Sunni theologians considered this a mystery, but ventured that Allah created both good and evil for human beings, forming a system with limits that defined the range of human accountability. Since Allah is limitless, this doesn't apply to himself, and therefore evil doesn't pertain to his nature or attributes. Here you see Islamic thinkers wrestling with precisely the same enormous issues that vexed Christian theologians, principally owing to their joint discovery of ancient Greek metaphysics.

The Emergence of Falsafah, or Philosophy

But this was only the beginning. Islamic thought enjoyed a sort of golden age in the tenth and eleventh centuries, with such intellectual heavyweights as Abu-Hamid Muhammad al-Ghazzali, Abu Ali ibn Sina (Avicenna), and Walid ibn Ahmad ibn Rushd (Averroës) building a large body of Islamic philosophy that played off themes in Sunni theology. These thinkers took advantage of the circulation of Greek philosophical texts in Arab and Persian cultures starting in the ninth century, and eventually gave birth to a revolutionary vision of the ultimate reality. In time, Sunni theologians rejected the mature ideas of kalam and falsafah, and Islamic philosophy tracked away from the traditional teachings in the orthodox Islamic schools throughout the Middle East, North Africa, and Spain.

Divinations

Al-Farabi's rediscovery of Aristotle in the early Middle Ages, and the development of Aristotelian thinking in the writings of ibn Sina and ibn Rushd, left a huge imprint in not only Muslim thinking, but in Jewish and Christian philosophy as well. Both Moses ben Maimon and Thomas Aquinas took their cues from Islamic fal-safah.

Abu Nasr al-Farabi

Among the earliest philosophers of the Islamic tradi-tion, al-Farabi (d. 980) borrowed heavily from parts of Aristotle's and Plotinus's ideas about God, envisioning the divine as an eternal, changeless entity that served as the first cause in a chain of causes. He strayed from the traditional Sunni doctrine that Allah created the world out of nothing (*ex nihilo*), and instead affirmed the Greek cosmological belief in emanation, by which the universe proceeded from the One in a series of successive releases that reached its end with the appearance of the earth. Al-Farabi affirmed the reverse emanation idea as well, whereby matter develops into successively higher forms (plants, animals), reaching its apogee in the human mind, the repository of divine reason. Plato and other Greeks taught al-Farabi that the exercise of reason enabled humanity to transcend matter and unite with the divine.

Abu Ali al-Husayn ibn Sina (a.k.a. Avicenna)

You can probably guess that al-Farabi and his ilk rattled a lot of people's cages in the ummah, particularly the orthodox Sunni theologians and jurists who took responsibility for defending revelation and the tradition of the Prophet. But there was more to come. In Bukhara, in present-day Uzbekistan, ibn Sina (980–1037) picked up al-Farabi's writings and affirmed his reading of Aristotelian metaphysics. He used Aristotle's concept of the Necessary Existent to show how God was both first cause in a chain of causation, and the Existent by which all other existences depend. Drawing from Neoplatonism, ibn Sina envisioned the universe proceeding from the divine in a series of emanations, which he identified as Intelligences, resulting in the final emanation of Active Intelligence—the source of the material world, including humanity. He believed human intelligence was the chief means by which people can work their way back to the divine; Muhammad, for example, was particularly receptive to the Active Intelligence and was rewarded with direct comprehensions of the ultimate, divine Intelligence.

Abu al-Walid Muhammad ibn Rushd (a.k.a. Averroës)

Ibn Sina influenced both Shi'ite and Sufi (Muslim mystic) thinking, which you'll learn more about in the next few chapters, but had few followers in the Sunni tradition. His system challenged the Sunni concept of creation ex nihilo, diminished Allah's role in the process of human-divine reconciliation, and stressed the importance of human reason in the pursuit of ultimate truth. In the face of attacks on al-Farabi and ibn Sina, ibn Rushd (1126–1198) of Córdova, Spain, came to their defense, attempting a thorough exploration of the kinship of faith and reason. Ibn Rushd was concerned to show that philosophy, together with the Qur'an, can lead us to a more satisfying concept of God than revelation alone. For example, thinkers struggled with the question of how God could create everything at once in some point in time if the divine, as eternal, isn't bounded by or structured by time. Ibn Rushd reasoned that this problem derived from a false extrapolation from human experience to the divine nature. With God, you can't assume a sequence of thought and action, as you can with humans who move through time from initial thought to subsequent action. God collapses these distinctions, and is both pure intention and pure cause at one and the same time.

Questions such as these gave ibn Rushd lots of points to ponder, and he rigorously tackled them in a remarkable body of work that influenced adventuresome thinkers within the Muslim ummah, especially the Sufis, and Jewish and Christian intellectuals as well. Traditionalists, though, found ibn Rushd's work and the work of al-Farabi and ibn Sina to be too far beyond the pale of acceptable talk about God. Traditionalist schools of theology shied away from the speculations of falsafah in favor of intensive study of the Qur'an and the hadiths of Muhammad, which they believed offered sufficient guidance to the ummah in following the correct path.

Shari'ah: Finding God in Islamic Law

Many of the great Muslim thinkers led double lives as philosophers and imams or, said another way, scholars and judges. Ibn Rushd is a great example, because he devoted his life to studying and explaining Aristotle to medieval Spanish Muslims while serving as a judge in Seville and Córdova. Muslim jurists such as ibn Rushd assumed responsibility for keeping alive the Islamic *shari'ah* (Arabic for "path to follow," in reference to the Muslim code of law). When presented with a case, ibn Rushd and others looked to four agreed-upon sources to make a determination: the Qur'an and hadiths of Muhammad, the consensus opinion (*ijma*) within the ummah, and commonsense analogies (*qiyas*). This process, called fiqh, produced legal doctrines across a spectrum of human activity, from marriage and divorce to taxation and contracts. In this way, Muslims learned to distinguish between what is obligatory, recommended, discouraged, and prohibited.

> **Word to the Wise**
>
> **Ijma** in Arabic means "consensus," specifically the unified opinion of the Muslim ummah, or precedent in Islamic legal tradition.

You can probably see that shari'ah bears a faint resemblance to the Jewish halakhah, which we encountered in Chapter 7. Both endeavor to ensure that every aspect of life is conducted in a manner consistent with available revelation and collected opinion about the revealed truth. No area of personal behavior or human relations should be exempt from purification and surrender to God. But in the first three or four centuries of Islamic history, Muslim jurists disagreed about the relative weight that should be given to each of the four sources of law, with jurists on the strict end of the spectrum advocating a literal application of the Qur'an and Muhammad's sayings. The argument over law reflects a larger problem that Islam and all the other great religions had to confront: How do you take the perfect revelations of an infinite God and apply them to the chaos of human affairs, using imperfect and finite human understanding?

Sunni jurists tended to take the surest road and simply read the Qur'an and the hadiths in their most literal sense. Of course, this paralleled their reaction to falsafah; Sunni imams tended to prefer the direct, unambiguous language of the Qur'an to the dangerous metaphysical sorties inspired by Aristotelian questions about ultimate reality. They didn't worry, as did the philosophers, about the face and hands of Allah in the Qur'an, or the concept of creation ex nihilo, but affirmed the ultimate reasonableness, as the Qur'an teaches, of otherwise "hidden reality," or "that which is beyond the reach of human perception and ordinary cognizance." (Surah 2.3) So if you find the Qur'an a little fuzzy on the subject of God's nature and attributes, don't blame God, but blame a fallible and limited human mind that can catch only glimpses of a perfect, infinite, and eternal entity.

The Least You Need to Know

- The Sunni tradition in Islam embraces 85 percent of Muslims worldwide.

- The Sunnis separated from the Shi'ite branch over the question of who should lead the ummah (the Muslim community) after Muhammad's death.

- Disputes among Sunni theologians erupted over whether Allah's essence could be distinguished from his attributes, and whether the Qur'an is an eternal or a created thing.

- Great Islamic thinkers such as al-Farabi, ibn Sina, and ibn Rushd borrowed the idea of emanation from Greek philosophers, which got them into trouble with traditional Sunni theologians.

- Shari'ah, or Islamic law, reflects the Muslim desire to conform every aspect of life to the will of Allah.

Chapter 18

God in the Shi'ite Tradition

In This Chapter

- ◆ Shi'ite beginning points in the post-Muhammad era
- ◆ Learn about the office of imam
- ◆ Muslim beliefs about the end of times
- ◆ Twelvers and Seveners
- ◆ What happens when the Mahdi arrives?
- ◆ Why Najaf, Kufa, and Karbala are holy sites

It's perfectly natural to ask the question: What's different about Sunni and Shi'ite concepts of God? You'll soon discover that as you go from one to the next, the differences don't seem all that great. Both uphold the tawhid (unity) of God, the eternal character of the Qur'an, Muhammad's role as recipient of revelation, and the Five Pillars, not to mention the application of shari'ah to every aspect of life. So what's the difference, then? The differences are lost on outsiders because they are rather subtle, but Sunnis and Shi'ites consider them quite significant; otherwise, the separation wouldn't have persisted to the present day.

The disagreement between Sunni and Shi'ia began in the seventh century, and involved questions of leadership following the death of Muhammad. Today, the continuation of the schism owes to differences of opinion about clerical authority. Of course, this is essentially the question of who's the best judge of the Qur'an's meaning. You can tell right away that this is a critical issue, since the Qur'an occupies a central place in the Muslim faith. Shi'ites give special emphasis to the figure of imam as both religious instructor and spiritual guide. Today, some Shi'ites believe that the imam is a spiritual being—a kind of divine manifestation—that guides them toward the esoteric meanings of Qur'anic passages. One of the consequences of this view is a rather distinctive way of perceiving divine immanence in a religion otherwise known for its emphasis on the transcendence of God.

Partisans of Ali

As you recall from the previous chapter, Muslims disagreed over who should lead the ummah after Muhammad's death. Abu Bakr and Umar enjoyed wide support as his successors, but then Uthman ibn Affan—of the Umayyad tribe that had previously persecuted Muhammad—came to office. After a lengthy and sometimes contentious reign, Uthman lay dead at the hands of a small group of his detractors, who preferred to see Ali, Muhammad's son-in-law, become caliph. Ali followed Uthman in the caliphate, but never enjoyed the universal support of the Muslim community. It appears that one of Uthman's fellow Umayyad tribesmen, Mu'awiyah, also claimed the title, dividing Muslim sentiment and setting the stage for a showdown.

Here the stories begin to differ, but it appears that Ali established himself at Kufa, in present-day Iraq, then engaged Mu'awiyah's forces in battle. Ali and Mu'awiyah agreed to submit the matter of succession to arbitration, which angered some of Ali's partisans, the so-called Kharijites who believed that the entire ummah should decide the question, not a select panel of arbitrators. One of the Kharijites killed Ali, thus handing the caliphate to Mu'awiyah. Ali's supporters then turned to his sons, Hasan and Husayn, but Hasan gave up his claims and retired to Medina. Husayn, however, permitted a cabal to organize a challenge to the rule of Mu'awiyah and the Umayyads. The Umayyads and their allies in Iraq acted swiftly against them, killing Husayn and his followers near Karbala in October 680 C.E.

Points of Departure

Husayn's death inspired the Kufa Muslims to even greater levels of devotion to the cause of succession through Ali's family line. Husayn had given Ali's partisans a martyr, which helped transform their faction into a popular movement. They alighted upon Muhammad ibn al-Hanafiya, one of Muhammad's natural sons, and claimed the caliphate on his behalf. For his part, al-Hanafiya wasn't very enthusiastic about serving in this role, and lived out his life in Medina, reconciled with the Umayyad caliphate centered in Mecca. But the movement in Kufa continued to grow. Some followed the lead of a mysterious figure named al-Mukhtar ibn Abu 'Ubayd at-Thaqafl, who declared al-Hanafiya to be the Mahdi, a kind of Islamic messiah that Muslims expected to arrive one day to establish an era of peace and justice. We'll discuss the concept of Mahdi in Islamic thought in a short while. Like Husayn, al-Mukhtar met a bloody fate, leaving Ali's partisans in a state of disarray. From this point, the party of Ali, or Shi'ia, disagreed on how to proceed. This is where the faction itself became factionalized.

> **Divinations**
>
> It's a reach to call Husayn's death in 680 C.E. the founding moment of Shi'a Islam, but it has special meaning to contemporary Shi'ites. Every year, Shi'ites commemorate his martyrdom with public rituals that feature battlefield reenactments of Husayn's decapitation, and men beating their heads bloody with swords. In some places where conservative Sunnis dominate government, the so-called Ashura rituals are banned.

The Extremists

If you want to sort out the early history of Shi'a Islam, be prepared for some confusion. Those who believed the line of succession should proceed through Ali disagreed among themselves about how to respond to the Umayyad dynasty in the late seventh and eighth centuries. And this led them into serious doctrinal disagreement. An example of this doctrinal disagreement is the group of extremists, under the leadership of Abdallah ibn Saba of Kufa, who perceived Ali to be divine and worshipped him as God. Of course, the orthodox Islamic position is that only Allah is God, and God is one. Today, you can find a small group of adherents living in Iran who perceive Ali as a manifestation of the divine, but Sunnis and most Shi'ites have disowned them.

Twelvers

Extremists aside, three larger factions of Shi'a Islam grew out of a controversy over which descendents of Ali should be considered rightful imams. The largest group of Shi'ites today are the Twelvers, who got their name from the belief that eleven true imams proceeded in a line from Muhammad, through Ali to his son Husayn, ending with Hasan al-Askari, who died in 873 C.E. They believe Hasan secretly had a son named Muhammad al-Mahdi al-Hujja (the twelfth imam), who was hidden in a cave in central Iraq in the same year, and from time to time came out of hiding to reveal himself to pious Shi'a adherents. Twelver Shi'ites believe that this hidden imam is actually the Mahdi, who provides special insight to Muslim leaders in anticipation of his eventual re-appearance on earth.

> **⚠ CAUTION**
>
> **Take Heed!**
>
> The Shi'ite Shahadah offers a window on the differences between Sunni and Shi'ite, because it stresses the importance of the first imam, Ali: "There is no god but Allah, Muhammad is the Messenger of Allah, Ali is the Friend of Allah. The Successor of the Messenger of Allah and his first Caliph."

Seveners

The Twelvers represent the largest body of Shi'ites; a somewhat smaller portion affirms only seven true imams (and there's even a Fiver Shi'ism as well!). Seveners also hold to the idea of the hidden imam and expect his appearance as Mahdi at some point in the future. The largest Sevener group, the Ismailis, believe that the last true imam to proceed in the line of Ali was Isma'il, who died in 755 C.E. Ismailis spawned an imaginative array of doctrines, including the idea that God revealed himself to a sequence of prophets beginning with Adam and ending with Muhammad. Each prophet had a secret partner, with the prophet revealing exoteric truth (religious doctrine), and his secret partner conveying esoteric truth (supernatural insight into divine reality embedded within the doctrine). Ismailis who held to this scheme perceived Muhammad and Ali as the last doublet, with Muhammad revealing the exoteric, and Ali the esoteric truth. They further believed that after Muhammad came six imams who received direct apprehensions of the divine, with a seventh imam, the long-expected Mahdi, to come one day to establish an earthly paradise. Earlier, Ismaili Shi'ism dominated North Africa and Egypt; today, it is concentrated in East Africa, Yemen, Pakistan, and India.

Role of Imam

Ultimately, Sunni and Shi'a differences boil down to divergent visions of the role of *imam*, which gives a subtle inflection to their understanding of the ways of Allah.

Sunnis see the role in a rather pragmatic light. Sunni imams oversee religious observances, lead community prayers, and offer leadership to the local mosque. The institution of imam in Shi'ism is another kettle of fish altogether. Here, the imams take on a more spiritual role, as guides to the hidden meanings of the Qur'an. All Muslims consider the acquisition of knowledge about the divine to be of paramount importance; in Shi'a Islam, however, the way a person acquires this knowledge takes on a rather unique form, connected to the figure of imam.

> **Word to the Wise**
>
> **Imam** means leader or model in Arabic. In Sunni Islam, imam refers to the person who supervises religious observances, while in Shi'a Islam the imamate relates to the dynastic succession of Ali, and to the doctrine of the hidden imam who provides spiritual insight to Shi'ite clerics.

A Guiding Light

Muslims of every stripe believe that the Prophet Muhammad possessed "excellent capabilities" that warranted his selection by Allah to receive the divine revelation. (Qur'an 74.1–2) Shi'ites go a little further, adding that these special capabilities passed along to Ali, the first male convert to Islam, then to successor imams in the eighth and ninth centuries. Of what do these special capabilities consist? Shi'ites teach that the imams bore within them the divine light, an inner manifestation of God that gave them direct access to the hidden secrets of the Qur'an. Only the imams possessed this light, and so only the imams could discern the esoteric truths embedded deeply within the exoteric language of the Qur'an. And this divine element within rendered imami interpretations of the Qur'an infallible.

Hidden Away

Shi'ites believe that for each generation after Muhammad, Allah provided an imam for the Muslim community to follow, someone gifted with special powers of spiritual cognition that enabled him to divine the fundamental mysteries of the Qur'an. Sunni caliphs considered Shi'ite imams to be threats to their rule, so they lashed out against them. Shi'ite tradition holds that each of the eleven imams were murdered during their lifetimes. Twelver Shi'ites hold that the eleventh imam, Hasan al-Askari, rightfully feared for his son Muhammad's life and hid him away in a cave. They believe that Allah favored him with an abnormally long life, and he reappeared on occasion to guide the faithful until his final disappearance around 939 C.E. Rather than dying a physical death, the hidden imam experienced an "occultation," a type of spiritualization that enabled him to exist in perpetuity. Today, the hidden imam offers inspiration and direction to his earthly agents, who wield spiritual authority on his behalf.

The Ulema

The notion of a hidden imam sets the Shi'ites apart from the Sunnis, and results in a divergence of opinion about how Allah's revelation to humanity in the Qur'an should be handled. The Sunnis believe that the Qur'an can be read by anyone. Whenever disputes arise, the Sunni *ulema*, or community of Islamic scholars who have been trained in the Qur'an and in the science of fiqh (legal reasoning), try to gain resolution by working together and forging consensus. For their part, the Shi'ite ulema agrees that the Qur'an can be read by anyone, but they hold that it's more profound insights are accessible only to those under the guidance of the hidden imam, who designated the Shi'ite ulema as his earthly deputy.

> **Word to the Wise**
>
> **Ulema** derives from the Arabic root, *ilm*, meaning knowledge, and refers to the community of learned scholars who are trained in the Qur'an and Islamic law.

Reflecting the divine order, the Shi'ite ulema is arranged hierarchically, with certain figures having a weightier opinion than others. Most Westerners will remember the Ayatollah Seyyed Ruhollah Khomeini (1900–1989), who led the Shi'ite rebellion against the Shah of Iran and helped to construct the first modern Islamic state. His title, "ayatollah," means "sign of God," and reflects the high stature accorded to ranking clerics in the Shi'ite ulema. Millions of Shi'ites revered him, and continue to revere him, for reaching the Shi'ite ideal of consolidating religious and political power in the hands of the hidden imam's earthly designates.

Divine Immanence

If you think about it, imamology in Shi'a Islam gives its adherents a way to talk about the continuing presence of Allah in the world. The hidden imam lacks a physical body, but is spiritually present, making himself available to Shi'ites who seek truths that are beyond normal human comprehension. Shi'ites can communicate to the hidden imam by leaving messages at the tombs of the early imams, most of which are located in present-day Iraq; Ali's shrine is in Najaf, while Husayn's is located in Karbala, and Hasan al-Askari's in Samarra. Thus, with the hidden imam, Shi'ites perceive a way to bridge the gulf between divine and human realities. It bears some resemblance to the Christian idea of a Holy Spirit, or the Jewish Kabbalah idea of Shekhina (divine presence), though Shi'ites insist that the hidden imam is not God, or part of God, but a perfect, sinless, metaphysical being that points to the ultimate source of truth in the universe: Allah as revealed in the Qur'an.

Continuing Revelation

With the idea of a hidden imam, you get a few other ideas that distinguish the Shi'ites from the Sunnis: continuing interpretive revelation and messianic expectation. As for the first idea, Shi'ites believe that Allah's revelation to humanity isn't closed, but continuous by means of the light granted to the imams, and carried forward by the hidden imam among us. This doesn't negate or even weaken the power of the Qur'an, but rather, gives its interpreters special power to discern the mysteries of the faith that lay behind its words and phrases.

Shi'ite doctrine veers in the direction of Sufism in this connection. We'll learn more about Sufism in the next chapter, but for now you'll understand Shi'ism's departures from Sunni Islam a little better if you recognize that Shi'ite clerics believe that Allah provides semimystical insight into the sacred text that transcends logic and reason. These insights add to the revelation that's available to humanity through philosophy, science, and other pursuits of the mind. And when the human mind errs through faulty or improper reasoning, the Shi'ite ulema provides correction, because the hidden imam helps them to look beyond the surface level of the Qur'an's language to divine the essence of its teaching.

Awaiting the Mahdi

So Shi'ites believe that the imam is an abiding spiritual presence that supplies continuous interpretive revelation. This way, the Muslim community possesses the means to follow the straight path taught to Muhammad and explained in the Qur'an. But there's more. Shi'ites associated the office of imam with the Day of Judgment foretold in the Qur'an:

> And the day when the Hour will arrive, on that day they will be sorted out. Then as for those who had believed and done deeds of righteousness, they will be welcomed with all honors and entertained in a stately and delightful Garden. But as for those who had disbelieved and cried lies to Our Messages and the meeting of the Hereafter, it is they who shall be given over to punishment. (Surah 30.14–16)

The hidden imam plays the role of the long-expected Mahdi in Shi'ism, the figure who will return one day to establish a new dominion on Earth, where the faithful and just are rewarded and the wicked condemned. The Mahdi isn't mentioned in the Qur'an, but seems to be implied by various references to the "rightly or divinely guided one" (which is essentially the English meaning of the Arabic root of *mahdi*). Scholars have detected an early linkage between the imam and the Mahdi in the proclamations of al-Mukhtar, whose followers, known as the Kaysaniyah, devised the earliest formulation of Shi'a Mahdi doctrine. From there Shi'ites generally perceived the hidden imam to be the rightly guided one whose earthly return will initiate the final reckoning and the end of times.

Mahdism invites Muslims to look to the future with great hope and expectation, especially during times when it's difficult to see any reason for it. Over the centuries, periods of suffering and oppression induced Muslims to declare certain charismatic leaders as the long-expected Mahdi. Scholars have documented dozens of episodes in which leaders adopted the title and developed popular followings, prompting the creation of Islamic states. One of the more famous cases occurred in the 1880s in the Sudan, when Muhammad Ahmad (1844–1885) took the title of Mahdi and together with his followers, defeated an occupying Egyptian army. The Mahdi established an Islamic state, declaring along the way that the duty of pilgrimage to Mecca was to be substituted for duty to wage holy war, or jihad, against unbelievers. After his death the Mahdi was entombed at Omdurman, which became a sacred place for Sudanese Muslims. And they defended this site with fanatical zeal when the Egyptians, with help from Lord Kitchener and the British Army, returned to fight the Battle of Omdurman (1898) for control of the region. Historians remember this battle for the thousands of Sudanese jihadists who were slaughtered in the first field test of modern machine gun technology.

Unity in the Ummah

Differences of opinion about the Mahdi and the imam might lead you to assume that there's little common ground among Muslims regarding their concept of God. Not true. Sunnis and Shi'ites reciprocally acknowledge one another as true followers of Islam. And most efforts to compare the division to Christian schisms such as Roman Catholicism and Eastern Orthodoxy, or Lutherans and Methodists, tend to distort rather than clarify the terms at issue.

Muslims find near unanimity on questions deemed to be essential to the faith: the unity of Allah, the perfection of the Qur'an, the role of Muhammad as seal of the prophets, and the Five Pillars of faith. Differences tend to occur on the margins. Shi'ites tend to affirm human freedom; Sunnis are more comfortable with predestination. Shi'ites believe the imam to have metaphysical dimensions; Sunnis talk about the imam as a prayer leader. Shi'ite observances feature the martyrdom motif, commemorating the deaths of Ali and Husayn; Sunnis take a pass on these rituals. Perhaps the most important differences among Sunnis and Shi'ites have little to do with their concepts of God, and more to do with race, ethnicity, and region. For example, Shi'ites are the dominant faction in Iran and Iraq, and large communities of Shi'ite Muslims inhabit Lebanon, Yemen, Syria, East Africa, Pakistan, and the northern territories of India. Elsewhere, Sunnis dominate.

> **Pearls of Wisdom**
>
> O God, I make Thee my quest and bear witness to Thy Lordship,
> acknowledging that Thou art my Lord
> and to Thee is my return.
>
> —From a prayer attributed to Imam Husayn

In many Islamic countries, Sunnis and Shi'ites live cheek by jowl. In Iraq, for example, efforts are underway to encourage Muslim unity in the wake of Saddam Hussein's campaign against the Shi'ite majority. Some Iraqi Christians even nominated the Shi'ite cleric Ayatollah Ayat-Ullah Ali Al-Sistani for the Nobel Peace Prize for 2005 for his efforts to encourage Iraqi citizens to work together. He runs a website, www.alsistani.org, which tries to forge understanding about Shi'ite beliefs and practices. When asked if a Shi'ite and Sunni could pray together, he replied: "There is no objection to standing in a Sunni congregational prayer," though he gave his response a familiar Shi'ite touch, noting that the Shi'ite should recite additional Qur'anic surahs and acknowledge the imam.

The Least You Need to Know

◆ Shi'ites differ from Sunnis in ascribing to the imams special powers of spiritual discernment.

◆ Shi'ite factions acknowledge only Ali and his line of descendants as imams, but disagree with each other about when the line of descent broke off.

◆ The doctrine of the hidden imam offers Shi'ites a way to perceive the spiritual presence of Allah in the world.

◆ Muslims look forward to the eventual appearance of the Mahdi, who will initiate the Day of Judgment foretold in the Qur'an.

◆ Sunnis and Shi'ites agree on the essentials: Allah is one, the Qur'an is perfect, the shari'ah is the rule of life, and the Five Pillars represent the straight path.

God in Islamic Mysticism

In This Chapter

- ◆ Mysticism in the hands of Muslims
- ◆ Exoteric and esoteric knowledge
- ◆ Reading the signs
- ◆ Sufi martyrs and mystics
- ◆ The best poetry in the world
- ◆ Sufism and the Islamic tradition

It's common for the people of God to grow tired of the rituals and doctrines of their traditions, and begin to seek what seems to be a more authentic, more personal experience of the divine. Even in my own tradition, which places a high value on theological rigor and liturgical formalism, you hear a faint cry of protest from time to time. Recently I enjoyed an ordination ceremony that included the old song, "Be Thou My Vision," in which the hymnist asked of God:

> Be Thou my Wisdom, and Thou my true Word;
> I ever with Thee and Thou with me, Lord;
> Thou my great Father, I Thy true son;
> Thou in me dwelling, and I with Thee one.

That last line contains a sentiment that you can find in most world religions, which scholars call mysticism. Mysticism is the impulse to seek hidden knowledge of God, or obtain a direct, unmediated experience of the divine presence. Within the Islamic tradition, mysticism, known as Sufism, has been alternately embraced and dismissed, though it is an impulse that traces its history to the beginnings of the faith. Many hands gave shape to Sufism, and in this chapter you'll encounter their remarkable stories and learn about their unique vision.

Kernels and Shells

We learned in Chapters 8 and 13 that Jewish and Christian traditions contain elements of mystical belief and practice. This kinship extends to the other major monotheistic faith, Islam, as well. Islamic mysticism took the name *Sufism*, which comes from the Arabic root for "wool," in reference to the crude garments worn by early Islamic ascetics who followed the mystical path. Mysticism is a curious, often misunderstood, discipline; those who practice it have a hard time explaining it to others in a way that doesn't immediately trigger suspicions.

With respect to the mystical experience, American psychologist and philosopher William James, in his famous book *Varieties of Religious Experience* (1902), said "no adequate report of its contents can be given in words." James described mysticism as more of a state of feeling than a state of intellect, which makes it impossible to adequately convey to another person the nature of the experience. He compared it to hearing a symphony; a few are gifted with a "musical ear" and will appreciate the symphony on a deeper and more intuitive level. For the rest of us, the symphony is just varying types of noise, with the occasional pleasing melody or moving rhythm thrown into the mix. Following this analogy, the unenlightened person can never appreciate what the mystic feels, and is "likely to consider him weak-minded or absurd."

Perhaps mysticism comes into clearer focus if we keep in mind the commonly held belief that God's essence is ineffable and God's ways are inscrutable. Human minds, being fallible and imperfect, cannot possibly comprehend the nature of the divine, so we've been told over and over throughout history. It follows that ordinary sense perception and patterns of human cognition will always fail to produce the knowledge of ultimate reality that we most ardently seek to possess. Islamic mystics teach that finding true knowledge about the divine is like finding a kernel wrapped in a husk or shell that's waiting to be cracked open or torn away—human reason alone can't do the trick.

There's an old tradition in the Western world of differentiating among exoteric and esoteric knowledge. Exoteric knowledge is the type you can gather merely by using your senses and engaging in commonsense reasoning. If you can follow a recipe for lasagna, then you've acquired exoteric knowledge. Esoteric knowledge, on the other hand, can be gained only by means of intuition, or perhaps an altered state of consciousness. On that latter point, spiritual advisors advocate a variety of methods for achieving an altered state of consciousness where direct apprehensions of God become possible: contemplation, yoga, ecstatic dances, hypnotism, and in the most extreme cases, hallucinogenic drugs (when used in religious ceremonies, they are called entheogens).

Signs and Signposts

Keep in mind the distinction between exoteric and esoteric knowledge, and you'll get a good grasp on the starting point for Sufism. Sufis believe that the Qur'an contains layers of meaning within each verse. Each features at least 7 meanings, and perhaps as many as 70. As you can see, to the Sufi way of thinking the Qur'an isn't just a bundle of information about Allah. It contains figures of speech, signs and symbols, allegorical passages, and so on, each pointing in some way to the esoteric truths of the divine, which require special disciplines of the mind and body to attain.

The Qur'an itself speaks frequently of signs. In Surah 30, for example, it describes the creation of the universe, the diversity of the nations, and the rhythms of nature as signs of Allah's benevolence and perfection. But Sufis go further, suggesting that particular words and phrases—structures of language—contain deeper, more mysterious realities than a surface reading would suggest. Here you see something of the spirit of Greek philosopher Heraclitus, who observed in the sixth century B.C.E.: "The Lord whose oracle is at Delphi neither reveals nor conceals, but gives a sign." Signs encode a matrix of meanings, not all of which are apparent at first blush. It sometimes takes a skillful interpreter to render the meanings of signs in all their richness and complexity. According to the Qur'an, "no one knows its true interpretation except Allah, and those who are firmly grounded in knowledge." (Surah 3:7)

Divinations

Ever heard of the whirling dervishes? They trace their roots to the Sufi brotherhood of Mawlawiyah, founded by the poet Jalal ad-Din ar-Rumi in thirteenth-century Konya (present-day Turkey). They dance and spin to music as part of their spiritual discipline, reflecting mysticism's close affinity to the artistic imagination.

So there's a bit of elitism in the mystical tradition, because not everyone can attain such dizzying heights of perception. But Sufis believe they are just following the very example of the Prophet Muhammad himself, who according to tradition experienced a sense of the divine presence on the Night of Power when he ascended through the seven heavens on his way to receiving the recitation. They reason that if you're going to follow the sunnah, or the way of the Prophet, then his mystical experience must be included.

A Philosopher's Second Career

Scholars have commented on the similarities between Sufism and earlier strands of thought that predate Islam, such as Christian Gnosticism and the Persian mystery religions of the late Roman Empire. But aside from the question of such influences, Sufism as we know it today developed in the first few centuries of Islamic history out of the peculiar dynamics of growth and change within the Muslim ummah. And no figure more clearly illustrates how the movement arrived at its present shape than Abu Hamid Muhammad ibn Muhammad Al-Ghazzali (1058–1111 C.E.), a Muslim philosopher and jurist who suffered a spiritual crisis and eventually became the most well-known Islamic mystic in history.

Early Excesses

Al-Ghazzali came on the scene long after Muslim zealots had moved in reaction to the perceived worldliness and intellectualism of Islamic leaders. Men such as Hasan al-Basri (642–728 C.E.) and Ibrahim ibn Adham (d. 770 C.E.) lived in extreme poverty as a way of exemplifying the self-denying ethics of the Qur'an and the hadiths of the Prophet. Those who live in extreme poverty because of religious commitment are known as ascetics. These ascetics inspired religious outsiders such as Bayazid al-Bistami (d. 874 C.E.) and Hussein ibn Mansur al-Hallaj (858–922 C.E.), who claimed ecstatic experiences of union with God that ran all the way to equating themselves with the divine; in fact, al-Hallaj was executed for proclaiming "I am the divine Truth!" It was a heady time for Sufi visionaries, but a dangerous one as well.

> **Pearls of Wisdom**
>
> For thirty years I went in search of God, and when I opened my eyes at the end of this time, I discovered that it was really he who sought me.
>
> —Bayazid al-Bistami

Correcting Falsafah

Al-Hallaj threw a scare into the Sunni clerics and jurists who felt besieged on other fronts by Shi'ite Ismailis and speculative philosophers such as al-Farabi and ibn Sina. You might recall al-Farabi and ibn Sina from Chapter 17. The Sunni ulema searched for talented scholars to respond to Shi'ite assaults on traditional belief, and they discovered al-Ghazzali, who distinguished himself as a brilliant student of kalam and fiqh at Nizamiyah, the best Sunni school of the age, in Baghdad. Al-Ghazzali knew the ins and outs of Ashari theology and consumed the writings of the early faylasufs (Muslim philosophers). His expertise earned him a post at the mosque at Nizamiyah, and at the age of 33 he began a very public ministry as refuter of unorthodox views.

As a student, al-Ghazzali nurtured a deep appreciation for Islamic theology and philosophy; however, after a few years of further study and reflection, he became disillusioned. Where the rational faylasufs promised clarity and certitude, al-Ghazzali found only deeper and more vexing questions. In *The Incoherence of the Philosophers*, he challenged the metaphysical beliefs of al-Farabi and ibn Sina, concluding that their beliefs lacked any rational basis. Metaphysical philosophy hadn't proven from logical reasoning, for example, that the material world was uncreated and eternal. Nor had it proven the fancy scheme of emanation that it attributed to God as the means by which the material world took its present shape. In the end, al-Ghazzali came to believe that the rational approach to finding God wasn't sufficient to chase away uncertainty and establish a true understanding of the divine.

A Crisis of Faith

Still, al-Ghazzali kept on searching. You might say he became obsessed with the nature of knowledge itself, which he documented in his famous books, *The Revival of the Religious Sciences* and *The Deliverer from Error*. In these texts, al-Ghazzali examined various ways of knowing, such as philosophical speculation, inspiration via the Shi'ite imams, and theological dogmatism of the Asharite variety. His journey was nothing short of a tour through the history and present state of Islamic epistemology. As he recounted, his journey triggered a personal crisis in 1095, which he described as an illness of the mind—a kind of brain cramp. One of the symptoms suggests a great deal about his feelings of discomfort with contemporary Islamic efforts to speak authoritatively about God: He couldn't speak at all. God had "shriveled" his tongue, thus preventing him from giving any positive instruction to his flock at Nizamiyah. Thus incapacitated, he left his post and embarked on a spiritual quest, which took him to Damascus, Mecca, and finally back to Nizamiyah.

What al-Ghazzali Saw

In effect, al-Ghazzali's excursion had a dual quality. As he journeyed through sacred places in Jerusalem, Hebron, Medina, and Mecca, he also took an inner journey, searching deeper and deeper into his own heart. Journeys lead to discovery, and he recalled later: "I arrived at Truth, not by systematic reasoning and accumulation of proofs, but by a flash of light which God sent into my soul." By going beyond sense perception and conscious awareness, al-Ghazzali obtained a direct, inner comprehension of the divine. Now he understood the esoteric meaning of the exoteric renderings of truth he previously encountered in Islamic kalam and falsafah. That was enough to convince al-Ghazzali to follow the discipline of mystical Sufism. Eventually he mastered Sufi teachings and organized his own school of Sufism, returning eventually to teach at Nizamiyah before his death in 1111.

The Inner Path

Where previous Sufis had exceeded the boundaries of orthodox Islam, al-Ghazzali instead cautiously developed his mystical beliefs within the context of conventional Sunni dogma and Islamic shari'ah. He spoke of the importance of sound doctrine and legal principles; his great achievement was to merge disparate strands of Islamic thought into an integrated whole by demonstrating how Sunni theological concepts and Islamic rationalism became complete by adding the mystical experience of the divine presence within.

Pearls of Wisdom

Mystics believe religion is incomplete without an inner experience of the divine, as in this Sufi verse:

> In your light I learn how to love.
> In your beauty, how to make poems.
> You dance inside my chest,
> Where no one sees you,
> But sometimes I do,
> And that sight becomes this art.
> —Jalal ad-Din ar-Rumi

Doing Mysticism the Sufi Way

Al-Ghazzali began his second career as a Sufi mystic by mastering its concepts and procedures. He found that much of the doctrine amounted to a focused sort of asceticism—denying fleshly appetites and cleansing the heart of impure thoughts and motives. He further discovered that the means of inner cleansing was *dhikr*, which means "remember" in Arabic. This is a Sufi discipline of meditation that trains the mind on Allah, which we'll go into in short order. But al-Ghazzali discovered quite soon that the doctrines were easier to master than the procedures: "What is most peculiar to them cannot be learned, but can only be reached by immediate experience and ecstasy and inward transformation." Here you learn something essential about Sufism—that the inner experience is the crucial ingredient of all higher forms of understanding, and yet this experience cannot be explained in a way that would satisfy the skeptic or the rationalist.

Eye of the Heart

Sufis speak rather cryptically of opening the "eye of the heart," which appears to be a kind of inner aperture of the soul that is similar to the "eye of the soul" spoken of Augustine in his *Confessions*. God uses this aperture to peer into one's inner being, moving past the feeble words and deeds that outwardly mark us as "religious" persons. We use this aperture to catch a direct, unmediated vision of the ultimate reality, bereft of the theological, doctrinal, and legal husks that shroud the kernel of the divine essence. According to twentieth-century philosopher and poet Frithjof Schuon, "God sees not only the outward, but also—or rather with greater reason—the inward, and it is this latter vision that is the more real one, or strictly speaking, the only real one, since it is the absolute or infinite Vision of which God is at once the Subject and the Object, the Knower and the Known." (*Eye of the Heart*, 1997)

A word of caution here: Esoteric traditions tend to discount religious doctrines and ritual practices as obstacles to be overcome. Sufis, following al-Ghazzali, have more respect for the Islamic tradition. The husk, as exoteric knowledge, might shroud the esoteric kernel within, but it is nevertheless a valuable form of knowledge. It is the thing that binds the ummah together, even as the *tariqah* ("way" or "path") pulls the individual away to prepare the heart for special revelation. Sufis perceive the exoteric knowledge to be the circumference of a circle, enclosing the esoteric knowledge within its boundary. That would make the tariqah the radius of the circle that connects the circumference to the center point.

Finding God in the Dhikr

The tariqah requires a discipline that lies outside the ability of most ordinary Muslims. Even the great al-Ghazzali struggled to master the practices of Sufism. To follow the Sufi way, you have to be initiated into the community and submit to the direction of a Sufi *shaykh* (master). The requirement is nothing short of what Muslims know as *tasawwuf*, or total conformity to the sunnah of the Prophet, not only in outward appearance but in inward purity of heart as well. Sufi shaykhs teach the method of remembrance—*dhikr* in Arabic—which entails intense concentration on the name of Allah. This notion of remembering Allah comes from the Qur'an,

which describes itself as a reminder to its readers of things already known, but forgotten. Through our worldly preoccupations we forget the divine source of our being, and dhikr becomes a duty thrust upon all of us. But the Sufis want to go beyond normal understanding. By allowing the remembrance of Allah to gradually take over our entire consciousness, selfish thoughts become displaced and the ground is prepared for an intuitive vision of the divine.

> **Word to the Wise**
>
> *Dhikr* means "remember" in Arabic, normally used in connection with the Muslim devotional practice of contemplating the name of Allah.

An Eclipse of Self

There's an important idea here that many mystical traditions seem to share—escaping or suppressing the ego. Mystics describe their union with God as an experience of the total eclipse of self. The self gradually ebbs and the divine presence wells up inside, seemingly taking over. In one of the hadiths of Muhammad, this divine takeover is described in vivid language:

> My slave approaches Me with nothing more beloved to Me than what I have made obligatory upon him, and My slave keeps drawing nearer to Me with voluntary works until I love him. And when I love him, I am his hearing with which he hears, his sight with which he sees, his hand with which he seizes, and his foot with which he walks.

> —Fath al-Bari, 11.340–41, hadith 6502

Here Allah covets the obedience of his people, and when they move in his direction, he responds with love, so much love that they begin to lose their individuality and become absorbed in him. Most Sufis deny the radical implication of this belief, which is to say the complete identity of the mystic with God, where each becomes indistinguishable from the other. Instead, Sufis speak of losing consciousness of the self or a cessation of normal patterns of cognition, as expressed in this stanza from the *Diwan of Shams-i Tabriz*, written by Sufism's—and maybe the world's—greatest poet, Jalal ad-Din ar-Rumi (1207–1273):

> That which the imagination hath not conceived,
> That which the understanding hath not seen,
> Visiteth my soul from Thee: hence in worship
> I turn toward Thee.

Here Rumi blurs the line between the two types of mystical experience: the acquisition of esoteric knowledge without conscious thought, and the direct sensation of the divine within. His poem also contains a hint of the Sufi mystics' main objective, which is to remove all the obstacles and barriers that divide human beings from God, especially ideas, concepts, and words. In al-Ghazzali's words, the mystical path requires "purification of the heart completely from what is other than God most high" and a consequent "complete absorption in God." (*Deliverer from Error*)

> **Take Heed!**
>
> According to traditional Islamic teaching, nothing created can be God, and God is One. Thus, Sufis walk a precarious line when they speak, as al-Ghazzali did, of mystical absorption into God. Sufis claim that the misunderstanding derives from our human failure to see all reality as a manifestation of the ultimate existent, God.

Ibn Arabi

Al-Ghazzali and Rumi lived in the eastern portion of the Islamic world and were influenced by Persian culture and language. Persia seemed to be a fertile ground for esoteric movements, going back to the mystery religions of the later Roman Empire and beyond. But just as important to Sufism was the Western mystic Muhyi al-Din ibn Arabi (1165–1240), who grew up in the shadow of the great Spanish Aristotelian ibn Rushd. There's a famous story that ibn Rushd once met the young ibn Arabi in Cordova, and brimming with spiritual power, ibn Arabi so affected ibn Rushd that he fell mute and began trembling. This meeting symbolizes the cross-fertilization of metaphysical reasoning and mystical experience in ibn Arabi's work, which totaled some 200 books, including his most famous books, *The Meccan Revelations* and *The Bezels of Wisdom*.

To understand ibn Arabi's concept of God, we'll have to use some rather evasive language. But he *was* a mystic after all, so there's no escaping it. It appears ibn Arabi was enchanted with the metaphysical speculations of the faylasufs, and began to describe all reality as a unity of being. In his scheme, God exists, and is the only true existent. Going further, everything that appears to exist is but an aspect of the divine unity. How can this be? Well, it's a riddle, but ibn Arabi speculated about an ultimate existent in which all other possible existents reside (that would be us human beings); this ultimate existent, the ineffable "unknown God," manifested itself as the God of revelation, or Allah, which longed to be known. So Allah breathed life into being, as a kind of reflection of himself. Mysticism comes into play in this scheme when Allah permits our escape from the impious notion that we're somehow distinct and separate beings apart from the divine, and gives us intuitive comprehensions of our unity with the One, the true existent.

The idea of the unity of being made ibn Arabi a bit, well, unconventional. But then there's the concept of the perfect human being, another of his innovations. Each person is a reflection of Allah, but some are more reflective than others. These special people manage to peer beyond the veil of humanity's seeming disconnectedness and disunity, and grasp their own oneness with the Absolute. Once they understand that they are manifestations of the underlying unified reality, they can resume their communion with the world, as perfect models for others to emulate. Ibn Arabi spoke of Muhammad as a perfect human being, in the sense of his self-realization of oneness with Allah, a spiritual polestar for the rest of humanity to use as a guide. And surely others would follow. This provides a basis for the distinctive Sufi doctrine of *awliya*, the cadre of spiritually gifted mystics, including the great shaykhs of Sufi history, who pass on into a type of sainthood after death and perform miracles and intercessions on behalf of the living.

> ### Word to the Wise
>
> Awliya, plural for *wali*, means guardians or friends; in orthodox Islam the word has legal and religious connotations, while in Sufism it is associated with the metaphysical power of the shaykhs, both living and dead.

Sufism and Traditional Islam

Ibn Arabi gave Sufism a firmer metaphysical framework, but didn't convince the Sunni ulema of his orthodoxy. That raises the question, are Sufis accepted within the broader Muslim community? Of course the answer is yes and no. Mystics such as al-Bistami (804–874 C.E.), who once proclaimed, "I saw the Ka'ba walking around me," were deemed sufficiently blasphemous to merit condemnation or even execution. Sunni theologians never got comfortable with the pantheistic tendencies of ibn Arabi or the famous Sufi mystic Yahya Suhrawardi (1155–1191), who was executed by the Sunni ulema for his apparent heterodoxy. Suhrawardi blended Zoroastrian cosmology, Greek Gnosticism, and Islamic esoteric thought to form the Ishraqiyah school of Sufism, which is a kind of theosophy that perceives various religious traditions as disparate lights, each partaking and reflecting the Light of Lights.

Al-Ghazzali played a significant role in tempering the excesses of Sufism and explaining its approach in language that the Asharite theologians could understand. Furthermore, Sufism developed institutionally through brotherhoods resembling Roman Catholic monastic orders, which are led by spiritually gifted shaykhs. These brotherhoods also helped to channel Sufism into more orderly directions. Today, the dominant Sufi brotherhoods are Chishtiyya, the Naqshbandiyya, the Qadiriyya, and the Mujaddiyya and are distributed widely throughout the Muslim world. In the beginning, these brotherhoods gave the Sunni ulema a visible target, then an instrument of regulation. Eventually, they imposed their own kind of internal order, thereby limiting the range of mystical possibilities to those sanctioned and encouraged by the brotherhoods.

It's safe to say that Sufism is an established, if marginalized, part of the Islamic tradition. Sunni imams and jurists understand the value of esoteric knowledge, but do not permit departures from the exoteric teachings made available to the ummah in the Qur'an and the sunnah of Muhammad. Strict Muslim traditionalists, such as the dominant Wahhabist sect (a fundamentalist branch of Sunni Islam) in control of most of the mosques and madrassas (schools) in Saudi Arabia, consider the Sufi idea of union with God to be the height of blasphemy. And Shi'ites dislike the Sufi practice of arranging deceased imams and shaykhs into a spiritual hierarchy. Where you see the Sufi influence most plainly is the popular belief among ordinary Muslims of the need for an inner, subjective experience of the divine.

The Least You Need to Know

- Mystics divide knowledge into exoteric (outer) and esoteric (inner) types.

- The mystical path seeks the attainment of esoteric or inner knowledge of the Absolute.

- Sufis work through shaykhs, spiritual leaders who have mastered the mystical path and return to guide others.

◆ Early Sufism derived from ascetic and ecstatic Islamic practices, but took a philosophical and poetic turn in the medieval writings of al-Ghazzali, ibn Arabi, and ar-Rumi.

◆ Most Islamic leaders are uncomfortable with the Sufi notion of unity with God.

20

God in Islamic Renewal Movements

In This Chapter

- ◆ Wahhabism and Mahdiyya
- ◆ Updating Allah for modern times
- ◆ Islamic fundamentalism 101
- ◆ Muslim Brotherhood
- ◆ Meet Sayyid Qutb, theorist of Islamic radicalism

In the passage of time, theologians, philosophers, and mystics contributed to a growing complexity and sophistication within the tradition started by the Prophet Muhammad in the seventh century. Their visions added new facets and angles to the original Islamic concept of God; for example, you can see outside influences at work in al-Farabi's and ibn Sina's discovery of Aristotle and Neoplatonism, or Suhrawardi's engagement with Persian and Greek religious traditions. Closer to our own time, the Muslim ummah confronted altogether new stimuli, spinning out movements for reform and renewal that were integral to the shaping of modern Islam.

Today, debates rage within the Islamic community over how to respond to secular forces such as scientific materialism, consumer capitalism, democratization, and cultural pluralism. Muslims aren't alone in this predicament—Christians, Jews, Hindus, Buddhists, and adherents to a wide variety of other faiths wrestle with the same question. There's quite an interesting parallel between the Islamic, Jewish, and Christian experiences: Each of the Abrahamic monotheisms developed modernist and traditionalist polarities, dividing the faithful into mutually suspicious and sometimes openly hostile camps. We encountered the Jewish and Christian polarities in Chapters 10 and 15; here you'll discover the Islamic polarities in the traditionalist visions of Wahhabism and Mahdiyya versus the modernizing efforts of progressive Sunni, Shi'ite, and Sufi clerics.

Islam and the West: A Thumbnail Sketch

From the very beginning, Islam harbored a divided conscience toward adjacent civilizations and cultures. It affirmed and incorporated the religious visions of Judaism and Christianity, and yet, as Muhammad's life demonstrated, Islam's intentions were not only spiritual and religious, but political and military as well. Under Muhammad, Islamic rule spread throughout the Arabian Peninsula, and under the first four caliphs, extended to Palestine, Syria, Persia, and Egypt. The Umayyads of the late sixth and early seventh centuries conquered North Africa, Spain, Asia Minor (Turkey), and northern India. Clearly, Muslim leaders had ambitions not unlike those of the Greeks, Romans, Persians, and other ancient Near Eastern empires, not to mention European colonialism closer to our own time.

Divinations

Islamic perceptions of the West are colored by the Crusades, which began in 1095 and proceeded in waves for the next two centuries. Europeans occupied Palestine and Syria for some 90 years before Muslim armies under Saladin defeated them in 1187. Among the more famous ruins you can still see today is the Krak des Chevaliers in Syria, which housed Crusader knights for 172 years.

Gradually, the Abbasid caliphate (successor to the Umayyads) disintegrated, having lost effective control of the Muslim empire first to the Fatimids, then the Seljuks of Central Asia, the Mameluks of Egypt, and finally the Ottoman Turks. The Ottomans converted to Islam and assumed the role of defenders of the faith. They protected Islamic holy sites (like Mecca and Medina) and instituted the shari'ah throughout their domain. In this way, they provided Arab and non-Arab Muslims alike a focal point of unity, which brought the Sunni ulema to throw its support behind them. By 1700, the Sunni religious establishment had gotten so cozy with the Ottoman political leadership, you couldn't really distinguish between them.

The downside of this arrangement became clear as the Ottoman Empire began to decay, and then overreact to growing Western pressures. Muslim clergy became associated with the ineffectiveness of the Ottoman state, as defeat after defeat humiliated Ottoman armies and navies, and as the political leadership lurched in the direction of political and military modernization in an effort to compensate for leadership failures. Ultimately, the forces of disintegration were too great for the Empire to bear, and the Ottomans were unable to fend off colonial intrigue and outright territorial annexation by Western powers such as Britain, France, and Germany.

Ottoman decline fractured any unity the Muslim ummah could claim to possess. Sunni clerics became targets of severe criticism for their perceived failure to bring about an Islamic social order in conformity with the Qur'an and guided by the shari'ah. By 1900, two movements for reform in Islam—Wahhabism and Mahdiyya—gained traction amid this widespread disaffection. These movements used language and tactics that fascinated Muslim writers and activists of the early and mid-twentieth century, who then provided the intellectual and doctrinal architecture of Islamic fundamentalism today. Historian Bernard Lewis wrote a famous book about souring relations between Islam and the West: *What Went Wrong?* (Oxford University Press, 2002). If you want an answer to Lewis's question, a good place to begin looking is Wahhabism.

Wahhabism

A sequence of events in the late 1600s produced the necessary stimulus for one of modern Islam's most influential renewal movements. Sultan Mustafa II directed one last military effort by the Ottomans to maintain control of the Empire's European possessions, but he suffered a bitter and embarrassing defeat in 1697 at the Battle of Zenta. The combined forces of Russia, Austria, Poland, and Venice extracted humiliating concessions from the Ottomans in the Treaty of Carlowitz (1699), including territories in Hungary, Croatia, Slovenia, and parts of the Ukraine. Though you never read about this in the history books, these concessions sent a shockwave throughout the Muslim world and prepared the ground for the advent of Wahhabism.

On the margins of the Ottoman Empire, but in the center of Islam in the Arabian Peninsula, Muhammad ibn Abd al-Wahhab (1703–1792) came of age having studied orthodox Sunni doctrines, and begun a career as scholar and teacher of traditional

Islam. He was known for teaching that Shi'ite imamology had added to, and therefore corrupted, the truths of the Qur'an and the purity of the Islamic faith as revealed to Muhammad. It seems he was trained in the most conservative methods of Islamic jurisprudence, the Hanbalite school, and was enchanted by the writings of an earlier purist, Ahmad ibn Taymiyya (1268–1328) who bitterly attacked the Mameluk Sultans of Egypt for failing to rid Islam of Shi'ite devotion to the deceased imams and the Sufi quasi-divinization of the shaykhs. The language of a corrupted Islam requiring purification became the predominant motif of Wahhabbism as it took root in the eighteenth century.

Wahhab succeeded in convincing provincial leaders in Arabia to adopt his program of renewal through purification, particularly the leader of al-Dar'iyah, Muhammad ibn Sa'ud. They formed a coalition to implement strict adherence to the most literal interpretations of the sunnah of the Prophet. Their unshakable commitment to the *tawhid* ("oneness") of Allah, for example, caused them to forbid the worship of great Islamic spiritual leaders and pilgrimage to their shrines. And they rejected the Sufi claim of an alternate path to God outside the instructions given by Allah in the Qur'an and developed in the shari'ah. But they also rejected unthinking acceptance of orthodox Sunni theology. The ideal, they claimed, was *ijtihad*. This refers to the exercise of independent judgment in Qur'anic interpretation, based on rigorous study of the entire Qur'anic revelation and the Prophet's hadiths (which offer guidance to those who seek the proper understanding of divine truth). Ijtihad, they believed, offered the only antidote to the ignorance and idolatry that pervaded the Muslim community under Ottoman rule. Of course ijtihad also necessitated strict adherence to the shari'ah in every aspect of religious, social, and economic life.

Word to the Wise

Ijtihad is an Islamic concept that refers to independent judgment in matters of Qur'anic interpretation.

The Saudi family, together with their allies among the Wahhabist mullahs, eventually gained control of most of the Arabian Peninsula, including the holy cities of Mecca and Medina. The Ottomans could no longer ignore the Saudi-Wahhabist threat to their power, and so the Ottomans suppressed the Wahhabists at the onset of the nineteenth century. But in the minds of many Arabs in the Peninsula, the short Saudi-Wahhabist reign in the eighteenth century was a kind of golden age, and Wahhabist partisans made small inroads toward a more general restoration over the next half century. In 1902, with the disintegration of the Ottoman Empire in full swing, Abd al-Aziz ib Abd al-Rahman (also known as ibn Sa'ud), conquered Riyadh, and proceeded to consolidate much of the Arabian Peninsula into the hands of the Saudi family. The Saudi family's work culminated with the 1932 declaration of the nation of Saudi Arabia, under the spiritual guidance of Wahhabist scholars and clerics.

Mahdiyya

Wahhabism wasn't essentially anti-Western, though it did teach resistance to beliefs and practices that the ulema considered un-Islamic, including those of a "foreign" derivation. In the main, Wahhabism had its sights on internal targets, namely Turkish and Egyptian rulers who weren't sufficiently committed to Islam in the eyes of Wahhabist mullahs. Similar dynamics produced the Mahdiyya (followers of self-proclaimed Mahdi Muhammad Ahmad) in the Sudan, though along the way it developed an overt hostility toward Western colonialism and Western culture. We discussed the theological content of Sudanese Mahdism in Chapter 18; it's sufficient to remind you here that the Mahdi figure in Shi'ite tradition has apocalyptic and eschatological value because of its association with the future reckoning at the end of history.

Sudanese Mahdism came about as a direct consequence of British colonial interference in Egyptian and East African politics. Britain opened the Suez Canal in 1869 and soon became dependent on this vital corridor for facilitating its Indian trade. Local pressures and Ottoman decline forced Britain to interfere more directly in Egyptian affairs, and by 1880 the British government had come to exercise something akin to a protectorate over Egypt. When Governor-General Gordon, Britain's colonial chief in the Sudan, retired in 1880, political uncertainty reigned up and down the Nile River valley.

In the year of Gordon's retirement, a remarkable figure appeared on the scene, a religious leader named Muhammad Ahmad ibn 'Abd Allah, who had risen to chief shaykh of the Sufi brotherhood Sammaniyah. He visited the people of Kordofan in central Sudan and learned of their suffering at the hands of pillaging army veterans, newly empowered slave traders, and unscrupulous tax collectors. To his way of thinking, the only solution for the Sudanese people was a return to the original vision of Muhammad in the seventh century. To this end he preached against an array of interconnected enemies—of course the British, but also an array of locals who sustained the regime, including Egyptian and Turkish collaborators and the Islamic leaders who gave them religious cover. To put a finer point to it, Muhammad Ahmad declared a jihad against the foreign infidels and their Muslim collaborators—perhaps the first jihad in the modern period declared against a Western power with the goal of instituting a purified Islamic state. (More on that later in this chapter.)

At this point Muhammad Ahmad revealed himself as the Mahdi, come to establish true justice and righteousness, and with the support of some Islamic clerics in the region, gathered an army of some 30,000 men for a military campaign against the Egyptians and British. The Ansar, as the Mahdi revolutionary army was called, rolled up victories against several Egyptian armies and even destroyed a British garrison at Khartoum under former governor Gordon. The Mahdi then instituted strict Islamic rule in a unified Sudan, which lasted for more than a decade as Sudanese Mahdist armies embarked on a failed campaign to spread the revolution to the rest of the Middle East. Severely weakened, the Mahdist regime couldn't withstand a British force under Lord Kitchener that reoccupied the region to prevent the French from assuming control of the Upper Nile region.

> **Divinations**
>
> Purification started right away in the Mahdi army. Muhammad Ahmad demanded his men follow the shari'ah, give up liquor and cigarettes, and maintain ritual separation from women. A strong martyr element entered the picture, since the Mahdi Muhammad Ahmad told the troops that service in the jihad replaced the Islamic requirement of pilgrimage to Mecca.

Allah for Modern Times

People who promoted Islamic renewal took aim at both European colonial officials and the Muslim leaders who supported the foreign presence. In the process, reformers created a potent combination of jihad and martyrdom, zeal in the cause of purity, and a vision for a universal Islamic caliphate. This combination fastened itself on the minds of subsequent purists who shaped modern Islamic fundamentalism. But this wasn't the only vision to emerge from Islam's encounter with the West in the nineteenth century. Some scholars and jurists charted a less militant course by reminding themselves and the West of Islam's contributions to civilization and asserting the value of critical reflection in theological and legal matters.

The problem the less militant thinkers identified was one of misunderstanding and prejudice. Western colonizers ridiculed the backwardness of the Middle East, including its main religious traditions, and compared the region unfavorably with the progressive, enlightened culture of Western Europe. While some Muslims rebelled against this Western characterization and responded with calls for purification and jihad, others asserted Islam's rich intellectual heritage and the essential rationalism of the faith. These thinkers, often referred to as Islamic modernists, were in fact convinced that Islam and the West had much to learn from each other, and they gave rise to a broader vision that embraced scientific and technological progress.

Muhammad Abduh

A good start on this topic is the famous Muhammad Abduh (1849–1905), a teacher at the al-Azhar mosque in Cairo. Abduh possessed a vision of Islam's future in which theology and modern science works hand in hand to clarify ultimate truth. In this effort, Abduh reminded both the West and the Muslim ummah that the original revelation to Muhammad was designed to dispel ignorance and superstition through a rational faith based on logical reasoning and demonstrable proofs. Ancient Muslims led the world in mathematics, astronomy, and medicine. And yet the orthodox responses to medieval falsafah resulted in a kind of intellectual rigor mortis, which was exacerbated by the Sufi tendency to set reason against intuition and experience. Abduh argued for a greater appreciation of the work of intellectuals in the Islamic tradition. As a member of the ulema, Abduh called for an interpretation of the shari'ah that would permit critical evaluation of Qur'anic revelation in light of changing times and circumstances, which of course is a far cry from the positions taken by the Wahhabists and Mahdiyya through the nineteenth century.

> ### Pearls of Wisdom
>
> Fazlur Rahman, a modernizing Islamic scholar, wrote: "The moral law and religious values are God's command, and although they are not identical with God entirely, they are part of him. The Qur'an is, therefore, purely divine."
>
> —*Islam* (University of Chicago Press, 1979)

Indian Variations

Scholars use Abduh as an illustration of a modernizing spirit among Muslims in the Middle East. Even more daring were Amir Ali (1894–1925) and Muhammad Iqbal (1877–1938), whose lives spanned the transition to the twentieth century. These thinkers from Muslim quarters in India stressed the liberal qualities of Islam. Ali's *Spirit of Islam* reminded Muslims of the Qur'an's broadmindedness and its language of inclusiveness. Where the diehards of Arabia and the Sudan preached jihad, Ali spoke of compassion for the poor and disinherited. He further counseled that the values of the Qur'an and the shari'ah were what counted, not the matrix of rules and procedures that the early Islamic leaders produced to activate these values. Put simply, the rules could drift with the culture.

To Muhammad Iqbal, individual Muslims should exercise independent judgment in order to bring new ideas and concepts to bear on the Qur'an. Like Christian process theologians, Iqbal perceived the human and divine as engaged in an evolving creative process in which God permitted individuals the freedom to deploy reason and imagination. This creative activity signaled an openness toward the Absolute and resulted in a fuller approximation of the divine will in the world. To Iqbal, the West was first to promote individualism, but had no means to prevent individualism from being perverted into narcissism, materialism, and capitalist exploitation. Utilizing the spiritual resources of Islam and exercising human creativity, Iqbal believed Muslims could model the kind of humane, orderly, and compassionate community called for in the Qur'an, and hoped for by Enlightenment and Romantic-era philosophers in the West.

The Muslim Brotherhood

Maybe Iqbal was on to something. After all, Europeans who lived through the political, social, and intellectual developments of the early twentieth century experienced a crisis of confidence in Western culture. And then came the shattering experience of World War I. At the war's close, events set in motion particular dynamics that gave rise to the modern Islamic fundamentalist movement, which called for renewal in a way utterly opposed to the modernist visions of Muhammad Abduh, Amir Ali, and Muhammad Iqbal.

What happened? Well, in 1920, British and French armies pushed into the Middle East to take control of territories formerly ruled by the Ottoman Empire (France in present-day Lebanon and Syria, Britain in Palestine, Jordan, and present-day Iraq). The League of Nations mandated independent Arab states, but under the tutelage of the old Western colonial powers. This mandate came right on the eve of the collapse of the Ottoman caliphate in 1923. To Muslims, these events signaled the dissolution of Islamic unity and the domination of the ummah by foreign—think infidel—powers.

> **CAUTION**
> **Take Heed!**
>
> It's become fashionable to claim that Islamic radicals acquired their violent, anti-Western attitudes from Europeans themselves. True, men such as Hassan al-Banna and Sayyid Qutb read Karl Marx and Friedrich Nietzsche, but this ignores the deeper roots of jihadist puritanism in Egypt, which go back as far as ibn Taymiyya in the fourteenth century.

Hassan al-Banna (1906–1949) witnessed these events, and like millions of other Muslims, recoiled in horror at the low state of the Islamic faith in the interwar years. Al-Banna witnessed the British occupation firsthand at Ismailia, on the Suez Canal. He became familiar with the literary works of the Islamic modernists, including the writings of Abduh, al-Afghani, and Rashid Riga, and knew the major ideas of the

Sufi shaykhs as well. These thinkers failed to create a popular impetus for reform and renewal. Nor did the modernists create the institutional mechanisms for the unification of the ummah across national boundaries. Hassan al-Banna tried to supply this deficiency with the Society of the Muslim Brothers.

The Muslim Brotherhood developed an outlook that combined Islamic renewal through purification and open resistance to Western influences in Islamic society. Soon, Muslim Brotherhood chapters opened in Syria, Lebanon, Palestine, and the Sudan, but their impact was most immediately felt in Egypt, where terrorists affiliated with the Brotherhood assassinated Prime Minister an-Nuqrashi in 1948 on charges of collaboration with the British occupation. The Egyptian government murdered al-Banna in response, and the Brotherhood replied with an attempt on President Gamal Abdel Nasser's life in 1954. Here you should remember the earlier example of ibn Taymiyya, whose calls for purity and jihad drew a repressive response from the Egyptian Mameluks before they ultimately accepted him as a renewer and restorer of the faith.

In the Shade of the Qur'an

Central to the efforts of the Muslim Brotherhood and other conservative renewal movements is the Muslim concept of *mujaddid*. Muslims believe Allah appoints a mujaddid about once a century to decontaminate Islam from various innovations and corruptions in belief and practice. Purifiers of all stripes lay claim to this title; agreement on who should bear it is elusive. But belief in the concept of mujaddid lies behind many of the recent Islamic renewal movements that want to turn back the clock to the seventh century and restore Islam to its supposed original purity.

One of the Muslim Brotherhood's intellectual heavyweights, Sayyid Qutb (1906–1966) aspired to the role of mujaddid. Qutb was educated in the United States and upon his return joined the Muslim Brotherhood. Eventually he was imprisoned and executed for his alleged role in the plot against Nasser, but while in prison he wrote *In the Shade of the Quran* (English trans., Wamy Intl. Inc., 1995), a thick commentary on the Islamic sacred text that ran to 15 volumes. The *Shade* is more than a commentary, though. It indicts Judaism for

> **Word to the Wise**
>
> **Mujaddid** is a reformer within Islam who is expected to appear once a century to purify the faith. **Aqidah** refers to a posture of rigidity in regard to doctrine or belief, commonly associated with Islamic fundamentalism.

failing to live up to its moral vision, and Christianity for distorting the message of Jesus. He identified a "hideous schizophrenia" in Western thought, a division between the spiritual and material worlds that God never intended. He claimed this division was the result of Christianity's importation of Greek philosophy into the writings of the apostles and early Christian theology. Worse still, Qutb blamed Muslim leaders for inviting philosophical dualism into Islam, and for accepting the Western concept of separation between sacred and secular domains of authority.

Of course, Qutb's prescription for an ailing Islam required the strict implementation of Qur'anic teachings in their most undiluted form, complete adherence to the shari'ah without accommodation to the modern temper, and physical struggle—jihad—for the soul of Islam against the Jewish Zionists, European materialists, American libertines, and Arab secularists who sought to dilute the faith and push it to the margins. Qutb liked to employ the concept of *aqidah*; in the words of Islamic scholar Ibrahim Abu-Rabi in a 2002 article in the online journal *Religioscope*, this implies "stability, fixity, [and] form as well as power to withstand all the different changes around you." (*Religioscope*, 2002) In the *Shade*, then, you get the intellectual and strategic playbook for Islamic fundamentalism, and legions of militants in the second half of the twentieth century answered Qutb's call to action.

Reform and Revolution

The Muslim Brotherhood served as a kind of clearinghouse for Islamic radicals in the 1960s, creating a network of like-minded purists who resented the complicity of Arab states with Western degeneracy. Inspired by the Brotherhood's return to the original Qur'an, conservative Shi'ites deposed the American-sponsored Shah of Iran in 1979, providing the region with a working model of Islamist revolution and the total conversion of society and politics to Islamic law.

Meanwhile, Islamic radicals stepped up their attacks on secular Arab governments. A new organization called Islamic Jihad assassinated Egyptian President Anwar Sadat in 1981 for making peace with Israel at the Camp David Accords; they would make repeated attempts to assassinate Egyptian ministers throughout the 1980s and 1990s. And thousands of Syrian citizens were killed in a 1985 Muslim Brotherhood uprising, which was brutally crushed by Hafiz al-Assad's army in the city of Hamah. Perhaps the movements most closely associated with Qutb's distinctive brand of jihadist puritanism are the Taliban of Afghanistan and Osama bin Laden's al-Qaeda organization. Taliban mujahedeen waged a successful jihad against the Soviet-sponsored government in the late 1980s and controlled the country until the U.S. invasion of 2002.

And of course Osama bin Laden, a veteran of mujahedeen operations in Afghanistan, exported jihad beyond the boundaries of the Middle East in his effort to purge Muslim territories of foreign influences, especially in his home country of Saudi Arabia.

So where's God in the Islamic renewal movements? Militant Islamic radicals believe the theologians, philosophers, mystics, and Westernizing secularists mixed Islam together with various foreign impurities to create some sort of alloy. You'll find Allah, they say, once the faith has been decontaminated. Other reformers say a different posture is required, one that creatively engages higher forms of thought in all cultures to reach a more complete understanding of ultimate reality. Most Islamic scholars reject both the rigid certainties of fundamentalism and the rationalizing speculations of modernism. They believe the nature of God is ineffable, but Allah can be perceived more clearly through critical reflection on the meaning of the Qur'an, within boundaries established by the sunnah of the Prophet Muhammad, generally accepted traditions of jurisprudence, and the consensus of the Muslim ulema.

The Least You Need to Know

- Wahhabism sought renewal by purifying Islam of Shi'ite imamology and Sufi notions of sainthood, and instituting strict adherence to the shari'ah.

- The Mahdiyya linked Islamic renewal with anti-Western jihad, which planted the seeds of modern fundamentalism.

- The stimulus for Islamic renewal came at the hands of European colonizers, who assumed control of much of the region amid the disintegration of the Ottoman Empire.

- A good place to begin understanding the tensions within modern Islam is to contrast the writings of Muhammad Abduh and Sayyid Qutb.

- The Muslim Brotherhood of the mid-twentieth century provided a network for spreading the militant Islamic vision of Sayyid Qutb.

Part 5

The Concept of God in Eastern Religions

If you know very little about Hinduism, Buddhism, Sikhism, Taoism, Shintoism, Neo-Confucianism, and other Eastern religious and philosophical traditions, then rest assured you're not alone. But you can enhance your understanding with a quick tour through the Eastern traditions, starting with the ancient Vedic religion that lies at the core of many Asian religious traditions. The early Brahmins, or religious leaders, gave us concepts such as atman and Brahman, karma and samsara (reincarnation), and the different yogas, or paths toward release from the cycle of rebirth. You'll also want to know how Hinduism and Buddhism evolved in the literary traditions of the Axial Age in the five or six centuries before the onset of the common era, because these developments are crucial to the shape of contemporary religious practice in South and East Asia. If you want to know more about Shiva and Vishnu, the Buddha's teachings, or the Tao of Taoism, this is a very good place to begin.

Chapter 21

The *Vedas* and Beyond

In This Chapter

- Roots of Hinduism and Buddhism
- Ideas about the "One"
- The Hindu idea of reincarnation
- Breaking the cycle of rebirth
- Karma, yoga, dharma, and other key concepts

And now for something completely different. If you're unfamiliar with Hinduism and Buddhism, you have to set aside many of your preconceptions about God before you can start to understand and appreciate the Hindu and Buddhist concept of the Absolute. Westerners who've grown comfortable with their father's or grandfather's monotheism quickly discover that many of the rules regarding the divine simply don't apply. Our minds are hardwired after thousands of years of Western philosophical tradition, so it's tough for many of us to grasp even the most elemental components of Eastern religions.

So if you're thinking in a Jewish, Christian, Muslim, or generally Western agnostic vein, get ready to set aside the language we typically use to describe the ultimate reality. If you're able to do so, great rewards await. Hinduism and Buddhism are rich traditions that offer unique perspectives on the problems of the human condition, the nature of realities external to the self, and the question of ultimate human destiny. In some Eastern traditions, you even discover how to speak of the Absolute without reference to a personalized divinity (such as Yahweh, Jesus, or Allah) at the center of existence. In this chapter, you'll learn that at the root of these visions lies a set of shared concepts, the earliest expression of which you find in the *Vedas* and the *Upanishads*—literary works of the ancient people of the Indian subcontinent. The ideas contained in these texts are the starting point for any discussion of the concept of the Absolute in Eastern religious traditions.

Architecture of Hinduism and Buddhism

Hinduism and Buddhism are sister traditions, or rather groups of traditions, that sprung from a common root in the Indus and Ganges river plains. Four or five thousand years ago, people living in these regions developed religious beliefs and practices that were not unlike the ancient polytheisms of the Near East, featuring multiple divinities associated with natural phenomena, ritual sacrifices supervised by a priestly class, and a mythological vision of the creation of the universe. These beliefs and practices are called Vedic religion, after their chief writings, the *Vedas*. Between 1000 and 600 B.C.E., the Vedic priests—brahmins—took a turn in the direction of what we now call Hinduism. The newer outlook gained expression in the *Upanishads* and other writings, which explained and interpreted the ideas contained in the liturgical hymns of the *Vedas*.

From the common root of Vedic religion and early Hinduism, the religious traditions of South and East Asia branched off into myriad directions, achieving the bewildering complexity you see in Hindu and Buddhist traditions today. That complexity belies Western expectations of what a religion should look like. Jewish, Christian, and Islamic teachers envisioned God as a unified, supreme, transcendent being, which resulted in centralizing tendencies within their faiths. Sunni Muslims policed the faith for violations of the tawhid (unity) of God; early Christians developed orthodox formulations of doctrine in early creeds; Hebrews had a common center in the Torah. In the Hindu and Buddhist traditions, there's no administrative hub like the Roman Catholic papacy, or a shared sense of national history and collective destiny as in rabbinical Judaism. Instead, what you get is an integrated set of concepts that link together an

> **Pearls of Wisdom**
>
> May the stream of my life flow into the river of righteousness. Loose the bonds of sin that bind me. Let not the thread of my song be cut while I sing; and let not my work end before its fulfillment.
>
> —*Rigveda* 11.28

array of traditions known to Westerners as Hinduism, Jainism, Buddhism, Sikhism, and so on. Our beginning point for understanding these concepts, then, is the expressions of the divine you find in the *Vedas*.

God in the *Vedas*

In their original form, the *Vedas* were orally transmitted hymns used in the religious ceremonies and observances of the ancient people of the Indian subcontinent. Grouped into four collections (*Rigveda*, *Samaveda*, *Yajurveda*, and *Atharvaveda*), they offered instructions and incantations for various participants in Vedic rituals; eventually they were written down in Sanskrit and passed along to successive generations.

Vedic Gods

If you read the *Vedas* in the most literal way, the gods appear in a form that bears a faint resemblance to other polytheisms and mythologies of the ancient world, with a pantheon including gods such as Indra, Varuna, Agni, and Soma. Indra gets generous coverage in the *Rigveda* for battling evil powers and defending the ancient Hindus from various enemies. Soma, on the other hand, is a little harder for Westerners to grasp, because he was associated with vegetation and with an intoxicating beverage made from plants, but also with the moon, whose crescent served as cup for the drink that nourished other gods. Varuna occupied a place of high importance as the divinity most responsible for protecting the order of the universe, which included keeping the earth intact and maintaining the separation of day and night.

But where did the gods come from? On this question the *Vedas* express a good bit of agnosticism:

> Who really knows? Who will here proclaim it? Whence was it produced? Whence is this creation? The gods came afterwards, with the creation of this universe. Who then knows whence it has arisen?

> Whence this creation has arisen—perhaps it formed itself, or perhaps it did not—the One who looks down on it, in the highest heaven, only he knows or perhaps he does not know. (*Rigveda* 10.129.6–7)

So rather than espousing an eternal god that created the universe, the Vedic texts conceived of the gods and everything else as coming from a common source, which the *Rigveda* describes as "the One." The term isn't to be understood as a supreme being or creator god, but rather, a sort of impersonal essence to which all things owe their origin, and to which all things are connected. The idea of an ultimate essence above and beyond the gods makes Vedic religion unique, and that idea is an important one in later Hindu and Buddhist traditions as well. Meanwhile, the Vedic gods, called *devas*, inhabited a heavenly realm above the sky, though some divinities were associated with natural phenomena, and lived in the atmosphere or upon the earth.

Gods and People

The *Vedas*, like other ancient religious texts, are imprecise on questions of the gods' locations or their specific roles in the universe. Nevertheless, the gods were thought to wield power over meteorological events and to control the natural rhythms of the earth. Because they could divert the rain or increase the herd's fertility, or perhaps even assist men in battle, the gods were the objects of petitions and sacrifices. Brahmins supervised intense religious observances that included purification rituals, invocation of Agni, the god of fire who consumed sacrificial animals, and sonorous incantations of sacred tones (called mantras). Brahmins facilitated the ritual by consuming soma, the intoxicating drink associated with the gods, which was thought to contain the divine presence.

> **Divinations**
>
> The *Vedas* tell the story of Purusha, a mythical giant who was divided into sections to make up the various parts of the universe, including gods. To some observers, Purusha is a representation of the later Hindu concept of Brahman, or universal spirit.

If the devas approved the ritual performance, they responded with the blessings of peace and prosperity. Proper sacrifices to Indra, for example, helped one's armies to victory; sacrifices to Parjanya, on the other hand, might produce a much-needed rainfall. The actions of people and of the gods were deemed necessary to sustain and uphold the *rta*, or the underlying order of the universe. All the rhythms of nature, including the change of seasons, the phases of the moon, the cycle of reproduction, and so on, were controlled by rta. The all-encompassing nature of rta extended to human affairs as well. It was rta that enabled people to live in peace with one another and to fulfill their mutual obligations. Rta offered a philosophical basis for moral action, or unchanging standards of human conduct that when observed, resulted in an orderly, just society.

The Way to Heaven

Rta was not itself a god or a creation of the gods, but the organizing principle of the cosmos and human society, which the gods and people together must sustain or risk lapsing into disorder and chaos. For those who performed religious observances in accordance with rta, there lay the possibility of greater earthly and heavenly rewards. Early Vedic mythology told of Yama and Yami, twin brother and sister who founded the human race. One day, Yama died and discovered the way to heaven where he assumed dominion over the assemblage of the dead. If you were a follower of Vedic beliefs and practices, you hoped to follow Yama to the heavenly realm; that is, if you lived according to rta and your survivors performed special rituals on your behalf. If you failed to do so, you experienced a kind of extinction as you dissolved into the earth's soil.

What actually goes to heaven? Well, the ancient Vedic texts spoke of *atman*, described as a sort of life force within that's released during cremation and ascends toward heaven along with the smoke of the funeral pyre. In its earliest usage, atman had associations with the physical act of breathing. This airy substance gave Vedic people a visual representation of how human beings progress into the afterlife. However, in later usage, atman grew less and less concrete and assumed a metaphysical quality, something closer in meaning to the Western concept of the soul. This tendency to see atman not as physical breath but as metaphysical force is the work of later brahmins who pushed Vedic religion in the direction of Hinduism, principally in the writings of the *Upanishads*.

> **Word to the Wise**
>
> **Atman** is the essence of Brahman within the inner being of each individual.

God in the *Upanishads*

So far the outlines of Vedic religion bear some familiarity with other ancient polytheisms. With the *Upanishads*, however, you begin to see development and change away from the religions of the ancient Near East. The *Upanishads* are oral traditions that emerged between 800 and 200 B.C.E., many of which were later committed to writing. The earliest *Upanishads*—a term that translates roughly from Sanskrit into English as "sitting for instruction"—are collected in a sort of canon, which taken together is known as Vedanta, or conclusion of the *Vedas*. In Hindu tradition, the *Upanishads* represent the maturation of Vedic thinking about the ultimate reality.

If you read the *Upanishads* in their most literal sense, the point of departure for those who began the tradition recorded in these texts was the question of whether the rituals and sacrifices of the Vedic system actually produced any meaningful or lasting benefit. Of course, this touched on the broader issue of what happens to the human soul after death. The gurus of the *Upanishads* wrestled with a central tension in late Vedic religion between the promise of blissful immortality in a heavenly realm and the painful cycles of rebirth and re-death associated with karma. The brahmins taught the doctrine of karma as a way to speak of the consequences of good conduct. If people fulfill their social, political, and religious duties (such as obedience to rulers or performance of sacrifices), they are rewarded with desirable goods such as wealth, stature, or beauty. People are reborn into the good traits that they earned as a result of moral action in previous lives (or the opposite—bad traits they earned from immoral action). This begs the question, how do you break the cycle?

The Path Supreme

The gurus wrestled with the question of karma, rebirth, and final destiny, and came to believe that religious observances were insufficient means to attain the state of eternal bliss. The *Mundaka Upanishad* noted the inadequacy of religious observances:

> Imagining religious ritual and gifts of charity as the final good, the unwise see not the Path supreme. Indeed, they have in high heaven the reward of their pious actions; but thence they fall and come to earth or even down to lower regions.

So people who perform rituals and sacrifices do good, but not good enough to avoid the cycle of rebirth and re-death because they focus on lower, material things and not higher, spiritual things. This idea of getting beyond the material, external forms of religion animates the prophetic voices of Isaiah and Jeremiah, and of course echoes Jesus' claim to have come to restore an inner dimension to the Jewish halakhah: "Think not that I have come to abolish the law and the prophets; I have come not to abolish them but to fulfill them." (Matthew 5:17) The *Mundaka Upanishad* continues:

> But those who in purity and faith live in the solitude of the forest, who have wisdom and peace and long not for earthly possessions, those in radiant purity pass through the gates of the sun to the dwelling place supreme where the Spirit is in Eternity. (*Mundaka Upanishad* 1.2)

Early Hindus now had a way to imagine escaping the cycles of rebirth and achieve the soul's ultimate destiny. There's a Sanskrit word for this: *moksha*, or "liberation." Various traditions within Hinduism developed methods for achieving liberation, such as yoga, which we'll discuss later in the chapter.

Unity with the One

By recasting Vedic ritualism in terms of lower and higher objects, early Hindu gurus developed a sweeping reconsideration of the structure of all reality and the nature of existence. At the center of their field of vision in the *Upanishads* lies the One of the *Vedas*, now perceived as Brahman. Brahman is tough to describe, because no words adequately do the job. The *Upanishads* contain passages where Brahman is spoken of as Spirit Supreme, the Creator, the Eternal, and even "an ocean of pure consciousness boundless and infinite." Throughout, Brahman is described as the source of all, and the spiritual power that sustains existence. Therefore, it is better to think of Brahman not as a thing, but as the divine essence by which things have their "thing-ness."

The gurus of the *Upanishads* perceived atman-Brahman as the key to transcending the cycle of rebirth and reaching our ultimate destiny. How one gets there is kind of tricky, because normal human cognition can never comprehend the incomprehensible. The Hindu gurus taught the necessity of gaining mystical comprehension of the divine, not mere knowledge. The *Katha Upanishad* observes: "His form is not in the field of vision: No one sees him with mortal eyes. He is seen by a pure heart and by a mind and thoughts that are pure. Those who know him attain life immortal. When the five senses and the mind are still, and reason itself rests in silence, then begins the Path supreme."

CAUTION

Take Heed!

Hinduism creates many misunderstandings among Westerners because it rejects doctrinal standardization, and accepts a multiplicity of expressions of the One at the center of existence. No less an authority as the *Rigveda* gave expression to Hindu universalism: "They call him Indra, Mitra, Varuna, Agni, or the heavenly sunbird Garutmat. The seers call in many ways that which is One; they speak of Agni, Yama, Matarisvan." (*Rigveda* 1.164.46)

The Absolute Within

At the level of knowledge we can only reach through mystical perception, we discover we are Brahman. The *Upanishads* explain it this way: "This is the Spirit that is in my heart, smaller than a grain of rice, or a grain of barley, or a grain of mustard seed, or a grain of canary seed, or the kernel of a grain of canary seed. This is the Spirit that is in my heart, greater than the earth, greater than the sky, greater than heaven itself, greater than all these worlds." (*Chandogya Upanishad* 3.14)

The *Upanishads* reveal a numinous vision of a Spirit Supreme that everywhere surrounds us and permeates our inner being. In the story of Nachiketas, as told in the *Katha Upanishad*, we get a greater sense of this idea of divine immanence: "The light of the Atman, the Spirit, is invisible, concealed in all beings." Nachiketas learned that certain gifted people can perceive Brahman in the form of atman: "It is seen by the seers of the subtle, when their vision is keen and clear." Here you have to be extra careful, since this isn't vision in the way we normally understand it. Nachiketas discovered that "Atman is beyond sound and form, without touch and taste and perfume. It is eternal, unchanging, and without beginning or end; indeed above reasoning." This kind of spiritual vision can be developed only through rigorous disciplines of meditation and contemplation. But if you acquire it, this vision enables you to escape the wheel of rebirth and enter the eternal state of bliss. Thus Nachiketas discerned the Path Supreme: "When consciousness of the Atman manifests itself, man becomes free from the jaws of death." (*Katha Upanishad*)

Yoga: The Path to God Within

Nachiketas found that the key to escaping the cycle of death and rebirth is to become conscious of the divine within one's inner being. And yet this key isn't for everyone to use. The *Katha Upanishad* taught "The path is narrow and difficult to tread, narrow as the edge of a razor." Nachiketas, in fact, was given the choice between two paths, the path of joy and the path of pleasure. The path of pleasure promises physical delights, financial gain, and social honor, but those who seek such things are fooled into thinking that this world is the only world, or that it's the best of all worlds. St. Augustine spoke of the same problem when he realized he "was in love with beauty of a lower order and it was dragging me down." (Augustine's *Confessions* 4.13)

The path of joy, the Path Supreme, requires you to take your eyes off the world's pleasures and rewards, and seek truth and wisdom. The best way to do this is to follow the techniques of yoga. The *Upanishads* present yoga as a way to realize the God within: "By the Yoga of meditation and contemplation the wise saw the power of God, hidden in his own creation." (*Svetasvatara Upanishad*) A series of later texts, the *Yoga Sutras* attributed to the Hindu guru Patanjali, offered wisdom on proper yoga technique, identifying various stages of the spiritual progression that lead to ultimate union with the One:

- Asana: moral restraint, proper physical posture

- Pranayama: regulation of breathing

- Pratyahara: restriction of sense perception

- Dharana: complete commitment of the mind

- Dhyana: concentration on spiritual truths

- Samadhi: awareness of union with the divine

These stages enable the seeker to attain the vision spoken of in the *Maitri Upanishad:* "When through self, by the suppressing of the mind, one sees the brilliant Self which is more subtle than the subtle, then having seen the Self through one's self, one becomes selfless. Because of being selfless, he is to be regarded as incalculable, without origin—the mark of liberation." (6.20) The last state produces a trancelike condition where reason and consciousness ceases and direct awareness of the ultimate source of being is attained. You can hasten the onset of these altered states of consciousness by chanting mantras or words that are thought to generate spiritual power, like the sacred om (or aum) with all its registers of meaning in Hindu theology. The power of spiritual tones has been accepted from the Vedic period to the present day, including the *Mundaka Upanishad:* "The bow is the sacred om, and the arrow is our own soul. Brahman is the mark of the arrow, the aim of the soul." (2.2)

Karma and the Variety of Human Destinies

Hindu spiritual teachings derived in part from Hindu folkways, including the practice of sorting people into various classes (called *varna*), which are thought to be social locations people earned by virtue of their actions in earlier lives. That's *karma* at work. The upper varna, such as priests and rulers, inherited a superior amount of good karma from past lives and therefore possessed greater spiritual power. Lower varna, such as artisans and workers, inherited a lesser amount of good karma and therefore possessed lesser spiritual power. If that seems unfair, then you're missing the point that karma holds people accountable for their actions, whether for good or ill, the consequences of which are repaid as the soul departs one life and enters another.

In a series of texts known as the *Dharmashastra*, or *Treaties on Dharma*, early Hindu gurus explained the concept of karma and the essential connection between the spiritual economy of good and evil and the social arrangements of the varna system. Whichever caste you were born into (there were roughly 2,000 different castes in the varna system), you acquired certain duties particular to that caste, which is known as *dharma*. The *Treatises* explained that you can't move up in the caste system in this life; you must perform the dharma for the caste you were born into in order to obtain good karma for the next life and possibly reappear in a higher caste. The implication is that certain people begin life with spiritual advantages that enable them to acquire good karma for the succession of lives to follow, or final liberation from the cycle of rebirth (moksha). In time, many reformers will question this belief, and we'll meet some of them in the next three chapters.

> **Word to the Wise**
>
> **Karma** is the law of cause and effect in Hinduism and Buddhism, which shapes the course of one's personal destiny. **Dharma** means "law" or "duty," and takes slightly different meanings in Hindu and Buddhist traditions. In Hinduism it refers to the obligations of one's caste, or perhaps "way of life," while in Buddhism it refers to the Buddha's teachings, which lead to enlightenment.

The Least You Need to Know

◆ Hinduism is not a religion, but an array of spiritual traditions that are connected by language, geography, and history.

◆ Hinduism and Buddhism are connected by virtue of shared concepts that have their beginnings in ancient Vedic religion of the Indus-Ganges river plains.

◆ The *Upanishads* speculated about the nature of existence and developed the Vedic concept of Brahman, which lies at the heart of the Hindu idea of God.

◆ Brahman is the ultimate source of being and Supreme Spirit of the universe, and atman is the essence of Brahman within one's inner being.

◆ Early Hindus taught that release from reincarnation comes about through a realization of God in one's inner being, which is gained through rigorous practices of yoga.

◆ Early Hindu gurus taught that one's actions produce good or ill effects in the next life through the operation of karma.

Chapter 22

God in Hindu Tradition

In This Chapter

- Multiple paths to salvation
- Classical Hindu gods such as Brahma, Vishnu, and Shiva
- Variations on a theme: Jainism, Buddhism, and Sikhism
- What's Krishna?
- Organizing Hindu belief
- Three hundred thirty million gods, and all are One

Hindus speak of karma and moksha, or liberation from the wheel of rebirth (the endless cycle of birth, life, death, and rebirth). They also speak of Brahman and gaining awareness of the divine element within through Samadhi, the method taught in the *Yoga Sutras*. But there's a much broader tradition of Hindu thought about God that includes belief in a kind of trinity, with Brahma (not to be confused with Brahman, the unfathomable One), Vishnu, and Shiva as members of a united godhead, and belief in various incarnations of Vishnu and Shiva. Shrines to dozens of Hindu gods, goddesses, and other spiritual beings are scattered throughout India and neighboring lands. This creates some difficulty for newcomers to Hinduism: if Brahman is the One at the center of all reality, then why do Hindus perceive so many different gods?

You'll find the answer isn't a simple one. Hinduism isn't really a religion so much as a variety of related spiritual traditions that accept the *Vedas* and the *Upanishads*, even as they disagree on questions of interpretation and emphasis. Over the centuries, Hindus came to accept more than one path to God. A good example of this sentiment comes from the *Bhagavad Gita*, which we'll explore in this chapter: "In any way that men love me, in that same way they find my love: for many are the paths of men, but they all in the end come to me." (4.11) Here you'll discover a variety of ways Hindu teachers have adapted this sentiment to changing times and circumstances.

God in the *Gita:* More Than One Path

The precise method for obtaining liberation vexed early Hindus. The *Upanishads* taught people to seek release from the wheel of rebirth through spiritual disciplines of meditation and contemplation, which encouraged many followers to abandon social obligations and worldly pursuits in favor of the spiritual life. Buddhists added a new wrinkle by teaching that release could be obtained only by extinguishing desires that produce stress and suffering. Again, such teachings tended to draw people away from ordinary, everyday matters. These trends toward spiritual pursuits led Hindus to question the value of moral action in the home, at the marketplace, and anywhere else that life must be lived.

Such thinking is behind one of the major texts of Hinduism, the *Bhagavad Gita*, which appeared sometime between the fourth and second centuries B.C.E. It takes the form of a dialogue between Arjuna, a great warrior, and his chariot driver, who claims to be, among other things, the Hindu god Krishna. The conversation begins when Arjuna, poised for battle, gazes on the enemy and sees among them people he knows and respects. Arjuna must kill them to fulfill his obligations as a member of the warrior caste, and yet his conscience won't permit it. Thus paralyzed, he turns to his charioteer for advice. In Krishna's response, Arjuna learns how to gain liberation by way of performing the duties of caste. In the process, Krishna teaches Arjuna—and generations of Hindus to follow—that devotion to a personal god is a viable path to release from samsara, the endless cycle of birth, life, death, and rebirth.

Karma Yoga: Way of Works

The *Gita* teaches Hindus that it is entirely possible to obtain release from samsara without having to sell your possessions and live in a trancelike state. Krishna tells Arjuna that he cannot avoid life, "for not even for a moment can a man be without action." (3.5) So Krishna reveals that it's possible to achieve salvation through karma yoga, or consecrated action. There's a right way and a wrong way to go about one's duties, and Krishna explains that the right way requires a renunciation of selfish desires and impure motives. Work for the good of the whole, not oneself. "He whose undertakings are free from anxious desire and fanciful thought, whose work is made pure in the fire of wisdom: He is called wise by those who see." Krishna concludes, "He has attained liberation: He is free from all bonds, his mind has found peace in wisdom, and his work is a holy sacrifice." (4.19, 23)

Dhyana Yoga: Way of Meditation

Krishna's path of consecrated action, which ordinary Hindus speak of as dharma, didn't intend to replace the vision of the *Upanishads* for a higher path of meditation and contemplation. It simply provided an alternative for those unable to follow the narrow path of mystical union. So Krishna affirms previous revelation:

> When the sage of silence closes the doors of his soul and, resting his inner gaze between the eyebrows, keeps peaceful and even the ebbing and flowing of breath; and with life and mind and reason in harmony, and with desire and fear and wrath gone, keeps silent his soul before final freedom, he in truth has attained final freedom. (*Bhagavad Gita* 5.27–28)

This path, known in the Hindu tradition as dhyana yoga, leads to a consciousness of the divine within. Of course, this requires vision of a supernatural variety, not unlike the Sufi idea of an "eye of the heart," as Krishna informs Arjuna: "Thou never canst see me with these thy mortal eyes: I will give thee divine sight. Behold my wonder and glory." (11.8)

Jnana Yoga: Way of Knowledge

Liberation is also possible for those who undertake rigorous study under the tutelage of Hindu sages. Krishna tells Arjuna that knowledge leads to understanding that one's finite self isn't one's true self, which in turn provides the necessary preparation for the sort of renunciation that enables the seeker to obtain liberation from the cycle of birth, death, and rebirth. "He who knows my birth as God and who knows my sacrifice, when he leaves his mortal body, goes no more from death to death, for he in truth comes to me." (4.9)

Bhakti Yoga: Way of Devotion

And toward the end of Arjuna's dialogue with Krishna, a fourth path becomes clear, the path of devotion to God. The *Gita* moves in this direction when Arjuna responds to seeing Krishna as the infinite, imperishable, omnipotent, transcendent, and immanent God of the universe. Arjuna surrenders himself to God and pledges to honor him: "My doubts are no more, my faith is firm; and now I can say, 'Thy will be done.'" (18.73) Hindus speak of this fourth path as bhakti yoga, or the path of love for God. With the appearance of the *Gita*, Hinduism reconnected with the concept of God in the Vedic tradition and gave sanction to religious devotion. The result? Hundreds of millions of Hindus today pursue the path to God that leads through worship and service to the divine in its innumerable manifestations.

Dimensions of Divinity

When Krishna revealed his true form to Arjuna, the warrior "saw in that radiance the whole universe in its variety, standing in a vast unity in the body of the God of gods." (*Bhagavad Gita* 11.12) He perceived a multitude of deities, many of which were known to the Vedic brahmins of the primitive Indus-Ganges civilizations. As you can imagine, the *Gita* connected with and intensified metaphysical speculation about Krishna's relationship with other gods in the Vedic pantheon, given that it also embraced the idea of Brahman established in the *Upanishads*. Some scholars of Hinduism, and many Hindus themselves, speak of the trimurti, which is Sanskrit for three forms and signifies an approach to harmonizing the various threads of Hindu thought regarding the nature and substance of the Absolute.

Trimurti

The doctrine of trimurti has been read into many Sanskrit religious texts. It appears as early as the work of the great Indian poet Kalidasa, particularly his *Kumarasambhava* from the fifth century C.E. The basic idea here is that God is one, Brahman, and assumes three different forms, identified in the *Vedas* as Brahma (not to be confused with Brahman), Vishnu, and Shiva. Remember, Brahman is a kind of essence, or ultimate source of being, which is completely unfathomable. Hindu mythologists perceived the god Brahma as Creator of the universe in all its material and spiritual aspects. In the Vedic tradition, Vishnu had lesser status among the gods, but gained stature over time and in the *Puranas*, a collection of Hindu mythology, Vishnu came to be perceived as the sustainer of the universe. Shiva, on the other hand, assumed a number of qualities, mostly associated with fertility and regeneration. Hindus sometimes worship Shiva in the form of a *linga*, or phallic symbol, which speaks to this linkage between Shiva and the generative powers of nature. But traditionally, Shiva was accorded some power in the cosmic cycles of creation and destruction, as the divine agent that brings about the final state of devastation in preparation for the world's rebirth.

Hindus permit the worship of a personal deity such as Ganesha, son of the gods Shiva and Parvati, which results in physical depictions of the divine.

(Courtesy of the Metropolitan Museum of Art)

Bhakti Traditions

Hundreds of millions of Hindus follow the bhakti path of religious devotion to a personal deity. There are lots of choices, but Hindus are pulled in the direction of two larger bhakti traditions, Vaishnava and Saiva-siddhanta, which perceive one or another of the trimurti as the ultimate supreme God of the universe. Adherents in the Vaishnava tradition select Vishnu or one of Vishnu's 10 established *avatars* as a personal deity, who becomes the object of offerings, prayers, meditation, pilgrimage, and other acts of devotion. Followers of the Saiva-siddhanta tradition worship Shiva or one of the many spiritual beings associated with Shiva, like Kali (Shiva's consort) or Ganesha (Shiva's son by another consort, Parvati).

Hindus speak of complete submission to the chosen deity and expect their discipline of bhakti yoga to provide the kind of release from samsara that is Hinduism's ultimate goal. You might find the avatars of Vishnu quite interesting; the list includes Krishna of the *Bhagavad Gita*, but also Matsya, a fish in Hindu mythology that saves the mortal man, Manu, from a world-destroying flood. It also includes Siddhartha Gautama, the guru who founded the Buddhist religion, and Kalki, an avatar who will come one day to destroy the wicked rulers of the earth and restore the brahmins to power. In Vishnu's avatars you can detect elements of other religions, whether it's the Hebrew story of Noah's Ark, or Shi'ite Muslim expectations of a Mahdi who will eventually appear to establish righteousness.

> **Word to the Wise**
>
> **Avatar** is an embodiment of the divine, particularly in Hindu Vaishnava traditions, some of which perceive incarnations of Vishnu in 10 different people or creatures.

Saguna and Nirguna Brahman

The bhakti traditions raise interesting questions about the relationship between the tangible deities of the *Puranas* on one hand, and the formless deities of the *Upanishads* on the other. Hindu teachers make the distinction between *saguna* and *nirguna* Brahman as a way to talk about the connections between the tangible versus formless visions. Saguna Brahman has particular dimensions or forms or attributes. That's God in an embodied form that adherents can connect with in a rather direct and personal manner. Nirguna Brahman has no form or attributes and is all-embracing. The concepts of saguna and nirguna demonstrate a pattern of thought evident in most religions, that is, declaring God to be indescribable and immeasurable and then proceeding with various descriptions and measures to satisfy our human need for a knowable God. Think of the concepts of saguna and nirguna as ways to account for a boundless and infinite divine who seeks to be known to otherwise bounded and finite human minds. And besides, most religions teach that to know God is good, but to experience God is better; here you have a way to account for a God who can be known as saguna Brahman, but must be experienced as nirguna Brahman.

One, Few, and Many

The question Westerners often ask regarding Hinduism is, do Hindus worship many gods, one god, or everything as god? It's important to recognize this as a Western question, because it imposes a kind of precision onto conversations about God that Hindu traditions have long resisted. After all, no less an authority than Mahatma Gandhi remarked that "God is One," and then went on to say, as quoted in Roger Eastman's book *Ways of Religion* (Oxford University Press, 1999), that "he is unfathomable, unknowable, and unknown to the vast majority of mankind." One strand of Hindu thought, Advaita Vedanta, developed a metaphysical scheme that Western observers might describe as monistic and pantheist, because it describes the physical world as maya, or illusion. Only a few can remove the veil of maya through rigorous mental discipline, and perceive the true reality of spiritual unity in the One. Most Hindus, however, adhere to the bhakti traditions, such as Vaishnava and Saiva-siddhanta, which perceive an ultimate, Supreme Being, and hold other deities in a lesser or subordinate status.

> **CAUTION**
>
> **Take Heed!**
>
> When you hear Hindus speak of innumerable gods, don't be mistaken. The *Mahabharata* mentions 33,333 gods, and the *Puranas* reveal 330 million divinities. But these are ways of expressing the Hindu belief that all gods are one and completely unfathomable.

The Cosmic Cycle

If Hindus see themselves as having an individual destiny bound up in karma, samsara, and moksha, they also believe the human race has a collective destiny, bound up in cosmic cycles of creation, development, eventual destruction, and rebirth. The micro-level idea of reincarnation thus has a corresponding macro-level circular pattern of history. Today, we find ourselves in a *yuga*, or era, characterized by decay and destruction. People are inattentive to sacred scripture, unhappy in their caste situations, and careless in their bhakti devotions. As a result, they live shorter lives and suffer through epidemics, wars, and apocalyptic natural disasters.

This is how Rani Moorthy, a Hindu adherent, made sense of the December 2004 South Asian tsunami, which killed over 200,000 people. In a comment noted in the BBC News, Moorthy said "we are born in an age of destruction, known as Kali Yuga, an age that lasts for perhaps 1,000 years." Kali Yuga follows a succession of eras characterized by freedom from suffering and proper performance of the dharma. Moorthy further reasoned, "We must go through a series of setbacks, obstacles, suffering, e.g. AIDS, and a propensity for natural disasters as nature shows its malevolent side." But this destructive pattern is necessary, Moorthy explained, since "mankind goes through this to be renewed." In other words, there's at least the promise of an eventual end of Kali Yuga in some climatic spasm of devastation, making way for the eventual reconstitution of the world into better and more fruitful conditions.

Hindu Metaphysics

In earlier chapters we encountered Jewish, Christian, and Muslim thinkers who struggled to express in words and concepts the elusive nature of ultimate reality, and in this respect Hinduism is no different. Clearly, metaphysics is a timeless pursuit, spanning cultural, linguistic, and racial boundaries and embracing all manner of religious visions. To get a flavor of the Hindu contribution to metaphysical speculation, we'll sample from the rich tradition of interpreting Hindu sacred literature.

Sankhya

The tradition of Sankhya formed in response to early *Upanishads*, essentially wrestling with the question of the relationship between matter (*prakriti*) and spirit (*purusha*). Sankhya developed a similar vision to what Christians would later know as Gnosticism, perceiving spirit as imprisoned in matter. By emphasizing the separation of matter and spirit, teachers of the Sankhya tradition were dualistic in their interpretation of the *Upanishads*, in contrast to the teachers of Advaita Vedanta. Sankhya further taught that people are essentially spirit beings who endure the attachment of matter to themselves like barnacles on the hull of a ship. If you find yourself in this situation, you can liberate your spirit from matter by working from personal experience toward greater levels of self-awareness and enlightenment.

Shankara

During the eighth century, a boy named Shankara came of age in a small village in Kerala in southern India, within a family of devout Shiva worshippers. He left home to pursue wisdom, and eventually came to doubt the prevailing sentiment, perhaps owing to the *Bhagavad Gita*, that religious devotion or performance of one's caste duties could lead to salvation. He began to advocate a purification of the faith and a restoration of the *Upanishads* vision of the unity of all reality. His school of thought, known as Advaita Vedanta, perceived reality as a unity, and Brahman-atman as the essence of that single reality. Advaita Vedanta developed a monistic vision because it rejected the separation of reality into dual spheres of matter and spirit. Since Shankara was a purist, he taught that release from the wheel of rebirth could be obtained only through jnana yoga (the way of knowledge), which succeeded only when the yogi recognized the illusory (maya) nature of the physical world.

> **Divinations**
>
> Among the more important concepts in the Hindu, Buddhist, and Jain traditions is *maya*, which is Sanskrit for "wizardry" or "illusion." Advaita Hindus believe that we've been tricked into believing that this world is actually real, when the only reality is Brahman-atman. We permit this illusion through ignorance, or *ajnana*, and overcome it through the acquisition of divine knowledge.

Ramanuja

Shankara's Advaita Vedanta philosophy influenced the spiritual leadership of Hinduism in India for generations, until the great Ramanuja (c. 1017–1137) reclaimed the tradition of worship of the great deities. Ramanuja received training in the Shankara school of philosophy but soon quarreled with his teachers over the question of whether the worship of personal deities led to release from samsara. Why, he wondered, should the Vedanta instructors preclude bhakti yoga when the sacred texts encouraged it, and millions of Hindus made it an important part of their everyday lives? And then Ramanuja received a vision of Vishnu and his consort Lakshmi, which left him a committed Vaishnavite. His unique contribution entailed wedding the metaphysical speculation of Advaita Vendanta with the impulses of folk religious practice. In the end, he offered Hindus a philosophical account of the religious teachings of the *Vedas*, blending bhakti and jnana yoga to show how individuals can perceive their unity with Brahman through devotion to Vishnu.

Challenges to Tradition

Hindu metaphysicians such as Shankara and Ramanuja wrestled with several major challenges to Vedic religion and the classic Hindu scriptures that extended the Vedic tradition. The classical Vedanta schools of Hindu thought were flexible and inclusive, but not enough to contain the centripetal forces that eventually spun off entirely new faiths, such as Jainism and Buddhism.

Jainism

The metaphysical teachings of the early Hindu gurus triggered a response by some who preferred to focus not on the gods, but on proper living to secure release from rebirth. The founder of Jainism, Nataputta Vardhamana (599–527 B.C.E.), carried the disciplines of renunciation, meditation, and contemplation to an extreme, even to the point of going naked rather than indulge himself with a monk's robe. His teachings and those of his followers outlined a rather unique point of view that perceived two principles, *jiva* and ajiva, within each and every person or thing in the universe (including plants and animals). Jiva is pure spirit, and ajiva is everything else, namely matter in its spatial and temporal aspects. Jiva is bound within ajiva, and the wheel of rebirth keeps your jiva from escaping into the infinite realm of peace. Karma comes into play here; when you fulfill your obligations with the proper intention, good karma filters into your life, "sticks" to your jiva, and lifts it to a higher plane upon rebirth. But the opposite is possible, too. When you ignore your duties or hurt other living things, bad karma drags your jiva down to a lower plane when it's reincarnated in the next life. Moksha is possible only for those who completely withdraw from earthly pursuits, thereby closing the inner door to karma and its potentially harmful effects. This gave rise to Jainism's chief ethical principle, *ahimsa*, or complete nonviolence. Jains respect life in its wide variety of forms, which makes them vegetarian by design.

> **Word to the Wise**
>
> **Jiva** is a word used in Jainism to describe the particular spirit of an individual, which loosely parallels the concept of atman in Hinduism and Buddhism.

Buddhism

Today's Buddhism traces its roots to another attempt to reform Hinduism in the sixth century B.C.E. Siddhartha Gautama (563–483 B.C.E.) grew up in a town in what is now

Nepal, on the northern border of India. He was raised in traditional brahmin style, and one day the sight of human suffering prompted him to seek release from samsara. Eventually, he became disappointed in the various spiritual disciplines practiced in his day, particularly the extreme asceticism common to Hinduism and Jainism. He discovered that suffering was the result of various human desires that could and must be extinguished in order for the individual to gain escape from rebirth. In his various teachings, Siddhartha came to doubt the Hindu concept of the eternal soul and rejected the idea that karma builds up through successive lives. And his vision of release into Nirvana bore little, if any, connection to the gods spoken of in the *Vedas*. Though Hindus worked to incorporate Siddhartha's teachings into the Vedanta tradition, Buddhism soon took on the form of a distinct religion. (You'll learn much more about the Buddha and the Buddhist tradition in Chapters 23 and 24.)

Sikhism

By tradition, Hindus perceive many paths to god, and accept all gods as modes, aspects, or manifestations of the One. One guru, Nanak (1469–1539 C.E.), went another direction and became the founder of Sikhism. As a child in Lahore, he received a Muslim education and learned Arabic before the age of 30, when he received a divine visitation telling him "there is neither Hindu nor Muslim, so whose path shall I choose?" Nanak went on to compose the sacred text of Sikhism, the *Adi Granth*, and develop a religious vision that was neither Hindu nor Muslim, but which resonated with both traditions. Nanak perceived God in ways that closely paralleled Muhammad's vision of Allah, as an omnipotent, eternal, transcendent Supreme Being and governor of the universe. He nevertheless affirmed the Hindu concepts of karma, samsara, and moksha, teaching that release from the wheel of rebirth could be obtained only through a Sufi-like mystical union with the divine. Sikhs today do not perform the Five Pillars of Islam or the physical exercises of Hindu yoga. They attend religious observances in temples, pray and recite the Adi Granth, and endeavor to demonstrate their love for God through acts of charity and devotion.

> **Pearls of Wisdom**
>
> Even as a tree has many branches and leaves, so is there one true and perfect Religion, but it becomes many as it passes through the human medium.
>
> —Mahatma Gandhi (1869–1948)

Hinduism Today

As Hinduism approached the modern age, it struggled with threats to its vitality from Mogul and British domination, assimilation to Western values, outbreaks of rebellion against the caste system, and the rise of militant secular nationalism in India. And yet Hinduism survived these threats and is thriving. Recent heroes such as Ramakrishna Paramahamsa, Mahatma Gandhi, and Rabindranath Tagore encouraged Hindus to rediscover the energies of the bhakti and jnana yoga traditions, while Swami Vivekananda and Maharishi Mahesh Yogi brought Hinduism to the West and secured millions of new devotees. As a matter of fact, the West seems to move in the direction of traditional Hindu teachings with each passing year, drifting toward the sort of pluralist vision summed up in Swami Vivekananda's speech before the World's Parliament of Religion in 1893: "But in the heart of everything the same truth reigns; the Lord has declared to the Hindu in his incarnation as Krishna, 'I am in every religion as the thread through a string of pearls. And wherever thou seest extraordinary holiness and extraordinary power raising and purifying humanity, know ye that I am there.'"

The Least You Need to Know

- Classical Hindu teaching envisioned more than one way to God.

- The Hindu ways to God include proper attendance to duty, oneness with the Absolute through contemplation, and religious devotion to a personal deity.

- Most Hindus follow the way of devotion (bhakti) by choosing a divinity to worship, usually associated with either Vishnu or Shiva.

- An avatar is an incarnation of God, normally applied to the many avatars of Vishnu.

- The major Hindu philosophers wrestled with the question of whether bhakti could provide release from the wheel of rebirth.

- Today, Hindus perceive the gods of all the world's religions to be essentially different versions of the One.

Chapter 23

God in Buddhist Thought and Practice

In This Chapter

◆ How the Buddha reached nirvana

◆ The Four Noble Truths about suffering and desire

◆ Attaining enlightenment through the Eightfold Path

◆ Do Buddhists believe in God?

◆ Buddha's teachings: dharma for beginners

◆ What Buddha meant when he said we have no soul

In a recent issue of *Time Magazine*, the editors settled on a list of 100 of the world's most influential people. The list is light on religious leaders from the major faiths, though a few managed to make it, including moderate Iraqi Shi'ia cleric Grand Ayatullah Sayyid Ali Husaini Sistani, influential Roman Catholic prelate Joseph Cardinal Ratzinger—now Pope Benedict XVI—and Evangelical Christian publishing phenom Rick Warren. And there, tucked in among the heroes and icons, you'll find the Dalai Lama, spiritual leader of Tibetan Buddhism and the winner of the

1989 Nobel Peace Prize. Few religious leaders have been consistently in the public eye over the last quarter century, and the Dalai Lama is one of them.

Many Americans know that the Dalai Lama advocates peaceful solutions to China's invasion and occupation of Tibet. But fewer understand what the Nobel Committee meant when it observed that he "developed his philosophy of peace from a great reverence for all things living and upon the concept of universal responsibility embracing all mankind as well as nature." And fewer still know anything about the central concepts of Buddhism that provide the architecture for this philosophy of peace. In this chapter, we'll learn about *duhkha*, *tanha*, and nirvana, and of course we'll discuss some differences between Hindus and Buddhists on the subjects of karma, reincarnation, and the nature of the human soul. As the Buddha himself might have said, prepare to be enlightened.

In the Beginning

Buddhism diverged from Hinduism in the sixth or fifth century B.C.E., but unlike schisms in other faiths, Buddhism's appearance had little to do with doctrinal issues or metaphysical questions. Its basic point of departure was the problem of human suffering, and the related matter of what could be done about it. At the outset, Buddhism downplayed, or even ignored, issues that took center stage in other religions, such as the manner and timing of the universe's creation, the origin and nature of the gods, and the boundaries between the material and spiritual worlds. The reason why suffering and its remedies stand in the middle of Buddhism's field of vision owes to the remarkable life of its founder, Siddhartha Gautama.

The Charmed Life of Siddhartha Gautama

Siddhartha Gautama (c. 563–483 B.C.E.) shares a few things in common with Jesus and Socrates; all three became famous for their wisdom, and yet none of them left behind any written texts. Therefore, much of what we know about the man who became the Buddha comes from his discourses (called *sutras*) that were orally transmitted and then written down in the centuries after his death, but also from various accounts of his life (and former lives) written by devoted followers. Separating the "real" Buddha from the Buddha as depicted in later Buddhist writings isn't easy to do, but there are a number of well-established points about his life that are important to understand in order to make sense of the tradition that venerates his life and work.

As a young man, Siddhartha enjoyed all the advantages that came along with privileged birth. He inherited his father's status as member of the ruling caste, the Kshatriyas (warrior kings), and astrologers foretold that he would either become the ruler of all India, or the spiritual savior of his people. His father wanted to protect him from the sort of suffering he was sure to endure as savior, so he took pains to insulate him from the cruel miseries of life outside the palace walls. He enjoyed the richest food, the finest clothing, and the grandest residences money could buy. Legend has it that his father made 40,000 con-

> **Divinations** _____
>
> Tales of the Buddha's former lives fill out the Buddhist idea of reincarnation. At one point he was Rupyavati, a woman who offered food to a starving woman and child by cutting off and donating her own breasts. For this act she had her breasts restored by Indra, chief of the Vedic gods, and for not seeking divine status through the act of charity she became a Buddha.

cubines available to him as well. He married a fabulously beautiful princess named Yasodhara who soon bore a son named Rahula. Soon, however, Siddhartha's curiosity overwhelmed him and he could tolerate his splendid isolation from the world no longer.

Witness to Suffering

On several outings from his palace, Siddhartha saw some things that shook him to the core. He came face to face with realities that he never dreamed existed, such as a frail old man leaning on a cane, or on a later trip, a gravely ill man lying on the road. To top it off, he and his driver made the gruesome discovery of a human corpse. Siddhartha realized that despite all efforts of his father to shield him from suffering and death, these were real facts of existence that nobody could deny. It was at this point that Siddhartha encountered the last of his Four Passing Sights, a wandering ascetic. This sight gave him the idea to embark on a personal quest to discover the path to freedom from pain, suffering, and death. At the age of 29, he left his sumptuous home and the attachments of family to live the spiritual life.

Two Unfruitful Paths

At the start of his journey, Siddhartha met several brahmin yogis, including Arada Kalama and Udraka Ramaputra, who drew his attention to higher things and taught him the difficult techniques of raja yoga, but he failed to find what he was looking for in the company of the gurus. So he turned to asceticism, thinking that release required a denial of one's physical urges. He and five others adopted a severe regimen of near starvation, marathon meditation sessions, and control of bodily impulses; during one stretch Siddhartha lived on six grains of rice a day, which nearly killed him. A young girl from a local village named Sujata nursed him back to health and when he recovered, he concluded that neither the brahmin yogis nor the ascetics got him sufficiently close to the ultimate goal of release from suffering and death.

An Awakening

What happened next shaped the way the Absolute has been perceived by humanity ever since; in fact, it's fair to say that the ensuring chapter in Siddhartha's life pushed the centuries-long conversation about God in an entirely new direction. One day, he found himself meditating under a ficus tree (or bo tree, from *bodhi*, meaning "enlightenment") next to the Ganges River in northeast India, near the present-day city of Patna. He determined never to leave until he discovered the way to defeat pain, suffering, and death: "I will not rise from this posture as long as my mind is not freed from the cankers without any remainder." (from the eighteenth-century Pali biography of Buddha, *Sangityavamsa*). Buddhists today call this location the Immovable Spot. Despite the wicked labors of Mara, a spirit perceived by Buddhists as a force behind ignorance and death, Siddhartha persevered, and "attained the undefiled supreme security from bondage, nirvana" (from an ancient text that records the Buddha's sayings, the *Ariyapariyesana Sutta*). His achievement of this state triggered cosmological events from the shaking of the earth to the flowering of every tree in the universe.

> **Take Heed!**
>
> Buddhists speak of nothingness and emptiness, which tempts Westerners to assume that Buddhists teach a doctrine of self-annihilation or extermination. On the contrary, the Buddha taught that the idea of an independent, supreme, eternal soul is a misunderstanding, and what must be extinguished is the ignorance and craving that puts this idea into our heads.

Reaching Nirvana

So, what happened? Well, it's hard to say, because Siddhartha spoke of his experience in terms familiar to us from our discussion of Jewish, Christian, and Islamic mysticism: "This *dharma* [I have] attained is profound, hard to see, and hard to understand, peaceful and sublime, unattainable by mere reasoning, subtle, to be experienced by the wise." But nirvana isn't like the Christian heaven, the Muslim al-akhirah (afterlife), or even the Hindu concept of moksha. The word comes from Sanskrit and Pali verbs for "blowing out." Gaining nirvana doesn't mean a total evaporation of the self into a state of nothingness, but an extinguishing of the inner desires, emotions, and feelings that bring about our attachment to the world. Siddhartha defined the release from our attachments as "the stilling of all formations, the relinquishing of all attachments, the destruction of craving, dispassion, cessation, nirvana" (from the *Ariyapariyesana Sutta*). In other words, when we free ourselves from the mental chains that bind us to the world, we achieve release from bondage to the cycle of birth, death, and rebirth.

Siddhartha as the Buddha

Having discovered the way to attain release from suffering and repeated cycles of birth and death, Siddhartha became the Buddha, Sanskrit for "Enlightened One." He remained in a state of nirvana for some 49 days before he was approached by Brahma Sahampati, the Hindu creator deity, with the idea of spreading the good news: "The world will be lost, the world will perish, since the mind of the *Tathagata* ("one who has thus gone"), accomplished and fully enlightened, inclines to inaction rather than to teaching the dharma" (from the *Ariyapariyesana Sutta*). The Buddha had acquired omniscience, and with his new godlike vision he observed a world full of sufferers, all of whom couldn't perceive the correct path because of the dust in their eyes. The Buddha welled up with compassion for these lost millions and resolved to show them the path to enlightenment. And that's how the Buddha gave rise to Buddhism.

Four Noble Truths

At the core of Buddhist teachings about the path to nirvana lies a set of interrelated dictums that passed into the Buddhist tradition as the Four Noble Truths, which the Buddha himself discovered under the bo tree. These truths form the kernel of the Buddha's message as recorded in the numerous sutras that contain his discourses, and they serve as the conceptual framework for much of Buddhist thought and practice from the end of the Buddha's life to the present day.

All Life Entails Suffering

The sutras explain that Buddha left his bo tree and preached his first sermon to his former ascetic compatriots in present-day Varanasi, famous as the home of Shiva in the Hindu bhakti tradition of Saiva-siddhanta. The first point of his sermon stressed the ubiquity of human suffering, or *duhkha*. He discerned that at every moment and every spot on the landscape, human beings are subject to anxiety, fear, pain, and grief; they feel deep within a gnawing sense of brokenness. Duhkha entails physical pain and death, but also despair and alienation, a sense of being out of sync with the deeper rhythms of the universe.

The Cause of Suffering Is Desire

The Buddha taught that it isn't sufficient to merely recognize that humans suffer—one must awaken to the ultimate source and true cause of suffering. On this subject he didn't resort to usual explanations such as disharmony among the gods or angry spirits in the landscape. Nor did he accept the traditional view that suffering came about as a result of human disobedience or unfaithfulness to God. Instead, he suggested *tanha* as the source. Tanha roughly translates from the Sanskrit as "desire," more specifically the desires that orient our being toward self-satisfaction and self-gratification. The trouble, then, lies in a mistaken view of the ego, as an autonomous, supreme, and indestructible self. Again, many religions would concur that designating oneself as the ultimate, eternal, and absolute entity of the universe will get you into trouble eventually.

Removing Desire Removes Suffering

Now for the remedy. The Buddha didn't prescribe confession and penance, sacrificial offerings to the gods, or an arduous pilgrimage. Instead, he taught that just as the source of your trouble lies within you, the remedy lies within you as well. Simply eliminate tanha, since escape to nirvana lies in "stilling of all formations, the relinquishing of all attachments, [and] the destruction of craving." One must become aware that the illusion of our inner being as an independent, self-contained, and absolute self keeps us from achieving eternal bliss. Buddhists speak of this as a "renunciation," meaning an extermination of all the illusions that result in ignorance of one's true nature and position within the universe.

Follow the Eightfold Path to Remove Desire

Sound easy? Perhaps, but the Buddha thought that only a few are ready for action, because they have only a little bit of dust in their eyes. The far greater number have their vision blocked with huge clods of dirt, and to rid themselves of ego-bloating desires requires some spiritual heavy lifting. It means nothing more, but nothing less, than a complete redirection of one's life, away from self-centered craving that leads to suffering, despair, and alienation, and toward the selfless detachment that leads to awareness, enlightenment, and eternal bliss. The Buddha, in fact, had a program in mind for this process. It's not a 10-step program, which you might find a motivational speaker pitching on a late-night infomercial; rather, it's a comprehensive approach to bringing one's mind and body into harmony with the ultimate reality of the universe, and the Buddha called it the Eightfold Path.

> **Divinations**
>
> Extinguishing desire is a theme in Christian writings too, as noted by the great mystic St. John of the Cross: "In order to be All, do not desire to be anything. In order to know All, do not desire to know anything. In order to find the joy of All, do not desire to enjoy anything."

The Eightfold Path

If many religions strive to refine our beliefs about metaphysical realities, Buddhism instead focuses our attention on the way we conduct our lives. The Buddha taught that we should understand the connection between our desires, feelings, and habits of thought, and the pain and suffering we experience as our lives lurch from crisis to crisis. These connections become clearer as we follow the Eightfold Path, working on each area of our mental, spiritual, and physical being, not in sequential order, but concurrently.

1. **Right views.** Escape from suffering and death is possible only by understanding the defectiveness of our point of view. The Buddha taught that we must become aware that as long as we put ourselves in the driver's seat, we invite more misery into our lives. This awareness shouldn't be thought of as correct doctrines about God, but rather, as right views about the nature of existence and what keeps us from achieving the ultimate goal of release from death.

2. **Right intent.** Knowing is one thing; wanting is another. Most of us live with the intention of pleasing ourselves, and most of us wind up being miserable. The Buddha teaches that nobody will escape the miseries of life and death unless they want to, which of course requires us to want something other than self-gratification.

3. **Right speech.** Getting one's thoughts and motives pointed in the right direction helps to put the mind in order. But there are other parts of our being that need attention as well, including those parts that interact with other living things. The Buddha taught that our speech should serve the cause of our freedom, rather than our continued imprisonment. We should stop using outrageous speech that magnifies our egos and belittles others, such as lies, slander, and verbal abuse. Then we should stop more subtle offenses, such as deceitful talk, shameless flattery, or idle gossip. These are self-indulgent habits that make it harder to suppress the inner fires of personal craving.

4. **Right conduct.** Speech is part of the equation, but so is action. Right conduct is behavior that has been conditioned by right views and proper motives. When you realize that there's no eternal, independent, sovereign "self" at the center of your existence, you start acting properly, with full appreciation for the interdependence of all living things. The Buddha listed several don'ts: Don't kill (even animals), lie, steal, cheat, fornicate, or drink alcohol. But he was more interested in the do's, such as loving and caring for everyone and everything that surrounds us.

5. **Right livelihood.** The Buddha worked from right conduct to the question of one's occupation. Does your profession promote evils such as war and violence, drug abuse, or sexual immorality? If so, you should consider a career change if your goal is release from the wheel of birth and death. Whatever career you choose, it should provide financial independence, leave you without debt or guilt, and promote the well-being of others.

6. **Right effort.** If speech, conduct, and livelihood put you in a right relation to the universe beyond, then the last three aspects in the Eightfold Path put you in a right relation to the universe within. The Buddha taught that people who attain nirvana discipline their minds with right effort, which he explained as laboring to extinguish mental states that focus our attention on ourselves at the expense of the larger reality that transcends us.

7. **Right mindfulness.** How do you extinguish mental states? Sounds impossible, right? A good starting point is to understand the typical cause-and-effect arrangement in which we permit our feelings, passions, and desires to infect our patterns of thought. Long hours of introspection, even meditation, are necessary to dredge the depths of the mind, to become aware of the specific points of misdirection that are soiling our lives. Only with these insights in mind is enlightenment even possible.

8. **Right concentration.** The other aspects of the Eightfold Path put you on the cusp of enlightenment; right concentration delivers the goods. Buddhists speak of a wholesale transformation or reconstitution as a clear view of the ultimate reality comes into focus. Through an intensive system of meditation and contemplation, concentration purges the mind of various impulses and feelings and then strives to go beyond mental states themselves. Nirvana comes when one loses consciousness of the self, obtains a direct comprehension of the fundamental nature of existence, and achieves freedom from attachment to the sources of suffering and death.

Rethinking Hindu Metaphysics

Experts will tell you over and over that the Buddha wasn't all that interested in speculation about the nature of God or the gods. He didn't deny God's existence, but believed the divine to be irrelevant to the essential problem of human suffering and the manner of liberation. The Buddha believed you could attain the deathless state without having to go through the gods, or even believing they exist. After the Buddha passed into nirvana for the final time around 483 B.C.E., his followers soon began to talk about gods, and in fact some suggested the Buddha himself was a god or even the Supreme Being. We'll discuss some aspects of Buddhist divinity in Chapter 24. For now you should keep in mind that the Buddha responded to queries about the gods with silence, an example of wisdom and humility in the face of questions that cannot be answered with the tools at hand.

Nirvana and God

There are, however, some elements of the Buddha's teachings that are crucial to understanding the Buddhist vision of the Absolute. In some ways, the Buddha spoke of nirvana as the Hindu brahmin might speak of Brahman, or a mystic might speak of God. In the book *The World's Religions* by Huston Smith (HarperSanFrancisco, 1991),

Edward Conze, noted scholar of Buddhism, is said to have scoured Buddhist scriptures for descriptions of nirvana and discovered terms such as unborn, immovable, imperishable, secure refuge, real Truth, supreme Reality, the Good, and so on. Those are attributes that theists typically assign to the divine. The Buddha taught that nirvana is the only permanent, enduring, and incorruptible reality.

Anatta

This perception of nirvana gave rise to a foundational principle in the Buddha's teachings that distinguishes the Buddhist Absolute from other concepts of God. When the Buddha described nirvana as a cessation, he conveyed the Buddhist idea that all is in a state of flux. We err when we fix our minds and attach our affections onto impermanent and changing entities, even our own inner being. The Buddha parted from the Hindu tradition in this important respect when he taught that there is no soul (*anatta*, Sanskrit for "no atman") that endures from life to life in a chain of reincarnation. According to the Buddha, to assume the soul's permanence is to hitch one's wagon to the self, thereby ensuring a perpetuation of cyclical rebirths and continued suffering.

> **Word to the Wise**
>
> **Anatta** is an essential Buddhist concept that translates from Sanskrit as no self or no soul, referring to the Buddhist rejection of the Hindu belief in the eternal nature of the soul.

So what endures? Buddhists use the metaphor of a chain of candles to explain the idea of reincarnation. If I light a candle, a flame appears on the wick. This flame can be passed from one candle to another in a chain of candles; if the candles are blown out behind the point of transfer, the flame continues to exist, but not as a permanent, enduring entity. As you can see, there's the illusion of endurance of the flame, but not the actual fact of a permanent, indestructible flame. The same goes with the soul in reincarnation. There's the appearance of a continuous self that leaps from life to life, when in actuality nothing permanent endures. Of course this affects the way we must understand karma in the Buddhist tradition. Karma is the causal consequences of past deeds, good or bad, but the Buddha warned against conceiving of it as a kind of medium for transferring the good or ill consequences of former actions into successive lives. Rather, the Buddha understood karma as the shadowy imprint of habits, tendencies, and predispositions in previous lives, which exert their influence in thoughts and deeds of present and future lives.

Skandas

The Buddha explained the workings of karma by elaborating the concept of *skandas*. The skandas, Sanskrit for "strands," are threads that, when woven together, comprise the fabric of our lives. Buddhists identify five skandas: the material substance of the body, the feelings we get when we sense the physical world, the cognition that helps to make meaning out of our senses and feelings, the fixed ideas in our minds that generate karma from cognitive processes, and consciousness of ourselves in contact with our surroundings. As you can see, these skandas are subject to influence by karmic echoes from former lives, but just like everything else, they themselves are in a state of flux and change. Karma tugs at our skandas, but it doesn't bind us to particular fates or predetermine our moral and spiritual destinies. There's an important sociological consequence to this revision of brahmin doctrine; the Buddha didn't believe you had to progress through the castes in a succession of lives in order to escape the wheel of rebirth. Escape could be accomplished within the compass of one lifetime, and each person possesses the means to make it happen.

Pratitya-Samutpada

Taken together, the concepts of anatta, karma, and skandas form a comprehensive vision of how the universe operates that doesn't require the active presence of God, or even the sort of "first cause" we discovered in Aristotelian metaphysics and popularized by the Scholastic philosophers of medieval Christendom. Buddha taught that everything is impermanent and transitory (*anicca*), and nothing is self-existent. All reality as we perceive it is caught in a web of begetting, flowing from ignorance and craving, and in turn creating the necessary conditions for the "arising" of ignorance and craving. This idea of "interdependent arising" or "dependent origination" is a distinct Buddhist concept (*pratitya-samutpada*) that helped the Buddha explain the function of karma in a universe without eternal souls. It helped him to make his point that the only way to depart from the "wheel of becoming" is to achieve the state of "cessation" in nirvana, which brings all begetting to an end in a blissful state of permanent stillness.

> ### Pearls of Wisdom
>
> Mind is the seed of everything, from which sprouts both existence and nirvana. Pay obeisance to it, for, like the wish-fulfilling gem, it gives you the fruit you desire.
>
> —From *Dohakhosa* (*Treasury of Songs*) by Kanha, a twelfth-century Indian Buddhist monk

Lingering Questions

The Buddha died at the age of 80 in 483 B.C.E., leaving his disciples to dwell over some of the silences that he so earnestly tried to maintain. Different schools of Buddhism emerged with differences of opinion on topics such as the continuing status of the Buddha and others who reached nirvana (the "never returners"), the essential nature of our interdependence with other living things, and the efficacy of prayer and other religious rituals. Some schools developed elaborate cosmologies with terrifying hells brimming with demons and ghosts. We'll discuss some of the lingering questions that split Buddhism into divergent streams in the next chapter, including the issue of whether there's a God or multiple gods. Keep in mind, though, that the Buddha steered away from vexing metaphysical issues and stormy theological debates during his time on Earth. Consider the popular representation of the Buddha; he sits lotus style, with a look of serenity on his face. And his hand, rather than pointing heavenward, symbolically touches the ground. You can interpret this gesture in a number of ways, but it's tempting to see it as a reminder that the means of our escape from suffering and death lies here, not in the celestial realms of the gods.

The Least You Need to Know

- Siddhartha Gautama became the Buddha when he attained nirvana, the state of release from suffering and death.

- The essence of Buddhism can be found in the Four Noble Truths, which outline the principles of duhkha and the manner of humankind's escape.

- The last of the Four Noble Truths, the Eightfold Path, explains how to refocus one's life to attain enlightenment.

- Nirvana is achieved once you become aware of the selfish desires that condition you to wrongly view your inner being as eternal, absolute, and supreme.

- Buddhists differ from Hindus on the subject of the soul: Hindus equate it with atman and consider it eternal, while Buddhists do not.

- The Buddha offered a vision of how to live the higher life, but remained largely silent on the subject of God.

Chapter 24

God in Buddhist Traditions

In This Chapter

- Three Jewels and two rafts
- Is the Buddha God?
- Stream-winners and never-returners
- Zen masters
- Parsing the dharma
- Mahayana schools from Tibet to Japan

For the most part, the Buddha kept silent in response to questions about the gods. Once he passed from the scene, however, his followers found lots of things to say about the nature of the divine. Just as in Islam and Christianity, the passing of Buddhism's founder led to division into various sects; one issue that divided Buddhists was whether the Buddha himself was actually God. Some said yes, others said no. And among those who affirmed his divinity, some went even further and perceived many other godlike beings that could help men and women escape from the cycles of rebirth. Other issues sharpened the divisions, such as whether the Buddha should be merely emulated or actively engaged through prayer, or whether a few could reach nirvana or many, and by what means.

Today, you'll find several major strands of Buddhism, which are the result of some early disagreements, but also the blending of Buddhism with other traditions as Buddhism spread to Tibet, China, Japan, Korea, and Southeast Asia. These strands perceive the Absolute in different ways, ranging from the worship of Amitabha Buddha in Pure Land Buddhism to the esoteric pantheism of Zen Buddhism. And just as you encountered the mujaddid of Islam (see Chapter 20), you'll find advocates of purification and renewal throughout Buddhism's history, and several of these movements persist to the present day. In this chapter, you'll discover an impressive array of ideas about God, inspired by the genius of Buddhism's founder.

Three Jewels

Buddha didn't leave history with a religious vision of God, but rather a path to self-liberation from the cycle of suffering and death. His followers, however, developed a religion out of Buddha's Four Noble Truths and the Eightfold Path, including the use of sacred spaces such as temples and *stupas*, religious icons of Buddhas and bodhisattvas (those who achieve enlightenment but postpone nirvana to help others), rituals of meditation and prayer, and the formation of monastic communities where the Buddha's ideas were taught and lived. Buddhists speak of three "refuges" or Three Jewels that together form the basic framework of the Buddhist religion: the Buddha, the dharma, and the sangha.

Divinations

One of the streams of Buddhism, Mahayana, injected a feminine component into the Absolute by developing works about Mahamaya, Supreme Wisdom personified and the mother of the Buddha (who was a virgin like Mary), and by recognizing female bodhisattvas like Tara, who is the object of meditation, prayer, and other devotional practices.

The Buddha

The Buddha gave humanity a powerful example of an individual who discovered the path to enlightenment, overcame pain, suffering, and death, and then returned to help others find the path to nirvana. His wisdom and compassion combined two of the most admirable human traits, and inspired legions of those frustrated with the brahmin priests to not only follow the Eightfold Path, but to venerate Buddha's life as well. Numerous stories of his life and depictions of his former lives circulated throughout India, enhancing Buddha's reputation and growing his legacy with each telling and retelling.

Some Buddhists would even come to perceive the Buddha as a savior, though without the need for his sacrificial death in atonement for sins, as with Jesus Christ. Others spoke of thousands of other Buddhas scattered widely throughout the universe, or of future Buddhas to come. This gives you a sense of how disagreement crept into the Buddhist community following the historical Buddha's final passage into nirvana. Nevertheless, all Buddhists affirm that the Buddha left behind a second jewel to keep them focused on the path to nirvana: the dharma.

The Dharma

Dharma derives from a Sanskrit root meaning "to hold," which in Hindu usage meant holding to one's duties. In Buddhist usage, the term referred to the thing that keeps a person on the way or path to nirvana. It includes the Four Noble Truths and the Eightfold Path, but a wide variety of other teachings regarding proper control of the mind and body, the organization of the sangha (see the following section), or a variety of other subjects. When they speak of dharma, Buddhists refer to what might be known to adherents of other religions as "truth" or "the truths." In one of his writings, the famous Buddhist master Buddhaghosa (fifth century C.E.) likened the Buddha to a doctor who "dissects away the cataract of delusion," and the dharma to the lancet that actually dissects the cataract away (*Paramatthajotika*, or *Illustrator of the Ultimate Meaning*).

Dharma is a tradition of teachings, disseminated first to the five ascetics whom the Buddha abandoned when he went to sit under his bo tree, and then to a wealthy merchant's son named Yasa and 45 of his friends. These disciples spread the dharma throughout India, orally at first, and then centuries later in palm-leaf manuscripts. Unlike Judaism, Christianity, and Islam, the sacred texts of Buddhism are voluminous. They've been organized into different genres, including *vinaya* (monastic rules), *sutras* (the Buddha's discourses), *jatakas* (accounts of the Buddha's former lives), *abhidharma* (explication of meditation and concentration), and others. This was the work of Buddhist monks, who assumed the task of authenticating, consolidating, and preserving the dharma. That gets us to the third jewel: the sangha.

Pearls of Wisdom

The Buddhist emphasis on annihilating selfish desires appears in this verse from Buddhist thinker Nagarjuna: "That which is virtuous in the beginning, middle, and end, which is infallible and constant, that is selfless. How can one imagine that to be I and mine."

—From *Hymn to the Dharmadhatu*

The Sangha

In his life, the Buddha presented an example for others to follow, not just in his attainment of nirvana, but in his normal, everyday routines and his interaction with others. The Buddha lived for 45 years after he became enlightened, which gave him plenty of time to develop a wide following. Many of his earliest followers were like himself—wandering ascetics who renounced the world and sought *moksha* (liberation from the worries and stresses of earthly living) by plying the techniques of yoga. The Buddha's disciples came to be known as the *sangha*, or "group." The sangha, technically the community of adepts who follow the Buddha's dharma, forms the third of the Three Jewels, which is known in the Buddhist tradition as the *triratna*.

The triratna shows up everywhere in Buddhism, and forms something akin to a creed or confession of faith. Buddhists recite: "I go for refuge to the Buddha. I go for refuge to the dharma. I go for refuge to the sangha." Say this three times and you're in. But just as Buddhists disagree over the status of the Buddha and the scope and content of the dharma, they also disagree on the nature and composition of the sangha. The specific issue in question is whether the sangha refers to the monks and nuns eligible for nirvana by virtue of their accomplishment of the first steps toward enlightenment, or the entire community of faith—monks, nuns, and laypersons combined. Is the sangha exclusive to the cloistered few, or does it include all those who labor toward nirvana? This question provides a good starting point for exploring the main division within Buddhism, between the Theravada and Mahayana sects.

Theravada Buddhism

In the earliest years of Buddhism, monks entered monasteries to chant, meditate, recite the dharma, and write commentaries on the Buddha's discourses. They assumed the role of protector of the tradition and taught the Buddha's dharma to those in the surrounding community who sought release from samsara. In exchange, laypersons provided the monks with food, clothing, medicines, and other items the monks required in order to maintain their intensive schedules of meditation and contemplation. Unfortunately, the senior monks (*theras*, hence the term Theravada) who directed the sangha believed that it was not likely that the laypersons providing these necessities would eventually reach nirvana. Elitism became distinctive to Theravada. This elitism prompted a reform movement that came to be known as Mahayana Buddhism, which we'll discuss in a few pages.

One Buddha at a Time

Besides their exclusivist tendencies, Theravada Buddhism cultivated other distinctive ideas over the centuries, and some of them are pretty important to know about if you want to appreciate the complexity of Buddhist beliefs about the ultimate reality. Keep in mind, however, that Buddhists of every stripe warn of the dangers of theological obfuscation, and reducing any school of Buddhism to a set of doctrines runs counter to the spirit of the tradition. Having said that, Theravada holds to the belief that there's only one Buddha at any given time, and focuses on the historical Buddha from the sixth century B.C.E. The result of this emphasis is a Buddha who is valued not for any presumed metaphysical qualities, but for his teachings.

The Buddha told his disciples that he wasn't the only Buddha, and that there were more Buddhas (awakened ones) to come. Theravadins understood this teaching in linear, sequential terms. They perceived that only one Buddha could be the Buddha at any given time, and that our Buddha is the historical figure formerly known as Siddhartha Gautama. There's one more Buddha coming, named Maitreya, who lives in the Tusita Heaven, but nobody knows when that Buddha will appear in the world.

Theravadins teach that the current Buddha isn't alive in the sense that we normally understand living, but continues in our imaginations as we meditate on his magnificent life. As the exceptional few reach the end of the Eightfold Path, they attain the status of an *arhat*, or saint who has attained enlightenment.

> **Word to the Wise**
>
> **Arhat** means one who is worthy, and refers to the saints who have achieved nirvana in the Theravada Buddhist tradition.

Phases of Enlightenment

The Theravadan system instructed the Buddha's disciples to become aware of the tanha (selfish desire) within that gives rise to duhkha (suffering). The theras coached their adepts to utilize techniques of meditation and concentration to peer deep inside and to realize that their inner being is temporary and contingent. If they followed the dharma correctly, they gained insight into the true nature of the human self and the false ideas that cloud their understanding. In this way, they were said to have taken the first major step toward enlightenment.

If you conjure up a mental picture of standing on the bank of a stream, looking across the water to the inviting shore beyond, then you catch something of the Buddhist meaning here. Theravadins believed that the process of crossing the stream would be complicated and required the completion of four different phases. In these phases, the seeker is first a stream-winner, and then a once-returner, never-returner, and finally an arhat. Stream-winners are those who have taken the first step toward the farther shore, where release from samsara occurs. But they still have plenty of work to do, since they could expect more rebirths, perhaps as many as seven. The next phase, however, holds greater promise because stream-winners who pursue the dharma become once-returners, coming back to live out another life and a final rebirth. Once-returners born into one last, final life move into phase three and become never-returners. Never-returners expect to achieve nirvana at the end of their present life, provided they follow the dharma. At the end, never-returners reach the fourth and final phase and become arhats. They have attained the central goal of Buddhism—nirvana—and will never again suffer the pain of human life and death.

Buddhaghosa and the *Path of Purification*

The theras, or senior monks, believed that the phases a monk must pass through before becoming an arhat were made more difficult because of the Buddha's passing into nirvana. Although Buddha left the dharma, the absence of his guiding presence made it more difficult to follow the Eightfold Path. One of the theras, writing a few centuries after the Buddha, observed that "the behavior of the *bhikkhus* [monks] now seems different from when the protector of the world, the best of men, was alive." He lamented, "because of the complete annihilation of good characteristics and wisdom, the conqueror's teaching, endowed with all excellent qualities, is destroyed." Sounding rather like Jeremiah or Amos of the Hebrew scriptures, he declared that "this is the time of evil characteristics and defilements, but those who are ready for seclusion possess the remainder of the true doctrine." (*Theragatha* or *Verses of the Elders*, c. second century B.C.E.)

Pearls of Wisdom

Mahayana Buddhism values compassion, as reflected in this prayer of the bodhisattva Santideva: "For as long as the vastness of space remains, and as long as the world exists, may I too subsist that long, destroying the suffering of the whole world."

—From the *Bodhicaryavatara*

We've encountered these calls for purification in the mujaddid of Islam. Buddhism's answer to Islam's Ahmad ibn Taymiyya of fourteenth-century Egypt might well be Buddhaghosa, a Burmese monk of the fifth century C.E., whose key text, *Path of Purification* (or *Way of Purity*) summarized the essential elements of the tradition that he and other Theravadins believed were being corrupted by the incorporation of novel ideas and practices. He worked to cleanse Buddhism of texts that didn't pass a strict test of authenticity, and to steer away from chatter about gods, demons, alternate worlds, and other phenomena that he thought were diversions from the main problem of the human mind and the skandas that produce the illusion of permanence and the impulses of self-gratification. Like other Theravadins, Buddhaghosa worked to invigorate the monastic system, because he believed that only monks could achieve the status of an arhat.

Mahayana Buddhism

As you can guess, some Hindus who were attracted to Buddhism found the elitism of the theras to run counter to the pluralist spirit of the age, best expressed in the *Bhaghavad Gita*'s discovery of many paths to release from samsara. That expansive vision carried over into Buddhism in the teachings of reforming monks who called themselves Mahayana, or greater vehicle, because they believed the theras were too exclusive in their understanding of who could reach nirvana. In derision, Mahayanas called the elders' faith Hinayana, or lesser vehicle; this insult was meant to criticize the smallness of the craft that the elders' teachings had designed in order to carry people to the farther shore. Of course the elders didn't like this label, and took the label Theravada to distance themselves from the Mahayana reformers.

Many Buddhas

In the Mahayana tradition, anyone can, in theory, become a Buddha, not just those who follow the strict monastic disciplines practiced by the Theravadin monks. The Mahayanas' concerns about the prevailing instruction led them in the direction of metaphysical speculation, and they disputed the linear and sequential belief, held by the theras, that there is only one Buddha at any given time. On the contrary, Mahayanas perceived many Buddhas inhabiting many worlds simultaneously. With the writing of the *Lotus Sutra* (c. 100 C.E.), a popular Sanskrit text soon translated into a variety of East Asian languages, some Buddhists came to think of the historical Buddha as a manifestation of a sort of "universal" Buddha who appears here and there, or even everywhere at once. This brought Mahayana monks to devalue the actual historical Buddha, Siddhartha Gautama, in favor of a more celestial concept of the Buddha, associated with the fundamental principles of order in the universe.

This sort of speculation led to the Mahayana doctrine of many Buddhas, typified by the five grand Dhyani Buddhas considered to be particularly helpful for visualizing the Buddha in meditation exercises. In the cosmic center of all reality one finds the Buddha Vairocana, with four other Buddhas dwelling in the four celestial quadrants:

Aksobhya in the eastern field, Ratnasambhava in the southern, Amitabha toward the west, and Amoghasiddhi in the north. Intense devotion to all or even one of these manifestations of the universal Buddha pushed Buddhism in new directions. Devotion to Amitabha of the western field brought about the movement we know as Pure Land Buddhism, which we'll meet later in this chapter.

Perfection of Wisdom

Around the time of the *Lotus Sutra*, Mahayana monks wrote a series of influential texts known as the *Perfection of Wisdom*, which permanently severed Buddhism into its two major streams. The *Perfection* tradition skewered the theras for being caught up in technicalities of the dharma and placing their faith too squarely on methods and concepts. One *Perfection* thinker, Nagarjuna (c. 150–250 C.E.) of India, argued that language requires oppositions and dualisms in order to function, which is testimony to its inherent shakiness as a vessel for truth. Human beings use the dualisms of language (*this* but not *that*) to "construct" a reality out of nothing, and when we discover our relative and arbitrary way of assigning meaning to things through words, we begin down the path toward true enlightenment. Here, we discover that true reality is emptiness—a void—and true release from samsara comes from purging oneself of any and all perceptions. These ideas gave Mahayana Buddhism its distinctive stress on the Buddha's exemplary actions, in contrast to Theravada Buddhism's emphasis on the Buddha's teachings.

The *Perfection of Wisdom* tradition is tough sledding for the novice, particularly the complexities of the *Heart Sutra* and *Diamond Sutra*. One of the major preoccupations of Mahayana writers was to rebuke the individualism inherent in Theravada doctrines, which is to say the ideal of the lone monk plying his way through successive lifetimes to reach the exalted status of the arhat. The Mahayana monks arrived at the belief, articulated neatly in the *Perfection* literature, that the arhat ideal subverted the true meaning of the Buddha's teachings about interdependent arising or dependent origination, which insisted on the interdependence of all things. They further accused the theras of corrupting the Buddhist vision of ultimate reality with false dualisms by believing that the arhat maintains some sort of existence when he passes into nirvana (if something can exist, it can not exist, in which case you have a dualism). Again, think emptiness, and you get some idea where the Mahayana were heading.

Rise of the Bodhisattvas

By rejecting the arhat ideal, Mahayana severed itself from Theravada, and in the process it produced an alternate ideal: the bodhisattva. A bodhisattva is a person who has traversed the Eightfold Path, achieved enlightenment, but postpones the blessings of enlightenment by helping others find the way. Mahayana teaches that to obtain nirvana is good, but to selflessly help others prior to winning the blissful state is the highest good. There's simply no greater act of compassion to be found anywhere in the universe. The Buddha himself provided the pattern, since he delayed nirvana to help a world full of sufferers obtain the same release from suffering that he himself had achieved.

The bodhisattva ideal reflects a type of anticlericalism among Mahayana Buddhists, who believed the establishment monks of early Buddhist monasteries harbored selfish and elitist tendencies. It also reflects the tendency within the tradition to venture into metaphysics, which itself was an important tradition in classical Hindu philosophy. Mahayana texts cast visions of parallel worlds and so-called Buddha-fields, which refer to fortunate worlds that enjoy the active presence of a Buddha. Those who fall short of nirvana in this life try to gain rebirth in a Buddha-field to better their chances of eventually reaching nirvana. Clearly, bodhisattvas assume an important position here as celestial beings that move between and within these parallel worlds, providing merit to the faithful through their grace and helping followers advance toward nirvana.

Certain Mahayana texts spoke of the bodhisattvas in terms that bear a striking familiarity to the deities of ancient Hinduism. Tales of celestial bodhisattvas proliferated in the Buddhist literary tradition, and figures such as Avalokiteshvara and Majushri became the focus of visualization exercises and even intercessory prayer. They even inspired shrines and temples, ritual observances, and visual representation in painting and sculpture. With the bodhisattvas, you get as close as you're going to get within Buddhism to the characterization of gods and deities you find in other ancient polytheisms, or contemporary bhakti traditions in Hinduism. Mahayana Buddhists envision compassionate bodhisattvas who hear prayers and offer assistance to nirvana. This connects to their overarching sense of the Buddha as a savior rescuing humanity. Theravadins, scholars note, perceive the Buddha not as a savior, but a saint worthy of emulation.

Mahayana Schools

Buddhism presents a bewildering complexity to the beginner because it's a rich tradition with 2,500 years of development behind it. It's also difficult to grasp because it deals with complicated psychological issues of consciousness, sense perception, cognition, and altered mental states, as well as philosophical questions of time and eternity, cause and effect, permanence and impermanence, and so on. It's important to remember that Buddhism interacted with local traditions in China, Japan, Korea, Southeast Asia, Indonesia, Tibet, and everywhere else, which gives it an additional layer of complexity. A quick look at some of the Mahayana schools will give you a sense of the richness of the tradition.

Vajrayana: Tantric Buddhism

The Mahayana tradition known as Vajrayana, or more commonly Tantric Buddhism (from *tantra*, meaning "text"), is the common form of Buddhism practiced in Tibet. It began in the eighth or ninth century C.E., as a result of Mahayana discussions of dualism and the turn toward spiritualism within the bodhisattva cults. Siddhas, or ascetics who lived near the Buddhist monasteries, taught that each person shares in the Buddha nature and is in fact a Buddha already. That we don't see this is a result of the illusion of duality caused by duhkha (suffering) and tanha (selfish desire). The historical Buddha insisted that enlightenment is within the grasp of each person, and so the siddhas concluded that the most direct path to enlightenment should be pursued. Numerous tantras emerged promoting different methods of reaching sudden enlightenment, but many of them shared the idea of concentrating on a Buddha or bodhisattva to the point of attaining a state of mental identification with that particular deity. To achieve this experience is to achieve enlightenment, and those blessed with it were at one point thought to wield godlike powers, such as invisibility, flight, or alchemy (turning metal into gold).

> **CAUTION**
>
> **Take Heed!**
>
> Tantric Buddhism has the reputation in the West of promoting ritual sex, which isn't exactly true. Part of the tantric discipline involves concentration on the unity of compassion and wisdom, sometimes visualized as male and female energies coming together to form a union. The discipline also includes use of geometric shapes and sacred tones.

Dhyana: Zen Buddhism

The origins of this very small but highly visible sect of Mahayana Buddhism lay in the sixth century C.E., when a sage named Bodhidharma carried Buddhist esoterism from India to China. From there, the so-called Ch'an sect moved into Japan (c. twelfth century) and became known as Zen. In the Zen tradition, adherents learn of the one-ness of all reality, which in fact is an emptiness. Zen teaches the famous dictum: "All is one, one is none, none is all." As noted in Edward Conze's *Buddhist Texts Through the Ages* (Philosophical Library, 1954), this derives from the *Heart Sutra*, a core text for Zen practitioners. The writer of the *Heart Sutra* says that "whatever is form, that is emptiness, whatever is emptiness, that is form. The same is true of feelings, perceptions, impulses and consciousness." Zen masters carry forward Nagarjuna's convictions about the inadequacy of language, using mental puzzles (koans) to disrupt the normal flow of cognition. These include the famous "What is the sound of one hand clapping?" and the less famous "If all things are reducible to the One, to what is the One reduced?" Intense concentration on these riddles kicks the mind out of its rut, and triggers flashes of insight into the true nature of self and the universe, unclut-tered by the useless forms (think *words*) we're so accustomed to using.

Sukhavati: Pure Land Buddhism

The strand of Buddhism known as Pure Land centers on the figure of Buddha Amitabha. In one of his former lives, Amitabha was a monk named Dharmakara who promised that once he obtained Buddhahood, he would build a Pure Land (sukhavati in Sanskrit) devoid of evil where the path to nirvana could be more easily traversed. Having accomplished his goal, he revealed certain vows one must take in order to be reborn in the Pure Land. This system developed in part out of the commonly held belief that the dharma weakened in power as humanity gave itself over to moral depravity, thereby sapping their ability to reach nirvana through intensive self-effort.

Devotees believe that the Buddha, ever compassionate, provided an alternate path to nirvana that leads through the Pure Land. Out of his infinite store of grace, the Buddha provides the merit required for rebirth in a buddha-field where the path to nirvana is easiest to trod, such as the Pure Land. In other words, the Buddha supplies merit that the seeker can't generate through his or her own efforts. Pure Land, then, substitutes the intense self-effort of classical Buddhism for the system of faith and grace more familiar to adherents of the Western monotheisms.

The Least You Need to Know

◆ The core of the Buddhist faith are the Three Jewels: the Buddha, the dharma (teachings), and the sangha (community).

◆ Disagreement about whether anyone but monks could achieve nirvana divided Buddhism into different streams.

◆ Theravada Buddhism advocates strict adherence to the earliest texts of the Buddhist dharma.

◆ Mahayana Buddhists believe that the theras are too exclusive in their understanding of who can reach nirvana.

◆ The Mahayana tradition, which is the more popular form of Buddhism, emphasizes the exemplary life and works of the Buddha and the many bodhisattavas who attained enlightenment.

◆ Tantric and Pure Land Buddhists practice intense concentration on a single Buddha or bodhisattva, giving Westerners the mistaken impression of religious devotion to a deity.

Chapter **25**

God in East Asian Religion and Philosophy

In This Chapter

- ◆ Heaven: chief deity of Chinese folk belief
- ◆ What's the Tao of Taoism?
- ◆ Confucianism and cosmology
- ◆ Buddhism in East Asia
- ◆ Gods in Japanese religion

Is there a higher power in the universe? Nearly everyone believes the answer to this question is yes. Philosophers, priests, shamans, gurus, mystics, and visionaries of every stripe look out into the heavens—or deep within their inner being—and perceive a force greater than themselves. Some see it in the changing of the seasons, the miracle of birth, or the patterns of planetary motion. Others see it in eureka moments of scientific discovery, and in the spark of inspiration that elevates composers, playwrights, and poets to heights of creativity. Still others find it in the completely baffling phenomenon of human consciousness, which experts have yet to explain using the research methods and scientific theories at hand.

We know the higher power is there, but the problem is, our efforts to describe it always fall short. In this chapter, we'll encounter some philosophical and religious traditions indigenous to East Asia, particularly China, Korea, and Japan, which accounted for the higher power with concepts like *ling* and *Tao*. As in Western philosophy and religion, conversations about the ultimate reality produced the same concerns about the adequacy of language and concepts to depict the higher power of the universe. As a result, East Asian religions accepted a high degree of cross-fertilization and intermingling in their visions of the Absolute, resting assured in the belief that if metaphysical realities can't be thoroughly mapped, then at least humanity can reach a state of harmony and balance.

Popular Belief in China

In ancient times, the people of East Asia cultivated a pervasive sense of spiritual realities, or *ling*, inhabiting the landscape. Immortal beings populated the region's mountains, streams, and forests, giving the earth a spiritual quality. The highest peaks of China were sacred not only because they provided the living spaces for countless deities, but also because they served as pillars holding aloft a weighty, drooping heaven that otherwise might collapse into the earth. Temples and shrines to these deities proliferated throughout the region; mountain temples drew pilgrims eager to petition the gods for divine favor. Taoist and Buddhist monks extended these traditions with temples on Wu Tai Shan, Hua Shan, and other sacred mountains.

Divinations

You might have heard of *kowtowing*, which is the posture adopted by worshippers of ancestral deities in the household rituals of Chinese folk religion. You simply lie on the floor with your face down and arms spread in a show of humility and submission before an image or another object associated with your deity.

Shang-Di: The Lord Above

The deities in ancient Chinese popular religion were thought to have been exceptional human beings whose souls persisted into immortality. One of the earliest civilizations in China, the Shang people, spoke of Shang-di, "the Lord Above," who was an immortal ancestor with power over the other deities. This henotheistic pattern (many gods, with one in charge) continued with the Taoist and Buddhist pantheons of the classical period; later emperors officially recognized a pantheon with the Jade August Supreme Lord wielding authority over a celestial bureaucracy that bore a striking resemblance to their own earthly dominion.

Heaven

In folk belief, the concept of *t'ien* played an important role as well. It means heaven, but not with the same connotations as the term acquired in the West. Heaven possessed the same characteristics as Shang-di, and in fact came to be seen as interchangeable with the concept of a Supreme Being that once created, and now governs, the universe. Chinese people also spoke of *t'ien ming*, or the "Mandate of Heaven." This concept offered a way to explain why people variously prospered or suffered; your sufferings were the result of disobeying t'ien ming, while your prosperity signified obedience to the cosmic force pervading the universe.

> **Word to the Wise**
>
> **T'ien** means "heaven" in Chinese popular religion, which exhibits many of the conventional attributes of a Supreme Being.

Yin and Yang

The idea of obeying or disobeying the Mandate of Heaven is linked to the concept of yin and yang, the tension of opposites that produces order and harmony in the universe. East Asian people everywhere perceived this tension of opposites in the form of earth and sky, male and female, good and evil, light and dark, strong and weak, and so on. The yin-yang binaries placed the structures and processes of the universe in creative tension, bringing separate, incomplete halves together to form an organic whole. Male is separate from female, and yet without female there is no male, and without male there is no female. Take away light and you can no longer call anything dark, since light creates for darkness an opposite by which darkness can be discerned. Yin-yang thinking carries with it the perception of generative power, human interconnectedness, and cosmic harmony, with clear implications for how human life should be lived.

Ancestor Spirits

East Asian religions taught that the dead proceeded to an afterlife where they dwelled as deities, receiving prayers and blessings from their living descendents. Ancestor deities became the focus of shrines and household religious observances; divination through village shamans offered men and women the chance to contact ancestor deities directly for assistance in overcoming illness or defeating enemies. These immortal souls must be sustained through continued offerings, as when Chinese families burn money or clothing for impoverished ancestor spirits who might otherwise suffer for want of attention. Much of this primitive folk religion persists to this day throughout East Asia, including China, where folk traditions survived Mao Zedong's campaign of religious suppression in the Cultural Revolution of the 1960s.

Taoism

The major faiths of Neo-Confucianism, Buddhism, and Taoism survived the Cultural Revolution as well, though in diminished form. These three traditions had wide popular followings throughout Chinese history, and until the Communist Revolution, enjoyed the support of the educated and powerful classes as well. Taoism, or Daoism, began as a philosophical investigation into the ultimate powers of the universe, and then acquired a religious character with visions of the afterlife and rigorous spiritual exercises. The Tao resists easy explanation, but a few words might suffice to highlight its distinctive quality.

Tradition has it that Taoism began its long career in the mind of Lao Tzu (551–479 B.C.E.), who reportedly lived during the lifetime of another famous Chinese sage, Confucius (discussed a little later in this chapter). Lao Tzu is famous for the work ascribed to him, *Tao Te Ching* (*The Way and Its Power*). As the central text of Taoism, its spare verses inspired hundreds of millions of people to search for harmony and balance in life through contact with the Tao, or the ultimate power in the universe.

Inadequacy of Words

But wait. Lao Tzu's main point about the Tao in *Tao Te Ching* is that it cannot be named or described: "I know not its name, so I style it 'the way.'" (25.56) Various passages account for the Tao in different ways, but mostly through negatives, as an entity that cannot be tasted, seen, or heard, or as an entity that is "silent and void." To speak of the Tao in positive terms is to speak of something other than the Tao. Of course this echoes a common sentiment in other faiths, expressed neatly in Justin Martyr's observation from Chapter 1 in this book, that "God cannot be called by any proper name."

Ultimate Reality

And yet Lao spoke as if the Tao were the source of the universe and the power that sustains its operation: "The nameless was the beginning of heaven and earth." (*Tao Te Ching* 1.2) In familiar negatives, Lao explained that the gods would deplete their powers without the Tao, since "it cannot be exhausted by use." (35.78) In effect, Lao Tzu made the Tao into the ultimate reality of the universe, along with implied warnings that it could not be said to exist as any mere object. This placed the Tao conceptually higher than the t'ien ming of Chinese folk religion. The Tao, after all, is not a "thing." The Tao is the answer to the Zen Buddhist question, if everything is reducible to the One, to what is the One reducible? Lao explained: "The way begets one; one begets two; two begets three; three begets the myriad creatures." (42.93) In this way, Lao steered away from the tendency among those who perceive a higher power of personifying and objectifying the formless nothing that makes all existent things possible.

> **Pearls of Wisdom**
>
> To know yet to think that one does not know is best;
> Not to know yet to think that one knows will lead to difficulty.
>
> —Lao Tzu, *Tao Te Ching*

Eastern religions tend to describe the Absolute in abstract terms like the Tao, giving rise to more abstract visual representations like the yin-yang symbol, surrounded by the I Ching hexagrams.

Wu Wei: No Action

Taoism, like other East Asian religions, emphasized the proper way to live over the proper way to think, which is not surprising given Lao's belief in the Tao's utter ineffability. People who read the *Tao Te Ching* learn that the cardinal rule of life is *wu wei*, which translates as "nonaction." They learn that the reason they suffer and die young is because they contend against other human beings and against the forces of nature. Through nonaction, understood as not striving against the power of the universe, they permit the Tao to flow through them, filling them with the life force and bringing them into harmony with the ultimate reality. "The most submissive thing in the world can ride roughshod over the hardest thing in the world—that which is without substance entering that which has no crevices." (*Tao Te Ching* 43.98) Here the author brings the paradoxes of the Tao and the idea of yin and yang into play; water is supple and weak, but it wears down the hardest rock over time. If you want longevity and prosperity, you need to set aside your willfulness and go with the flow. The cosmic power of the universe will then channel through your being and give you the earthly blessings you seek.

You can see this ethic of wu wei and going with the flow in many Chinese cultural practices. You maybe have seen men and women practicing t'ai chi in a neighborhood park. This is a Taoist practice of slow, rhythmic motion designed to channel energy (chi) through the body. You might have heard of feng shui, the art of arranging space. Feng shui masters carefully select building sites and design interior spaces in order to maximize the natural energies of place and locale. This achieves the Taoist goal of balancing yin and yang by placing the individual into an environment conducive to proper energy flow. Acupuncture redirects energy within the body to injured or energy-starved places, thus maximizing the body's own self-healing potential. In all, practitioners believe that if you resist the irresistible, you will lose.

Confucianism

Taoism stands next to Confucianism as major indigenous systems of belief and practice in China. According to tradition, Lao Tzu and Master K'ung (known in the West as Confucius) lived during the same period of Chinese history, a period of constant warfare among territorial rulers and the collapse of ethical standards of human conduct. As such, Confucius (551–479 B.C.E.) spent little time teaching about metaphysical realities; instead, he stressed the ethical principles necessary for a just social and political order. In this way, Confucianism is properly viewed not as a religion, but a system of ethics, a system that enjoyed popularity throughout Chinese history and even won adherents in Korea, Japan, and Vietnam.

Confucian Virtues

Philosophers of the Axial Age, the period between 800 and 400 B.C.E. that saw a worldwide transformation of religion, tried to find an answer to the question, What does it mean to live well? Confucius expressed his main preoccupation in *The Analects:* "It is these things that cause me concern: failure to cultivate virtue, failure to go deeply into what I have learned, inability to move up to what I have heard to be right, and inability to reform myself when I have defects." (7:3) This motive led him to fashion a moral and ethical system designed to help its adherents live well, and to fulfill the Mandate of Heaven. Here are the main components:

◆ *Ren* (or *jen*) provides the starting point. Roughly, ren means humaneness, or respect and compassion for other human beings; those who live according to ren recognize the inherent worth of others.

- *Shu*, or reciprocity, may be familiar to Westerners who know the Golden Rule: Do unto others as you would have them do unto you.

- *Li* is the means to accomplish ren and shu—perhaps the central concept in Confucianism. Li refers to the customs, manners, or ritualized behaviors that promote orderliness in social and political relations.

- *Hsiao* relates li to family and household, and translates as "filial piety." Confucius stressed the importance of cultivating a sense of loving commitment to one's grandparents, parents, siblings, and children, as well as paying homage to ancestor spirits.

- *Yi*, or righteousness, pulls the Confucian virtues into a seamless web. Those who possess this quality perform their duties and obligations out of an inner sense of what is right; the yi in this connection is like a moral compass that induces us to act the proper way without even thinking about it.

> **Divinations**
>
> Want to learn more about Confucianism? Confucius's timeless principles of right conduct can be found in the book *The Analects*, which forms part of the larger corpus of Confucianism, the *Four Books*. You can get *The Analects* in a modern, English-language Penguin edition at www. amazon.com.

Legacies of Confucianism

At bottom, Confucius wasn't a prophet, seer, or priest; he didn't claim to see God, or to speak on God's behalf. In *The Analects* he summed up his life's journey in simple terms: "At 15 I set my heart on learning; at 30 I firmly took my stand; at 40 I had no delusions; at 50 I knew the Mandate of Heaven; at 60 my ear was attuned; at 70 I followed my heart's desire without overstepping the boundaries of right." (2:4) To his way of thinking, selfishness and strife had gotten the human race out of sync with heaven, and he taught his fellow citizens to be unselfish, broadminded, forgiving, and respectful to one another as a way to restore cosmic unity.

Mencius and Hsun Tzu

Such was the power of Confucius's teachings that soon political leaders of China adopted his ethical system and reverence. Confucianism became the state religion during the Han dynasty (205 B.C.E.–200 C.E.), complete with shrines, icons, and sacrifices. By this time, Confucian masters such as Mencius (371–289 B.C.E.) and Hsun Tzu (298–238 B.C.E.) developed Confucian thought even further, adding doctrines regarding the essence of human nature; Mencius argued that human beings are essentially good by nature, while Hsun Tzu argued the position of human depravity. To Mencius, moral failure is the result of a person's inability to perfect the good within; Hsun Tzu believed it was the result of an inability to acquire the virtues necessary to overcome one's innate evil impulses.

Neo-Confucianism

Confucianism enjoyed a revival during the Song dynasty (960–1271 C.E.), following a centuries-long decline in the face of Buddhist and Taoist expansion. Neo-Confucian thinkers during the late Song period pushed harder in the direction of cosmology than the Great Sage (Confucius) was prepared to go. They perceived a Great Ultimate, which in a state of movement gave rise to yang, and in a subsequent state of stillness gave rise to yin; these opposing principles generated the constituent elements of earth, fire, water, wood, and metal, which formed the basic building blocks of existence. The Great Ultimate served a function similar to Plotinus's idea of the One, which lay at the center of a process of emanation that produced all creation. The Great Ultimate was Neo-Confucianism's answer to the Tao, since those who spoke of it described it as the principle of heaven and earth and all other things. Later Neo-Confucians associated this Great Ultimate with Confucius' li, or principle, which directed the creation of myriad things by means of *qi* (or chi), the generative power that animated all living things. These later Neo-Confucians borrowed from Buddhism the practice of meditation, whereby the individual works toward perfect awareness of li, expanding the chi within, which leads to a direct and immediate experience of the Great Ultimate.

Confucianism and Modernity

Closer to our own time, Confucianism contended with a variety of pressures that brought it to the brink of extinction. In the eighteenth and nineteenth centuries, contact with the West introduced China to the ideals of individualism and equality, and millions of ordinary people found those ideals more attractive than the Confucian virtues of commitment to family and right conduct toward superiors and inferiors. Christianity came along during this period and threw the Confucian system into bold relief. Christianity offered Chinese converts a personal relationship with a loving

God, and a degree of proof that Christian societies enjoyed the favor of heaven by virtue of their economic, political, and military success.

Christianity influenced Hong Xiuquan (1814–1864), who blended Christian apocalyptical thinking (the end is near!), socioeconomic egalitarianism, and moral purification in a religious movement known as T'ai P'ing. Severe persecution of the Taipings by the Manchu rulers led to civil war (1850–1864), resulting in 20 million deaths. Half a century later, Confucianism received a lukewarm endorsement by Western-leaning statesmen such as Sun Yat-Sen and Chaing K'ai Shek; after 1949, Mao Zedong and his communist operatives waged a campaign against Confucian teachings because they believed Confucianism promoted oppressive social hierarchies and elitism in education. But recently, the leaders of the People's Republic of China embraced Confucian ideals amid the collapse of Maoism in the 1980s and 1990s, thus restoring Confucianism to its traditional place in the highest councils of Chinese government.

> **CAUTION**
>
> **Take Heed!**
>
> Is Confucianism a system of belief about God or gods? Scholars can't agree on the answer to this question, since Confucius's main preoccupation was achieving social and political harmony. However, Confucius spoke tenderly of the Way of Heaven, or the Tao, and performed customary sacrifices to the divine.

I Ching

Confucianism survived into our own time because political elites believe it evokes some of the glory of past dynasties and offers a focal point of national unity. At the popular level, its vitality owes not only to Confucianism's doctrines of family loyalty, but also to the practice of divination within the Confucian tradition. This practice derives, in part, from *I Ching (Book of Changes)*, one of the five canonical texts in the Confucian canon. This text explains how you can understand the future by interpreting the meaning of certain geometrical figures. These figures, called hexagrams, contain solid and broken lines arranged in various patterns by means of casting lots; once composed, these hexagrams are keyed to passages in *I Ching* that explain their portent. In effect, they serve the function of an oracle, whereby participants discern the energies of yin and yang behind the geometric symbols and plan their course of action accordingly. *I Ching* is just one of many traditions that utilize sacred geometry or numerology in their attempts to bridge the chasm between the human mind and the ultimate reality of the universe.

East Asian Buddhism

Chinese civilization produced three major faiths: Taoism, Confucianism, and Chinese versions of Buddhism. Buddhism in East Asia developed along Mahayana lines (see Chapter 24), with special shrines, rites, and observances for the most widely revered Buddha, Avalokiteshvara. Chinese Buddhists perceived Avalokiteshvara as the female deity Guanyin, the goddess of compassion and mercy. Devotion to Guanyin won widespread adherence before the Communist Revolution in the twentieth century, and has surged in popularity in today's post-Maoist environment. Further east, Japanese Buddhism developed a variant of Mahayana Avalokiteshvara worship, in which Avalokiteshvara is perceived as Kannon with scores of shrines and temples throughout the Japanese islands.

To be sure, East Asian Buddhism in its various Mahayana forms triggered responses from Taoist and Confucian teachers. Confucian officials in China persecuted Buddhism nearly out of existence during the ninth century, on the grounds that Buddhist monasteries promoted anti-state and anti-family values. The survival of Mahayana Buddhism in later periods, especially after the anti-Buddhist campaigns of Japan's Meiji Emperor (1867–1912) and Mao's Cultural Revolution, testifies partly to the resilience of the Buddhist tradition, but also to the power of the basic religious impulse within each individual. Throughout the ages and across cultures, people sense a power greater than themselves and strive to experience it directly. Guanyin and Kannon offer East Asian Buddhists a way to act on this impulse in private devotion to tangible, personalized deities.

Japanese Visions

Many of the trends that shaped popular views of the divine in China were at work in Japan as well. The indigenous religion in Japan is known as Shinto, meaning "way of *kami*." Kami, or gods, are everywhere—in the landscape itself, in the forces of nature, and in various living creatures. Kami could also be ancestral deities, or loved ones who have died and passed into the spirit world. Shinto priests supervise the worship of a pantheon of gods with a Supreme Being at the summit, known as Amaterasu, goddess of the sun. In an odd twist, Japanese tradition perceives Amaterasu as female, with the earth god understood as male. As we learned in Chapter 3, most polytheistic and

Word to the Wise

Kami are the gods of traditional Japanese religion, known as Shintoism.

henotheistic schemes designate the genders of the sun and earth gods as male and female, respectively.

In the Shinto tradition, adherents visit family and neighborhood shrines and pray to the local kami, seeking to discern the divine *makoto*, or "will of the gods." These petitioners make requests and perform acts of devotion, hoping to receive guidance on how to live in harmony with the divine will. They even speak of the necessity of faith in kami in terms not unlike Western monotheisms. This impulse to develop a vital faith in the divine can also be detected in the Japanese version of Pure Land Buddhism (Jodo Shu), in stark contrast with the ethic of self-effort you find in the Zen variety. Shinto is alive and well today, despite the forces of modernization that have pushed Japanese culture in a secular direction. That's also true for the so-called New Religions that have attracted millions of converts through an enhanced group life, riveting visions of the apocalypse, or renewed emphasis on supernatural phenomena.

The New Religions of Japan are what you'd call synthetic, blending Taoist, Buddhist, Shinto, and even Hindu or Christian ideas together in interesting and creative ways. But that's been the spirit of East Asian religion for thousands of years. Most Chinese, Japanese, Korean, Taiwanese, and others perceive a supreme power in the universe; in different times and places, this power bore the name Shang-di, Tao, Great Ultimate, Guanyin, and Amaterasu, among others. By a variety of means, such as meditation, ritual observances, pilgrimage, divination, and even yoga, East Asians seek this power in order to achieve a state of harmony and balance with it. And in contrast to the exclusive loyalties expected of Western monotheists, East Asian traditions exhibit greater permissiveness as the faithful engage the supreme power in its multitudinous forms. It is altogether common to see a Chinese citizen pay homage to ancestor deities, spend hours in Buddhist-style meditation, and ponder the deeper meanings of the *Tao Te Ching*.

The Least You Need to Know

- T'ien is the central concept in popular Chinese religion, meaning "heaven," which has the features Westerners typically associate with God.

- The Tao (or Way) is impossible to describe, and it's safer to refer to it as Nothing than as Something; and yet Taoists believe it's the ultimate reality of the universe.

◆ In Confucianism and Neo-Confucianism, li means "principle," in reference to the rituals that create order in human affairs.

◆ East Asian Buddhists tend toward the Mahayana end of the spectrum, with special emphasis on devotion to the Buddha Guanyin (China) and Kannon (Japan).

◆ Millions of East Asian people worship ancestral deities at family and neighborhood shrines.

Part 6

Keeping the Faith

Not more than two or three generations ago, quite a number of people doubted whether belief in God would survive in the modern era. This part details the modern case against God, mounted by intellectuals and activists of the nineteenth and twentieth centuries. As it turns out, comparatively few have been persuaded by the case against God. Millions embrace faith because they're convinced that belief is more intellectually defensible than disbelief; millions more sense spiritual realities that cannot be explained using the language of modern science. Their continued faith tells us that belief in God offers meaning, hope, and purpose in uncertain times. But our religions can also be a source of trouble and uncertainty; we often forget that our visions of God are fragmentary and incomplete, and we sometimes allow conflicting perspectives to lapse into sectarian and inter-religious violence.

26

The Case Against God in the Modern World

In This Chapter

- ◆ Certainty and uncertainty in religious belief
- ◆ Enlightenment rationalism and French atheism
- ◆ The great conversation about God in modern Germany
- ◆ Is anything real beyond what we can see?
- ◆ Challenges to orthodox concepts of God

Not that long ago, it became fashionable in European and American societies to deny the existence of God and to complain about the ideas and lifestyles of God's chief advocates. Atheism crystallized as an intellectual fad during the Enlightenment, a philosophical doctrine in nineteenth-century Positivism and Marxism, an official state ideology in the Soviet Union (and Maoist China, too), and finally, a diffuse cultural ethos in the secularizing West. To be sure, defenders of the faith stepped up with an unflinching case for continued belief in God.

But even if we take atheism out of the picture, people throughout the world appeared to be shrinking the space they allowed God to inhabit in their busy social, professional, and political lives. Over the last few centuries, the faithful watched with growing concern as millions became disenchanted with traditional religious beliefs and practices and followed secular faiths like nationalism and consumerism, which promised earthly fulfillment with no moral constraints or spiritual obligations. In this chapter, you'll get a sense of why some believers are convinced that the greatest threat to belief in God has come not from the tiny rivulet of exhibitionist atheism, but from the rising tide of disinterest in otherworldly pursuits, running right down to the present day.

How Can We Know Anything for Sure?

If you're like most people, your first instinct is to question whatever it is that you're told to believe. Everybody wants proof, and when we don't get it we remain skeptical. This is especially true for things that are mysterious and incomprehensible, like God.

The Trouble with Proof

The question of proof is very much at the center of much Western thinking about the divine. It goes way back to ancient Greece and Rome, since Thomas Aquinas relied on Aristotle to explain how rational people could continue to believe in God in the face of our natural skepticism. Soon, however, John Duns Scotus and William of Ockham influenced the way we talk about proof of God's existence by widening the gap between what we can know for certain and what we must accept on faith (see Chapter 14). Proof seemed elusive for thinkers who tried to enlist it in the service of Christian belief, and this experience shaped the perspective of philosophers in the coming centuries. This was certainly true of French philosopher Michel de Montaigne's cautions about saying anything definitive about God, which we learned about in Chapter 5.

Pascal's Wager

One of Montaigne's countrymen, Blaise Pascal (1623–1662), contributed to suspicions about reason. Pascal happened to be a child prodigy in mathematics and engineering, and one day at the age of 31, he had a direct, supernatural experience of the power of God. He came away from his encounter convinced of the inability of reason to prove the divine, let alone comprehend its nature or essence. This point of view lay behind Pascal's wager, in which the mathematician argued the probability against the certainty of God's existence. Pascal wrote, "God is, or He is not. But to which side shall we incline? Reason can decide nothing here. There is an infinite chaos which separated us." (*Pensées*, c. 1658) You can't know for certain whether God exists, but given the likelihood and the stakes, it's a safe bet: "If you gain, you gain all; if you lose, you lose nothing. Wager, then, without hesitation that He is."

> **Pearls of Wisdom**
>
> Blaise Pascal wrestled with certainty and uncertainty in the area of religious belief as few others in history have done. Lots of comments about faith have been attributed to him, including this one: "Faith certainly tells us what the senses do not, but not the contrary of what they see; it is above, not against them."

The Cartesian Moment

If you listen closely, you might hear Pascal saying that the odds are even that God exists at all. That's quite a startling admission for someone living in the mid-seventeenth century. Other intellectuals of the period weren't ready to give up on certainty in favor of mathematical probabilities, including the most influential of them all, René Descartes (1596–1650). You might remember him for his famous line, "I think, therefore I am." This notion came in the wake of an intellectual crisis in which Descartes questioned the reliability of all forms of knowledge, whether from established authorities, sense experience, or commonsense reasoning.

The one saving grace, Descartes supposed, was that he had in his mind the thought that he exists. This thought provided sufficient certainty that he did exist, and that other truths could be deduced from this single, self-evident truth. For example, he proposed that his mind could conceive of a self-existent, limitless, and perfect God. According to Descartes, an *idea* of a perfect God that doesn't correspond to an *actual* perfect God is a logical impossibility, since nonexistence would render God less than perfect. And the idea of an infinite God could only come from a Supreme Being, since the finite human mind could never conceive of such a thing by itself. This gave Descartes the kind of certainty he needed to rescue belief from the clutches of doubt.

A Scientific Revolution

Descartes utilized reason to deduce God's existence and to account for God's attributes. Others, such as Johannes Kepler and Francis Bacon, had been working along similar lines, trying to discern the principles of order in the universe by means of the faculties of mind; that is, by sense experience. By the late seventeenth century, this rational process reached its high point with Isaac Newton's discovery of the laws of motion. As a consequence, intellectuals now understood the universe in mechanistic terms, and preferred to describe its workings with mathematical, rather than theological, language. Enlightened thinkers such as Rousseau, Voltaire, and Jefferson weighed in with talk of the laws of nature and nature's God, setting aside miracles, the Trinity, and other Christian teachings that defy rational explanation.

Divinations

Atheism and religious disinterest are important legacies of the Enlightenment in modern France. A 2004 poll found that only 12 percent of the population attends religious services of any faith more than once a month; 31 percent describe themselves as atheists, and 26 percent as indifferent to religion. In what used to be the most ardently Roman Catholic society in the world, church officials identify only 8 percent of the population as practicing Catholics. (U.S. Department of State, September 15, 2004)

The Advent of Atheism

It was in the context of the European Enlightenment that a few intellectuals firmly rejected the principles of theism and argued the position of God's nonexistence. As Alister McGrath recounts in his excellent study, *The Twilight of Atheism: The Rise and Fall of Disbelief in the Modern World* (Doubleday, 2004), early eighteenth-century critics (known as philosophes) struggled to rescue a reasonable concept of the Supreme Being from the evils of clerical hypocrisy, sectarian partisanship, oppressive dogmatism, and mindless superstition. Eventually, the philosophes began to despair of ever fixing these problems, and some drifted into principled atheism.

Julien Offroy de La Mettrie (1709–1751) and Paul-Henri Dietrich, baron d'Holbach (1723–1789) believed the concept of God to be a fabrication of the human mind and the source of incorrect thinking about the natural world. Flouting centuries of conventional wisdom, they reasoned that no God is required in order to understand the inner workings of nature. What these and other atheists had produced, in effect, was an early version of naturalism, a variant of materialism that would find eloquent spokesmen among the educated elites of Europe and America in the nineteenth and twentieth centuries.

Scientific Naturalism

Naturalism is the belief that all phenomena can be explained in terms of natural laws and natural causes. Most atheists in Western societies adhere to a form of naturalism. *Materialism* agrees, and adds that our thoughts, feelings, ideas, concepts, and so on are functions or operations of matter and energy. Yet materialists can still claim to perceive the divine by identifying the sum total of physical reality as God. We'll see in short order that some intellectual elites were unsatisfied with these trends in eighteenth-century higher thought. Several of these thinkers gave us the school of philosophy we know as idealism, which holds the view that there's a higher reality beyond the physical world, composed of ultimate concepts and principles—absolutes—that provide the key to our understanding.

> **Word to the Wise**
>
> **Naturalism** refers to the belief that all phenomena can be explained in terms of natural causes and natural laws with no reference to spiritual causes.

The Idealists

Descartes, Baruch Spinoza (whom we met in Chapters 2 and 9), and the Enlightenment philosophes wrestled with the fundamental issue of what we can know for certain about the highest reality of the universe. The Scottish philosopher David Hume (1711–1776) pushed this issue much farther than anyone could have imagined. His philosophical theory, known as radical empiricism, broke the presumed link between cause and effect that lay at the heart of Newtonian physics, throwing the entire system of universal natural laws into question.

Hume interpreted reality as a function of individual sense perception and personalized experience; of course, this wrecks the whole idea of a deity that operates universally across time and space. Hume liked neither the philosophes' depiction of God as a Cosmic Designer, nor the traditional theistic perception of an omniscient, omnipotent, infinite Supreme Being, personally involved with humankind and the natural world. In his book *The Blind Watchmaker* (W.W. Norton, 1994), Richard Dawkins, one of the most well-known atheists living today, quotes Hume as saying, "I have no explanation for complex biological design. All I know is that God isn't a good explanation, so we must wait and hope that somebody comes up with a better one."

Kant to the Rescue

A response to Hume became critical, if only to salvage the idea that one can obtain knowledge, and that this knowledge can help us understand more clearly the ultimate reality of the universe. Religion, philosophy, science, ethics, and most other systems of thought hung in the balance. Into this debate entered German philosopher Immanuel Kant with his *Critique of Pure Reason* (1781), which countered Hume's theory of knowledge with the assertion that the human mind does possess certain a priori categories—a kind of mental hardwiring—that enables it to discern patterns, establish relationships, and form theories. In other words, we're not left with mere sense perception and individualized experience, since these a priori categories enable the thinking person to organize their perceptions and experiences in meaningful ways.

> **Take Heed!**
>
> Be careful not to place rational skeptics in the same category as outright atheists. Folks like Rousseau and Voltaire weren't atheists in the technical sense, but progressive thinkers who thought they were "cleansing" the concept of God of those things that couldn't be proven through reason.

Kant's insights lifted science above the rocky shoals of radical empiricism, but he offered only modest help to the theologians; Kant, in fact, expressed doubt that the mind possessed the a priori categories necessary to make definitive statements on metaphysical topics such as time and eternity, the source of being, and the absolute subject of knowledge. Given the categories our minds actually do possess, we are fundamentally incapable of comprehending what a nontemporal and nonspatial being would be like.

G. W. F. Hegel's Absolute Spirit

That's where another German philosopher, G. W. F. Hegel (1770–1831), comes into the picture. The Enlightenment thinkers designated God as the Cosmic Designer (or less anthropomorphically, the Supreme Being) who fashioned the laws of nature, but left nature to run of its own accord. In response to this impersonal, distant, changeless deity, Hegel offered a different vision. He thought that God, whom he dubbed the Absolute Spirit, was evident in natural phenomena, in thoughts and ideas, and in human history.

Kant had written extensively about thoughts and ideas, and Hegel agreed with Kant that the human mind isn't limited to mere sense perception and experience. But Hegel went further, claiming that each human mind contains the means necessary to appreciate the Absolute Spirit in its manifestation as universal Mind. According to Hegel, when thinking people discover some truth about nature, they have a direct and immediate experience of Absolute Spirit. In Hegel's system, Absolute Spirit has the potential to become manifest in human experience, which occurs in the process of scientific discovery and flashes of philosophical insight. With each successive advance in human understanding, Hegel reasoned, Absolute Spirit inches closer and closer to a full realization in human experience.

What you get in Hegel, then, is a fundamentally knowable deity, inextricably bound within the web of human experience, and moving in the direction of actuality in the dynamic process of human growth and development. Of course you can probably detect an element of Jewish Kabbalah (see Chapter 8), and a foreshadowing of Christian process theology (see Chapter 15) in Hegel's view of God as dependent on humanity in form and substance.

Atheism's Modern Architects

Kant and Hegel are important figures in the preservation of a philosophically in-formed understanding of the Absolute. But they couldn't stem the tide of skepticism that emerged from French atheism and the radical empiricism of David Hume and his second-generation disciples, known as positivists. A group of nineteenth-century German scholars emerged whom experts typically consult to understand the dimensions of disbelief in the modern era.

Arthur Schopenhauer: God as an Illusion

It isn't a coincidence that Germany played host to a good bit of modern rethinking of the Western concept of God. Germany produced Martin Luther, Gottfried Leibniz, Immanuel Kant, and Georg Hegel, each of whom contributed to the ongoing conversation about God in Western civilization. Arthur Schopenhauer (1788–1860), a philosopher who lived most of his life in Frankfurt, rebuked Kant's and Hegel's confidence in human reason, and instead reduced all of reality to human will in his famous book *The World as Will and Idea* (1817).

According to Schopenhauer, beneath the intellect, beneath ideas, beneath concepts, there lay only one driving force: the basic human impulses and desires that inform our judgment and direct our choices. Whatever else we believe in, Schopenhauer argued, was mere illusion, including God. He went on to teach a Buddhist-style renunciation of human desires as the only way to live in peace and contentment, which he thought might be enhanced by aesthetic appreciation of visual arts and musical compositions.

Ludwig Feuerbach: God as a Projection

Like Schopenhauer, Ludwig Andreas Feuerbach (1804–1872) considered the Western idea of God to be essentially illusory. In his book *The Essence of Christianity* (1841), Feuerbach went even further, ascribing the religious vision of Western Christianity to humanity's self-created notions of sinfulness and inadequacy. He believed that human beings see themselves as finite, and therefore cast a vision of God as infinite; they see themselves as corrupt and sinful, and project a vision of God as perfect and holy.

These tendencies to see humanity as limited and immoral, Feuerbach reasoned, resulted in a completely externalized and transcendent God, and a hopelessly negative human self-image. As a corrective, Feuerbach taught the need to take all the good qualities that people have long attributed to the divine, and reinvest them in themselves. In other words, you have to get rid of God in order to elevate and enrich humanity. As he wrote in *The Essence of Christianity*, "religion is the dream of the human mind," and "God is man, and man is God."

Karl Marx: God as a Drug

Schopenhauer and Feuerbach made religion an object of serious scholarly reflection, and they concluded that much of our concept of God is of human rather than divine origin. In other words, they concluded that God exists because people have led themselves to believe in such a divine being, not because such a divine being has revealed itself to humanity.

The ground had been prepared for the thunderous pronouncements of Marx and Nietzsche, which together formed the creed of contemporary disbelief. Marx, a German social critic, historian, and standard-bearer for the international communist movement, reduced all of reality to material conditions and forces. He was an ardent student of Hegel and was influenced greatly by his thinking, but Marx denied that Absolute Sprit was the prime initiator and ultimate terminus of the historical process.

Instead, Marx believed that history is driven by conflict between owners of wealth (capitalists) and their workers. He believed that the ultimate resolution of this conflict will be achieved through a worker's rebellion, which will lead to the attainment of an earthly utopia. Marx believed that capitalists nurtured belief in God in order to tranquilize the poor into accepting their own economic exploitation.

Religion, Marx famously quipped, is "the opium of the people." And so millions of his readers came to believe that rabbis, priests, and ministers had duped them into believing that true fulfillment lay in not in this life, but in an afterlife in heaven or paradise. Joining with Marx and other communist leaders, communist supporters pressed for fulfillment through collective action, designed to advance the social and economic status of the industrial working class.

Friedrich Nietzsche: God Is Dead

Perhaps more than any other thinker, Friedrich Nietzsche (1844–1900) succeeded in synthesizing the ideas of Schopenhauer, Feuerbach, and Marx into a highly persuasive and influential philosophy of life. Nietzsche felt that Christianity perverted reality when it designated the normal human impulses of self-assertion, self-promotion, and self-expression as vices that must be disciplined and controlled. In famous books such as *Thus Spoke Zarathustra* (1885), *Beyond Good and Evil* (1886), and *Twilight of the Idols* (1888), Nietzsche foretold the end of this distorted reality.

> Perhaps the most solemn concepts which have occasioned the most strife and suffering, the concepts "God" and "sin," will one day seem to us of no more importance than a child's toy and a child's troubles seem to an old man—and perhaps "old man" will then have need of another toy and other troubles—still enough of a child, an eternal child. *(Beyond Good and Evil)*

Nietzsche observed in modern Germany an important trend: The pursuit of business, leisure activities, and family life contributed to a general indifference to God, or as he wrote in *Beyond Good and Evil*, "it seems that they have no time at all left for religion."

It was this indifference to Christian faith and practice that led Nietzsche to his famous dictum, "God is dead; but considering the state the species Man is in, there will perhaps be caves, for ages yet, in which his shadow will be shown." (*Ecce Homo*, 1888) Clearly, Nietzsche had nothing but contempt for Christianity, but his contempt also applied to other systems of thought based on the perception of eternal absolutes, such as Kant's theory of knowledge.

Nietzsche taught a philosophy of *nihilism:* There are no moral or spiritual absolutes. If you want to be rescued from the intellectual and psychological enslavement of traditional morality, you must do it yourself. The exceptional person who manages to escape blind conformity to slavish moral codes and acts according to his or her own will to power, Nietzsche called übermensch or overman. Nietzsche gave the West a new secular creed of individual self-determination and a sophisticated way to reject belief in a higher reality beyond the material world and a personal God who demands obedience and devotion.

> **Word to the Wise**
>
> **Nihilism** is the rejection of metaphysical truths—such as any article of belief in God—along with denial of moral absolutes and transcendent values.

A Material World: Darwin and Freud

Nietzsche would probably have been Public Enemy Number One in Western societies if Charles Darwin (1809–1882) hadn't beaten him to the title. Scores of religious leaders streamed to the defense of traditional Christian cosmology in the face of Darwin's account of natural selection and human evolution in *Origin of Species* (1859) and *Descent of Man* (1871). We learned in Chapter 15 that Darwinism perceived a world in motion driven by blind chance with no apparent design or intention.

Darwin understood the implications of his theories for conventional ideas about creation, and he fueled the growth of the sort of indifference that Nietzsche discerned in the 1870s and 1880s. The whole arc of development from Newton to Locke to Schopenhauer to Marx to Darwin to Nietzsche worked against the traditional view of a divinely created universe, sustained by the ongoing presence of a supernatural force or being. It wasn't so much that God had died, as that people no longer felt a need to reference God in order to make the natural world and human affairs seem comprehensible.

> **Divinations**
>
> Charles Darwin went to Cambridge University to study theology, but detoured into botany and geology. It took him a while to lose his faith, starting with doubts about the mythic account of creation in Genesis, and maturing in a rejection of rational proofs for the existence of God. His disenchantment was complete by the end of his life. In his autobiography, he speculated that belief in God evolved as a genetic trait, much like a monkey's "instinctive fear and hatred of the snake."

Just 100 years ago it was the norm among the educated classes to compartmentalize the divine into an increasingly small space. But to traditionalists, the worse was yet to come. The one thing that most thinkers throughout history were sure was the product of divine intelligence was the human mind. Imagination, creativity, intuition, reason, and other faculties of the mind were so mysterious and complex as to defy materialist explanations. But Sigmund Freud (1856–1939) claimed to correct this deficiency in his pathbreaking work, notably *The Interpretation of Dreams* (1900), *The Ego and the Id* (1923), and *Civilization and Its Discontents* (1930).

Freud affirmed the nineteenth-century consensus among the educated elite that human behavior is driven by nonrational impulses such as fears and desires, but he went on to develop a way to talk about these impulses that helped people understand their source and function. By using concepts like id and ego, Freud claimed that our mental states are shaped by primal instincts such as self-preservation or sexual gratification, which are conditioned, sometimes rather unhealthily, by society's need for cooperation and self-discipline. As for God, Freud dismissed the divine Other in the materialist fashion of Feuerbach and Nietzsche before him, as a childish projection of an individual's instinctual desire for paternal love and protection.

Scientific Study of Religion

The architects of atheism mustered a pretty compelling brief in the case against God by the time Freud ended his professional career in the period between World Wars I and II. The most fashionable segments of Western society appeared to follow Freud in his summary dismissal of religion as "comparable to a childhood neurosis." (*Future of an Illusion*, 1927) In the nineteenth and early twentieth centuries, scientists and philosophers preached that no belief could be entertained without hard, empirical evidence, and this article of faith won a harvest of true believers. Perhaps you'll find no greater measure of the acceptance of this belief than the so-called search for the historical Jesus.

The idea behind this movement is to investigate the historical basis for Christian beliefs about Jesus Christ, which isn't a new movement at all. But what gave the modern quest its peculiar character was an empirical mindset and, in a few notorious cases, partisan atheism. Modern scholarship wanted an objective biography of Jesus Christ, and began with a presumption of disbelief in miraculous occurrences that couldn't be proven either true or false using the tools of modern science.

During the Enlightenment period, a succession of German scholars—Johann Jakob Hess, Ernst August Opitz, Johann Adolph Jakobi, Johann Gottfried Herder, and Herman Samuel Reimarus—wrote biographies of Jesus reflecting a growing critical posture and rational spirit. But when David Friedrich Strauss published *Life of Jesus* (1836), scholarship confronted a fork in the road. Strauss rather severely challenged the Gospel accounts of Jesus, claiming that the writers cloaked his life in mythology, especially the question of Jesus' messiahship, for which Strauss could find no basis in Jewish history. Strauss also questioned Gospel accounts of supernatural occurrences, from the Incarnation to the Transfiguration to the Resurrection, saying that they were without rational or scientific warrant.

As we've seen in previous chapters, the people of faith responded to new movements in science, philosophy, and religious studies by creatively adapting their beliefs and incorporating the insights of modern scholarship. In the next chapter, you'll encounter voices which sought to preserve a traditional concept of God in all its supernatural and metaphysical splendor.

The Least You Need to Know

- Several efforts to rescue knowledge from radical skepticism, as the work of Descartes and Kant, were critical to ongoing belief in God.

- The intellectual movements of the eighteenth and nineteenth centuries led many educated people in Western societies to reject religious explanations for the natural world.

- Modern scholarship tended to produce disenchantment and disillusionment with conventional doctrines of Judaism and Christianity.

- The ideas of Marx, Nietzsche, and Freud established parameters for the twentieth-century debate about the existence of God.

- Modern Biblical and religious scholarship encouraged many people in the West to reject supernatural explanations for the origins of sacred texts and religious practices.

Chapter 27

Rescuing Belief in Uncertain Times

In This Chapter

- ◆ Believers respond to the case against God
- ◆ The seductive allure of certainty
- ◆ Rediscovering the supernatural and miraculous
- ◆ Finding God amid tragedy and despair
- ◆ God always heals; religion sometimes hurts

Recently, a book appeared with the provocative title, *Can a Smart Person Believe in God?* by Michael Guillen (Nelson Books, 2004). Before the nineteenth century, such a question would have been considered profane, and foolish, too. Yet this question is taken seriously today, and probably most people think it deserves an answer. That's a measure of the success of the modern case against God. In the last century, the most highly educated segments of Western society formed a loose consensus around the idea that what can be known for certain are scientifically verifiable facts, and not much else. This left little room for miraculous events, spirits and specters, and faith-based explanations for the creation of the universe.

Somehow, many of us internalized Mark Twain's famous quip: "Faith is believing what you know ain't so." Our hearts insist that there must be something out there, beyond the reality we can perceive with our senses, and yet our minds caution that such a thing is a scientific impossibility. So can we ever escape this predicament? Can we commit to belief in the divine without the sort of proof that would convince a philosophical skeptic, or a professional scientist? In this chapter, you'll encounter a wide range of voices that spoke in favor of God amid widespread disbelief and disinterest in the modern world. And we'll encounter others who struggled to understand God's mysterious ways in the face of terrible, earth-shattering events like world war, apocalyptic disasters, and genocide.

The Will to Believe

As thinking creatures, we're beguiled by the idea of certainty. Nobody wants to be proven a fool by accepting beliefs that might turn out to be false or unfounded. As St. Augustine once wrote, "Anxiety about what I could believe as certain gnawed at my heart all the more sharply as I grew more and more ashamed that I have been misled and deluded by promises of certainty for so long, and had talked wildly, like an ignorant child, about so many unconfirmed theories as though they were beyond question." (*Confessions* 6.4) This position presents several options: believe in the face of uncertainty, reject any belief that can't be proven beyond the shadow of a doubt, or suspend judgment until more evidence can be obtained.

In recent times, the option to believe in the face of certainty increasingly fell out of favor. Millions seemed to follow Mark Twain in his cynical view of faith as belief in something we know is false. Mark Twain's contemporary, philosopher William James of Harvard University, addressed this very problem in an 1896 speech to the Philosophy Clubs of Yale and Brown universities, called "The Will to Believe." If you want to learn how one terribly smart person answered the question of how one can believe in the face of uncertainty, James's speech is an excellent place to begin. What he offers is a "defense of our right to adopt a believing attitude in religious matters, in spite of the fact that our merely logical intellect may not have been coerced."

> ### Pearls of Wisdom
>
> When I first knew you, you raised me up so that I could see that there was something to be seen, but also that I was not yet able to see it. I gazed on you with eyes too weak to resist the dazzle of your splendor.
>
> —St. Augustine, *Confessions*, 7.10

How can this be done? James starts his speech by criticizing Pascal's wager (see Chapter 26) as the "last desperate snatch at a weapon against the hardness of the unbelieving heart," and pointing out that if he was in God's shoes, he would "take pleasure in cutting off believers of this pattern from their infinite reward." Belief shouldn't arise from a calculation of odds, but from personal volition—an act of will. Furthermore, we should not only know what we believe, but why we believe it. The problem is that objective evidence and certainty elude our grasp; James wonders, "where on this moonlit and dream-visited planet are they found?"

Try as you might, you'll never find a test of truth that all human beings can agree upon: "The intellect, even with truth directly in its grasp, may have no infallible signal for knowing whether it be truth or no." This shortcoming in human knowledge left nineteenth-century skeptics to conclude that it's better to go on disbelieving forever rather than accept a lie. And here's where James's speech strikes against the religious skeptics and scientific empiricists of his age. He rejects the disbelievers' command "that we shall put a stopper on our heart, instincts, and courage, and *wait*— acting of course meanwhile more or less as if religion were *not* true till doomsday, or till such time as our intellect and senses working together may have raked in evidence enough." The command to suspend belief in the face of insufficient empirical evidence is itself a kind of belief. If you follow this logic, you are betting the field against the religious hypothesis, whereas the believer is betting the religious hypothesis against the field.

To James's way of thinking, those who wager against the religious hypothesis, suspending belief until the day of certainty arrives, choose to worship the "the queerest idol ever manufactured in the philosophic cave." In effect, they decide to put off making a decision until absolute certainty pulls into view. But they'll wait forever, given the imperfections of human reason and the impossibility of a universal test of truth upon which everyone can agree. James teaches that everyone takes a "leap in the dark," whether you choose to believe in God, or choose to leave the biggest riddles of existence unanswered. In the end, James finds comfort in the words of Fitz-James Stephen: "'We stand on a mountain pass in the midst of whirling snow and blinding mist, through which we get glimpses now and then of paths which may be deceptive.'" What do we do? "'Act for the best, hope for the best,'" and if death is the end of existence, "'we cannot meet death better.'"

A Reason to Believe

Like many other thinkers in the modern era, James concluded that the case against God hinged on a highly questionable view of proof, since the religious skeptic applied the test of certainty to beliefs about God, but not to other systems of knowledge, such as science. Today we're a little more savvy in this regard; in 2005, when Nobel Prize–winning physicist Charles Townes won the Templeton Prize, awarded annually to a person who makes the largest contribution to religion, the prize committee noted that both science and theology are "human perspectives trying to explain and to find meaning in the universe, [and] both are fraught with uncertainty."

But James seemed to hint, and others affirmed, that belief in God has a rational foundation. Prominent Roman Catholic writers such as Jacques Maritain (1882–1973) helped to develop an influential movement known as Neo-Thomism, which reminded Europeans of the broader conception of proof in the Western intellectual tradition that included philosophically sound reasoning as well as empirically verifiable data. The Neo-Thomists joined forces with popular writers such as G. K. Chesterton (1874–1936) and C. S. Lewis (1898–1963), who argued that traditional Christian beliefs are defensible precisely because they satisfy our commonsense and intuitive understanding of the world as logical, but not so perfectly logical as to preclude mystery and miracle.

In response to the God-deniers, Lewis wondered, where did Nietzsche derive his ideas about justice and injustice, or bondage and freedom? Lewis argued that these judgments against religion must have some foundation in moral absolutes, which testifies to the truth of the religious vision. He contended that when humanity uses reason to disprove God, they wind up proving God's existence because they can find no other plausible explanation for where reason itself came from. Against Freud and many others who rooted reason, consciousness, and morality in material conditions, Lewis said in *Miracles* (1947) that "rationality is the little telltale rift in Nature which shows that there is something beyond or behind her." Indeed, "the rational and moral element in each human mind is a point of force from the Supernatural working its way into Nature."

CAUTION

Take Heed!

The supposed war between science and religion is a matter of perception, not fact. Of course both communities have extremists who deny the "other side" its proper role in the advance of human understanding. Moderate voices recognize the value of each, and view science and religion as the two barrels of a pair of binoculars. Without both, we get a skewed perspective on the world's material and spiritual realities.

Seekers

Chesterton and Lewis reminded readers of the existence of spiritual realities that can't be detected by the tools of modern science. As a matter of fact, a quiet rebellion against the contraction of the religious vision in Western Europe had been brewing for some time. Enlightenment dissidents such as William Blake (1757–1827) had little use for the mechanistic view of the universe touted by avant-garde intellectuals and instead celebrated imagination and intuition. Frederich Schleiermacher (1768–1834), a German minister and theologian, resonated with Romantic poets like Blake in *On Religion: Speeches to Its Cultured Despisers* (1799), which maintained that religion is the "feeling and intuition of the universe," and that humanity's special gift is its "sense of the Infinite in the finite." Nobel Prize–winning writer Henri Bergson (1859–1941) gave intuition a shot of intellectual respectability in *Two Sources of Morality and Religion* (1932), a book that celebrated the creative power of spiritual visionaries.

Thomas Merton (1915–1968), a Roman Catholic monk and writer of popular spiritual texts, provides an illustration of this increasing appreciation of intuition and mystical religious experience. As a young student in France and the United States, Merton cycled through the intellectual fashions of nihilism, Marxism, and Freudianism, convinced that he had "suddenly risen above all the errors and stupidities and mistakes of modern society." As he remembered later, "I became a true citizen of my own disgusting century: the century of poison gas and atomic bombs. A man living on the doorsill of the Apocalypse, a man with veins full of poison, living in death." Merton realized that "my soul was simply dead. It was a blank, a nothingness." (*The Seven Storey Mountain*, 1948)

Divinations

Women's spirituality has been a subject of intense research and commentary in recent years. Some helpful starting points include the work of Kathleen Norris (*The Cloister Walk* [G. K. Hall, 1996]), Anne Lamott (*Traveling Mercies: Some Thoughts on Faith* [Pantheon Books, 1999]), and Asra Nomani (*Standing Alone in Mecca: An American Woman's Struggle for the Soul of Islam* [HarperSanFrancisco, 2005]).

So how did Merton revive his soul? He visited churches and spoke with great teachers. He read voraciously, including many of the books we've learned about here. He came to appreciate intuition in the writings of William Blake and Neo-Thomism in the work of Jacques Maritain. A Hindu mystic named Bramachari turned Merton on to St. Augustine's *Confessions* and Thomas à Kempis's *Imitation of Christ*. Christian theology and experiential piety offered Merton the nourishment his soul required; from here Merton converted to Christianity, embraced the contemplative life in a Trappist monastery, and wrote books advocating the spiritual path to wisdom and truth. And he found in Christianity and Buddhism what he couldn't find in Marx, Nietzsche, and Freud—the ethical principles you need to combat evils like violence and racial injustice.

Merton's writings and appearances further encouraged a legion of seekers to move in the direction of contemplation and mysticism. You might say that divine revelation found a new life in the twentieth century. There are lots of ways to measure this resurgence. Over the last century, a Pentecostal and Charismatic revival washed across the Protestant and Catholic communities, bringing literally hundreds of millions of Christians in every part of the world to celebrate miraculous visitations of the Holy Spirit, who gives believers the power to speak in different languages, heal the sick, and exorcise demons.

Protestant Evangelicals such as Carl F. H. Henry and Karl Barth came to the defense of the divine inspiration of scripture against the humanistic trends in Biblical interpretation. Catholic pilgrims flock to shrines where the Blessed Virgin Mary has reportedly been seen or experienced. Everywhere you look you see a resurgence of interest in the supernatural, even in popular culture. Television is rife with programming such as CBC's *Joan of Arcadia*, the story of a teenage girl who experiences God in the form of ordinary people, and NBC's *Medium*, a story about a woman who uses her psychic powers to catch criminals. New religions in the East, such as Shinreikyo in Japan, stress the wonder of miracles.

It's easy to account for this renewed interest in the supernatural: The idea of divine revelation offers people a way to understand things that simply defy explanation. Even in the most advanced fields of science, such as particle physics, we're confronted with inexplicable phenomena; quantum mechanics leaves scientists to ponder the intrinsic randomness inherent in the behavior of particles and forces. To cite another example, a well-received book titled *The Mysterious Flame: Conscious Minds in a Material World* (Basic Books, 2000) by Rutgers philosopher Colin McGinn says that the human mind is not equipped to answer the question of how and why it has consciousness. Cognitive scientists are hard at work on the subject, but for now it looks like we have to take it as a given. These developments leave us scratching our heads, reminding us of Albert Einstein's famous quote, uttered in frustration over quantum mechanics: "The theory yields much but it hardly brings us closer to the Old One's secrets. I, in any case, am convinced that he [God] does not play dice."

Help in Times of Need

Belief in miracles satisfies our inner sense of something larger than ourselves, some unfathomable power, that provides direction, purpose, and meaning to existence. In a chaotic world, we rely on God to help us make sense of tragedy, suffering, and despair.

Meaning in Tragedy

When tragedy befalls us, conversation about God offers a way for us to find meaning and purpose. Take, for example, Jewish responses to the Holocaust. Elie Wiesel's acceptance speech at the 1986 Nobel Prize ceremony posed the essential question: "Where was God in all this?" In *After Auschwitz* (The John Hopkins University Press, 1992), Richard Rubenstein offered a response, declaring that God died at Auschwitz: "To see any purpose in the death camps, the traditional believer is forced to regard the most demonic, anti-human explosion in all of history as a meaningful expression of God's purposes. The idea is simply too obscene for me to accept." Wiesel offered a more mainstream *theodicy* by recalling the story of Job from Jewish scriptures: "His ordeal concerns all humanity. Did he ever lose his faith? If so, he rediscovered it within his rebellion. He demonstrated that faith is essential to rebellion, and that hope is possible

Word to the Wise

Theodicy means defense of God, which surfaces in discussions about the problem of evil in Western monotheism.

beyond despair. The source of his hope was memory, as it must be ours. Because I remember, I despair. Because I remember, I have the duty to reject despair."

Wiesel and Rubenstein pursued questions that have become all too familiar to us, as when Archbishop Rowan Williams of the Church of England asked in response to the December 2004 South Asian tsunami, "How can you believe in a God who permits suffering on this scale?" The BBC News documented the loss of faith of one South Asian woman, Malar, who lost her son Manimaran in the tragedy. She said, "When the tsunami hit I ran to the church and begged for the life of my son. All I got was his dead body. God cheated me." Malar's bitter indictment joined a chorus of angry renunciations of belief; and yet millions of others found meaning through traditional religious teachings. A Hindu woman, Gita Mahishwuarn, made sense of the tragedy by telling the BBC News that Hinduism holds out hope that one's current life isn't the final stage of one's existence, and that other lives, potentially greater and more rewarding, will follow. "Within the cycle of life there has to be birth, creation, preservation, and then destruction in order for life to continue," she remarked.

Both Elie Wiesel and Gita Mahishwuarn found in their respective traditions a way to wrest meaning from tragedy, and in the process discovered the hope that carries us through our darkest hours.

Pearls of Wisdom

The great poet of Islamic Sufism, Rumi, offers a compelling portrayal of separation and restoration:

> Listen to the story told by the reed, of being separated.
>
> "Since I was cut from the reedbed, I have made this crying sound.
>
> "Anyone separated from someone he loves understands what I say, anyone pulled from a source longs to go back."

A Reason to Go On Living

Whether we're speaking of escape from suffering in Buddhism, release from the cycle of reincarnation in Hinduism, or eternal life in heaven in Christianity, religious belief gives us a reason to go on living in a spirit of hopeful expectation.

Christianity, along with Judaism, Islam, and many other religions, perceives deities that listen and respond to humankind. They resonate with the vision offered by David in Psalm 23: "Even though I walk through the valley of the shadow of death, I fear no evil; for thou art with me; thy rod and thy staff, they comfort me." (v. 4) But even traditions like Theravada Buddhism or Taoism, which perceive the Absolute in quite impersonal terms, offer spiritual disciplines that still our troubled minds, or sacred texts that nourish our impoverished souls. And nearly all traditions offer comfort in the form of the community of the faithful, which provides guidance, prayer, fellowship, inspiration, healing, and even material support when the need arises.

Power for Living

In the speech we learned about earlier, William James referred to each person as a "small active center" who bears some connection to the ultimate reality of the universe. Depending on your tradition, this could mean that the cosmic struggle between good and evil is playing out in your very soul, or the essence of your inner being is one with the universal world spirit. The permutations are legion. What's important here is that our religious visions of God connect finite beings with the infinite being or reality of the universe, giving humanity its essential dignity, its reason for existence, and its source of power.

There are many ways to illustrate this power, some of which defy rational explanation. It's the power that sustained Mother Teresa, who served the poorest of the poor in the slums of Calcutta for 50 years. It's the power that made it possible for the late John Paul II to face death with dignity and grace, while offering worldwide spiritual leadership to hundreds of millions of Christians. It's the power that guided Mahatma Gandhi, Martin Luther King Jr., and Desmond Tutu to fight for social justice, and the power that enables believers to withstand persecution without surrendering their faith. But perhaps it's also the unfathomable power that can positively affect rates of conception in fertility clinics when unknowing mothers receive prayers from anonymous sources, as several scientific studies have shown. And maybe it's the power that Buddhists speak of when they describe the mind's ability to see the true nature of reality through meditation or visualization exercises.

The Politicization of God

Belief in God gives us meaning, hope, comfort, and power. Along the way, our religious traditions have made the world a better place. In 2005 Pope Benedict XVI was surprised to find a self-described atheist and postmodern theorist, Jürgen Habermas, agreeing with him that Judaism and Christianity produced great benefits for Western civilization, and Christianity's role in human progress should be acknowledged in the constitution of the European Union. Even so, religions can sometimes bring the darker parts of our nature to the surface.

Take Heed!

Don't assume that belief in God automatically results in violent fanaticism. If you travel to Teheran, for example, you might encounter Dr. Abdol Karim Soroush (b. 1945), a Muslim scholar known for his humanistic perspectives on sacred literature. His books *Attributes of the Pious* and *Wisdom and Subsistence* contribute to a very long tradition of scholarship in the Islamic tradition.

As you've read about in this book, our most spiritually gifted sages warn us time and time again that we shouldn't equate our limited and faulty concepts of God with the actual Supreme Being of the universe. Adherents sometimes ignore this sound advice and use incomplete concepts of God as wedges of separation, leading to sectarian strife and, regrettably, religious warfare. Where God comforts and heals, religions sometimes confuse and divide. This is especially true when God is enlisted in the cause of human projects like the creation of governments or the realignment of territorial boundaries. Nonreligious ideologies such as Nazism and Communism produced a vast harvest of death in the twentieth century, and yet we still must count the human costs that have resulted from the politicization of God.

Some numbers might help put human costs into perspective. In Ireland, the troubles between Roman Catholics and Ulster Protestants from 1966–1999 produced 3,636 deaths and over 30,000 injuries. In Nigeria, some 10,000 people have died in recent clashes between Christians and Muslims jockeying for electoral advantage in a budding democracy. Thousands perished in India following the destruction of the Babri Mosque in Ayodhya in 1992, which triggered waves of violence between Hindu and Muslim adherents. Uganda suffers today from the ongoing rebellion of the Lord's Resistance Army, which mutilates people who stand against their efforts to create a government based on the Ten Commandments. And this is to say nothing of the ongoing hostilities in the Middle East, where Jewish and Muslim extremists target moderate leaders within their own ranks merely on the grounds that these leaders have negotiated with their sworn enemy.

Today, people in the West cringe in fear of nuclear terrorism, now justified by radical Muslim clerics on the basis of their reading of the shari'ah, or Islamic law. They, and all of us, need to be reminded of the one thing that nearly all systems of belief about God agree upon: the need for humility in the face of the simple, yet undeniable fact that the human mind cannot possibly grasp the totality of God. I'm reminded of the Christian convert John Bunyan, who was plagued by a desire to have complete certainty about the things of God. At the end of a long spiritual journey, he achieved peace when he realized, "God had a bigger mouth to speak with, than I had heart to conceive with." Let's remember that God cannot be fully captured by any concepts or words we could devise for this purpose. Or in the words of Alfred Lord Tennyson …

> Our little systems have their day;
> They have their day and cease to be,
> They are but broken lights of Thee;
> And Thou, O Lord, art more than they.

—*In Memoriam*

The Least You Need to Know

- ◆ Gifted scholars and intellectuals discovered that the case against God rested on faith in certain unverifiable assumptions.

- ◆ The resurgence of belief in God in the contemporary world owes to the hope and healing that people find in God.

- ◆ One of the shared motifs in the world's religions is the idea of separation between humanity and the Absolute, with various methods of restoring this broken relationship.

- ◆ God provides comfort, healing, and hope, but sometimes our traditions fuel sinful patterns of animosity, hatred, and intolerance.

- ◆ A near-consensus opinion through all of history is that God is hard to understand; this should remind us to be humble about what we say and do on God's behalf.

Resources

Websites

These websites provide useful information on various topics on the subject of God, including many that feature encyclopedia-type articles written by experts in the field.

Buddhist Studies WWW Virtual Library
www.ciolek.com/WWWVL-Buddhism.html

The Catholic Encyclopedia
www.newadvent.org/cathen

Dictionary of the History of Ideas
http://etext.lib.virginia.edu/DicHist/dict.html

Encyclopedia Mythica
www.pantheon.org

Encyclopedia of Religion and Society
http://hirr.hartsem.edu/ency/index.html

Encyclopedia of Religious Knowledge
www.ccel.org/s/schaff/encyc/encyc13/htm/TOC.htm

Hindu Resources Online
www.hindu.org

Islam 101
www.islam101.com

Jewish Encyclopedia
www.jewishencyclopedia.com/index.jsp

The Jewish Virtual Library
www.jewishvirtuallibrary.org/jsource/index.html

Overview of World Religions Project
http://philtar.ucsm.ac.uk/encyclopedia

Religion Online
www.religion-online.org

A Shi'ite Encyclopedia
www.al-islam.org/encyclopedia

The Stanford Encyclopedia of Philosophy
http://plato.stanford.edu/contents.html

Wabash Guide to Resources in Theology and Religion
www.wabashcenter.wabash.edu/Internet/front.htm

World Wide Encyclopedia of Christianity
www.ccel.org/php/wwec.php

Books

It's hard to find a topic that generates more literature than the subject of God. The list of books is practically endless, ranging from introductory surveys of the various religious traditions to highly specialized works that explore particular areas of belief and practice. Here's a sampling that will help improve your understanding.

General Works

These books range broadly through the religious traditions to illustrate various ways that God has been perceived and experienced.

Armstrong, Karen. *A History of God: The 4,000 Year Quest of Judaism, Christianity and Islam*. New York: Ballantine Books, 1993.

Eastman, Roger. *The Ways of Religion: An Introduction to the Major Traditions*. Oxford: Oxford University Press, 1999.

Eliade, Mircea. *The Sacred and the Profane: The Nature of Religion*. New York: Harcourt, 1987.

James, William. *The Varieties of Religious Experience: A Study in Human Nature*. New York: Penguin Classics, 1983.

Kirsch, Jonathan. *God Against the Gods: The History of the War Between Monotheism and Polytheism*. New York: Viking Compass, 2004.

Moses, Jeffrey. *Oneness: Great Principles Shared by All Religions*. New York: Ballantine Books, 2002.

Otto, Rudolf. *The Idea of the Holy*. Oxford: Oxford University Press, 1958.

Peters, F. E. *The Children of Abraham: Judaism, Christianity, Islam*. New ed. Princeton: Princeton University Press, 2004.

Sire, James W. *The Universe Next Door: A Basic Worldview Catalog*. Downers Grove, Ill.: InterVarsity Press, 2004.

Smith, Huston. *The World's Religions: Our Great Wisdom Traditions*. San Francisco: HarperSanFrancisco, 1991.

Judaism

These books offer introductions to Biblical Judaism, the Rabbinic tradition, Jewish mysticism, and Jewish responses to modernity.

Ben-Sasson, H. H. *A History of the Jewish People*. Tel Aviv: Dvir Publishing House, 1969.

Cahill, Thomas. *The Gifts of the Jews: How a Tribe of Desert Nomads Changed the Way Everyone Thinks and Feels*. New York: Anchor Books, 1999.

Cohn-Sherbok, Dan. *The Vision of Judaism: Wrestling with God*. St. Paul, Minn.: Paragon House Publishers, 2004.

Cooper, David A. *God Is a Verb: Kabbalah and the Practice of Mystical Judaism*. New York: Riverhead Books, 1998

Dimont, Max I. *Jews, God, and History*. New York: Signet, 1994.

Eisen, Arnold M. *Rethinking Modern Judaism: Ritual, Commandment, Community*. Chicago: University of Chicago Press, 1999.

Friedman, Richard E. *Who Wrote the Bible?* San Francisco: HarperSanFrancisco, 1997

Kadushin, Max. *The Rabbinic Mind*. Binghamton, New York: Global Publications, 2001.

Miles, Jack. *God: A Biography*. New York: Vintage, 1996.

Neusner, Jacob. *Four Stages of Rabbinic Judaism*. London: Routledge, 1999.

Sachar, Howard M. *A History of Israel: From the Rise of Zionism to Our Time*. 2nd ed. New York: Knopf, 1996.

Sarna, Nahum M. *Exploring Exodus: The Origins of Biblical Israel*. New York: Schocken Books, 1996.

Scholem, Gershom. *On the Kabbalah and Its Symbolism*. New York: Schocken Books, 1969.

Smith, Mark S. *The Early History of God: Yahweh and the Other Deities in Ancient Israel*. 2nd ed. Grand Rapids, Mich.: Wm. B. Eerdmans Publishing Company, 2002.

Telushkin, Joseph. *Jewish Literacy: The Most Important Things to Know About the Jewish Religion, Its People and Its History*. New York: William Morrow, 1991.

Christianity

In these books you'll encounter the key themes in the origin and progress of Christian thought, from the time of Jesus to the present day.

Brown, Peter. *Religion and Society in the Age of St. Augustine.* Chicago: Faber and Faber, 1972.

Brown, Raymond E. *An Introduction to the New Testament.* New York: Doubleday, 1997.

Burkett, Delbert. *An Introduction to the New Testament and the Origins of Christianity.* Cambridge: Cambridge University Press, 2002.

Chadwick, Henry. *Early Christian Thought and the Classical Tradition: Studies in Justin, Clement, and Origen.* Oxford: Oxford University Press, 1984.

Fox, Robin Lane. *Pagans and Christians.* New York: Knopf, 1987.

Grenz, Stanley J., and Roger E. Olson. *Twentieth-Century Theology: God and the World in a Transitional Age.* Downers Grove, Ill.: InterVarsity Press, 1992.

Horsley, Richard A. *The Message and the Kingdom: How Jesus and Paul Ignited a Revolution and Transformed the Ancient World.* Minneapolis, Minn.: Augsburg Fortress Publishers, 2002.

Johnson, Paul. *A History of Christianity.* New York: Touchstone, 1976.

McGrath, Alister E. *Christian Theology: An Introduction.* 3rd ed. London: Blackwell Publishers, 2001.

————. *Reformation Thought: An Introduction.* 3rd ed. London: Blackwell Publishers, 1999.

Pelikan, Jaroslav. *The Christian Tradition: A History of the Development of Doctrine.* 4 v. Chicago: University of Chicago Press, 1978.

Price, James L. *The New Testament: Its History and Theology.* New York: Macmillan, 1987.

White, L. Michael. *From Jesus to Christianity: How Four Generations of Visionaries and Storytellers Created the New Testament and Christian Faith.* San Francisco: HarperSanFrancisco, 2004.

Wright, N. T. *Christian Origins and the Question of God.* 3 v. Minneapolis, Minn.: Augsburg Fortress Publishers, 1992–2003.

Islam

Here are some good starting points for an investigation into the life of the Prophet Muhammad, the nature of the Qur'an, the history of Islamic thought, and revitalization movements within the Islamic faith.

Armstrong, Karen. *Muhammad: A Biography of the Prophet.* Reprint ed. San Francisco: HarperSanFrancisco, 1993.

Aslan, Reza. *No God But God: The Origins, Evolution, and Future of Islam.* New York: Random House, 2005.

Delong-Bas, Natana. *Wahhabi Islam: From Revival to Reform to Global Jihad.* Oxford: Oxford University Press, 2004.

Esposito, John L. *What Everyone Needs to Know About Islam.* Oxford: Oxford University Press, 2002.

Fakhry, Majid. *A History of Islamic Philosophy.* 2nd ed. New York: Columbia University Press, 1987.

Mitchell, Richard P. *The Society of the Muslim Brothers.* Oxford: Oxford University Press, 1993.

Nasr, Sayyed Hossein. *Islam: Religion, History, Civilization*. San Francisco: HarperSanFrancisco, 2003.

———. *The Heart of Islam: Enduring Values for Humanity*. New York: HarperCollins, 2002.

Pickthall, Mohammad. *The Meaning of the Glorious Koran*. Rev. ed. Beltsville, Md.: Amana Publications, 2002.

Schuon, Frithjof. *Understanding Islam*. Bloomington, Ind.: World Wisdom Books, 1998.

Stoddart, William. *Sufism: The Mystical Doctrines and Methods of Islam*. Rev. ed. St. Paul, Minn.: Paragon House Publishers, 1986.

Taji-Farouki, Suha. *Modern Muslim Intellectuals and the Qur'an*. Oxford: Oxford University Press, 2004.

Watt, William Montgomery. *Islamic Fundamentalism and Modernity*. London: Routledge, 1990.

Hinduism

Hinduism is a rich and multifaceted tradition, and you'll learn more about the various schools and movements of Hinduism in these highly regarded books.

Babb, Lawrence. *Redemptive Encounters: Three Modern Styles in the Hindu Tradition*. Berkeley: University of California Press, 1986.

De Bary, William Theodore, ed. *Sources of Indian Tradition*. 2 v. New York: Columbia University Press, 1988.

Eck, Diana. *Darshan: Seeing the Divine Image in India*. Chambersburg, Penn.: Anima Books, 1985.

Hopkins, Thomas. *The Hindu Religious Tradition*. Belmont, Calif.: Wadsworth Publishing Company, 1982.

Jaffrelot, Christophe. *The Hindu Nationalist Movement in India*. New York: Columbia University Press, 1996.

Jones, Kenneth W. *Socio-Religious Reform Movements in British India*. Cambridge: Cambridge University Press, 1994.

Kinsley, David. *Hinduism: A Cultural Perspective*. Englewood Cliffs, N.J.: Prentice-Hall, 1982.

Klostermaier, Klaus K. *A Survey of Hinduism*. Albany: State University of New York Press, 1989.

Koller, John. *The Indian Way*. New York: Macmillan, 1982.

Larson, Gerald James. *India's Agony Over Religion*. Albany: State University of New York Press, 1995.

Mascaró, Juan, trans. *The Bhagavad Gita*. London: Penguin Books, 2003.

———, trans. *The Upanishads*. London: Penguin Books, 1965.

O'Flaherty, Wendy Doniger, trans. *The Rig Veda: An Anthology of One Hundred Eight Hymns*. London: Penguin Books, 1981.

Prabhavananda, Swami. *The Spiritual Heritage of India*. Hollywood, California: Vedanta Press, 1980.

———. *How to Know God: The Yoga Aphorisms of Patanjali*. Hollywood, Calif.: Vedanta Press, 1996.

Radhakrishnan, S. *The Hindu View of Life*. London: Allen & Unwin, 1964.

Zimmer, Heinrich. *The Philosophies of India*. Princeton: Princeton University Press, 1969.

Buddhism and Eastern Religions

Hundreds of millions of people follow paths in Buddhism and East Asian religions, and Westerners can find helpful information about these complex traditions in the following highly accessible books.

Govinda, Lama Anagarika. *Foundations of Tibetan Mysticism*. York Beach: Me.: Samuel Weiser, 1969.

Johnson, Willard. *The Buddhist Religion*. Belmont, Calif.: Wadsworth Publishing Company, 1982.

Kapleau, Philip. *The Three Pillars of Zen*. New York: Anchor Books, 1989.

Koller, John M., and Patricia Joyce Koller. *Asian Philosophies*. 3rd ed. Upper Saddle River, N.J.: Prentice Hall, 1998.

Lancaster, Lewis R., ed. *Contemporary Korean Religion*. Berkeley: Institute for East Asian Studies, 1992.

Lau, D. C., trans. *Lao Tzu: Tao Te Ching*. London: Penguin Books, 1963.

Lopez, Donald S., Jr., ed. *Buddhist Scriptures*. London: Penguin Books, 2004.

———. *Religions of China in Practice*. Princeton: Princeton University Press, 1996.

MacInnis, Donald E. *Religion in China Today*. New York: Orbis, 1989.

Pine, Red, trans. *The Heart Sutra*. Washington, D.C.: Shoemaker & Hoard, 2004.

———. *The Diamond Sutra: The Perfection of Wisdom*. New York: Counterpoint, 2001.

Reader, Ian. *Religion in Contemporary Japan*. Honolulu: University of Hawaii Press, 1991.

Suzuki, Shunryu. *Zen Mind, Beginner's Mind*. New York: John Weatherhill, 1970.

St. Ruth, Diana, and Richard St. Ruth. *The Simple Guide to Theravada Buddhism.* Folkestone, Kent (U.K.): Global Books, Ltd., 1998.

Watson, Bruce, trans. *The Lotus Sutra*. New York: Columbia University Press, 1993.

Wilhelm, Richard, and Cary F. Baynes, trans. *The I Ching, Or Book of Changes.* 3rd ed. Princeton: Princeton University Press, 1997.

Williams, Paul. *Mahayana Buddhism: The Doctrinal Foundations*. London: Routledge, 2001.

Yao, Xinzhong. *An Introduction to Confucianism*. Cambridge: Cambridge University Press, 2000.

Glossary

Advaita Vedanta   Hindu philosophical school that perceives all of existence as a single, unified reality.

agnosticism   Belief that one cannot know conclusively whether or not God exists.

anatta   Buddhist concept of no self or no soul, which denies the eternal spiritual identity of the individual.

animism   Belief that everything in the universe is filled with spirit, from the Latin word *anima* for "breath of life."

anthropomorphism   Act of assigning to God human traits such as compassion, jealousy, determination, and even angst, or depicting the divine in human form.

aqidah   Posture of fixity in regard to doctrine or belief, commonly associated with Islamic fundamentalism.

arhat   One who is worthy, in reference to the individual who has achieved nirvana in the Theravada Buddhist tradition.

asceticism   From the Greek for "athletic training," referring to the denial of bodily pleasures as a means to experience directly the divine.

Ashkenazim   Jews living in diaspora (dispersion) influenced by Germanic and Slavic cultures.

atheism   Belief that gods or spiritual beings do not exist.

Atman   Hindu concept of the unchanging essence of Brahman within the inner being of each individual.

avatar   Embodiment of the divine; in Hindu Vaishnava traditions, Vishnu takes the form of 10 different people or creatures.

awliya   Guardians or friends; in orthodox Islam, a legal and religious relationship, and in Sufism, the metaphysical power of the Shaykhs, both living and dead.

Baptism of the Holy Spirit   Belief among some Christians in the divine presence, which confers powers of healing, prophecy, or speaking in tongues.

bhakti   Hindu practice of devotion to a particular god, such as Shiv, or to one of the avatars of Vishnu.

bodhisattva   One who has achieved the Buddhist ideal of nirvana, but returns to help others find the path to enlightenment.

Brahman   Hindu concept of the universal world spirit.

brahmin   Member of the highest caste in Hindu society, believed to possess the greatest degree of spiritual purity.

Buddha   One who is enlightened or awakened and is destined to escape the cycle of rebirth in the blissful state of nirvana; used most often in reference to Siddhartha Gautama.

canon   Writings that are accepted as authoritative, mainly because they meet some standard of holiness or divine inspiration.

chi   *See* **qi**.

covenant   Agreement between two parties; used within Judaism to describe the relationship between Yahweh and the ancient Hebrew people.

Deism   Belief that God is revealed through reason and scientific inquiry, rather than supernatural or scriptural revelation; from the Latin *deus* for God.

devas   Gods of ancient Vedic religion prior to the period of the *Upanishads* and the appearance of Buddhism.

dharma   Law or duty; in Hinduism, the obligations of one's caste, or "way of life," and in Buddhism, the Buddha's teachings, which lead to enlightenment.

dhikr   Arabic for "remember," used in connection with the Muslim devotional practice of contemplating the name of Allah.

dualism   Distinction between mind and body, or good and evil, but most often, a division of reality into two realms, matter and spirit.

duhkha   Buddhist concept of human suffering, caused by selfish desire or craving.

Eightfold Path   Buddhist plan for achieving salvation, or release from the wheel of rebirth.

emanation   Idea that lower principles and realities flow out from some ultimate, absolute principle or reality.

falsafah   Movement in medieval Islamic and Jewish philosophy that explored the rational foundation of belief.

fiqh   Practice of legal reasoning in relation to the religious laws of Islam.

Five Pillars of Faith   Islamic concept of religious duties required of all members, including confession of faith, prayers, fasting, almsgiving, and pilgrimage.

fundamentalism   Modern religious movements that seek to preserve traditional beliefs and practices in response to perceived weakening of religious commitment.

hadiths   Recorded sayings of the Prophet Muhammad.

hajj   One of the Five Pillars of Faith in Islam; the pilgrimage to Mecca to visit the Ka'bah with stops at other holy sites in Saudi Arabia.

halakhah   Jewish teachings about right living, including proper diet and dress, to reflect God's righteous involvement with humanity.

Hasidism   Early modern Jewish movement that included intense devotionalism and mystical religious experience.

Haskalah   Modern movement within Judaism that promoted adaptation and assimilation to secular culture.

henotheism   Type of religious belief and practice in which many gods are perceived, but one is elevated to the status of supreme or chief deity.

hsiao   Confucian virtue of loving commitment to one's grandparents, parents, siblings, and children, and devotion to ancestor spirits.

ijma   Consensus; the unified opinion of the Muslim ummah, or precedent in Islamic legal tradition.

ijtihad   Independent judgment in matters of Qur'anic interpretation.

imam "Leader" or "model" in Arabic; in Sunni tradition, Imam is the supervisor of religious observances, and in Shi'ia (also called Shi'ite) tradition, the Imamate refers to the dynastic succession of Ali and the doctrine of the hidden Imam who provides spiritual insight to Shi'ia clerics.

immanence Idea that God is present within every living thing; usually contrasted with transcendence, in which God is seen as distinct and separate from creation.

incarnation Process by which the divine takes on a human form, which is derived the Latin word *carn*, meaning "flesh."

jen *See* **ren.**

jinn Desert spirits recognized by Bedouin tribes of pre-Islamic Arabia.

jiva Concept in Jainism used to describe the particular spirit of an individual.

Ka'bah Shrine in the center of Mecca that is considered by Muslims to be the most sacred place in the world.

Kabbalah Mystical tradition within Judaism.

kalam Arabic for "speech," used in reference to theology in Islam.

Kali Yuga Hindu and Buddhist concept of an era of destruction and weakened spiritual power.

kami Gods of traditional Japanese religion, known as Shintoism.

karma Law of cause and effect in Hinduism and Buddhism, which shapes the course of one's personal destiny.

li Customs, manners, or ritualized behaviors that promote orderliness in social and political relations in the Confucian tradition.

ling Concept in Chinese religion of a sense of spiritual beings in the surrounding environment.

Logos Concept in early Judaism, Christianity, and Neo-Platonism used in reference to God's creative power and mode of revelation.

Mahayana Sect within Buddhism that advocates adaptation of the faith to local conditions, and teaches a more flexible path to nirvana including visualization of deities.

Mahdi Figure within the Islamic tradition who will return one day to establish a new dominion on Earth.

makoto   Concept of mandate of heaven or will of the gods in Shinto tradition.

mantra   Sacred tone or tones used in Hindu and Buddhist yoga exercises, which are thought to enhance the powers of concentration, leading to ultimate perception of ultimate reality.

Mara   Spirit perceived by Buddhists as a force behind ignorance and death.

Maya   Hindu concept of the illusory nature of experience.

Messiah   Hebrew for anointed one; Greek for Messiah is *Christ*, hence Jesus Christ in Greek Christian texts.

metaphysics   Philosophical study of the ultimate nature of reality or being.

mitzvoth   Various religious observances in Judaism, outlined in the Torah, which are commanded by God as the proper means of observing the covenant.

moksha   Hindu concept of liberation from the cycle of reincarnation and the attainment of the soul's ultimate destiny.

monism   Philosophical and religious concept in which reality is depicted as unified and indivisible.

monolatry   Type of religious belief and practice in which many gods are recognized, but only one is the object of worship.

monotheism   Belief in the existence of one Supreme Being, as in the Jewish, Christian, and Muslim concepts of God.

mujaddid   Reformer of Islam who purifies and renews the faith; one appears every 100 years.

mysticism   In the philosophical sense, a pursuit of hidden or secret knowledge; in the religious sense, a direct experience with the divine or ultimate reality.

naturalism   Belief that all phenomena can be explained in terms of natural causes and natural laws.

nihilism   Rejection of metaphysical truths—such as any article of belief in God—along with denial of moral absolutes and transcendent values.

nirguna Brahman   Hindu idea of Brahman as being indescribable, with no forms or attributes.

nirvana   Sanskrit for "blowing out"; Buddhist idea of extinguishing inner desires, emotions, and feelings that bring about our attachment to the world, leading to the blissful state of deathlessness.

orthodoxy   Idea of right belief in religions with official doctrines that adherents are expected to support.

panentheism   Belief that everything that exists in the universe is a part of God, but not all of God.

panpsychism   Belief that all reality is mind or consciousness, and each person is an instance of the universal consciousness.

pantheism   Notion that everything that exists in the universe is God, including all physical matter and its properties.

polytheism   Type of religious belief and practice in which many gods are perceived and worshipped.

predestination   Belief that God has chosen some souls for eternal life, and others for eternal damnation.

Pure Land   Sect of Mahayana Buddhism that teaches devotion to bodhisattvas who have prepared fields of rebirth where nirvana can be more easily obtained.

purusha   Hindu philosophical concept of human spiritual essence, which is trapped in *prakriti* (human flesh).

qi (or **chi**)   Generative power or life force that animates and sustains all living things.

Qur'an   Sacred text of Islam, from the word "recitation" in Arabic.

ren (also **jen**)   Confucian virtue of humaneness, or respect and compassion for other human beings.

rta (RIT-ah)   The ancient Vedic concept of an underlying order of the universe, supported and sustained by the gods.

sacramentalism   Religious rites in Christianity that are thought to convey the grace of God to believers, or symbolize unity of faith in Jesus Christ.

saguna Brahman   Hindu idea of Brahman as having particular dimensions, forms, or attributes.

samsara   Cycle of reincarnation in Hinduism and Buddhism.

Sephardim   Jews living in diaspora (dispersion) influenced by Mediterranean culture.

sephiroth   Hebrew for "numerations," in reference to the Jewish Kabbalah idea of the emanation of God's attributes.

Shahadah   Muslim confession of faith, one of the Five Pillars of Faith in Islam.

Shang-di   Early Chinese concept of Supreme Being, or chief deity in the classic Chinese pantheon of gods.

shari'ah   Straight path, or the laws of the Islamic faith.

shaykh   Master of Sufism within the tradition of Islamic mysticism.

Shi'ite (also **Shi'ia**)   Minority sect within Islam that recognizes the leadership line of Muhammad's descendents—the imams—over the Muslim ummah.

skandas   In Buddhism, the five core elements of the individual, subject to karmic echoes from former lives.

Social Gospel   Theological movement in modern Christianity that advocated social and political action on behalf of the poor and disadvantaged.

spiritualism   Any system of belief in nonmaterial realities, such as spirits, gods, souls, or a universal mind; also used in reference to the practice of communicating with the spirits of the dead.

Sufism   From the Arabic word for "wool," used in reference to the mystical tradition within Islam.

sunnah   Recorded deeds of the Prophet Muhammad.

Sunni   Majority sect within Islam that follows the sunnah and recognizes the leadership of a traditional succession of caliphs over the Muslim ummah.

syncretism   Practice of fusing different religious or philosophical concepts into one integrated system.

Talmud   Collection of opinions about the meaning of the Torah within the Jewish rabbinical tradition.

Tanak   Entire body of ancient Hebrew scriptures, comprised of the Torah and the books of history, prophetic teachings, wisdom, and poetry.

tanha   Buddhist concept of selfish desire or craving, which leads to suffering and continued rebirth.

Tantra Sect of Mahayana Buddhism that utilizes intensive meditation exercises to achieve enlightenment.

Tao Way or road; in Taoism, the ultimate, nameless reality of the universe that makes all existent things possible.

tariqah Way or path, used in reference to particular orders within Islamic Sufism.

tawhid Islamic concept of unity in reference to the singleness of God.

teleology Study of purpose or final causes, such as origins of the universe, the destiny of humankind, and the resolution of the struggle between good and evil.

theism System of belief in which God is depicted as the sole creator and sustainer of the universe, unified in form, perfect in nature, and distinct from the material world.

theodicy Defense of God, usually in response to claims that the principles of theism cannot account for the problem of evil.

theophany Special appearance of God in the presence of a human being, such as God's visitation with Moses on Mt. Sinai.

Theravada Sect within Buddhism that stresses purity of the faith and teaches a rigorous, exclusive path to nirvana.

t'ien Concept of heaven in Chinese religion, which serves many of the functions of a God or Supreme Being.

Torah When used in reference to a body of written texts, means the ancient Hebrew books of Genesis, Exodus, Leviticus, Numbers, and Deuteronomy.

Trinity Concept in Christian theology that conceives of God as one substance or essence in three persons or aspects.

triratna Buddhist concept of three jewels that lead to salvation—the Buddha, the dharma (Buddha's teachings), and the sangha (the Buddhist community).

ulema Community of Islamic scholars trained in the Qur'an and in shari'ah, or Islamic law.

ummah World-wide community of faithful Muslims.

Upanishads Sacred texts of ancient Hinduism that expanded upon and interpreted the *Vedas*.

Vedas   Earliest writings of the Hindu people, including hymns to the gods of the ancient pantheon and instructions for ritual observances.

Wahabbism   Sect within Islam that advocates a return to the original purity of the faith.

wu wei   Cardinal rule of life in Taoism—nonaction—that permits the Tao to flow through one's inner being.

Yi   Confucian virtue of righteousness, or the inner desire to do what is right.

yoga   Sanskrit for "union," used in reference to Hindu and Buddhist techniques for achieving release from the cycle of reincarnation.

Zen   Sect of Mahayana Buddhism that uses meditation rituals, including word puzzles, to induce flashes of insight that lead to enlightenment and nirvana.

Zionism   Beliefs regarding the Jews and the land promised to Abraham, and more recently, a political movement to secure Jewish control of Palestine.

Zoroastrianism   Ancient version of monotheism that sprang up in Persia, or present-day Iran.

Index

ninety-nine names, 190
path to heaven, 191
sacred language, 189
signs, 221-222
social vision, 194-195
Tawhid, 190
Qutb, Sayyid, 239-240

R

Rabbi Akiba, 86
rabbinical schools, 78-79
radicals of Islam, 240-241
Ramanuja, 263
Ramses II, 64
Rashi's Commentaries, 82
realms of pantheism, 15
reason
    atheism, 50-51
    living, 324
    questioning, 164
Reform Judaism, 111-112
Reformation, 165-169
reincarnation, 276
religious scholarship, 315
ren, 296
renewal movements of Islam
    Mahdiyya, 235-236
    Wahhabism, 233-235
renunciation, 272
repentance, 125
resurrection of Jesus, 132-133
revelation of the divine,
    322-323
revivalists, 176
Rig-Veda, 32
Roman Catholic Church,
    151-152
rta, 248
Rubenstein, Richard, 323
Ruether, Rosemary Radford,
    180
Rule of St. Benedict, 150
Russell, Bertrand, 54-55

S

sacramentalism, 151-152
sacred places, 16-17

Sadducees, 76
saguna Brahman, 260-261
Saiva-siddhanta tradition, 260
Samaritans, 77
sangha, 282
Sankhya, 262
Schleiermacher, Frederich, 321
scholarship of religion, 315
Scholasticism, 160-163
schools of Mahayanas, 288-289
Schopenhauer, Arthur, 311
Science of Judaism, 105
scientific revolution, 308
secular Judaism, 115
seekers, 321-323
Seleucids, 75
Sephardim, 108
sephiroth, 90
Sermon on the Mount, 123
Seveners, 212
Shammai the Elder, 78
Shang-di, 292
Shankara, 263
shari'ah, 206-207
shaykhs, 226
Shi'ites
    caliph challenge, 199,
        210-211
    compared to Sunnis, 217
    continuing revelation, 215
    Day of Judgment, 216
    extremists, 211
    imams, 213-214
    leadership, 198
    Mahdi, 216
    Seveners, 212
    Twelvers, 212
    ulema, 214
Shinto, 300-301
Shiva, 259
shu, 297
Siddhartha Gautama, 268-269
    asceticism, 270
    as Buddha, 271
    Immovable Spot, 270
    nirvana, 271
    witnessing suffering, 269
signs of Sufism, 221-222
Sikhism, 265
sin, 125, 191

Sire, James W., 6
skandas, 277
skepticism, 49
    atheism, 308
    Descartes, 307
    Idealists, 309-310
    naturalism, 309
    Pascal's wager, 306
    proof, 306
    religious scholarship, 315
    scientific revolution, 308
    theism, 4
Social Gospel, 174
Solomon, 70
Soma, 247
soul, 276
sources of knowledge, 162
Spinoza, Baruch de, 104
spirituality of women, 322
St. Teresa of Avila, 154
Stoics, 38
Strauss, David Friedrich, 316
Sudanese Muslims, 216
Sufism, 220
    acceptance, 229
    al-Ghazzali, 222-224
    awliya, 228
    dhikr, 226
    escaping the ego, 226-227
    eye of the heart, 225
    ibn Arabi, 227-228
    inner cleansing, 225
    shaykhs, 226
    signs, 221-222
    tasawwuf, 226
Sukhavati, 289
Sumerians, 23-24
sunnah, 193
Sunnis
    al-Ash'ari, 202-203
    caliph challenge, 200
    compared to Shi'ites, 217
    jurists, 207
    leadership, 198
    role of imams, 213
    theology, 203-204
    ulema, 214
supernatural, 322
synagogues, 74
syncretism, 49-50